THE CAMBRIDGE COMPANION TO
AMERICAN POETRY SINCE 1945

The extent to which American poetry reinvented itself after World War II is a testament to the changing social, political, and economic landscape of twentieth-century American life. Registering an important shift in the way scholars contextualize modern and contemporary American literature, this *Companion* explores how American poetry has documented and, at times, helped propel the literary and cultural revolutions of the past sixty-five years. Offering authoritative and accessible essays from fourteen distinguished scholars, the *Companion* sheds new light on the Beat, Black Arts, and other movements while examining institutions that govern poetic practice in the United States today. The text also introduces seminal figures like Sylvia Plath, John Ashbery, and Gwendolyn Brooks while situating them alongside phenomena such as the "academic poet" and popular forms such as spoken word and rap, revealing the breadth of their shared history. Students, scholars, and readers will find this *Companion* an indispensable guide to postwar and late-twentieth-century American poetry.

Jennifer Ashton is Associate Professor of English at the University of Illinois at Chicago, where she teaches literary theory and the history of poetry. She is author of *From Modernism to Postmodernism: American Poetry and Theory in the Twentieth Century* and has published articles in *Modernism/Modernity*, *Modern Philology*, *American Literary History*, and *Western Humanities Review*.

A complete list of books in the series is at the back of this book.

T0381826

THE CAMBRIDGE
COMPANION TO

AMERICAN POETRY
SINCE 1945

THE CAMBRIDGE
COMPANION TO
AMERICAN POETRY
SINCE 1945

EDITED BY
JENNIFER ASHTON
University of Illinois at Chicago

CAMBRIDGE
UNIVERSITY PRESS

CAMBRIDGE
UNIVERSITY PRESS

University Printing House, Cambridge CB2 8BS, United Kingdom

One Liberty Plaza, 20th Floor, New York, NY 10006, USA

477 Williamstown Road, Port Melbourne, VIC 3207, Australia

314-321, 3rd Floor, Plot 3, Splendor Forum, Jasola District Centre, New Delhi - 110025, India

103 Penang Road, #05-06/07, Visioncrest Commercial, Singapore 238467

Cambridge University Press is part of the University of Cambridge.

It furthers the University's mission by disseminating knowledge in the pursuit of education, learning and research at the highest international levels of excellence.

www.cambridge.org
Information on this title: www.cambridge.org/9780521147958

First published 2013

A catalogue record for this publication is available from the British Library

Library of Congress Cataloging in Publication data
The Cambridge companion to American poetry since 1945 /
[edited by] Jennifer Ashton.
p.   cm. – (Cambridge companions to literature)
Includes bibliographical references and index.
ISBN 978-0-521-76695-1 (hardback) – ISBN 978-0-521-14795-8 (pbk.)
1. American poetry – 20th century – History and criticism.
1. Ashton, Jennifer, 1964–
PS323.5.C27   2012
811´.509–dc23   2012016512

ISBN 978-0-521-76695-1 Hardback
ISBN 978-0-521-14795-8 Paperback

CONTENTS

Notes on Contributors   *page* ix
Acknowledgments   xiii
Chronology of Publications and Events   xv

1. Periodizing Poetic Practice since 1945   1
   JENNIFER ASHTON

2. From the Late Modernism of the "Objectivists" to the
   Proto-postmodernism of "Projective Verse"   16
   MARK SCROGGINS

3. Confessional Poetry   31
   DEBORAH NELSON

4. Surrealism as a Living Modernism: What the New York
   Poets Learned from Two Generations of New York Painting   47
   CHARLES ALTIERI

5. The San Francisco Renaissance   66
   MICHAEL DAVIDSON

6. Three Generations of Beat Poetics   80
   RONNA C. JOHNSON

7. The Poetics of Chant and Inner/Outer Space: The Black Arts
   Movement   94
   MARGO NATALIE CRAWFORD

8. Feminist Poetries   109
   LISA SEWELL

9. Ecopoetries in America   127
    NICK SELBY

10. Language Writing   143
    STEVE MCCAFFERY

11. American Poetry and Its Institutions   158
    HANK LAZER

12. The Contemporary "Mainstream" Lyric   173
    CHRISTINA PUGH

13. Poems in and out of School: Allen Grossman and Susan Howe   187
    OREN IZENBERG

14. Rap, Hip Hop, Spoken Word   202
    MICHAEL W. CLUNE

15. Poetry of the Twenty-First Century: The First Decade   216
    JENNIFER ASHTON

    Index   231

NOTES ON CONTRIBUTORS

CHARLES ALTIERI teaches in the English Department at UC Berkeley. His most recent books are *The Particulars of Rapture* (Cornell University Press, 2004) and *The Art of Twentieth-Century American Poetry: Modernism and After* (Blackwell, 2009). He has just completed a book manuscript, *Wallace Stevens and the Phenomenology of Value*.

JENNIFER ASHTON teaches in the University of Illinois at Chicago and is one of the founding editors of nonsite.org. She is the author of *From Modernism to Postmodernism: American Poetry and Theory in the Twentieth Century* (Cambridge University Press, 2005) and a contributor to *The Cambridge History of American Women's Writing*, edited by Dale Bauer (Cambridge University Press, 2012). Her scholarly articles have appeared in *ELH*, *Modernism/Modernity*, *Modern Philology*, *ALH*, *Western Humanities Review*, and the international online arts journal, *Interval(le)s*.

MICHAEL W. CLUNE is Assistant Professor of English at Case Western Reserve University. He is the author of *American Literature and the Free Market, 1945–2000* (Cambridge University Press, 2010). Elements of his new book project, *Writing Against Time*, have appeared in *Representations, Criticism,* and *Behavioral and Brain Sciences*.

MARGO NATALIE CRAWFORD is the author of *Dilution Anxiety and the Black Phallus* (Ohio State University Press, 2008) and the coeditor, with Lisa Gail Collins and Alondra Nelson, of *New Thoughts on the Black Arts Movement* (Rutgers University Press, 2006). She is associate professor of African American literature and visual culture at Cornell University.

MICHAEL DAVIDSON is Distinguished Professor of Literature at the University of California, San Diego. He is the author of *The San Francisco Renaissance: Poetics and Community at Mid-Century* (Cambridge University Press, 1989), *Ghostlier Demarcations: Modern Poetry and the Material Word* (University of California Press, 1997), *Guys Like Us: Citing Masculinity in Cold War Poetics* (University of

Chicago, 2003), and *Concerto for the Left Hand: Disability and the Defamiliar Body* (University of Michigan, 2008). His most recent book, *Outskirts of Form: Practicing Cultural Poetics*, was published in 2011 by Wesleyan University Press. He is the editor of *The New Collected Poems of George Oppen* (New Directions, 2002). He is the author of five books of poetry, the most recent of which is *The Arcades* (O Books, 1998). He is the coauthor, with Lyn Hejinian, Barrett Watten, and Ron Silliman, of *Leningrad* (Mercury House Press, 1991). He has written extensively on disability issues, most recently "Hearing Things: The Scandal of Speech in Deaf Performance," in *Disability Studies: Enabling the Humanities*, ed. Sharon Snyder et al. (Modern Language Association, 2002); "Phantom Limbs: Film Noir and the Disabled Body," *GLQ* 9:1–2 (2003); *Universal Design: The Work of Disability in an Age* of Globalization, *The Disability Studies Reader*, ed. Lennard Davis (Routledge, 2010); and "Pregnant Men: Modernism, Disability, and Biofuturity in Djuna Barnes," *Novel* 54.3 (Summer 2010).

OREN IZENBERG is the author of *Being Numerous: Poetry and the Ground of Social Life* (Princeton University Press, 2011). He is Assistant Professor of English at the University of California, Irvine.

RONNA C. JOHNSON is Lecturer in English, Women's Studies, and American Studies at Tufts University, where she has been Director of Women's Studies. She studies Jack Kerouac, Joyce Johnson, Lenore Kandel, and Brenda Frazer, as well as other Beat writers, often focusing on gender in Beat movement discourses. She is currently finishing the book *Inventing Jack Kerouac: Reception and Reputation 1957–2007* (Camden House Press). Her essay, "Beat Transnationalism Under Gender: Brenda Frazer's Troia: Mexican Memoirs," appears in *The Transnational Beat Generation*, ed. Nancy M. Grace and Jennie Skerl (Palgrave Macmillan, 2012). She has written, with Nancy M. Grace, *Breaking the Rule of Cool: Interviewing and Reading Women Beat Writers* (University Press of Mississippi, 2004), a sequel to their *Girls Who Wore Black: Women Writing the Beat Generation* (Rutgers University Press, 2002). Johnson is a cofounder and Vice President of the Beat Studies Association.

HANK LAZER is the author of sixteen books of poetry, including *Portions* (Lavender Ink, 2009), *The New Spirit* (Singing Horse Press, 2005), *Elegies & Vacations* (Salt Publishing, 2004), and *Days* (INK-A! Press, 2002). *Lyric & Spirit: Selected Essays 1996–2008* was published by Omnidawn in 2008. He coedits the Modern and Contemporary Poetics Series for the University of Alabama Press. Lazer is Associate Provost for Academic Affairs, Executive Director of Creative Campus, and Professor of English at the University of Alabama.

STEVE MCCAFFERY is author of more than thirty-five volumes of poetry and four critical books. A fifth, *The Darkness of the Present: Poetics, Anachronism and the Anomaly*, will appear through the University of Alabama Press in late 2012. He is

David Gray Professor of Poetry and Letters at SUNY Buffalo and Director of the Poetics Program.

DEBORAH NELSON is the author of *Pursuing Privacy in Cold War America* (Columbia University Press, 2002) and the forthcoming *Tough Broads: Suffering in Style*. She received her PhD from the City University of New York and teaches at the University of Chicago, where she is the Deputy Provost for Graduate Education.

CHRISTINA PUGH is an Associate Professor in the Program for Writers at the University of Illinois at Chicago. She has published two books of poetry: *Restoration* (Northwestern University Press, 2008) and *Rotary* (Word Press, 2004, winner of the Word Press First Book Prize). Her awards have included the Lucille Medwick Memorial Award from the Poetry Society of America and a fellowship in poetry from the Illinois Arts Council.

MARK SCROGGINS is Professor and Director of Graduate Studies in the English department at Florida Atlantic University. He is the author of *Louis Zukofsky and the Poetry of Knowledge* (University of Alabama Press, 1998) and *The Poem of a Life: A Biography of Louis Zukofsky* (Counterpoint, 2007). His most recent collections of poetry are *Torture Garden: Naked City Pastorelles* (Cultural Society, 2011) and *Red Arcadia* (Shearsman, 2012).

NICK SELBY is Professor of American Literature and Head of the School of American Studies at the University of East Anglia. His book *Poetics of Loss in* The Cantos *of Ezra Pound* was published in 2005 by Edwin Mellen Press, and he has published three other books, on Herman Melville, T. S. Eliot, and Walt Whitman, as well as numerous essays on topics concerned with American poetry, poetics, and culture. A new book, *Dazzling Geographies: American Poetics in Ezra Pound, Gary Snyder and Jorie Graham*, which examines the relationship between American poetics and ideas of the land, is forthcoming. He is the editor of *Comparative American Studies*.

LISA SEWELL is the author of *The Way Out* (Alice James, 2002), *Name Withheld* (Four Way Books, 2006), and *Long Corridor* (Seven Kitchens Press, 2009). With Claudia Rankine, she has edited two collections of essays on contemporary poetry and poetics: *American Poets in the 21st Century: The New Poetics* (Wesleyan University Press, 2002) and *Eleven More American Women Poets in the 21st Century: Poetics Across North American* (Wesleyan University Press, 2012). She teaches in the English Department at Villanova University.

ACKNOWLEDGMENTS

This volume's strength rests entirely on the shoulders of its thirteen distinguished contributors, whose work will speak eloquently for itself. They have succeeded together in producing a far more nuanced, surprising, and useful vision of American poetry since 1945 than I could have imagined even in my wildest fantasies. It's a tremendous privilege to find my own work in the same pages as theirs. I would like to thank Matthew Brown, Matthew Corey, Chad Heltzel, and Jennifer Moore, who made indelible contributions to this *Companion* with their superb editorial and research assistance. Their work on this volume was partially funded with the financial support of the UIC English Department, authorized by my department head, Mark Canuel, whose moral support and encouragement have been important to me throughout the preparation of this volume, and of the Cambridge University Press offices of my editor Ray Ryan, who have demonstrated saintly levels of patience and generosity. As ever, I owe my deepest thanks for the development of my ideas to Ruth Leys and Michael Fried, Oren Izenberg and Sonya Rasminsky, Edward and Katherine Ashton, and to my husband, Walter Benn Michaels.

1945   Pulitzer Prize: Karl Shapiro, *V-Letter and Other Poems*
Gwendolyn Brooks, *A Street in Bronzeville*

1946   Elizabeth Bishop, *North & South*
William Carlos Williams, *Paterson*, Book I
Lorine Niedecker, *New Goose*

1947   Pulitzer Prize: Robert Lowell, *Lord Weary's Castle*
Robert Duncan, *Heavenly City, Earthly City*
Wallace Stevens, *Transport to Summer*

1948   Pulitzer Prize: W. H. Auden, *The Age of Anxiety*
Ezra Pound, *The Pisan Cantos* and *The Cantos of Ezra Pound*
Theodore Roethke, *The Lost Son and Other Poems*

1949   Pulitzer Prize: Peter Viereck, *Terror and Decorum*
Charles Olson, "The Kingfishers"
Kenneth Patchen, *Red Wine & Yellow Hair* and *To Say If You Love Someone*
Kenneth Rexroth, *The Signature of All Things* and *The Art of Worldly Wisdom*

1950   Pulitzer Prize: Gwendolyn Brooks, *Annie Allen*
National Book Award: William Carlos Williams, *Paterson: Book III and Selected Poems*
Charles Olson, "Projective Verse" appears in *Poetry New York* (no. 3)
E. E. Cummings, *XAIPE: 71 Poems*

1951   (May) In New York City, Leo Castelli curates the 9th Street Art Exhibition, exhibiting paintings by Willem de Kooning, Jackson Pollock, Barnett Newman, and Mark Rothko

(Summer) Charles Olson named as rector of Black Mountain
College
Pulitzer Prize: Carl Sandberg, *Complete Poems*
National Book Award: Wallace Stevens, *The Auroras of
Autumn*
Cid Corman, ed. *Origin* magazine
Langston Hughes, *Montage of a Dream Deferred*

1952   (August) John Cage premieres 4'33"
Pulitzer Prize and National Book Award: Marianne Moore,
Collected Poems
Robert Creeley, *Le Fou*
Archibald MacLeish, *Collected Poems, 1917–1952*
W. S. Merwin, *A Mask for Janus*

1953   Pulitzer Prize and National Book Award: Archibald MacLeish,
Collected Poems, 1917–1952
John Ashbery, *Turandot and Other Poems*
Larry Eigner, *From the Sustaining Air*
Kenneth Koch, *Poems*
Charles Olson, *In Cold Hell, In Thicket*
Theodore Roethke, *The Waking*

1954   Pulitzer Prize: Theodore Roethke, *The Waking*
National Book Award: Conrad Aiken, *Collected Poems*
Robert Creeley, ed. *Black Mountain Review*
Anthony Hecht, *A Summoning of Stones*

1955   (October) The Six Gallery reading showcases the poetry of
Allen Ginsberg, Phillip Lamantia, Michael McClure, Gary
Snyder, and Philip Whalen
Pulitzer Prize and National Book Award: Wallace Stevens,
Collected Poems
Lawrence Ferlinghetti, *Pictures of the Gone World*
Adrienne Rich, *The Diamond Cutters*

1956   (Autumn) Black Mountain College closes
Pulitzer Prize: Elizabeth Bishop, *Poems: North & South/A
Cold Spring*
National Book Award: W. H. Auden, *The Shield of Achilles*
John Ashbery, *Some Trees*
John Berryman, *Homage to Mistress Bradstreet*
Allen Ginsberg, *Howl and Other Poems*
Denise Levertov, *Here and Now*

1957   (October) Judge Clayton W. Horn rules that Lawrence
        Ferlinghetti is not guilty of obscenity for publishing *Howl
        and Other Poems* by Allen Ginsberg
        Pulitzer Prize and National Book Award: Richard Wilbur,
        Things of This World
        Donald Hall, Robert Pack, and Louis Simpson, eds., *New
        Poets of England and America*
        Frank O'Hara, *Meditations in an Emergency*
        Wallace Stevens, *Opus Posthumous*

1958   Pulitzer Prize and National Book Award: Robert Penn Warren,
        Promises: Poems 1954–1956
        Gregory Corso, *Bomb* and *Gasoline*
        Lawrence Ferlinghetti, *A Coney Island of the Mind*
        Bob Kaufman, *Abomunist Manifesto*

1959   Pulitzer Prize: Stanley Kunitz, *Selected Poems 1928–1958*
        National Book Award: Theodore Roethke, *Words for the Wind*
        Ted Joans, *Funky Jazz Poems*
        Robert Lowell, *Life Studies*
        Gary Snyder, *Riprap and Cold Mountain Poems*
        Louis Zukofsky, '*A*,' 1–12

1960   Pulitzer Prize: W. D. Snodgrass, *Heart's Needle*
        National Book Award: Robert Lowell, *Life Studies*
        Donald Allen, ed., *The New American Poetry 1945–1960*
        Robert Duncan, *The Opening of the Field*
        Charles Olson, *The Maximus Poems*
        Anne Sexton, *To Bedlam and Part Way Back*
        Gwendolyn Brooks, *The Bean Eaters*

1961   Pulitzer Prize: Phyllis McGinley, *Times Three: Selected Verse
        from Three Decades*
        National Book Award: Randall Jarrell, *The Woman at the
        Washington Zoo*
        LeRoi Jones, *Preface to a Twenty Volume Suicide Note*

1962   Pulitzer Prize and National Book Award: Alan Dugan, *Poems*
        John Ashbery, *The Tennis Court Oath*
        Cid Corman, *Sun Rock Man*
        Robert Creeley, *For Love: Poems 1950–1960*
        Denise Levertov, *The Jacob's Ladder*
        William Carlos Williams, *Pictures from Brueghel and Other
        Poems*

Barbara Guest, *Poems: The Location of Things, Archaics, The Open Skies*

1963   Pulitzer Prize: William Carlos Williams, *Pictures from Breughel*
National Book Award: William Stafford, *Traveling Through the Dark*
James Wright, *The Branch Will Not Break*

1964   Pulitzer Prize: Louis Simpson, *At the End of the Open Road*
National Book Award: John Crowe Ransom, *Selected Poems*
Ted Berrigan, *The Sonnets*
Robert Lowell, *For the Union Dead*
Frank O'Hara, *Lunch Poems*
A. B. Spellman, *The Beautiful Days*
Jack Spicer, *Language*

1965   Pulitzer Prize: John Berryman, *77 Dream Songs*
National Book Award: Theodore Roethke, *The Far Field*
Charles Olson, *Proprioception*
Sylvia Plath, *Ariel*
Charles Reznikoff, *Testimony: The United States (1885–1890): Recitative*
A. R. Ammons, *Corson's Inlet* and *Tape for the Turn of the New Year*

1966   Pulitzer Prize: Richard Eberhart, *Selected Poems*
National Book Award: James Dickey, *Buckdancer's Choice: Poems*
Amiri Baraka, *Black Art*
Diane di Prima, *Poems for Freddie*
James Merrill, *Nights and Days*

1967   Pulitzer Prize: Anne Sexton, *Live or Die*
National Book Award: James Merrill, *Nights and Days*
Ted Berrigan, *Many Happy Returns*
Robert Creeley, *Words*
Nikki Giovanni, *Black Feeling, Black Talk*
Lenore Kandel, *Word Alchemy*
W. S. Merwin, *The Lice*
James Wright, *Shall We Gather at the River*

1968   Pulitzer Prize: Anthony Hecht, *The Hard Hours*
National Book Award: Robert Bly, *The Light Around the Body*
Amiri Baraka and Larry Neal, eds., *Black Fire*
Gwendolyn Brooks, *In the Mecca*

Ed Dorn, *Gunslinger*
Robert Duncan, *Bending the Bow*
Audre Lorde, *The First Cities*
Lorine Niedecker, *North Central*
George Oppen, *Of Being Numerous*
Charles Reznikoff, *Testimony: The United States (1891–1900)*:
  Recitative
Mark Strand, *Reasons for Moving*

1969   Pulitzer Prize: George Oppen, *Of Being Numerous*
National Book Award: John Berryman, *His Toy, His Dream,*
  His Rest
John Berryman, *The Dream Songs*
Robert Creeley, *Pieces*
James Schuyler, *Freely Espousing*

1970   Steve McCaffery, bpNichol, Rafael Barreto-Rivera, and Paul
  Dutton form the sound-poetry group, *The Four Horsemen*
Pulitzer Prize: Richard Howard, *Untitled Subjects*
National Book Award: Elizabeth Bishop, *The Complete Poems*
Amiri Baraka, *It's Nation Time*
Clark Coolidge, *Space*
Michael S. Harper, *Dear John, Dear Coltrane*
Audre Lorde, *Cables to Rage*
Haki Madhubuti, *Don't Cry, Scream*
Sonia Sanchez, *We a Baddddd People*

1971   Pulitzer Prize: William S. Merwin, *The Carrier of Ladders*
National Book Award: Mona Van Duyn, *To See, To Take*
(Winter) Robert Grenier and Barrett Watten publish the first
  volume of *This*
June Jordan, *Some Changes*
Galway Kinnell, *The Book of Nightmares*
Stanley Kunitz, *The Testing Tree*
Charles Simic, *Dismantling the Distance*

1972   Pulitzer Prize: James Wright, *Collected Poems*
National Book Award: Frank O'Hara, *The Collected Works*
  of Frank O'Hara and Howard Moss, *Selected Poems*
H. D. (Hilda Doolittle), *Hermetic Definition*
Allen Ginsberg, *The Fall of America: Poems of these States,*
  1965–1971
George Oppen, *Collected Poems*

1973 Pulitzer Prize: Maxine Kumin, *Up Country*
National Book Award: A. R. Ammons, *Collected Poems, 1951–1971*
Frank Bidart, *Golden State*
Muriel Rukeyser, *Breaking Open*

1974 Pulitzer Prize: Robert Lowell, *The Dolphin*
National Book Award: Allen Ginsberg, *The Fall of America: Poems of these States, 1965–1971* and Adrienne Rich, *Diving into the Wreck: Poems 1971–1972*
A. R. Ammons, *Sphere: The Form of a Motion*
Leslie Marmon Silko, *Laguna Woman*
Gary Snyder, *Turtle Island*

1975 Pulitzer Prize: Gary Snyder, *Turtle Island*
National Book Award: Marilyn Hacker, *Presentation Piece*
Charles Reznikoff, *Holocaust*
Denise Levertov, *Freeing the Dust*
Kenneth Koch, *The Art of Love*
Anne Waldman, *Fast Speaking Woman*

1976 Pulitzer Prize and National Book Award: John Ashbery, *Self-Portrait in a Convex Mirror*
Lorine Niedecker, *Blue Chicory*

1977 (Summer) Steve McCaffery edits *The Politics of the Referent*, a special issue of *Open Letter*
Pulitzer Prize: James Merrill, *Divine Comedies*
National Book Award: Richard Eberhart, *Collected Poems, 1930–1976*
John Ashbery, *Houseboat Days*
Jayne Cortez, *Mouth on Paper*
Ronald Johnson, *radi os I-IV*

1978 Pulitzer Prize and National Book Award: Howard Nemerov, *Collected Poems*
Rae Armantrout, *Extremities*
Robert Grenier, *Sentences*
Lyn Hejinian, *Writing Is an Aid to Memory*
Audre Lorde, *The Black Unicorn*
Adrienne Rich, *The Dream of a Common Language*

1979 Pulitzer Prize: Robert Penn Warren, *Now and Then*
National Book Award: James Merrill, *Mirabell: Book of Numbers*

National Poetry Series: Sterling Allen Brown, *The Collected Poems of Sterling A Brown*; Joseph Langland *Anybody's Song*; Roberta Spear, *Silks*

Mei-Mei Bersenbrugge, *Random Possession*

Robert Hass, *Praise*

Denise Levertov, *Collected Earlier Poems*

Steve McCaffery and bpNichol, *Sound Poetry: A Catalogue*

Charles Reznikoff, *Testimony: The United States (1885–1915): Recitative*

1980 Audre Lorde, Barbara Smith, and Cherríe Moraga found Kitchen Table: Women of Color Press

Pulitzer Prize: Donald Justice, *Selected Poems*

National Book Award: Philip Levine, *Ashes: Poems New and Old*

National Poetry Series: George Barlow, *Gumbo*; Larry Levis, *The Dollmaker's Ghost*; Robert Peterson, *Leaving Taos*; Reg Saner, *So This Is the Map*; Michael Ryan, *In Winter*

Louise Glück, *Descending Figure*

Lyn Hejinian, *My Life*

Sharon Olds, *Satan Says*

Alicia Ostriker, *The Mother-Child Papers*

1981 MacArthur Fellowships: A. R. Ammons, Joseph Brodsky, Derek Walcott, and Robert Penn Warren

Pulitzer Prize: James Schuyler, *The Morning of the Poem*

National Book Award: Lisel Mueller, *The Need to Hold Still*

National Poetry Series: Jonathan Aaron, *Second Sight*; Cyrus Cassells, *The Mud Actor*; Denis Johnson, *The Incognito Lounge and Other Poems*; Nami Shihab Nye, *Hugging the Jukebox*; Sherod Santos, *Accidental Weather*

Charles Bernstein, *Disfrutes*

Carolyn Forché, *The Country Between Us*

Michael Palmer, *Notes for Echo Lake*

Bob Perelman, *Primer*

Ron Silliman, *Tjanting*

1982 Pulitzer Prize: Sylvia Plath, *The Collected Poems* (posthumous)

National Book Award: William Bronk, *Life Supports: New and Collected Poems*

National Poetry Series: Joanne Kyger, *Going On: Selected Poems 1958–1980*; Jane Miller, *The Greater Leisures*;

Donald Revell, *From the Abandoned Cities*; Susan Tichy, *The Hands in Exile*; John Yau, *Corpse and Mirror*
Jayne Cortez, *Firespitter*
Larry Eigner, *Water/Places/a Time*
Joanne Kyger, *Going On: Selected Poems, 1958–1980*
Bernadette Mayer, *Midwinter Day*
James Merrill, *The Changing Light at Sandover*
Hannah Weiner, *The Code Poems*
Charles Wright, *The Southern Cross*

1983   MacArthur Fellowships: Brad Leithauser and A.K. Ramanujan
Pulitzer Prize and National Book Award: Galway Kinnell, *Selected Poems*
National Poetry Series: Wendy Battin, *In the Solar Wind*; Stephen Dobyns, *Black Dog, Red Dog*; Mary Fell, *The Persistence of Memory*; James Galvin, *God's Mistress*
A. R. Ammons, *Lake Effect Country*
Charles Bernstein, *Islets/Irritations*
Frank Bidart, *The Sacrifice*
Elizabeth Bishop (posthumous), *Collected Poems 1927–1979*
Joy Harjo, *She Had Some Horses*
Gary Snyder, *Axe Handles*
John Yau, *Corpse and Mirror*

1984   MacArthur Fellowships: Robert Hass, Charles Simic, and Galway Kinnell
Pulitzer Prize: Mary Oliver, *American Primitive* and John Ashbery, *A Wave*
National Poetry Series: Amy Bartlett, *Afterwards*; Kathy Fagan, *The Raft*; Robert L. Jones, *Wild Onion*; Nathaniel Mackey, *Eroding Witness*; Bruce Smith, *Silver and Information*
Bruce Andrews and Charles Bernstein, eds., *The L=A=N=G=U=A=G=E Book*
Mei-Mei Bersenbrugge, *The Heat Bird*
Robert Duncan, *Ground Work: Before the War*
Kenneth Rexroth, *Selected Poems*
Yusef Komunyakaa, *Copacetic*

1985   MacArthur Fellowship: John Ashbery
Pulitzer Prize: Carolyn Kizer, *Yin*

National Poetry Series: Stephen Dunn, *Local Time*; Alice Fulton, *Palladium*; Reginald Gibbons, *Saints*; Jack Myers, *As Long as You're Happy*

Amy Clampitt, *What the Light Was Like*

Susan Howe, *My Emily Dickinson*

Sonia Sanchez, *Homegirls and Handgrenades*

Gjertrud Schnackenberg, *The Lamplit Answer*

1986   MacArthur Fellowships: Daryl Hine and Jay Wright

Pulitzer Prize: Henry Taylor, *The Flying Change*

National Poetry Series: Barbara Anderson, *Junk City*; John Engels, *Cardinals in the Ice Age*; Mark Halliday, *Little Star*; Sylvia Moss, *Cities in Motion*; Charlie Smith, *Red Roads*

Philip Dacey and David Jauss, eds., *Strong Measures: Contemporary American Poetry in Traditional Forms*

Alice Fulton, *Palladium*

Li-Young Lee, *Rose*

1987   MacArthur Fellowships: Douglas Crase, Richard Kenney, Mark Strand, and May Swenson

Pulitzer Prize: Rita Dove, *Thomas and Beulah*

National Poetry Series: Jeffrey Harrison, *Singing Underneath*; Marie Howe, *The Good Thief*; William Olsen, *The Hand of God and a Few Bright Flowers*; Jeffrey Skinner, *A Guide to Forgetting*; Cole Swensen, *New Math*

Gloria Anzaldúa, *Borderlands/La Frontera: The New Mestiza*

Rachel Blau DuPlessis, *Tabula Rosa*

Robert Duncan, *Ground Work II: In the Dark*

Jorie Graham, *The End of Beauty*

1988   Pulitzer Prize: William Meredith, *Partial Accounts: New and Selected Poems*

National Poetry Series: Emily Hiestand, *Green the Witch-Hazel Wood*; David Mura, *After We Lost Our Way*; Len Roberts, *Black Wings*; Lee Upton, *No Mercy*; Paul Zimmer, *Great Bird of Love*

Ted Berrigan, *A Certain Slant of Sunlight*

Michael Palmer, *Sun*

Leslie Scalapino, *way*

1989   MacArthur Fellowship: Allen Grossman

Pulitzer Prize: Richard Wilbur, *New and Collected Poems*

National Poetry Series: Tom Andrews, *The Brother's Country*; Thomas Centolella, *Terra Firma*; David Clewell, *Blessings in Disguise*; Roland Flint, *Stubborn*; Carol Snow, *Artist and Model*
Ed Dorn, *Abhorrences*
Robert Hass, *Human Wishes*
Bernadette Mayer, *Sonnets*
Thylias Moss, *Pyramid of Bone*

1990   MacArthur Fellowships: Jorie Graham and John Hollander
Pulitzer Prize: Charles Simic, *The World Doesn't End*
National Poetry Series: John Balaban, *Words for My Daughter*; Billy Collins, *Questions about Angels*; Roger Fanning, *The Island Itself*; Thylias Moss, *Rainbow Remnants in Rock Bottom Ghetto Sky*; Laura Mullen, *The Surface*
Frank Bidart, *In the Western Night: Collected Poems*
Alice Fulton, *Powers of Congress*
Amy Gerstler, *Bitter Angel*
Joy Harjo, *In Mad Love and War*
Derek Walcott, *Omeros*

1991   Debut of the World Wide Web as a publicly available service
MacArthur Fellowships: Alice Fulton and Eleanor Wilner
Pulitzer Prize: Mona Van Duyn, *Near Changes*
National Book Award: Philip Levine, *What Work Is*
National Poetry Series: Stuart Dischell, *Good Hope Road*; Lynn Emanuel, *The Dig*; Judith Hall, *To Put the Mouth to*; James Richardson, *As If*; David Romtvedt, *A Flower Whose Name I Do Not Know*
John Ashbery, *Flow Chart*
Billy Collins, *Questions about Angels*
Robert Creeley, *Selected Poems*
Joanne Kyger, *Just Space: Poems, 1979–1989*
Adrienne Rich, *An Atlas of the Difficult World*

1992   MacArthur Fellowships: Amy Clampitt and Irving Feldman
Pulitzer Prize: James Tate, *Selected Poems*
National Book Award: Mary Oliver, *New and Selected Poems*
National Poetry Series: Gerald Burns, *Shorter Poems*; Mark Doty, *My Alexandria*; Terry Ehret, *Lost Body*; Mark Levine, *Debt*; Lawrence Raab, *What We Don't Know about Each Other*

Sherman Alexie, *The Business of Fancydancing*
Bruce Andrews, *I Don't Have Any Paper So Shut Up*
Charles Bernstein, *A Poetics*
Thom Gunn, *The Man with Night Sweats*
Lyn Hejinian, *The Cell*

1993   MacArthur Fellowships: Thom Gunn, Ann Lauterbach, and Jim Powell
Pulitzer Prize: Louise Glück, *The Wild Iris*
National Book Award: A. R. Ammons, *Garbage*
National Poetry Series: Rafael Campo, *The Other Man Was Me: A Voyage to the New World*; Martin Edmunds, *The High Road to Taos*; Karen Swenson, *The Landlady in Bangkok*; Rachel Wetzsteon, *The Other Stars*; Kevin Young, *Most Way Home*
Jorie Graham, *Materialism*
James Schuyler, *Collected Poems*
Alex Preminger and T. V. F. Brogan, eds., *The New Princeton Encyclopedia of Poetry and Poetics*

1994   MacArthur Fellowship: Adrienne Rich
Pulitzer Prize: Yusef Komunyakaa, *Neon Vernacular: New and Selected Poems*
National Book Award: James Tate, *A Worshipful Company of Fletchers*
National Poetry Series: Erin Belieu, *Infanta*; Pam Rehm, *To Give It Up*; Matthew Rohrer, *Hummock in the Malookas*; Samn Stockwell, *Theater of Animals*; Elizabeth Willis, *The Human Abstract*
Ted Berrigan, *Selected Poems*
Michael Fried, *To the Center of the Earth*
Louise Glück, *Proofs & Theories*
Paul Hoover, ed. *Norton Anthology of Postmodern American Poetry*

1995   MacArthur Fellowship: Sandra Cisneros
Pulitzer Prize: Philip Levine, *The Simple Truth*
National Book Award: Stanley Kunitz, *Passing Through: The Later Poems*
National Poetry Series: Heather Allen, *Leaving a Shadow*; Marcus Cafagna, *The Broken World*; Daniel Hall, *Strange Relation*; Juliana Spahr, *Strange Response*; Karen Volkman, *Crash's Law*

Lucie Brock-Broido, *The Master Letters*
Billy Collins, *The Art of Drowning*
Alice Fulton, *Sensual Math*
Michael Palmer, *At Passages*
Rosmarie Waldrop, *A Key into the Language of America*

1996   MacArthur Fellowships: Richard Howard and Thylias Moss
Pulitzer Prize: Jorie Graham, *The Dream of the Unified Field*
National Book Award: Hayden Carruth, *Scrambled Eggs and Whiskey*
National Poetry Series: Jeanne Marie Beaumont, *Placebo Effects*; A. V. Christie, *Nine Skies*; Jeff Clark, *The Little Door Slides Back*; Barbara Cully, *The New Intimacy*; Mary Leader, *Red Signature*
Robert Duncan, *Ground Work*
Mark Jarman and David Mason, eds., *Rebel Angels: 25 Poets of the New Formalism*
Susan Howe, *Frame Structures*
Ronald Johnson, *ARK*
Reginald Shepherd, *Angel, Interrupted*

1997   MacArthur Fellowship: Susan Stewart
Pulitzer Prize: Lisel Mueller, *Alive Together: New and Selected Poems*
National Book Award: William Meredith, *Effort at Speech: New and Selected Poems*
National Poetry Series: Sandra Alcosser, *Except by Nature*; Bartine Bellen, *Tales of Muraski and Other Poems*; Robert Gibb, *The Origins of Evening*; Lisa Lewis, *Silent Treatment*; Heather Ramsdell, *Lost Wax*
Kim Addonizio, *Jimmy & Rita*
Frank Bidart, *Desire*
Brenda Hillman, *Loose Sugar*
Lisa Robertson, *Debbie: An Epic*

1998   MacArthur Fellowships: Linda Bierds, Edward Hirsch, and Ishmael Reed
Pulitzer Prize: Charles Wright, *Black Zodiac*
National Book Award: Gerald Stern, *This Time: New and Selected Poems*
National Poetry Series: Rigoberto Gonzalez, *So Often the Pitcher Goes to Water Until It Breaks*; Harry Humes,

Butterfly Effect; Joan Murray, *Looking for the Parade*; Ed Roberson, *Atmospheric Conditions*; Lee Ann Roripaugh, *Beyond Heart Mountain*
Anne Carson, *Autobiography of Red*
Robert Creeley, *Life and Death*
Alice Notley, *Mysteries of Small Houses*
Charles Wright, *Appalachia*

1999   MacArthur Fellowship: Campbell McGrath
Pulitzer Prize: Mark Strand, *Blizzard of One*
National Book Award: Ai, *Vice: New and Selected Poems*
National Poetry Series: Tenaya Darlington, *Madame Deluxe*; Eugene Gloria, *Drivers at the Short-Time Motel*; Corey Marks, *Renunciation*; Dionisio D. Martinez, *Climbing Back*; Standard Schaefer, *Nova*
Rafael Campo, *Diva*
Wanda Coleman, *Bathwater Wine*
August Kleinzahler, *Green Sees Things in Waves*
Michael Palmer, *The Danish Notebook*
Leslie Scalapino and Lyn Hejinian, *Sight*

2000   MacArthur Fellowships: Anne Carson and Lucia M. Perillo
Pulitzer Prize: C. K. Williams, *Repair*
National Book Award: Lucille Clifton, *Blessing the Boats: New and Selected Poems 1988–2000*
National Poetry Series: Jean Donnelly, *Anthem*; Susan Atefat Peckham, *That Kind of Sleep*; Spencer Short, *Tremolo*; Rebecca Wolff, *Manderley*; Susan Wood, *Asunder*
Kay Ryan, *Say Uncle*

2001   Pulitzer Prize: Stephen Dunn, *Different Hours*
National Book Award: Alan Dugan, *Poems Seven: New and Complete Poetry*
National Poetry Series: Betsy Brown, *Year of Morphines*; David Groff, *Theory of Devolution*; Terrance Hayes, *Hip Logic*; Elizabeth Robinson, *Pure Descent*; Ruth L. Schwartz, *Edgewater*
Christian Bök, *Eunoia*
Alice Fulton, *Felt*
Allen Grossman, *How to Do Things with Tears*
Nada Gordon and Gary Sullivan, *Swoon*
Rod Smith, *The Good House*

2002   Lilly Pharmaceuticals heiress Ruth Lilly bequeaths $100 million to *Poetry: A Magazine of Verse*
Pulitzer Prize: Carl Dennis, *Practical Gods*
National Book Award: Ruth Stone, *In the Next Galaxy*
National Poetry Series: Julie Kane, *Rhythm and Booze*; W. B. Keckler, *Sanskrit of the Body*; Eleni Sikelianos, *The Monster Lives of Boys and Girls*; Gabriel Spera, *The Standing Wave*; Meredith Stricker, *Tenderness Shore*
Rachel Blau DuPlessis, *Drafts 1–38*
Myung Mi Kim, *Commons*
Major Jackson, *Leaving Saturn*
Harryette Mullen, *Sleeping with the Dictionary*
Claudia Rankine and Juliana Spahr, eds., *American Women Poets in the 21st Century: Where Lyric Meets Language*

2003   Establishment of The Poetry Foundation
Pulitzer Prize: Paul Muldoon, *Moy Sand and Gravel*
National Book Award: C. K. Williams, *The Singing*
National Poetry Series: Stephen Cramer, *Shiva's Drum*; Andrew Field, *Citizen*; Raymond McDaniel, *Murder (a violet)*; John Spaulding, *The White Train*; Mark Yakich, *Unrelated Individuals Forming a Group Waiting to Cross*
Kenneth Golsmith, *Day*
K. Silem Mohammad, *Deer Head Nation*
C. D. Wright, *One Big Self*

2004   MacArthur Fellowship: C. D. Wright
Pulitzer Prize: Franz Wright, *Walking to Martha's Vineyard*
National Book Award: Jean Valentine, *Door in the Mountain: New and Collected Poems, 1965–2003*
National Poetry Series: David Friedman, *The Welcome*; Tyehimba Jess, *leadbelly*; Corinne Lee, *PYX*; Ange Mlinko, *Starred Wire*; Camille Norton, *Corruption*
Jen Bervin, *Nets*
Michael Fried, *The Next Bend in the Road*
D. A. Powell, *Cocktails*
Christina Pugh, *Rotary*
Claudia Rankine, *Don't Let Me Be Lonely*
Srikanth Reddy, *Facts for Visitors*
Matthew Rohrer, *A Green Light*
Cole Swensen, *Goest*

2005   Pulitzer Prize: Ted Kooser, *Delights and Shadows*
National Book Award: W. S. Merwin, *Migration: New and Selected Poems*
National Poetry Series: Steve Gehrke, *The Resurrection Machine*; Nadine Meyer, *The Anatomy Theater*; Patricia Smith, *Teahouse of the Almighty*; S. A. Stepanek, *Three, Breathing*; Tryfon Tolides, *An Almost Pure Empty Walking*
Elizabeth Alexander, *American Sublime*
Jennifer Moxley, *Often, Capital*
Kay Ryan, *The Niagara River*
Anne Winters, *The Displaced of Capital*
John Yau, *Ing Grish*

2006   Pulitzer Prize: Claudia Emerson, *Late Wife*
National Book Award: Nathaniel Mackey, *Splay Anthem*
National Poetry Series: Laynie Browne, *The Scented Fox*; Noa Eli Gordon, *Novel Pictorial Noise*; Laurie Clements Lambeth, *Veil and Burn*; Martha Ronk, *Vertigo*; William Stobb, *Nervous Systems*
Joshua Clover, *The Totality for Kids*
Noah Eli Gordon, *Inbox*
Terrance Hayes, *Wind in a Box*
Tao Lin, *you are a little bit happier than i am*
Alice Notley, *Grave Light: New and Selected Poems 1970–2005*
Frederick Seidel, *Ooga-Booga*

2007   MacArthur Fellowship: Peter Cole
Pulitzer Prize: Natasha Tretheway, *Native Guard*
National Book Award: Robert Hass, *Time and Materials*
National Poetry Series: Joe Bonomo, *Installations*; Oni Buchanan, *Spring*; Sabra Loomis, *House Held Together by Winds*; Donna Stonecipher, *The Cosmopolitan*; Rodrigo Toscano, *Collapsible Poetics Theater*
Rae Armantrout, *Next Life*
Mary Jo Bang, *Elegy*
Matthea Harvey, *Modern Life*
Natasha Trethewey, *Native Guard*
Susan Howe, *Souls of the Labadie Tract*
Rod Smith, *Deed*

2008   Pulitzer Prize: Philip Schultz, *Failure*
National Book Award: Mark Doty, *Fire to Fire: New and Collected Poems*
National Poetry Series: Anna Journey, *If Birds Gather Your Hair for Nesting*; Douglas Kearney, *The Black Automaton*; Adrian Matejka, *Mixology*; Kristin Naca, *Bird Eating Bird*; Sarah O'Brien, *catch light*
Anne Boyer, *The Romance of Happy Workers*
Kevin Davies, *The Golden Age of Paraphernalia*

2009   MacArthur Fellowship: Heather McHugh
Pulitzer Prize: W. S. Merwin, *The Shadow of Sirius*
National Book Award: Keith Waldrop, *Transcendental Studies: A Trilogy*
National Poetry Series: Julie Carr, *Sarah – Of Fragments and Lines*; Colin Cheney, *Here Be Monsters*; Carrie Fountain, *Burn Lake*; Erika Meitner, *Ideal Cities*; Jena Osman, *The Network*
Rita Dove, *Sonata Mulattica*

2010   Pulitzer Prize: Rae Armantrout, *Versed*
National Book Award: Terrence Hayes, *Lighthead*
National Poetry Series: Lauren Berry, *The Lifting Dress*; Billia Billiter, *Stutter*; James Grinwis, *Exhibit of Forking Paths*; M. A. Vizsolyi, *The Lamp with Wings: 60 Love Sonnets*; Laura Wetherington, *A Map Predetermined and Chance*
Ben Lerner, *Mean Free Path*
Anne Carson, *Nox*
Timothy Donnelly, *The Cloud Corporation*
John Koethe, *Ninety-Fifth Street*

1

JENNIFER ASHTON

Periodizing Poetic Practice since 1945

The *Cambridge Companion to American Poetry since 1945* is organized to represent the most important poetic developments in the period (between 1945 and the present) and to do so in the context of the social, political, professional, and, above all, aesthetic forces that shaped those developments. But in the discourse of literary history, the designation "Post 45" is a comparatively new attempt at the periodization of the twentieth and early twenty-first centuries, and its canons are still in the making. The chapters of the volume are designed to provide a variety of vantages on the poetic production of the period, and the categories that organize them are thus not all taxonomically equivalent to one another. Although a certain number of the chapters are devoted to the major schools or movements in American poetry since 1945 – Confessionalism, the New York School, Language writing – recognizable as such either through an established body of criticism or through claims made and acknowledged by the poets themselves, other chapters take a very different angle of approach. Devoted to particular ways of being or becoming a poet or to important institutional formations that do not fit neatly within the terms of a movement or school, these chapters – for example, on creative writing programs in the United States, on discursive formations such as the idea of the "mainstream," or on two instances (Allen Grossman and Susan Howe) of what one might call the career of the "academic poet" – are intended to fill out, in ways that a survey driven only by important movements could not, a detailed picture of the major poetic projects, formal innovations, and aesthetic legacies that have defined American poetry in the latter half of the twentieth century and the first decade of the twenty-first.

Furthermore, although various dichotomies – between mainstream and marginal or avant-garde, between academic and nonacademic, between practice and theory – have played a significant role in the recent history of American poetry, the essays that make up this volume are concerned as much with understanding that history as the attempt to deal with a set of common problems, as with the effort to taxonomize the solutions. The hope is that as students and scholars of the period read in and across this volume, they will become well acquainted with the range of aesthetic and philosophical questions that poetry of the last six decades has asked and the answers it has given: Who or what determines the meaning of a poem (language as a system of rules, as ideology, as inventive practice? the poet's intention? the material or historical situation in which the poem was produced? the reader's response to the poem?)? In what ways do poems seek to represent persons, whether it be the poet himself or herself, some other imagined speaker of the poems, or someone to whom the poem is addressed? What, if any, kinds of value can poetry bestow on persons or objects in the world? To what extent do poems belong to the world of experience that we inhabit, and to what extent should they be understood as categorically distinct from that world? In what ways do poetic uses of language distinguish it from "ordinary" uses of language? How ordinary is ordinary language to begin with?

Many of these questions are obviously abstract, but readers of this *Companion* will quickly see that they are asked and answered in the context of sometimes overwhelmingly concrete historical developments. The question of poetry's ability to confer value on persons, for example, is crucially reformulated by the actual genocides of the mid-twentieth century and by the potential for total annihilation made vivid by the invention of the nuclear bomb. The question of the poem's speaker and of its audience is also given a new valence, both by the rise of new social movements (such as the civil rights movement, feminism, and the mobilization for rights and recognition denied on the basis of other ascriptive and legal categories such as sexuality, disability, or citizenship status) and by the questions about the very identities that produce and are produced by those movements. And, more generally, the globalization of markets and the saturation of local cultures by marketed and marketable objects and ideas has given new meaning to many of the legal, scientific, political, and religious questions that have always been a subject of poetic discourse: Which uses of language count as public versus which count as private, say, or what sorts of ethical responsibilities acts of speech do or do not entail.

We begin a little over a decade before 1945, with an avant-garde movement that traces its lineage directly to two major modernist predecessors, Ezra Pound and William Carlos Williams, and indirectly to a third, Gertrude Stein. Both Williams and Pound were important mentors to Louis Zukofsky, the coiner of the term "objectivists" and the major figure associated with it, and it is partially through the mediations of the poets who gathered, however briefly, under that umbrella that they and Stein have crucially influenced some of the avant-garde movements that are absolutely central to the period covered by this volume. Thus, while the Objectivists have one foot planted in the modernism of the preceding generation, they also antici-pate the claims made by Charles Olson in his 1950 manifesto "Projective Verse" that would help establish the ideal of the "open text" as one of the foundations of postmodern poetry.[1] Mark Scroggins's detailed, comprehen-sive account in Chapter 2 reveals the extent to which the influence of the objectivists, particularly as funneled through Olson, had expansive effects in the generations following, from Allen Ginsberg and the Beats, to Robert Duncan and the San Francisco Renaissance, to Amiri Baraka and the Black Arts movement, to the Language writers of the 1970s through the 1990s, as subsequent chapters on all four of these movements make clear.

Launched with the February 1931 "Objectivists" issue of *Poetry: A Magazine of Verse*, edited by Zukofsky at the request of Harriet Monroe, the imagined project of the Objectivists as defined by Zukofsky was an explicit response to the Imagist project that Pound had announced in the same venue two decades earlier. But if the questions raised by Imagism focused on the role of technique in the achievement of poetry, the ques-tions raised by Objectivism had to do with distinguishing such techniques from the ontology of the poetic achievement itself. Thus, whereas technique is, for Pound and Imagism, the "test of a man's sincerity" and, in turn, of the poem's success, "sincerity" (technique in precisely Pound's terms, and as such a formal rather than a psychological category) becomes, for Zukofsky and Objectivism, subordinate to and ontologically distinct from the ideal achievement of poetry, namely the poem's "rested totality": its composi-tional integrity.[2] In this respect, the idea of the objective in poetry is never far from music – hence Zukofsky's famous formula, the sign of the inte-gral indicating "Lower limit speech / Upper limit: music."[3] Moreover, the role played by individual words in the poem imagined on the model of the musical composition generates another set of questions central to much of the poetry covered by this volume: How do we understand the relationship between the meaning of words and their phonic and graphic forms – or, more broadly, between the materiality of language and its communicative uses?

As crucial to a proper understanding of this movement as its formal prin-ciples are the left political commitments of its poets, a number of whom were actively involved with, if not signed members of, the Communist Party. At the same time there is a manifest anxiety in the work regarding the political efficacy of poetry. For Zukofsky and Lorine Niedecker this would take the form of a sustained critique of one of the major formal devices of poetry – metaphor – as an effort to test its adequacy to the representation of material poverty. In the case of Oppen, it would take the form of nearly two and a half decades of silence after the publication of his first book of poetry in 1934 – the refusal or inability to write during a long period of intensive political activism for the Communist Party and labor causes in New York, followed by a life of exile in Mexico until 1960. But for these poets, and indeed for the poetry that has come to be identified as Objectivist, the project of foregrounding the materiality of the word in the poem becomes an analog for the representation of the material conditions of objects and persons in the world. This same project would be taken up with no space for analogy, and no ambivalence, several decades later in the work of Language writers such as Charles Bernstein, Lyn Hejinian, and Ron Silliman, who would argue that such reading and writing entails a kind of unalienated labor, capable of granting poet and reader alike direct access to the means of poetic production.

Published nearly two decades after the "Objectivists" issue of *Poetry*, Charles Olson's "Projective Verse" was in part an explicit response to the Objectivist project descended from Zukofsky and Niedecker. For Olson, the commitment to the objective involved a latent commitment to the subjective, which needed to be made patent as the quite literal vitality of the poem. Between typewriter and page Olson saw the poet's own breath shaping the arrangement of the words in the poem, the resulting material form of the poem as the trace of the visceral presence of the poet *as subject*. Understanding the argument of the Projective response to Objectivism turns out to be crucial not only to extending the materialist implications of the latter and the legacy it drew from Pound and Williams, but also the extent to which something like "breath" would become representative of a bodily and performative engagement that was by no means unique to Olson – it was as central to the Beat poetry of Jack Kerouac and Bob Kaufman as to the California Renaissance of Jack Spicer and Robert Duncan or the Black Arts poetics of Amiri Baraka and Nikki Giovanni.

If the musical model for the formal project of the Objectivists would have been a Bach cantata or, in homage to Pound, a Provençal chanson, the equivalent for the Beat movement is the "barbaric chant." Drawing on Walt Whitman – indeed, making the poetry as well as the personality of Whitman more central to poetic thought than ever before – Allen Ginsberg, Gregory Corso, Lawrence Ferlinghetti, Jack Kerouac, Diane di Prima, and other Beats represented a lifestyle as much as a poetics and a sustaining model for the counterculture of the late 1960s. The career of Ginsberg and the successive public performances of "Howl" effectively chart the transition from a Beat counterculture of individual rebellion – openly exploring sexuality (gay and straight), taking drugs, studying Buddhism and Hinduism – to a Hippie counterculture in which sex and drugs turn into communitarian enterprise. The inseparability of poetry, sex, spiritualism, and political activism that mark Ginsberg's own transition from Beat poet to Hippie are the hallmarks of the larger counterculture movement as well, as it became increasingly driven by organized protests against the war in Vietnam. But while chanted word plays its role in demonstration, it can hardly be said to have been invented by the Beats or the Hippies; the rhythms of the speeches of the civil rights protests of the 1950s and early 1960s – that is, the rhythms also of the black preacher's sermon – were essential to the emphasis on oral utterance in Beat poetry, as was the elevation of breath as the unit of the line in Charles Olson's "Projective Verse" and LeRoi Jones's (later Amiri Baraka) "How You Sound??" In this respect, a complete account of the movement must engage these influences as well as the consequences that Beat poetry's transformations of chant, in turn, had in the emergence of spoken word as a genre and slam contests as a format for its performance.[4]

Often understood as a reaction against the imperative to impersonality in the modernism of Eliot, Pound, and Moore, the thematic concerns of the poetry of the 1950s and 1960s that would come to be called "confessional" – psychological depression, suicidal impulses, domestic oppression or abuse, and alcoholism, for example – move into the realm of public utterance what might otherwise remain confined to the most private exchanges between family members, between analyst and client, or between priest and parishioner (hence the term "confessional"). Unlike the romantic vision of the poem as the spontaneous outpourings of the poet – not heard but overheard (to borrow from William Wordsworth and John Stuart Mill), and so produced by an ideally unselfconscious speaker – the speech acts of confessional poems are supremely self-conscious in their depiction of deeply personal thoughts and situations. As Deborah Nelson shows in Chapter 3, these poetic projects take place both in the context of an increased popular interest in what in everyday life does and does not count as private, even of (in the wake of McCarthyism) what is and is not properly accessible to the State. In this respect, confessional poetry must also be understood as itself a project of working out poetic definitions of the "personal" and the "private" as such, as well as their relation to one another and to poetic discourse more generally.

If the degree to which confessional poetry counts as personal is the degree to which it lays bare the most emotionally fraught or potentially scandalous desires and impulses of the poet, the poetry for which Frank O'Hara coined the term "Personism" in 1960 – namely, his own – challenged itself to make art out of the poet's most mundane desires and impulses. But the "I do this, I do that" statements about everyday activities that were O'Hara's stylistic hallmark were understood by him not so much as efforts to achieve a detailed sense of the particular person who was Frank O'Hara, but rather as a means of achieving – as Oren Izenberg has argued – something like the representation of personhood as such. Solicited for Donald Allen's 1960 anthology, *The New American Poetry*, Frank O'Hara's Personism prescribed a poetics that is rooted, on the one hand, in the idea of impulse ("you go on your nerve"), and thus in the most personal and idiosyncratic of choices. On the other hand, in "opposing the personal removal for the poet" (an opposition O'Hara also identifies closely with the abstract canvases of Jackson Pollock, Joan Mitchell, and other contemporary painters), Personism aspires to "true abstraction."[5] For O'Hara, this commitment to abstraction – not through the impersonality of the poet but through something like his presence in the poem as the expression of personal choice (think also of Pollack describing himself as *in* the painting while pouring and dripping the paint) – is ultimately a way of distinguishing the poem and the work of art more generally from the experiential world of the reader / viewer. In Chapter 4, Charles Altieri brings an important and long-missing focus to the relationship among New York School poets, such as O'Hara, Barbara Guest, and John Ashbery, and painters of the same moment who were reviving figurative modes at a time when abstract expressionism was dominant. Altieri calls our attention to the work of Fairfield Porter, Larry Rivers, and Jane Freilicher to show how poets – precisely in their contact with these painters and their work – were developing new ways of imagining expressivity in art.

Taking place on the opposite coast at roughly the same time as the New York School was emerging as something that could be called a "school," the California Renaissance was striking in its confluences with the Beat movement as well as the Black Arts movement. Indeed as Michael Davidson's, Ronna Johnson's, and Margo Crawford's chapters all show, there is considerable overlap among the poets whose names are synonymous with these movements. But as Davidson makes clear in Chapter 5, the California Renaissance is also striking in that its scope extends well beyond the 1950s and 1960s; poets associated with the later developments of Language writing – Clark Coolidge, Lyn Hejinian, Michael Palmer, and Kit Robinson, among others – also rightly belong to it. It would be hard not to see the community of writers who collaborated on one another's work, founded magazines and small presses, and gave readings together in the Bay Area during the 1970s and 1980s as an important extension of the poetic ideas of the "open text" (another legacy of Black Mountain) that became solidified in conversations among Kenneth Rexroth, Madeline Gleason, Robert Duncan, Jack Spicer, and Robin Blaser in the 1950s and 1960s. But the latter poets' investigations of the material features of language as a kind of architecture of thought – taking on the shape of archetypal myth in Duncan and of something like raw information in Spicer – require discussion on their own terms. For one thing, at the time when the circle around Rexroth and Duncan was forming, there was as yet no vivid sense of the San Francisco Bay area as a geographical center for poetry, as there had long been for New York, and as there would be by the time the Language writers of the West Coast were coalescing into a community. In this respect, the geographical designation functions similarly to that of the New York School. But for the San Francisco Renaissance poets, there was also the added sense (a distinctively American one, it is worth noting) of a new frontier – or as Duncan might have put it, of "opening the field." Or, to use a term that would matter even more to the next generation of writers in the Bay area, we might say that the place was in this instance foundational to the very idea of the "open text."

Emerging contemporaneously with the Beat movement and with the poetic activity that came to be identified with the San Francisco Renaissance – and involving no small number of their poets – the Black Arts movement can be seen as a reinvention of the celebration of blackness in the Harlem Renaissance and of the questions of cultural aesthetics that it raised, but in the context now of a radical, even militant, politics. Indeed the movement is driven in part precisely out of a sense (articulated most vividly in Harold Cruse's *Crisis of the Negro Intellectual*) that the intellectual and artistic efforts of the Harlem Renaissance, whatever forms of recognition and respect they may have garnered for African-American culture, had been a political failure.[6] LeRoi Jones – who would renounce his "slave" name in the late 1960s and rename himself Amiri Baraka, and whose 1967 anthology, *Black Fire* (coedited with Larry Neal), would effectively establish a Black Arts canon – charts his own career in terms of a renunciation of a more or less detached aesthetics for one inextricable from political action.[7]

The continuity between the Black Arts movement and its poetic predecessors is visible in Jones's significant career as editor or contributing editor of several very important small magazines in the 1950s and early 1960s (*Kulchur*, *Yugen*, and *Floating Bear*, in particular). Here, in collaboration with Diane di Prima and others, Jones solicited work from a remarkably diverse range of poets, including Louis Zukofsky, Charles Olson, Frank O'Hara, Allen Ginsberg, Robert Creeley, Denise Levertov, and Gary Snyder. Indeed, the significance of a number of the foundational statements of American avant-garde poetry in the latter half of the twentieth century – O'Hara's "Personism" and Olson's "Projective Verse" in particular – cannot be fully understood without reference to Baraka's early poetic and editorial career and the later political transformations undertaken by him and by the Black Arts movement in general (and vice versa).

But if his 1959 manifesto "How You Sound??" alludes unmistakably to his correspondence with Olson, and if Baraka's poetry, both early and late, manifests an emphasis on the body similar to what one finds in Olson and in much of the performance-based work associated with Black Mountain, the poetry of Baraka would increasingly insist on aspects of that body that in Olson were at best incidental. For Baraka, the vital source of the poem is not just a body, but a raced body, a black body. When Baraka points to the sounds made by John Coltrane and others who would represent the "New Music" in jazz (Pharoah Sanders, Albert Ayler, Sun Ra, among others), it is to imagine their art precisely as a kind of projection through the breath, but he would also insist that that projection sounded different to black listeners than it did to white ones. For unlike Olson's "Projective Verse," the wailing and shrieking bursts of the New Music solo are understood by Baraka not so much as a projection of the artist in his visceral particularity (à la Olson), but of the artist expressing, by means of his raced body, the collective protest of a people united by oppression, first under slavery, then under Jim Crow, and finally, after the de jure (if not de facto) abolishment of both, under the continued economic and social consequences of that history.

The point of the new Black Arts and theater collectives at the time – the Umbra Workshop, for example, or the Black Arts Repertory Theater School and others modeled on it such as Black Arts West and Black Arts South – in identifying and promoting a distinctively black aesthetic was not (or not merely) self-expression, or even collective expression, but political action and change: hence the anthemic function of works such as Baraka's "It's Nation Time!," Giovanni's "The True Import of Present Dialogue, Black vs. Negro," or The Last Poets' "The Revolution Will Not Be Televised," written to be performed before an audience and to move people not only to shout back but to act.[8] The call-and-response form that dominated these perform-ances was a model for the Beat movement as it persisted through the antiwar protests of the late 1960s, as well as for the later spoken word performances and slam contests that would become increasingly popular toward the end of the twentieth century. In Chapter 7, Margo Natalie Crawford probes beneath the surface of poems by major spokespersons of the movement to reveal a dialectical movement between the personal and the social, the indi-vidual and the collective.

Arising in the context of second-wave feminism in the United States following World War II – in the midst of the best-selling publication of Betty Friedan's *Feminine Mystique* (1963), the formation of a Presidential Commission on the Status of Women and of the National Organization of Women, the (successful) proposal to include discrimination on the basis of sex in the Civil Rights Act of 1964, and the (eventually unsuccessful) proposal of an Equal Rights Amendment to the U.S. Constitution – the feminist poetry discussed by Lisa Sewell in Chapter 8 does not present anything like a unified front.[9] But what the work has in common – and shares with the events listed earlier – is a broad critique of male hegemony, more specifically of patriarchal structures that were understood to have consistently misrepresented or altogether denied representation to women. For poets like Muriel Rukeyser or Alicia Ostriker, for example, the translation of this critique into poetic discourse meant thematizing, in rich detail, thoughts and feelings offering privileged access to experiences unique to women's lives. Maternal bonds and conflicts, female friendship, and the struggle to voice those experiences using the forms of a male-dominated poetic tradition are among the recurring themes of their work. Poetry also becomes a means here of thinking through other identity categories as they relate to gender and sex. The major figure in this context is Adrienne Rich, whose feminist projects both outside and inside poetry would become synonymous with a wider critique of heteronormativity. And when that project is in turn aligned with a broader critique of white supremacy, we begin to see efforts to negotiate multiple racial or ethnic identities – for instance, African American (Audre Lorde), Chicana (Cherríe Moraga), Native American (Joy Harjo) – as well as the constraints of gender. The earlier poetry in Chapter 8 engages with feminism by thematizing various aspects of women's experiences. The question of whether there is a distinctive form as well as content for women's poetry emerges in a much more pervasive way in the 1980s and 1990s with the advent of various identity-based "innovative" poetries that emphasize linguistic experiment and rupture as strategies for combating ideological formations around race, gender, and sex.

The ecology movement in the United States ignites at roughly the same time as second-wave feminist and civil rights movements of the 1960s. After the publication of Rachel Carson's *Silent Spring* in 1962, the question of the pastoral in poetry begins to be raised not as it had been in the modernist context – as a question about what counts as the alternative to the urban (as in Frost or the Southern Agrarians) or about how the urban might itself count as pastoral (as in Hart Crane or William Carlos Williams) – but in the context of a nature that is for the first time defined by the endangerment posed by human presence.[10] In the work of poets like A. R. Ammons or Wendell Berry, ecology, specifically as it involves human uses and transformations of nature, becomes an allegory for a kind of poetic economy grounded in the metaphorical transformation of meaning. For a poet like Gary Snyder, meanwhile, the poetic technique of personifying nature as a means of communicating human thoughts and feelings becomes a project of granting nature itself the standing of personhood, with the poem as the proper means of acknowledgment. In 1972, the legal theorist Christopher Stone asked the question "Should Trees Have Standing?" – asking, in effect, whether lawyers should be allowed to represent their interests in court.[11] The answer of Snyder and other poets in the strongest "ecopoetic" tradition has been that, whether or not the lawyers do, the poet will. In Chapter 9, Nick Selby situates the work of recognizable ecopoets alongside those whose work might appear less obviously ecologically engaged, even as he offers an incisive analysis of the theoretical frameworks that have emerged around ecopoetry under the name of "ecocriticism."

From Olson's "Projective Verse" and Jones's "How You Sound??" and the poetic movements that extend from their moment of inception, we can see how impossible it would be to give a full account of poetry in the United States in the second half of the twentieth century without taking identity – racial, cultural, sexual – into account; however, one could as easily argue that the same applies to poetry from the preceding half-century as well. But from a purely material perspective, it would be equally impossible to give a full account of poetry in the United States in the second half of the twentieth century without taking up the development and proliferation of the MFA program in creative writing, and this would not be true for the preceding decades. Beginning with the Iowa Writers' Workshop, founded in 1936, the institution of the workshop, while it certainly has own its precedents and models in various writing groups and collaborative endeavors that have occurred throughout the history of poetry, nevertheless marks, in its remarkable proliferation throughout the academic system in the United States in particular, something distinctive to post-1945 American poetry. The phrase "workshopping a poem," ubiquitous in poetic discourse during the period of concern in this volume, would have been unimaginable for most of the first half of the twentieth century and earlier. Hank Lazer's treatment of the newly professionalized contexts of poetry asks us to consider both the constraints and the openings these institutional formations have created for poets. The remaining chapters of this volume are all inflected in some way by the role of academic programs in poetic discourse whether by virtue of an avowed antagonism, as in the case of rap and spoken word, or a kind of rivalry, as with the early Language movement, or by virtue of the kinds of choices that have developed in the context of the workshop itself (with the emphasis it places on exercises, disciplinary constraints, etc.).

The concept of the "workshop poem" could never have emerged without expansion of the academy in the latter half of the twentieth century, and neither could our idea of the "academic poet." In Chapter 13, Oren Izenberg disables the pejorative connotations of the term and reveals how two exemplary poets, Allen Grossman and Susan Howe, start from a sense of the poetic vocation in its largest sense. The particularity of the American poem for Howe links to the materiality of its sites of production and the circumstances of the American writer (Emily Dickinson, Charles Sanders Peirce, anonymous members of an obscure religious sect), whose representation requires disciplined archival research in order to do justice to the conditions under which their poetic thinking took place. For Grossman, the universality of the poetic project hinges on the predication of all language on loss and the assertion of value in persons that the mourning of loss entails. Both of these projects are inexplicable without the institutional context of the academy or the kind of literary scholarship that gets taught and promoted there; at the same time neither of these bodies of work typifies anything that might come to mind when we speak of academic poetry on the one hand or academic criticism on the other. What Howe and Grossman each offer, albeit in completely different forms, is to establish, systematically and completely, the grounds of necessity for poetry – and further to exemplify its necessity in a cumulatively coherent body of work, one to which poetry is obviously central but that also importantly includes theoretical texts (like Howe's *The Birth-Mark* and Grossman's *Summa Lyrica*) that have themselves become central to contemporary critical thought.[12]

From John Ashbery's "Self-Portrait in a Convex Mirror" to Jorie Graham's "Self-Portrait as..." poems in *The End of Beauty and* several poems entitled "Notes on the Idea of the Self" in *Materialism*, to Louise Glück's mythological restaging of patently autobiographical material in *The Triumph of Achilles*, to C. D. Wright's *One Big Self*, a collaborative project with a photographer and inmates of several prisons in the South, one of the major questions of the period in U.S. poetry since 1945 has been how to explain the predominance of poems exemplifying or resisting, embodying or dissolving, the idea of a self in the act of expression.[13] Why, to put the question even more generally, does U.S. poetry seem to be preoccupied with either affirming or repudiating one notion or another of the "lyric," along with its corollary categories of "speaker" and "tone" (themselves largely academic products of the New Criticism at the mid-century)? In Chapter 12, Christina Pugh examines work that has, for critics and poets alike, and for celebrators and detractors alike, come to count as paradigmatically "lyric." Whereas, on the one hand, creative writing programs are at least as responsible as the work of critics writing on contemporary poetry for the promulgation of twentieth-century ideas about the lyric, and if Language writing has been responsible for one of the most powerful sustained critiques of lyric, Pugh helps establish what it is we have meant by lyric in the late twentieth and early twenty-first centuries, even as she elegantly dismantles many of the late-twentieth-century assumptions that have divided poetic activity between an avant-garde and a mainstream.

In the eyes of those for whom "mainstream" is a real category (and a pejorative one), the kinds of poems written by, say, Charles Wright or Louise Glück look problematic precisely by virtue of the qualities that for a critic like Helen Vendler represent the prospect of continuity in the lyric tradition: an authoritative voice, the display of privileged access to the highest forms of thought, the purpose of conferring special insight or experience upon a reader. The lyric transformation of the reader's soul that Vendler famously celebrates becomes, for poets like Bob Perelman or Lyn Hejinian, the imposition of a false hierarchy in which "the poet," as Perelman puts it, "is firmly in the driver's seat ... firmly in control of all the meaning," and the poem, far from effecting any transformation, leaves reader and poet alike "unaffected by the word."[14] The Language movement, then, represented in part an effort to recuperate the capacity of words to affect us and did so by enabling readers to confront language as a material presence – visual, aural, sensual – and in so doing to participate actively in bringing the poem into being. In effect, Language writing so imagined is something like the inverse of Olson's "Projective Verse"; where the Projective poet asserted his visceral self through the breath into the word, with Language writing, the word now comes into being through the reader's visceral encounter with it. What makes that visceral encounter possible are various strategies for disrupting our conventional patterns of thought and meaning: disjunctive syntax, nonsense syllables, ruptured words, erasures and overwritten texts. If the New Criticism is central to the lyric that language poetry opposes, it is the advent of French poststructuralist theory, especially deconstruction, that provides the theoretical (and to some extent political) foundation for Language writing, a poetics of indeterminacy founded on the idea of the word as a material or even bodily trace. The question of what kind of a thing a text or poem is now becomes a function neither of what the poet might have intended by its words nor of what the conventions of grammar and meaning might seem to require of them, but rather of the reader's irreducibly subjective experience in her encounter with those words. Understood as a political act, the critique of the linguistic structures that is at the heart of Language writing is also intended to put poet and reader on equal footing. But more than that, in its most utopian versions, the idea that the reader's experience of the materiality of the word is the compositional agency that makes the poem becomes for Language writing a powerful vision of the possibility of revolution, of disabling the power of ideological formations and giving the reader full agency over the production of the work. Steve McCaffery, often identified with Language writing as one its foremost practitioners, offers in

Chapter 10 a critically nuanced history of the full range of creative practices that came to be associated with the term "Language," and does so without losing sight of the theoretical and aesthetic differences and disagreements that helped propel those projects.

Another commitment to the agency of the audience, also in the interest of eradicating hierarchies of power, is obvious in the context of the spoken word movements of the 1980s through the present. But as Michael Clune makes clear in Chapter 14, the rap music that came to prominence during the same period is designed to cut the audience out of the performance, however impossible a project that would seem to be in the context of the rapper's video and live appearances. Despite this fundamental divide, and despite the fact that the practitioners of rap, hip-hop, and spoken word alike would want to insist on the points of divergence in their history and the institutions and markets in and against which they have developed, these modes of verbal performance share sufficient formal and theoretical similarities to merit their discussion in a single chapter.

Part of what has defined the spoken word movements, including slam competition, is their wholesale rejection of academic institutions and paradigms for the promotion and understanding of the poetry. In the case of rap and hip-hop, of course, the idea of resisting the academy is absent altogether, because the singer and audience alike often represent a world where the academy is irrelevant (because it is inaccessible) to begin with; resistance is rather to the state (in the form of the police, for example) and on behalf of the market (sometimes in drugs, sometime in clothes and jewelry, and always in music itself). But spoken word, hip-hop, and rap represent important work for this volume precisely because the kinds of questions they raise – particularly about the relationship between poet/speaker/singer and audience, between the uttered and the written – are of central concern both to the history of poetry broadly construed and to its most recent American manifestations. What emerges in the discourse about both spoken word and rap is rhetoric emphasizing the importance of authentic self-expression (being "real") even as the words of the poems themselves and the theatrical features of their performance present distinctive strategies for obfuscating or obscuring the presence of the person speaking the poem. Perhaps most vividly, the lyrics of recent rap songs, as Clune's analysis demonstrates, have mobilized the tropes of conspicuous consumption – the image of gold ("bling") in particular – as a technology, paradoxically, for blinding the sight of the viewer and disabling the possibility of social recognition in the wake of a long history of political efforts to promote recognition, efforts that have largely failed to achieve social justice for black people.

The final chapter of this volume returns to the visual surface of the page (occasionally extending to the computer screen). A number of younger poets operating in the wake of the Language writers' powerful efforts to discredit the conventions of voice and epiphany in the "mainstream workshop lyric," even as Language poetry itself seemed to have become the "official verse culture" (to recall Charles Bernstein), have raised the question of whether the very idea of poetic innovation remains viable. As one of the *chefs d'état* of the movement, Bob Perelman, put it himself, "The gestures that Language poetry triumphantly says are still radical are actually super codified now."[15] And because many of the answers to that question have also constituted a more or less direct response to the Language writers' commitment to innovation, the question resides along the axis of the relationship between poems and their material sources (language, media, the poet or the reader's own embodied experience) on the one hand and the works' material and ideological effects on the other. What movements ranging from Flarf (Google-search-based poetry) to the resurgence of conceptual writing *as* a movement, and also what some newly published projects by distinguished poets of the an earlier generation (C. D. Wright, Cole Swensen), have had in common is an effort to revisit questions about the relationship between the poet's agency and the possibilities of language, producing new ways of either embracing or rejecting subjectivity as sources for the poem. Indeed, what the poetry of the First Decade shows is how central those sometimes contradictory relations to the very idea of subjectivity – and more specifically, to an idea of "lyric" – have remained. Thus, the First Decade matters to this volume, not because it represents major departures from the work of preceding generations or ushers in the next big movement (although Chapter 15 will offer two examples of what these might look like), but because it makes visible the cohesiveness of the American poetic project since 1945, an era of literary production that still includes our present moment.

NOTES

1. Charles Olson, "Projective Verse," in *Collected Prose*, ed. Donald Allen and Benjamin Friedlander (Berkeley, Los Angeles, and London: The University of California Press, 1997).
2. Ezra Pound, "A Retrospect," in *Literary Essays of Ezra Pound* (New York: New Directions, 1968), 9; Louis Zukofsky, "An Objective," *Prepositions+: The Collected Critical Essays*, ed. Charles Bernstein (Hanover and London: University Press of New England, 2000), 13.
3. Louis Zukofsky, "A" (Berkeley and Los Angeles: The University of California Press, 1978), 138.
4. LeRoi Jones, "How You Sound?" in *The New American Poetry, 1945–1960*, ed. Donald Allen (New York: Grove Press, 1960).

5. Frank O'Hara, "Personism: A Manifesto," in *The Collected Poems of Frank O'Hara*, ed. Donald Allen (Berkeley, Los Angeles, and London: The University of California Press, 1995), 498.

6. Harold Cruse, *The Crisis of the Negro Intellectual* (New York: The New York Review of Books, 1967).

7. Amiri Baraka and Larry Neal, eds., *Black Fire: An Anthology of Afro-American Writing* (1968; Baltimore: Black Classic Press, 2007).

8. Amiri Baraka, *The LeRoi Jones/Amiri Baraka Reader*, ed. William J. Harris (New York: Thunder's Mouth Press, 1991); Nikki Giovanni, *The Collected Poetry of Nikki Giovanni* (New York: William Morrow, 2003); The Last Poets, *The Last Poets*, Varese Sarabande. CD, 2002.

9. Betty Friedan, *The Feminine Mystique* (New York: W.W. Norton, 2001).

10. Rachel Carson, *The Silent Spring* (New York: Houghton Mifflin, 2002).

11. Christopher D. Stone, *Should Trees Have Standing?: Law, Morality, and the Environment* (Oxford: Oxford University Press, 2010).

12. Susan Howe, *The Birth-Mark: Unsettling the Wilderness in American Literary History* (Hanover and London: University Press of New England, 1993); Allen Grossman and Mark Halliday, *The Sighted Singer: Two Works on Poetry for Readers and Writers* (Baltimore: The Johns Hopkins University Press, 1992).

13. John Ashbery, *Self-Portrait in a Convex Mirror* (New York: Penguin, 1976); Jorie Graham, *The End of Beauty* (New York: Ecco Press, 1987); Graham, *Materialism* (New York: Ecco Press, 1993); Louise Glück, *The Triumph of Achilles* (New York: Ecco Press, 1987); C. D. Wright, *One Big Self: An Investigation* (Port Townsend, WA: Copper Canyon Press, 2007).

14. Cited in Lee Bartlett, "What Is 'Language Poetry'?" *Critical Inquiry* 12.4 (Summer 1986): 741–752, 743.

15. Bob Perelman, *IFLIFE* (New York: Roof Books, 2006), 32.

FURTHER READING

Altieri, Charles. *The Art of Twentieth-Century American Poetry: Modernism and After*. Oxford: Blackwell, 2006.

Hoover, Paul. *"Introduction" Postmodern American Poetry: A Norton Anthology*. New York: W.W. Norton, 1994.

Von Hallberg, Robert. *Poetry, Politics, and Intellectuals: A History of American Poetry, 1945–1995*. Sacvan Bercovitch. "Poetry, Politics, and Intellectuals." Volume 8, Poetry and Criticism 1940–1995. Cambridge University Press, 1996. Cambridge Histories Online. Cambridge University Press. Accessed November 8, 2011, http://histories.cambridge.org/extract?id=chol9780521497336_eg2

2

MARK SCROGGINS

From the Late Modernism of the "Objectivists" to the Proto-postmodernism of "Projective Verse"

The Objectivist "movement" is most properly viewed as a second-generation moment in American modernist poetry, a short-lived alliance of poets sharing an admiration for the modernist poetics of Ezra Pound and William Carlos Williams and tenuously united under a theoretical banner for a brief period of the 1930s. The Objectivists were active and prominent in American avant-garde circles for only a few years before falling out of the public eye for some two decades, but the Objectivist "nexus" proved to have a tenacious and highly influential half-life. When Charles Olson, himself deeply indebted to Pound and Williams, published his influential 1950 statement of poetics, "Projective Verse," he (probably unwittingly) restated some of the essential tenets Louis Zukofsky had laid down in the various Objectivist manifestos. Olson was an enormously powerful and charismatic figure, and the poets surrounding him – what would later come to be known as the "Black Mountain" group or the "Projectivist" poets – would form a core audience for the reemergence of the original Objectivists, particularly Zukofsky, George Oppen, and Lorine Niedecker, into public prominence. These two generationally separated groups, then, would combine synergistically to make one of the most important "fire-sources" of postwar American avant-garde poetry.

While the word "objectivist" has a philosophical pedigree (Alfred North Whitehead had used it in *Science and the Modern World* [1925]), it first appears in reference to poetry in the February 1931 issue of *Poetry: A Magazine of Verse*, "'Objectivists' 1931." Ezra Pound had persuaded Harriet Monroe, the magazine's editor, to allow his young New York protégé Louis Zukofsky to edit a "special number" of the magazine; Monroe, in turn, had insisted that Zukofsky present his selection of poets under the rubric of a "movement" or "group": clearly she was thinking back to the critical and popular interest aroused by Pound's "Imagists" in the years before the First World War.

So far as he knew, Zukofsky was not participating in any distinct "movement" at the time; he simply wanted to present a selection of work by younger poets whom he found vital and exciting. But under the pressure of Monroe's insistence and an impending deadline, he retooled an essay he had written a year earlier on the work of his friend, Charles Reznikoff, retitling it "Sincerity and Objectification: *With Special Reference to the Work of Charles Reznikoff*," and presented the poets he had chosen as "Objectivists." He had no illusions that his contributors were working together as a group, or would even recognize themselves as "Objectivists." As he told his friend, the poet Carl Rakosi, the whole business was "Foolish – but may excite the reading booblik, hysterectomied & sterilized readers of 'Poetry.'"[1]

While he might deprecate the business of movement formation, Zukofsky was entirely serious about the principles of poetics he laid out in "Sincerity and Objectification." "Sincerity" is a kind of hygiene or askesis of composition, a "preoccupation with the accuracy of detail in writing"; it is writing that is "the detail, not mirage, of seeing, of thinking with the things as they exist, and of directing them along a line of melody."[2] "Thinking with the things as they exist" demands a fidelity to both the objects of the poet's perceptions and the words with which the poet deals. Compositional sincerity rejects both the outright inventions of fiction – the poetry Zukofsky promotes is based on observation rather than imagination – and the mediations of inherited mythology, such as the grail-quest myths underpinning Eliot's *The Waste Land*. Zukofsky would write later, at the height of Eliot's influence, that:

> The poet wonders why so many have raised up the word "myth," finding the lack of so-called "myths" in our time a crisis the poet must overcome or die from, as it were, having become too radioactive, when instead a case can be made for the poet giving some of his life to the use of the words *the* and *a*, both of which are weighted with as much epos and historical destiny as one man can perhaps resolve.[3]

"*No myths*," Kenner comments, "might be the Objectivist motto."[4]

The concept of "sincerity" clearly owes much to the poetic dicta Pound had issued in *Poetry* magazine back in 1913 on behalf of the "Imagist" movement: "Use no superfluous word.... Go in fear of abstractions.... Use either no ornament or good ornament." Indeed, as Pound emphasized then, "I believe in technique as the test of a man's sincerity."[5] "Objectification," on the other hand, is a *formal* principle; according to Zukofsky, it is "the arrangement, into one apprehended unit, of minor units of sincerity – in other words, the resolving of words and their ideation into structure." To achieve objectification in writing is to produce a poem which is a "rested totality," "writing ... which is an object or affects the mind as such."[6] What "objectification" adds to the various Imagist strictures is a principle of overall poetic form, the notion that the ideally realized poem – and Zukofsky is quick to point out that very few poems, even those of his ostensible subject Reznikoff, achieve such realization – is not merely the result of a painstaking fidelity both to the poet's perceptions and to the language at hand, but achieves "rested totality," a tangible objecthood in the reader's mind.

Such "tangibility" has various analogues in the other arts (visual, sculptural), but Zukofsky's own poetic practice pursues in particular the parallels between poetry and music, not merely in his shorter poems labeled "songs" but in the movements of his long poem "A", which aim to mimic the structures of repetition and variation in the baroque fugue. "Sincerity," then, with its emphasis on directing words "along a line of melody," and "objectification," with its definition of the poem as "writing (audibility in two-dimensional print) which is an object or affects the mind as such," put two important questions put into play: (1) the relationship between language's material, audible or tangible aspect, and (2) its communicative function. Pound's critical writings consistently emphasize this communicative function – "Great literature is simply language charged with meaning to the utmost possible degree."[7] Zukofsky, in contrast, with the examples of Gertrude Stein and James Joyce's "Work in Progress" (*Finnegans Wake*) perhaps in mind, pays rather little attention to notions of readerly clarity.

That stance would put Zukofsky at odds later in the 1930s with fellow leftist writers promoting an aesthetic of "social realism," and while he associated with the editorial staff of the Communist *New Masses* and even published a few brief pieces there, he found it impossible to convince agit-prop-minded editors that a poetics deeply invested in modernist innovation had anything concrete to contribute to the class struggle.[8] Zukofsky's fellow Objectivist George Oppen had Marxist convictions as strong as Zukofsky's own, and a poetics as recalcitrantly modernist, but Oppen had no desire either to modify his work to conform to Party standards or to argue for its political value. Instead, he would abandon poetry and devote himself to concrete political organizing for much of the 1930s. "I did not write 'Marxist' poetry," he later recalled; "I made a choice. Stopped, for the crisis, writing."[9]

It is tempting to read the left-wing modernism of the Objectivists – in particular the early Zukofsky, Oppen, and Niedecker – as little more than a demonstration of the ideological ductility of modernist poetics in general. In this view, such works as Oppen's *Discrete Series*, Zukofsky's "'A'-8" or "'A'-9," and Niedecker's Mother Goose–derived political lyrics are merely the ideological flip side of Pound's more reactionary Cantos: both bodies of poetry turn the instrument of a paratactic, collagist poetics to a cultural-political end, and whether that end is socialist or authoritarian depends on the personal inclinations of the poet. But such an equation can only result from a superficial reading of the poetries in question. While the Objectivist poets share with Pound a poetics of the image, of the juxtaposition of textual materials from different realms of discourse, and of the "luminous detail" – the datum that "give[s] one a sudden insight into circumjacent conditions, into their causes, their effects, into sequence, and law"[10] – these poets' emphasis on the tangible "objectification" of the poem, and indeed their ongoing project of foregrounding the materiality of the word in the poem, becomes a sustained analogue for the representation of the material conditions of objects and persons in the world. The leftist poetics of "thinking with the things as they exist," in contrast to the nostalgia of Pound's cultural archaeology, involves a continuous quest for elements of the Utopian precisely in the concrete details of the here and now: in Walter Benjamin's words, "splinters of messianic time."[11]

When, six months after the publication of the "'Objectivists' 1931" *Poetry* issue, Zukofsky defends that issue in the lecture "'Recencies' in Poetry," he emphasizes that "Objectivist" does not name a movement in contemporary poetry ("The interest of the issue was in the few recent lines of poetry which could be found, and in the craft of poetry, NOT in a movement"[12]). There is, in short, no such thing as "Objectivism"; sincerity and objectification are neither new nor revolutionary concepts, but rather transhistorical principles of poem-making. While he showed consistent diffidence about the conceptual foundations of the "group" he had reluctantly named, Zukofsky was more than willing to see how much mileage he and his colleagues could get out of the "Objectivist" moniker. The "'Objectivists' 1931" issue of *Poetry* had attracted considerable publicity, and in its wake Zukofsky and fellow Objectivist George Oppen founded To, Publishers, a press based in France (where Oppen was living), which would put into print works by Pound, Williams, and the Objectivist poets themselves. In 1932, To, Publishers issued the Zukofsky-edited An *"Objectivists" Anthology*, which narrowed down the rag-bag of poets included in the *Poetry* issue and presented larger selections of their work (including the first seven movements of Zukofsky's long poem *"A"*). But Oppen, who was the press's major funding source, was forced to fold To, Publishers in late 1932. A year later he, Zukofsky, Reznikoff, and Williams formed The Objectivist Press, a collectively edited venture that, after publishing works by Oppen, Williams, and Reznikoff, trailed off in 1936.[13]

In addition to the four "core" Objectivist poets – Zukofsky, Oppen, Rakosi, and Reznikoff – literary history has added Niedecker, a Wisconsin poet who, inspired by the *Poetry* issue, commenced a long relationship with

Zukofsky. (The Northumbrian Basil Bunting, one of Zukofsky's closest correspondents, has also occasionally been included with the group.) Rachel Blau DuPlessis and Peter Quartermain are quite right in identifying the Objectivists as less a "movement" or even a "group" than a "nexus," a historically contingent confluence of a number of disparate poets, and their retrospective critical categorization. The four original Objectivists shared certain sociological commonalities: they were all male, Jewish, and roughly of the political left; they also were all born in the first decade of the century (except for Reznikoff, a decade older than Zukofsky). But far from espousing a common poetic "program" in 1931, they were writing a wide range of disparate poetries: Zukofsky, always highly attuned to the musical qualities of language, was experimenting in casting contemporary life into song-forms and into the recurrent structures of the fugue; Reznikoff's poetry, deeply influenced by his legal training, often took the form of "testimony," and his short poems, usually set in New York City, adapted Imagism to a precise, laconic realism; Rakosi's early work, hearkening back to Wallace Stevens, is often colorful and playful, though Zukofsky's influence turned him in more angular, compressed directions; Oppen wrote a startlingly minimal poetry of urban observation which aimed in part to tease out the oppressive economic structures underlying the phenomena of the "jazz age."

As DuPlessis and Quartermain usefully summarize it, "the term 'Objectivist' has come to mean a non-symbolist, post-imagist poetics, characterized by a historical, realist, antimythological worldview."[14] It *has come* to mean that – but only in the backward glance of literary history. For one thing, by the end of the 1930s, the Objectivists had for the most part entirely fallen off of the map of American poetry. Sometime after The Objectivist Press published his *Discrete Series* in 1934, Oppen, convinced that his poetic vocation and his leftist political commitments were incompatible, had given up poetry entirely. Rakosi had similarly stopped writing, both because of his ambivalence concerning the political value of poetry and the sheer pressures of work. Zukofsky continued to forge ahead with *"A"* and his shorter lyrics, but the economic circumstances of the Depression had stifled most of the little magazines that had previously published his work; in 1940, he and his wife Celia issued a mimeographed edition of *First Half of "A"-9*, and in 1941 and 1946 two collections of his short poems were published (probably underwritten by Zukofsky himself) by James A. Decker of Prairie City, Illinois – to little public notice. Niedecker's poetry grew astonishingly over the 1930s and 1940s, moving from a surrealist note to a politically inflected "Mother Goose" idiom, and then to a concise but oblique American "folk" voice; but little of this work saw print until 1946, when she too had a collection published by Decker (again to little notice). Only Reznikoff, who had self-published his earliest books, continued to issue collections of poetry, seemingly unperturbed by the lack of public attention.[15] Over two decades, then – from the late 1930s through the mid-1950s – the Objectivist moment became a minor footnote to the history of American poetry.

Only slightly younger than Zukofsky and his Objectivist comrades, Charles Olson came to poetry in mid-life after a varied career in scholarship and politics. Olson sensed early on that Pound and Williams were the most important American modernist poets, and he visited Pound at St. Elizabeth's mental hospital in Washington on a number of occasions from 1946 to 1948. (Olson's notes on those meetings indicate that he was familiar with Zukofsky's name, if not with his writings.[16]) Olson came to public prominence by dint of a pair of texts: the poem "The Kingfishers" (1949) and the extraordinarily influential essay "Projective Verse" (1950). "The Kingfishers" is something of a belated response to T. S. Eliot's 1922 *The Waste Land*, in which Olson acknowledges Eliot's cultural pessimism but rejects the solutions at which his poetic career arrived. "These fragments I have shored against my ruins," *The Waste Land*'s speaker laments, surveying the "heap of broken images" of quotations from and allusions to the Western canon that make up the poem. Within half a decade, Eliot himself would embrace Christianity as a unifying cultural and spiritual principle. Olson's "The Kingfishers" concludes with the line "I hunt among stones": if contemporary culture presents a panorama of "broken images," Olson implies, the poet's remedy is to work backward, archaeologically, *beyond* the impasse of the Western mind (which Olson dated to the classificatory project set in train by Plato and Aristotle). Olson's mature work, then, is an attempt to recover a holism lost at the very beginning of Western civilization.[17]

"Projective Verse," which was first published in *Poetry New York* in 1950, and excerpted at length the next year in Williams's *Autobiography*, is a broadside blast at late-1940s American poetry, a poetry which, in Olson's view, had backtracked from the innovations of Pound and Williams to a traditional, "closed" formalism, "that verse which print bred."[18] In contrast, Olson offers a theory of "projective" or "open" verse, a concept of poetic form rooted not in a historical tradition of rhyme and meter but in the poet's own physical *body*. (Olson's editors point out that while "Projective Verse" is an act of *literary* theorizing, Olson's ultimate interest is "phenomenological," as is made most clear in his short prose volume of 1965, *Proprioception*.)[19] "Projective Verse" falls into two parts: first, Olson's description of what the act of composing "projective or OPEN verse" involves – a poetics, that is; and then a consideration of "what stance toward reality brings such verse into being, what that stance does, both to the poet and to his reader."[20]

"Projective verse" rejects all previous rules for poetic line, stanza, and overall form; instead it treats the space of the potential poem as a "field" open for composition in any direction. Its paramount formal rule is a principle Olson learned from his younger correspondent Robert Creeley, that "FORM IS NEVER MORE THAN AN EXTENSION OF CONTENT." Projective verse must manifest speed, energy, vigor: "ONE PERCEPTION MUST IMMEDIATELY AND DIRECTLY LEAD TO A FURTHER PERCEPTION," as Olson quotes his friend Edward Dahlberg. "[G]et on with it," Olson exhorts, "keep moving, keep in, speed, the nerves, their speed, the perceptions, theirs, the acts, the split second acts, the whole business, keep it moving as fast as you can, citizen." The basis of this open-form, almost frenetically energetic composition is the poet's own somatic totality, in which the brain and the heart are organs among other organs rather than the disembodied "spirit" or "mind" of Cartesian dualistic thought. "The HEAD" gives rise to "the SYLLABLE," but only in conjunction with "the EAR," as "the HEART" determines "the LINE," but only in conjunction with "the BREATH."[21]

It is in the brief second part of "Projective Verse," where Olson outlines the "stance toward reality" such verse manifests, that he explicitly mentions the Objectivists. Pound and Williams are the clear progenitors of the poetics he describes, and "it is no accident that Pound and Williams both were involved variously in a movement which got called 'objectivism.' But that word was then used in some sort of a necessary quarrel, I take it, with 'subjectivism.'" Olson himself, to avoid such philosophical connotations, would call his "stance" "Objectism":

> the getting rid of the lyrical interference of the individual as ego, of the "subject" and his soul, that peculiar presumption by which western man has interposed himself between what he is as a creature of nature (with certain instructions to carry out) and those other creations of nature which we may, with no derogation, call objects.[22]

The Projectivist poet, then by overcoming the "lyrical interference of the ego" and letting the body, especially the *voice*, participate fully in the poem's composition, can achieve a larger perspective on the phenomena of the world, a deeper insight into the heart of events.

Olson's memory of what the Objectivists were up to in the 1930s is clearly fuzzy. Far from pursuing a "necessary quarrel" with "subjectivism," Zukofsky was careful to place "'Objectivists' in quotes: no infringement, i.e. of philosophical etiquette, intended";[23] and he *never* used the nominal "Objectivism." (Perhaps Olson picked up "objectism" from correspondence or conversation with Williams, who was laxer with his terms.[24]) But

"Projective Verse" coincides rather closely with Zukofsky's Objectivist manifestos at several moments. Olson's rejection of the "closed" forms of traditional meter, line, and stanza echoes Zukofsky's assertion that "each poem has its own laws"; and Olson's enthusiasm for the typewriter – "For the first time the poet has the stave and the bar a musician has"[25] – is anticipated in the non-typing Zukofsky's endorsement of typography as an element of the poem, "if print and the arrangement of it will help tell how the voice should sound."[26] Olson's account of how projective verse involved "getting rid of the lyrical interference of the individual as ego, of the 'subject' and his soul" parallels Zukofsky's rather more arcane description of the poem "as object.... Perfect rest – or nature as creator, existing, perfect, experience perfecting activity of existence, making – theologically, perhaps – like the Ineffable –".[27] And Zukofsky's description of sincerity as writing that is "the detail, not mirage, of seeing, of thinking with the things as they exist" is almost uncannily echoed in Olson's assertion that "the objects which occur at every given moment of composition (of recognition, we can call it) are, can be, must be treated exactly as they do occur therein and not by any ideas or preconceptions from outside the poem." While "Projective Verse" presents no principle of overall form that directly parallels "objectification," Olson's sense of the poet's necessary fidelity to immediate thought and perception strongly evokes Zukofsky's principle of compositional "sincerity," and Olson's assertion that "every element in an open poem" must be "taken up" "just as solidly as we are accustomed to take what we call the objects of reality" provides a sense of the tangibility of the poet's materials that closely follows Zukofsky's.[28]

When he read "Projective Verse," Zukofsky was convinced that Olson had done him a disservice: while dismissing the original Objectivist "movement" and misreading Zukofsky's writings, he had restated many of the Objectivist principles as his own – in the process gaining them a far wider audience.[29] Olson's untidy but enormously energetic prose, his dynamic teaching and conversation, and the attraction of his radical poetics made him a flashpoint and personal influence in twentieth-century American poetry second only perhaps to Pound himself. In 1951, Olson became the rector of Black Mountain College, a small liberal arts institution in North Carolina, and in his five years there he set about engineering a renaissance in American poetry. The "Black Mountain" or "Projectivist" poets in Olson's orbit were not all present at Black Mountain, but Creeley and Robert Duncan taught at the college, and among the students were Jonathan Williams, Edward Dorn, Joel Oppenheimer, and John Wieners. Olson had been in intense correspondence with the Boston poet Cid Corman, serving as informal, logorrheic, and often hectoring editorial advisor for Corman's fledgling journal *Origin*.

The English-born Denise Levertov was brought into Olson's orbit by way of her friendship with Creeley. All of these poets pursued some variation of "composition by field," and many of them composed statements of poetics, all of which can be read as the lineal descendents of "Projective Verse."

The prominence that Olson's influence had come to assume in avant-garde poetics by the end of the 1950s is evident in Donald Allen's groundbreaking 1960 anthology, *The New American Poetry, 1945–1960*. Allen's anthology, a riposte to the formalist, New Criticism–inspired selections of Donald Hall, Robert Pack, and Louis Simpson's *New Poets of England and America* (1957), presented the work of forty-four "outsider" poets, many of them published only in periodicals. Crucially, Allen presented his selections in rough "groups" – Black Mountain poets, San Francisco Renaissance, Beats, New York Poets. By far the largest of Allen's groups is the Black Mountain poets, and Olson, who appears first in the anthology ("The Kingfishers"), is given approximately four times as much page space as the average poet included, while "Projective Verse" leads off a selection of "Statements on Poetics" at the end of the volume. *The New American Poetry*, reprinted numerous times throughout the 1960s and 1970s (by the mid-1960s it had gone through eight printings, with 40,000 copies in print), became something of a Bible of American counterpoetics, a foundational document for various postmodern movements – and Olson is its most prominent prophet.[30]

The poets in Olson's circle, it is safe to say, spearheaded the "rediscovery" of the Objectivists. Duncan had been in correspondence with Zukofsky since 1947, and introduced Creeley to his work in 1955. Creeley published Zukofsky in *Black Mountain Review*, and he and Duncan communicated their enthusiasm for Zukofsky's work to their students at Black Mountain College. Jonathan Williams, who had worked with Olson at Black Mountain and had printed the first collection of Olson's *The Maximus Poems* under his Jargon Society imprint, went on to publish Zukofsky's *Some Time* (1956) and Niedecker's *T&G: Collected Poems 1936–1968* (1969). Corman, the first series of whose *Origin* (1951–57) was largely a platform for Olson's writing, devoted much of the second series of that periodical (1961–64) to Zukofsky's work, and in 1959 Origin Books issued the first half of Zukofsky's long poem, *"A" 1–12*. Levertov, who in 1959 cited Creeley and Duncan as "the chief poets among my contemporaries," became poetry advisor to the publisher W. W. Norton and facilitated the publication of Zukofsky's *ALL: The Collected Short Poems* (1965).[31]

The other Objectivists reemerged into the public eye in the first part of the 1960s. Oppen, living in Mexico but shortly to return to the United States, began writing poetry again in 1958; similarly, Rakosi resumed writing in the mid-1960s, spurred by a correspondence with English poet Andrew Crozier.

Along with Reznikoff, these two former Objectivists found a publishing outlet in James Laughlin's New Directions, which (initially in collaboration with the *San Francisco Review*, edited by Oppen's half-sister June Oppen Degnan) issued a half-dozen of their books over the course of the 1960s.[32] Public recognition came in the form of a Pulitzer Prize in Poetry for Oppen's *Of Being Numerous* in 1968, the same year that L. S. Dembo began the process of critical and scholarly consecration by inviting Zukofsky, Oppen, Rakosi, and Reznikoff to gather for a conference on the Objectivist "movement" at the University of Wisconsin. Zukofsky by this point was bitterly estranged from Oppen and refused to participate, so Dembo brought each poet to campus *seriatim*, collecting his conversations with them in the journal *Contemporary Literature* as "The Objectivist Poet: Four Interviews."[33]

By the end of the 1960s, then, both the Objectivists – a second generation of "high modernists" – and the Projectivists – a first generation of "postmoderns" (Olson himself had been among the first to use that term) – were active forces in the avant-garde of American poetry. The dozen or score of poets who were either associated with Black Mountain or who were now being mentioned as resurgent Objectivists wrote in a bewildering variety of idioms: the outward-spiralling, continents- and geological age-spanning reach of Olson's *Maximus Poems*; Creeley's compact, tightly engineered and oblique lyrics; Duncan's richly allusive and mystical poems, which drew as deeply on Romantic tropes and voicings as they did on modernist traditions of parataxis and collage; Oppen's profoundly philosophical meditations on community, history, and the human condition; and the increasingly complex later movements of *"A"*, a poem that shared the historical scope and Cantos-like referentiality of *The Maximus Poems*, but which in its densely woven textures and idiosyncratic formal structures was the polar opposite of Olson's.

All of the Projectivists and the Objectivists shared an ongoing investment in foregrounding the materiality of their language. Such foregrounding was pressed to an extreme in Zukofsky's translation (with his wife Celia) of Catullus (1969), which aims to preserve the *sound* of Catullus's Latin – "tries to breathe with him," as Zukofsky puts it – often at the expense of the original's lexical meaning, and usually at the expense of recognizable English syntax.[34] Zukofsky's late work, from the middle sections of *"A"* to the posthumously published *80 Flowers* (1978), becomes an almost continuous web of quoted, translated, and transliterated texts, obdurate blocks of tantalizing, polysemic textuality.

Such texts, along with Gertrude Stein's earlier experiments in "cubist" writing, Olson's dense but fragmentary poems, and the scattered obliquities of such poets in the Black Mountain orbit as Larry Eigner, would become primary influences on Language writing, the bicoastal avant-garde tendency that emerged in the 1970s and 1980s. A quarter-century's retrospect enables one to see that Language writing, despite the phalanx of unifying essays and manifestos issued throughout the 1980s by its practitioners (among them Lyn Hejinian, Charles Bernstein, Ron Silliman, and Barrett Watten), is no more tight-knit a "movement" than the Objectivists or the Black Mountain poets had been. But running throughout the Language writers' work is an emphasis on the poem's textuality and on the poetic possibilities of manipulating the word as a material unit. This emphasis announces itself as early as Robert Grenier's 1971 pronouncement "I HATE SPEECH" in the first issue of *This*, a journal he coedited with Watten – a statement that Silliman claims heralds "a new moment in American writing."[35] Grenier is by no means disowning Olson's equation of the poet's line with his or her physical breath, nor the explorations in speech-based poetics carried out by Creeley, Duncan, and various Objectivists; rather he is rejecting the formally slack, conversational, unreflexive first-person poetics that he and other Language writers saw as dominating American verse culture with the rise of the MFA industry.

For most of the Language writers, an investment in the materiality of the poetic text goes hand in hand with a leftist politics, and indeed various Language poets have made forceful arguments for the political charge inherent to their own disruptions of syntax and poetic frame. Such claims have rightly sparked vigorous arguments, many of them at first glance little more than rehashing of the Brecht/Lukács/Adorno debates of mid-century.[36] What is striking is the degree to which the Language writers, however overreaching their early claims about the political resonance of their poetics may sometimes seem, have, like the Objectivists before them, steadfastly worked to uncover the parallels and connections between a materialist politics and a poetics of linguistic materiality: if the Objectivists pursued a poetics of *liberation*, one might hazard, the Language writers have for the most part pursued a poetics of *critique*.

Even though the Objectivist-Projectivist nexus now appears less a "strain" in American poetry than an *environment*, a vast and almost inescapable background to much of the innovative writing of our fin-de-siècle, a number of poets outside of the Language movement have made especially personal use of the inheritance of Black Mountain and the writing of the poets briefly associated in the February 1931 *Poetry*. There are, of course, a number of confirmed "Olsonians," poets whose work is deeply invested in Olson's mannerisms and habits of thought, such as Donald Wellman, Gerrit Lansing, and Don Byrd, among others. More interesting, however, is Susan Howe, whose work is predicated in large part on Olson's liberation of the page space for free composition, and who, like Olson, is fascinated with the traces of the historical past. But Howe's poetics, unlike Olson's, do not concern themselves with a perhaps imaginary pre-lapsarian state of being in the world; instead they pursue the textual and historical traces of what Western patriarchy has persistently tried to eliminate or suppress: the extravagant, the antinomian.

What one might call a second generation of Objectivist poets – among them Michael Heller, Norman Finkelstein, Michael Palmer, and Rachel Blau DuPlessis – have pursued poetic projects deeply indebted to Oppen, Zukofsky, and Niedecker for models of musical clarity, concision, and formal invention. At the same time, these latter-day Objectivists have matured in the shadow of Black Mountain, and the formal and tonal restraint they inherit from the first generation of Objectivists is enlivened by a very Olsonian sense of exploration, of the poem as a field in which anything, in the long run, might find its place.

If Olson and Zukofsky during their own lifetimes could find little common ground in the politics of the innovative poetry "scene," their combined inheritance is perhaps best illustrated in the career of Ronald Johnson, whose early introduction to contemporary poetry came by way of his partner, Jonathan Williams, who had studied with Olson at Black Mountain and who published both Zukofsky and Niedecker. Johnson's long poem *ARK* is a formally various and high-spirited celebration of the intertwined systems of physics and the human sensorium, and pays particular homage to both Olson and Zukofsky – "The Minimalist and The Maximus," as Johnson calls them in an explanatory note.[37] Johnson's poem, while it presents itself as a Blakean visionary poetry, and while it may be read as an idiosyncratically *spiritual* poetry, is a studiedly *apolitical* work: his long poem, he insists, does *not* include history. While the combined Objectivist-Projectivist nexus has been central to American innovative poetry of the second half of the twentieth century, *ARK* demonstrates that the works of those poets can be read (merely) as a formal and musical provocation; later generations of poets are always in danger of overlooking or erasing the social text inherent in the Objectivists'

NOTES

1. Cited in Mark Scroggins, *The Poem of a Life: A Biography of Louis Zukofsky* (Emeryville, CA: Shoemaker & Hoard, 2007) 112.
2. Louis Zukofsky, "Sincerity and Objectification," *Prepositions+: The Collected Critical Essays* (Hanover, NH: Wesleyan University Press, 2000) 199, 194.
3. Ibid., 10.
4. Hugh Kenner, *A Homemade World: The American Modernist Writers* (1975; Baltimore: Johns Hopkins University Press, 1989) 187.

5. Ezra Pound, "A Retrospect," *Literary Essays*, ed. T. S. Eliot (1935; New York: New Directions, 1968) 4–5, 9.

6. Zukofsky, 194.

7. Pound, 23.

8. See Mark Scroggins, "The Revolutionary Word: Zukofsky, *New Masses*, and Political Radicalism in the 1930s," *Upper Limit Music: The Writing of Louis Zukofsky*, ed. Mark Scroggins (Tuscaloosa: University of Alabama Press, 1997) 44–63.

9. Cited in Peter Nicholls, *George Oppen and the Fate of Modernism* (Oxford: Oxford University Press, 2007) 19.

10. Ezra Pound, *Selected Prose 1909–1965*, ed. William Cookson (New York: New Directions, 1973) 22.

11. Walter Benjamin, "On the Concept of History," *Selected Writings Volume 4, 1938–1940*, ed. Howard Eiland and Michael W. Jennings, trans. Edmund Jephcott et al. (Cambridge, MA: Belknap Press of Harvard University Press, 2003) 397.

12. Zukofsky, 214.

13. On the publishing history of the "movement," see Tom Sharp, "The 'Objectivists' Publications," *Sagetrieb* 3.3 (Winter 1984): 41–47, and Scroggins, "The 'Objectivists' and Their Publications," *Z-Site: A Companion to the Works of Louis Zukofsky*, www.z-site.net/biblio-research/Objectivists-Publications.php

14. Rachel Blau DuPlessis and Peter Quartermain, "Introduction," *The Objectivist Nexus: Essays in Cultural Poetics* (Tuscaloosa: University of Alabama Press, 1999) 3.

15. For the publishing history of these latter poets, see Scroggins, *The Poem of a Life*, Jenny Penberthy's introduction and textual notes to Niedecker, *Collected Works* (Berkeley: University of California Press, 2002), and Seamus Cooney's textual notes to Reznikoff, *Poems 1918–1936* (Santa Barbara, CA: Black Sparrow Press, 2976) and *Poems 1937–1975* (Santa Barbara, CA: Black Sparrow Press, 1978).

16. See Olson, *Charles Olson and Ezra Pound: An Encounter at St. Elizabeths*, ed. Catherine Seelye (1975; New York: Paragon House, 1991). The most comprehensive examination of Zukofsky and Olson's relationship is in Anne Day Dewey, *Beyond Maximus: The Construction of Public Voice in Black Mountain Poetry* (Stanford, CA: Stanford University Press, 2007) 223–225n.4.

17. Charles Olson, *The Collected Poems of Charles Olson, Excluding the Maximus Poems*, ed. George F. Butterick (Berkeley: University of California Press, 1987) 93.

18. Olson, "Projective Verse," *Collected Prose*, ed. Donald Allen and Benjamin Friedlander (Berkeley: University of California Press, 1997) 239.

19. Ibid., 424n.

20. Ibid., 239.

21. Ibid., 239–242.

22. Ibid., 247.

23. Zukofsky, 214.

24. See *The Autobiography of William Carlos Williams* (New York: Random House, 1951) 265, where Williams writes of "Objectivism."

25. Olson, *Collected Prose*, 245.

26. Zukofsky, 211.

27. Ibid., 207.

28. Olson, *Collected Prose*, 243.

29. Scroggins, 264–265.

30. Robert von Hallberg, *American Poetry and Culture, 1945–1980* (Cambridge, MA: Harvard University Press, 1985) 14.

31. *The New American Poetry: 1945–1960*, ed. Donald Allen (New York: Grove Press, 1960) 412.

32. Over the 1960s, New Directions published Oppen's *The Materials* (1962), *This In Which* (1965), and *Of Being Numerous* (1968), Rakosi's *Amulet* (1967), and Reznikoff's *By the Waters of Manhattan: Selected Verse* (1962) and *Testimony: The United States, 1885–1890, Recitative* (1965).

33. Scroggins, 407–408.

34. Zukofsky, *Prepositions*, 225.

35. Ron Silliman, ed., *In the American Tree: Language, Realism, Poetry* (Orono, ME: National Poetry Foundation, 1986) xv.

36. See Theodor Adorno et al., *Aesthetics and Politics* (London: New Left Books, 1977); an early but vigorous and still representative debate about Language writing is the exchange among Jerome J. McGann, Charles Altieri, and Jed Rasula in *Politics and Poetic Value*, ed. Robert von Hallberg (Chicago: University of Chicago Press, 1987).

37. Ronald Johnson, *ARK* (Alburquerque, NM: Living Batch Press, 1996), "A Note" (n.p.).

FURTHER READING

Allen, Donald, ed. *The New American Poetry 1945–1960*. New York: Grove Press, 1960.

Benjamin, Walter. *Selected Writings Volume 4, 1938–1940*. Ed. Howard Eiland and Michael W. Jennings, trans. Edmund Jephcott, et al. Cambridge, MA: Belknap Press of Harvard University Press, 2003.

DuPlessis, Rachel Blau, and Peter Quartermain, eds. *The Objectivist Nexus: Essays in Cultural Poetics*. Tuscaloosa: University of Alabama Press, 1999.

Johnson, Ronald. *ARK*. Alburquerque, NM: Living Batch Press, 1996.

Kenner, Hugh. *A Homemade World: The American Modernist Writers*. 1975; Baltimore: Johns Hopkins University Press, 1989.

Nicholls, Peter. *George Oppen and the Fate of Modernism*. Oxford: Oxford University Press, 2007.

Olson, Charles. *The Collected Poems of Charles Olson, Excluding the Maximus Poems*. Ed. George F. Butterick. Berkeley: University of California Press, 1987.

Collected Prose. Ed. Donald Allen and Benjamin Friedlander. Berkeley: University of California Press, 1997.

Pound, Ezra. *I Gather the Limbs of Osiris, Selected Prose 1909–1965*. Ed. William Cookson. New York: New Directions, 1973.

Literary Essays. Ed. T. S. Eliot. 1935; New York: New Directions, 1968.

Scroggins, Mark. *The Poem of a Life: A Biography of Louis Zukofsky*. Emeryville, CA: Shoemaker & Hoard, 2007.

Silliman, Ron, ed. *In the American Tree: Language, Realism, Poetry*. Orono, ME: National Poetry Foundation, 1986.

Von Hallberg, Robert. *American Poetry and Culture, 1945–1980*. Cambridge, MA: Harvard University Press, 1985.

Williams, William Carlos. *The Autobiography of William Carlos Williams*. New York: Random House, 1951.

Zukofsky, Louis. *Prepositions+: The Collected Critical Essays*. Hanover, NH: Wesleyan University Press, 2000.

3

DEBORAH NELSON

Confessional Poetry

Robert Lowell's "Skunk Hour," one of the best-known poems from his epoch-defining collection, *Life Studies* (1959), begins with "Nautilus Island's hermit/heiress" "thirsting for the hierarchic privacy / of Queen Victoria's century."[1] Two stanzas later, the speaker of the poem appears making a furtive trip to lover's lane to spy on teenagers making out in their cars. This latter image is confessional poetry as we have known and sometimes loved it: a mentally unstable poet in an act of self-exposure. We see his perversion ("I watched for love-cars") and his mental anguish ("My mind's not right"). We see his guilt ("I myself am Hell, / Nobody's here –").[2] If we have come to this last poem in the collection having read Lowell's narrative sketch of his childhood, "91 Revere Street," the unflattering poems about his parents and grandparents, and the even less flattering poems about his mental illness and his marriage, we might be tempted to see this poem as simply one more private moment confessed to the reader. But we would misunderstand something fundamental to confessional poetry and to the period in which it was written if we failed to note the contrast Lowell sets up between the hermit heiress and the speaker in this, the concluding poem in the volume. "Skunk Hour" tells us that even though barely fifty years separate Queen Victoria's century from the moment in which Lowell was writing, some fundamental shifts had taken place in the conception of privacy. There was no single self-evident and self-evidently valuable concept of privacy. Instead there were priva*cies* (a "hierarchic" one, for instance) and different relationships to its value (one character thirsts for it, the other gives it – and takes it – away). To call these poems "private," which was the term of choice for critics for several decades, is not to settle a question about confessional poetry, but to identify one of its preoccupations. What is privacy? And for whom?

"Confessional poetry" was first coined by the critic M. L. Rosenthal in 1959 in one of the more influential reviews ever written.[3] Lowell was the central figure of his study, but Rosenthal grouped him with Sylvia Plath, John Berryman, and Anne Sexton. W. D. Snodgrass would round out the cohort of those poets thought to be *the* Confessional Poets, who are now routinely said to be part of a "confessional movement" but only loosely so. Compared to other poetic or artistic movements of this period – the Black Mountain or Beat poets, for instance – no confessional poet imagined him- or herself to be part of a movement. The poets never congregated *as* the confessional poets; they almost universally disliked the term as it applied to their own work.[4] The idea of a poetic movement is to some degree the useful fiction that has organized the study of late-twentieth-century poetry since the publication of Donald Allen's tremendously influential anthology, *The New American Poetry, 1945–1960*.[5] While "movement" applies only as an analogy to this group, it is true that the confessional poets knew one another, often – though not always – through Lowell, who taught Sexton, Plath, and Snodgrass; they met in his classes at Boston University and Harvard, at his home, and more generally in Boston, where confessional poetry can properly be said to find its roots.

To the extent that we want to consider it a movement, confessional poetry ends in the mid-1970s. In 1973, Lowell published the last and most controversial of his confessional works, *The Dolphin*, which incorporated letters from his soon-to-be ex-wife, the highly regarded writer and editor Elizabeth Hardwick, in sonnets written for his soon-to-be next wife, heiress to the Guinness fortune, Lady Caroline Blackwood.[6] By 1975, when Sexton's last collection, *The Awful Rowing Toward God*, was published posthumously, she, Berryman, and Plath were all dead and by their own hand.[7] Snodgrass had moved away from the signature personal poems of his 1959 collection, *Heart's Needle*, and new forms of anti-confessional and even anti-lyric poetry were in the ascendance.[8] Nonetheless, confessional poetry had an unparalleled impact on poetry writing of the late twentieth century, and by the mid-1970s it had achieved a kind of dominance, deeply influencing creative writing schools across the country and later generations of confessional writers, producing a set of conventions for personal self-revelation, and most importantly retraining our appetite for and expectations of personal revelation in poetry. A poet like T. S. Eliot, who had formulated the modernist theory of poetic impersonality that so shaped poetic output until the publication of *Life Studies*, could now be read as confessional because confession was no longer just a writing practice; it was a paradigm for reading as well.[9]

The turn toward confession in poetry startled many contemporary readers because the reigning orthodoxy of the mid-century was impersonality. Eliot's famous declaration of the impersonality of the poet, along with William Carlos Williams's dictum, "no ideas but in things," put the psyche of the poet firmly out of view, irrelevant to the poetic project.[10] This theory of impersonality was taken up and elaborated not only by the generation of poets that followed them, but also by the most important critics of the day, the so-called New Critics, whose theories of poetic autonomy were imbibed by many readers new to the form, who were attending college courtesy of the G.I. Bill. By the mid-1950s, those strictures against the personal were felt to be arid by poets with many different aesthetic theories and practices. Lowell called his own refusal of the impersonal, *Life Studies*, his "breakthrough back to life."[11]

But this term – "confessional" – represented, of course, a far longer history and a much broader reach within the period when confessional poetry emerged. Confessional writing is part of a religious tradition that dates back to Augustine and became part of a therapeutic tradition even before the advent of psychotherapy, which certainly shaped and accelerated the outpouring of personal self-revelation in the twentieth century. Moreover, in confessional poetry, both religious belief and Freudian psychotherapy play very important roles. Confession, with or without the motivation of penance or psychic pain relief, also represents one of the most varied and intense forms of artistic experimentation in the latter half of the twentieth century. It is impossible to imagine this period without considering the popularity of the memoir and the autobiographical novel, the exhibitionism of performance art, the subjective viewpoint of the New Journalism, and self-portraiture in photography and the fine arts more generally, to say nothing of the personal revelations of talk shows, tabloids, and, in the twenty-first century, personal blogs and social media. Likewise in the political realm, most importantly in the feminist movement but also the civil rights and gay liberation movements, speaking personally was considered a crucial form of intervention into the public sphere and the political process. In many of these cases, the personal voice was a rebuke to what was increasingly viewed as a fraudulent objectivity or a false universality.

Poetry, quite naturally, participated in this general cultural trend, and what we term confessional poetry could be understood, in these broader terms, to have considerably larger membership than the so-called confessional poets. Two of their contemporaries, Allen Ginsberg and Frank O'Hara, for instance, experimented in sometimes similar ways with their personal experience. Ginsberg, a notable influence on Lowell, felt called to witness the exploits, sexual and otherwise, of the "best minds of [his] generation."[12] "Howl" (1956) was easily as scandalous as anything the confessional poets ever wrote and was put on trial in one of the era's most famous obscenity cases. O'Hara also used the material of his everyday life, his lunch-hour strolls, in his best-known collection, *Lunch Poems* (1964), which also casually mentioned his circle of friends and their social gatherings.[13] This is to say that autobiographical poetry more generally, and sometimes even what we might call confessional, was quite widespread.

What made confessional poetry confessional, as opposed to just personal or autobiographical, was the nature and context of its revelations. There is, first of all, the urgency and "rawness" of the revelations. This is, in key respects, a distinction of form, not content. In accepting the National Book Award for *Life Studies*, Lowell made a contrast between the "raw and the cooked," by which he meant to signal the difference between a more relaxed and conversational style in *Life Studies* and his previous, syntactically overwrought, often opaque lines. The directness – the relaxation of iambic pentameter or the loosening of the rhyme scheme (without its abandonment) – created an impression of casual and intimate conversation. Lowell also meant to mark the difference between this more informal style and the technically expert poems that filled the magazines and journals of the 1950s. Rawness could also describe Sylvia Plath, albeit in a different way. One of Plath's most original contributions to the history of poetry is the emotional force of her poetry, particularly the intensity of rage in *Ariel* (1965), which was conveyed by an alternation in tone between fury and detachment.[14] The mixed ferocity and coldness of Plath's work in poems such as "Lady Lazarus" or "Lesbos" is the aspect of her work least dulled by time and the conventionalization of confession. Berryman's antic, sometimes scatological humor, and the polyvocality of his *77 Dream Songs* (1964) speaker (the shifting between rhetorical modes like dialect, ad-speak, poetic high tradition) might also be thought to be raw.[15] It was certainly not decorous in either the social or the poetic meaning of that term.

If the form of these poems can be thought raw, so, too, can the content, the "shameful" material the poems discussed. The revelations of confessional poetry were extreme and transgressive, particularly with respect to norms of white, middle-class, heterosexual society. Sexton, Lowell, Plath, Berryman, and Snodgrass made poems about marital failure and infidelity (hetero) sexual transgression, abortion, rage, mental illness, and drug and alcohol abuse. They wrote about the body, often in its most degraded or vulnerable states. Sexton is arguably the most important voice in this respect. Her poem, "Menstruation at Forty" (1966), would hardly raise eyebrows now, but many critics of the time were shocked and repelled.[16] Perhaps most importantly, however, it was their depiction of the emotional violence of the middle-class family that disrupted their readers' expectations. Taken together, a directness of address, which produced the impression of candor and intimacy with the reader, and the shameful, dishonorable (Rosenthal's term), or merely private nature of the content were a potent mix. It is thus important to keep both the form and content innovations of confessional poetry in mind. Critics mistook the informal address and the private content for a kind of transparency and artlessness, which made the poems appear to be mere outpourings of feeling and information unmediated by craft. In other words, the poems were initially viewed more as confession than poetry. In the past twenty years or so, critics began to examine the poems not so much for their content but for the artistry that creates the pose or performance of sincerity, the theatricalization of intimacy.[17]

Following closely on the charge that confessional poetry – shameful, artless, shocking – was not poetry at all came the criticism that it was merely private. Unlike the politically engaged poetry that also began to flourish in the 1960s, confessional poetry reported the conflicts internal to the family and to the self, which suggested to many readers that it had nothing to tell them about the tumultuous and rapidly changing world in which it existed. In this line of criticism, it was not the sordidness of its revelations that mattered, as it had been upon initial publication, but their triviality and banality. In the face of the Vietnam War or the civil rights movements, who cared that Lowell's father was a failure? That Sexton was unfaithful to her husband? That Plath had an Electra complex? That Berryman was an alcoholic? That Snodgrass was on his third (or was it fourth?) marriage? Nonetheless, this complaint overlooks the extreme political importance of privacy and private life in the high period of the Cold War.

There is a great deal more to say about the emergence of confessional poetry at this moment than how it reflected a generational swing of the pendulum from impersonality to emotionally intense revelations of shameful and mostly personal and familial dramas. Why should transgressing the boundaries of private life have been so stimulating to so many writers and so many readers? These poets were, as some critics have emphasized, celebrities, with all the attendant issues of publicity. *Life Studies* sold in pharmacies; during readings, Anne Sexton's fans yelled encouragement at her like groupies; Sylvia Plath's brief life occasioned at least six biographies and a major motion picture starring Gwyneth Paltrow. The point is not that they ushered in an era of extreme self-exhibitionism; rather they were caught up in the wave that made their revelations part of a larger aesthetic and political impulse. As Americans everywhere began to think about their privacy, few had as much insight into its paradoxes as the confessional poets.

The Kitchen Debates

This is something I would never find
in a lovelier place, my dear,
although your fear is anyone's fear,
like an invisible veil between us all...

and sometimes in private,
my kitchen, your kitchen,
my face, your face.[18]

Anne Sexton, "For John Who Begs Me
Not to Inquire Further" (1959)

Two "kitchen debates" from 1959 help us understand how confessional poetry participated in a wider examination of the meaning and value of privacy in the Cold War. By extension, we can also think about what it means to look at poetry historically without either exaggerating its influence on or diminishing its relevance to the concerns of its time. In what is considered her poetic manifesto, "For John Who Begs Me Not to Inquire Further," Anne Sexton set her side of a debate over the limits of poetic self-disclosure in a kitchen. And in an actual kitchen, part of a model home built by U.S. contractors for a Moscow exhibition, leaders of the two Cold War superpowers, Vice President Richard Nixon and Soviet Premier Nikita Khruschev, debated the comparative value of capitalism and communism. Pairing these debates should not be taken to mean that Sexton had Nixon on her mind, nor Nixon Sexton. The first is improbable and the second unimaginable. Thinking historically about poetry does not require the poet's intimate connection to public figures or events, but instead takes stock of their sensitivity to the charged concepts and metaphors of their moment. In 1959, kitchens – and the homes that enclosed them – were visible in U.S. public discourse in a variety of contradictory ways. We do not ordinarily imagine either the poetic tradition or the fate of the free world to rest on kitchens. But the common backdrop clearly warrants some investigation.

A much-recounted episode in the Cold War, perhaps because it is as unlikely as it is illuminating, the "Kitchen debate" between Nixon and Khrushchev was broadcast on all three networks in the United States (ergo there was nothing else to watch) and several days later in Moscow. The model home, touted as affordable to any American, was stocked with entertainment and labor-saving devices, a display of the technical wizardry and material plenitude of American capitalism. But the home was a significant symbolic choice for other reasons as well. Cold War discourse had long enshrined the home as the centerpiece of U.S. democracy, the site of the citizen's autonomy, liberty, and sovereignty. The home was where citizens retreated from the public world, the place where they could be themselves, think their own thoughts, make decisions about their own lives, and enact their own projects. It was also the space of the nuclear family, whose idealization in the Cold War is difficult to overstate. Elaine Tyler May, the first historian to link the foreign policy of Cold War containment to the domestic politics of postwar rebuilding, uses the bomb shelter beneath the suburban home to explain the ambiguity of the home's symbolic promise in the 1950s.[19] A *Life Magazine* photograph of a smiling newlywed couple descending into a bomb shelter filled with canned goods for their honeymoon epitomized for May contradictory impulses in the large-scale retreat from public life into the privacy and security of the home. Celebrated as the quintessential site of liberty and autonomy, the home was less conspicuously a space of fear and anxiety.

The doubleness of the home lies at the heart of the Cold War privacy paradox: at the same time that more Americans than ever were living in single-family homes and presumably enjoying their privacy, these same citizens experienced conspicuously, even surprisingly, high levels of exposure and invasion. If the "enemy within" – a term for communists in the United States – could reside untouched and unremarked in the protected space of privacy, and if that enemy could annihilate American freedoms along with American lives, the space of privacy would have to be invaded. Cold War security anxieties justified the forced confessions of the House Un-American Activities Hearings and those of Senator Joseph McCarthy just as it did the FBI's massive collection of dossiers on suspected subversives. These files included dossiers on public figures like Albert Einstein and Frank Sinatra; private citizens like public school teachers and Hollywood filmmakers; and writers and poets like Lowell, Ginsberg, Faulkner, Hemingway, Steinbeck, Auden, and many more.

In the shadow of these politically motivated intrusions, myriad threats to privacy seemed to be emerging on all fronts, and countless books and articles reported them from the end of the 1950s to the late 1960s. Among the things counted as a threat or a source of anxiety were surveillance equipment like "spike mikes" and telescopes, job testing, psychological surveys, government dossiers, closed-circuit television, peep holes in men's rooms, Fourth Amendment violations by law enforcement, consumer polls, educational records, databases and computers more generally, satellites and television, psychoanalysis, suburban neighborhoods, celebrity profiles, news reporting, and more. This list, drawn from this explosion of writing and from a 1966 Senate subcommittee hearing on privacy cited by Supreme Court Justice William Douglas in a legal opinion,[20] shows how varied and far-reaching the death of privacy seemed to be. Some of this list could be described broadly as technological and some of it as organizational, some of it experiential and some of it abstract, but as nearly every commentator noted, it was not any single invasion but the totality of them that seemed to suggest there was no realm of privacy for the U.S. citizen. One feature of this debate, but only a minor one at the time, was the willing abandonment of personal privacy by writers, celebrities, politicians, and ordinary citizens. Myron Brenton in

The Privacy Invaders (1964), for instance, noted that this willingness was alarming because then people would not object to intrusions on their privacy in nearly every area of their lives. Privacy was not only being invaded from without; it was eroding from within. Moreover, the Cold War provided a narrative to this experience: the end of privacy was the end of the free world.[21] As privacy violations mounted, the United States was beginning to resemble its ideological enemy, the Soviet Union, which was routinely characterized as a totalitarian state, one hallmark of which, in U.S. popular discourse, was the lack of a private sphere.

These battles over privacy – what it was, whom it protected, and under what conditions – were fought before the Supreme Court many times between the late 1950s and the mid-1970s. Two kinds of cases, in particular, focused directly on the issue: one was Fourth Amendment cases that sought protection for the home from invasive search techniques enabled by new technologies, and the other was birth control cases that adjudicated the state's interest in the individual's decisions about bearing children. They came together momentously in 1965 in a case called *Griswold v. Connecticut* in which the court declared the home a "zone" of privacy. In naming a legal right to privacy, which did not exist before this ruling, *Griswold v. Connecticut* seemed to answer American anxieties about the death of privacy. "Would we allow the police to search the sacred precincts of marital bedrooms for telltale signs of the use of contraceptives?" asked Justice Douglas in the most memorable image of this landmark case. The specter of policemen searching bedrooms epitomized the Cold War anxieties of the police state, which the Justice had worried about since the McCarthy era.[22] His image was all the more striking, however, because no policeman had ever entered a marital bedroom on such a search; instead, Lee Buxton, a doctor and provider of medical services at Planned Parenthood, and Estelle Griswold, its executive director, had provided information about birth control to women at a clinic. Various incarnations of this case had been argued before the Supreme Court between 1959 and 1965 when the Court declared that the constitution implied a right to privacy in the "penumbra" the Bill of Rights.[23] It may be no surprise that *Griswold* was a controversial decision in the legal community; privacy was a right inferred, but not explicitly stated anywhere in the Constitution. It will be far less surprising, however, that this right met with immediate and widespread popular acceptance.

Keeping in mind Douglas's phrase, "the sacred precincts of the marital bedroom," let's return to Anne Sexton's "For John Who Begs Me Not to Inquire Further." Confessional poetry represents a counter-discourse of privacy, one that undermined the sanctity of the home and deflated the value of privacy by attending to its deprivations. Written after her teacher and mentor, John Holmes, objected to the "the source and subject" of the poems in her first book – her stay in a mental hospital – Sexton defended her choices by elaborating the transpersonal nature of her private distress.[24] The poem's simple but profound intuition is that Sexton's poetry made Holmes uncomfortable not because its subject was so alien to him, but because it mirrored something in his private life ("my kitchen, your kitchen, / my face, your face"). He had objected to the "selfishness" of "forcing others to listen to you" and giving them nothing.[25] Sexton interpreted his resistance otherwise. Having voiced her experiences of mental breakdown, emotional violence, and secret humiliation in the public realm of poetry, Sexton believed her listener could no longer deny such things in his own home. In so doing, the sanctity of the home, its freedom and its pleasures, gets turned upside down. The home becomes isolated instead of private, secret instead of merely withdrawn from scrutiny, defined by loneliness and coercion rather than sovereignty and autonomy.

While confessional poets produced a great number of poems that echo the paranoia of the privacy discourse, they consistently imagined the home as a place that was defined by its *lack* of privacy.[26] Sexton's "Self in 1958" (1966) elaborates this story. In the poem, the speaker describes herself as a "plaster doll" who ends the poem by asking:

> What is reality
> To this synthetic doll
> Who should smile, who should shift gears,
> Should spring the doors open in a wholesome disorder
> And have no evidence of ruin or fears?[27]

The expectation of being watched necessitates a carefully crafted scene of authentic private life; "wholesome disorder" creates a fiction of authenticity because it is not too perfect, but neither is it imperfect enough to invite further inspection. Because the door "*should* spring" open, the self is always prepared for exposure, having subjected itself to an ongoing surveillance that anticipates that exposure. Similarly, Plath frequently makes the home, and especially the kitchen, into a kind of stage. "Lesbos," for instance, depicts the home as neither private nor public: inside it is "all Hollywood," with "stage curtains" and "coy paper strips" for a door, but it is also "windowless," so lacking a view to the outside world.[28] The kitchen is paradoxically a theatrical space of performance rather than a private space of self-making.

The universality of private experience, perhaps especially in its darkest moments, animates these postwar experiments with the autobiographical, and most certainly those of the confessional poets, particularly the poetry of women, whose access to universality was considerably less certain. Plath would come to this conclusion in the pages of her journal. She understood as one of the grounds of her writing that "[her] problems are universal enough to be made meaningful."[29] Note that Plath does not take for granted this universality; by saying the problems can be "made meaningful" she presupposes the private self as a work of art, something that requires aesthetic fashioning to be recognizable. Sexton's and Plath's bids to enter the public sphere from the space of the private, the domestic, the marginal, the embodied, and the enraged made them generational icons for speaking of the stunted possibilities of women confined to, not protected by, the home. When Betty Friedan's *Feminine Mystique* was published in 1963, launching second-wave feminism, Sexton and Plath were already exploding the myth of happy suburban home and pointing to the enforced silence among and between women that sustained that myth.[30]

The Privacy of the Body

As soon as *Griswold v. Connecticut* established a constitutional right to privacy in the zone of the home, a series of cases challenged that limit. What happened to a citizen's privacy outside of the home? Were only married couples and their bedrooms entitled to protection from policing? Among others, two cases clarified these issues: *Katz v. US*, which established that citizens had expectations of privacy outside the home (in this case on public telephones) and *Eisenstadt v. Baird*, which allowed that individuals, not just married couples, had rights to self-determination in their decisions to use birth control. As privacy law evolved, then, privacy became mobile, contextual, and embodied. Once this happened, the gendered dimensions of privacy were set to manifest themselves, and did so with the court's decision that privacy lay "*between* a woman and her doctor" in *Roe v. Wade* (1973). We will return to that shortly.

By the time *Roe* was handed down in 1973, confessional poetry was all but finished. Nevertheless, in numerous poems written throughout the privacy debate that began in the late 1950s, confessional poets had explored the body and used it to comment on and define the nature of privacy for men and women. One of the most important ways they did so was in what I have called "operation poems," a small but distinct subgenre in which the issues of inside and outside, surface and depth, power and coercion are explored in relation to the confessional project.[31] Looking back at this work, it is astonishing to see how well these poets understood the conditions under which men and women could claim or relinquish their privacy. Some of these operation poems were obviously metaphors for the confessional project. John Berryman, for instance, in his "67th Dream Song," writes:

> I don't operate often. When I do,
> persons take note.
> Nurses look amazed. They pale.
> The patient is brought back to life, or so.

The poem ends:

> I am obliged to perform in complete darkness
> operations of great delicacy
> on my self.[32]

Berryman is talking about a medical procedure, invoking nurses and patients, but we are not in much doubt that the "operations of great delicacy / on my self" are the 77 Dream Songs. His sly humor works on several levels. It is not clear that the patient who survives this operation actually lives; perhaps the surgeon can only mummify – that is, preserve – a lifeless form. Confessional poetry, because it exposed the poets' intimate others, was always in danger of destroying someone else, or at the very least wounding them. What we are sure of, however, is that in this poem, the poet is the surgeon, whether cutting into someone else or himself. The surgery on the self is especially risky, on the one hand, because it takes place in unlit places – that is, where the poet has no sight, much less insight – but on the other hand, the darkened arena reduces risk as well because the poet/surgeon cannot be seen.

If Berryman's is the most obviously metaphorical, it has been somewhat less clear to readers that the many other operation poems allegorize the confessional act as well. What does it mean that so many confessional poets wrote poetry about surgery? Surgery is an act of penetration, one that troubles the inside/outside dichotomy of the self in the most literal way. Unless the confessional poets had an unusual number of surgical procedures, it seems obvious that the operation poem is meant to reveal something about the poetry of private life. While the exposure of the body is primarily associated with Sexton and Plath, male poets also exposed their bodies, but critics either failed to notice or perhaps could not see it, and for good reason. When male poets cut into the body, something happens that limits or even eliminates their exposure. For one, they tend to keep the scalpel in their own hands; for another, the act of exposure transposes their gender.

Snodgrass's "The Operation" (1959), for example, turns the operation into an act of castration.[33] As his body is shaved in preparation for surgery, the razor moves ominously from his abdomen to his groin. As he is rendered hairless, exposed, Snodgrass is slowly transformed: "White as a child, not frightened. I was not / ashamed. They clothed me, then, / in the thin, loose, light, white garments, / The delicate sandals of poor Pierrot, / A schoolgirl first offering her sacrament." He is first "a child" and then no longer himself (the line breaks on "I was not"); he is then "poor Pierrot," a liminal figure that is neither male nor female, and last he is a "schoolgirl" whose first sacrament is confession.[34] Masculinity seems unable to withstand or remain intact in the act of exposure. To lose one's privacy is to become a woman or a child. In recovery from the operation, which he has performed on himself (he is the "blank hero" who "enacts [his] deed" in the operating arena even if he is also "shackled and spellbound"), he "wakens into women," thus restoring his masculinity by implying the restoration of his virility.

In contrast, Sexton's "The Operation" (1962), which responded to Snodgrass's, opens with powerful and coercive doctor. Beginning with the moment of diagnosis, Sexton submits with a paradoxical willingness to the doctor's invasion: "while I, who must, allow the glove its oily rape, / to hear the almost doctor over me equate / my ills with hers / and decide to operate."[35] The verb is the tell here: "must allow." Allowing appears to suggest consent, but the imperative of "must" makes that consent dubious, and "oily rape" renders it nonsensical. When her body is shaved for surgery, the result is also to lose herself, not to infantilization or feminization, but to genericization: "All that was special, all that was rare / is common here. Fact: death too is in the egg. / Fact: the body is dumb, the body is meat...."[36] Sexton, no longer an individual, is identifiable only as a member of a species, a body that is information, readable but not capable of telling its own story. The problem of being read rather than speaking forms the center of Sexton's doctor/patient poems more generally. "Unknown Girl in a Maternity Ward" (1960) revolves around the complicated refusal the girl makes to the "enamel" (that is impenetrable) doctor's unceasing efforts to force her to confess the name of the father of her newborn child.[37] Addressing the child, she finally answers the doctor's questions: "I speak. It is you my silence harms"; and yet, her answer is nothing. She will announce her resistance: "name of father – none" and therefore "name you bastard."[38] She has given everything away in this poem, including her child, by answering with no answer. Refusing to submit to the doctor's coercion of confession, her poem shows that to give nothing away is to lose everything.

If Snodgrass and Berryman kept the scalpel in their own hands, for Plath and Sexton, the condition of self-expression is always mediated by powerful doctors. One of Plath's most famous poems, "Lady Lazarus," also works through this dilemma of speaking in the context of coercion. The speaker refuses to be "Herr Doktor's" "opus" or "valuable" and so "melts into a shriek," thus garbling her speech to make it unreadable and unusable to him.[39] Thinking of confessional poetry's interest in doctors and surgeons, it is perhaps not difficult to imagine how they might have responded to Justice

Blackmun's compromise in *Roe v. Wade*. Arguing for a right to abortion under the rubric of privacy meant placing that right "between a woman and her doctor." She could, indeed had to, confess her story as a condition of her autonomy. It was he, the doctor, who would ultimately decide what she did with her body. As *Doe v. Bolton* (1973), which followed *Roe*, made clear, it was the doctor's judgment being upheld, not the woman's: "Medical judgment may be exercised in light of all factors – physical, emotional, psychological, familial, the woman's age – relevant to the well-being of the patient … this allows the attending physician the room he needs to make his best medical judgment" (192). The presumptively male doctor's reason and compassion undergird the woman's right, thus avoiding, as Justice White complained in his dissent, the woman's "convenience, whim, or caprice." Confession, therefore, is mandated in the enactment of female rights to privacy.

Conclusion

Should it surprise us that lyric poetry provided an ideal form in which to consider and elaborate the conditions and the costs of privacy? If we remember that the lyric has been defined since the nineteenth century as a "self overheard speaking to itself," the anxieties of privacy in the Cold War – of being overheard anywhere and at any time – make the lyric a suitable and even necessary place to think about privacy and self-exposure. Withdrawing into privacy to conduct a conversation with oneself is one of the most powerful images of autonomy that we have. The freedom of expression of the lyric – where the speaker has no obligations to others because there are no listeners other than self – translates into the freedom of self-creation where the speaker can – indeed, by the New Critical standards of that historical moment, must – transcend the constraints of time, place, and social location. The confessional poets, by exploring the realms of the not merely private, but *too* private aspects of selfhood, submerged themselves in those aspects of domestic life that curb autonomy and limit self-making. In an era when so many worried so deeply about incursions into privacy, their example helps us understand why others would relinquish it and interrogate its fictions and its promises. As privacy became suddenly visible in U.S. culture at the end of the 1950s, it quickly became clear that we no longer knew what it was. Privacy would be defined and redefined, exalted and protested, violated and protected in ever-changing ways as the twentieth century came to an end. We still imagine that we have privacy, even though it has died a thousand deaths, and we still cannot agree on its uses and its value.

NOTES

1. Robert Lowell, *Life Studies* (New York: Vintage Books, 1959), 83.
2. Ibid., 84.
3. Originally published as "Poetry as Confession" in the November 19, 1959 issue of *The Nation*, this article also formed the basis of *The Modern Poets: A Critical Introduction* (New York: Oxford University Press, 1960) and was later collected in *Our Life in Poetry: Selected Essays and Reviews* (New York: Persea Books, 1991).
4. Anne Sexton both denied being a confessional poet and declared herself the only one. See Jo Gill, "Anne Sexton and Confessional Poetics," *The Review of English* 55.220 (June 2004): 425–445, 425.
5. Donald Allen, ed., *The New American Poetry, 1945–1960* (New York: Grove Press, 1960).
6. Robert Lowell, *The Dolphin* (London: Faber, 1973).
7. Anne Sexton, *The Awful Rowing Toward God* (Boston: Houghton Mifflin, 1975).
8. W. D. Snodgrass, *Heart's Needle* (New York: Knopf, 1959).
9. T. S. Eliot, "Tradition and the Individual Talent," in *The Sacred Wood: Essays on Poetry and Criticism* (London: Methuen, 1920), 47–59.
10. This line first appeared in a poem called "A Sort of Song," published in *The Wedge* (Cummington, MA: The Cummington Press, 1944); it appeared again in *Paterson. Book One* (New York: New Directions, 1946).
11. Frederick Seidel, "Robert Lowell: The Art of Poetry 3," *Paris Review* 7 (Winter–Spring 1961): 59–65, 64.
12. Allen Ginsberg, *Howl and Other Poems* (San Francisco: City Lights Books, 1956), 9.
13. Frank O'Hara, *Lunch Poems* (San Francisco: City Lights Books, 1964).
14. Sylvia Plath, *Ariel* (1966; New York: Harper Perennial, 1999).
15. John Berryman, *77 Dreamsongs* (New York: Farrar, Straus and Giroux, 1964).
16. Anne Sexton, *The Complete Poems* (Boston: Houghton Mifflin, 1981), 137–138.
17. See, for instance, Christina Britzolakis, *Sylvia Plath and the Theatre of Mourning* (Oxford and New York: Clarendon Press, 1999).
18. Sexton, *The Complete Poems*, 35.
19. Elaine Tyler May, *Homeward Bound: American Families in the Cold War Era* (New York: Basic Books, 1988).
20. Douglas dissenting in *Osborne v. U.S., Lewis v. U.S., Hoffa v. U.S.*, U.S. 323, 87 S. Ct. 439 (1966).
21. Myron Brenton, *The Privacy Invaders* (New York: Coward-McGann), 1964.
22. In lectures delivered at Franklin and Marshall Law School, published as *The Right of the People* (New York: Doubleday, 1958), Douglas laid out a rationale for a right to privacy in relation to Cold War–era McCarthyism, and much of its reasoning finds its way into his *Griswold* opinion.
23. The "penumbra," which means "shadow," was composed of "emanations" from the First, Fourth, Fifth, and Ninth Amendments.
24. See Diane Middlebrook's account of this episode in "Housewife into Poet: The Apprenticeship of Anne Sexton," *The New England Quarterly* 56.4 (December 1983): 483–503.

25. Ibid., 493.
26. In 1962 alone, Plath wrote no fewer than eight poems that registered the pervasiveness of surveillance: "Eavesdropper," "The Detective," "Purdah," "The Other," "Words heard, by accident, over the phone," "The Courage of Shutting Up," "A Secret," and "The Jailer." These poems were originally marked for inclusion in *Ariel* but were cut by her husband and literary executor, Ted Hughes, in the original edition.
27. Sexton, *The Complete Poems*, 155.
28. Plath, *Ariel*, 33.
29. Sylvia Plath, *The Journals of Sylvia Plath: 1950–1962*, ed. Karen V. Kukil (London: Faber and Faber, 2000), 569.
30. Betty Friedan, *The Feminine Mystique* (1963; New York: W. W. Norton, 1983).
31. Deborah Nelson, *Pursuing Privacy in Cold War America* (New York: Columbia University Press, 2002).
32. Berryman, *77 Dreamsongs*, 74.
33. Snodgrass, *Heart's Needle*, 16–17.
34. Ibid., 16.
35. Sexton, *The Complete Poems*, 56.
36. Ibid., 57.
37. Ibid., 24–25.
38. Ibid., 25.
39. Plath, *Ariel*, 9.

FURTHER READING

Allen, Donald, *The New American Poetry, 1945–1960*. New York: Grove Press, 1960.

Breslin, Paul. *The Psycho-Political Muse: American Poetry since the Fifties*. Chicago: University of Chicago Press, 1987.

Britzolakis, Christina. *Sylvia Plath and the Theater of Mourning*. Oxford: Clarendon Press, 1999.

Brunner, Edward J. *Cold War Poetry: The Social Text in the Fifties Poem*. Urbana: University of Illinois Press, 2001.

Davidson, Michael. *Guys Like Us: Citing Masculinity in Cold War Poetics*. Chicago: University of Chicago Press, 2004.

Forbes, Deborah. *Sincerity's Shadow: Self-Consciousness in British Romantic and Mid-Twentieth Century American Poetry*. Cambridge, MA: Harvard University Press, 2004.

Friedan, Betty. *The Feminine Mystique*. 1963; New York: Dell, 1983.

Garrow, David. *Liberty and Sexuality; The Right to Privacy and the Making of Roe v. Wade, 1923–1973*. New York: Maxwell Macmillan International, 1994.

Gill, Jo, ed. *Modern Confessional Writing: New Critical Essays*. New York and London: Routledge Press, 2006.

May, Elaine Tyler. *Homeward Bound: American Families in the Cold War Era*. New York: Basic Books, 1988.

Nelson, Deborah. *Pursuing Privacy in Cold War America*. New York: Columbia University Press, 2002.

Packard, Vance. *The Naked Society*. New York: David McKay, 1964.

Ramazani, Jahan. *The Poetry of Mourning: The Modern Elegy from Hardy to Heaney*. Chicago: University of Chicago Press, 1994.

Rogin, Michael. *Ronald Reagan, The Movie and Other Episodes in Political Demonology*. Berkeley and Los Angeles: University of California Press, 1987.

Rose, Jacqueline. *The Haunting of Sylvia Plath*. Cambridge, MA: Harvard University Press, 1992.

Vendler, Helen. *The Given and the Made: Strategies of Poetic Redefinition*. Cambridge, MA: Harvard University Press.

4

CHARLES ALTIERI

Surrealism as a Living Modernism: What the New York Poets Learned from Two Generations of New York Painting

For Frank O'Hara, the way to a fully contemporary art had to run through Jackson Pollock. But how could writing adapt Pollock's collapsing of distinctions between foreground and background or his capacity to focus so intensely on the energies embodied in the varied material qualities a line could possess? O'Hara's solution was to treat Pollock's later work not as a rejection of his earlier explicit surrealism but rather as a realization of a surrealist spirit that could thrive by rejecting what had become tired surrealist imagery trying to express an ever-receding unconscious: "Cubism was an innovation; Surrealism an evolution. The former dealt with technique, the latter with content.... Surrealism enjoined the duty, along with the liberation, of saying what you mean and meaning what you say beyond any fondness for saying or meaning."[1]

Surrealism becomes a dynamic Modernist demonstration of how art could free itself not just from representational ideals but also from the psychological accoutrements of those ideals – especially the fantasy that to represent the world seems to entitle the artist also to judge it and to parade those judgments as wisdom. Against this fantasy, Pollock managed to achieve a completely literal understanding of the modernist distinction between an art of representation and an art of presentation. The space of painting could become "a field of incident," "exploring possibilities for discovery" by the artist as he or she elaborates an ongoing process of decisions and the adjustments they necessitate in tracking the self's energies and the relationships those energies were making possible.[2] Such tracking could not produce the analytic powers that Cubism and constructivist abstraction developed out of Cézanne. But it could elaborate moments where the imagination finds itself literally dwelling in sites of being that intensify strange conjunctions and states.

Viewing Pollock this way made a major difference in how writers represented their own modernity because they could explore their capacities to replace scenic representation by the energies of line that provided an immediacy of saying what one means "beyond any fondness for saying and meaning." So younger poets could write in the spirit of Pollock without simply copying Pollock's project. More important, these poets could explore a version of Pollock's freedom to foreground the self's energies without binding that self to scenes of confessional sincerity. Instead one could see one's art participating in what had become the major version of international modernism. Pursuing that freedom in "saying what you mean" then enabled the writers to find allies and guides in a second generation of New York painting that had taken the enormous risk of returning from abstraction to figuration. Both writers and painters could treat the turn to figuration not as a conservative flight from the pressures of innovation but rather as a means to bring freedoms derived from abstract expressionism into conjunction with energies basic to quotidian life.

The filiations between New York School poets and painters were nowhere more evident than in the interests painters took in the poets as portrait subjects – in part because ideas and ideals of portraiture were changing radically under the new dispensation represented by O'Hara's reading of Pollock. The new art offered various models for self-portraiture that could refuse the imaginary satisfactions of the finished portrait that tells someone what he or she will have to look like. And the pursuit of this immediacy could recast the entire social role portraits might play. The classical portrait cannot but remind audiences of the patronage system ultimately responsible for what status and freedom artists had achieved in Western society. But now the New York painters were responding to friendship, not to dependency on the whims of their financial masters. Therefore portraits could take on a new intimacy – not by stressing psychological depth but rather as a record of how figuration might provide an expressive register of what the painter feels for and about the subject in the moment of the painting. Tone becomes as central in painting as it had been in literature, because an entire tradition must be treated self-consciously and submitted to the interpretive power of a spontaneous and evocative use of color that places abstract expressionist techniques within quotidian life. Conversely that sense of stylizing the quotidian as a means of honoring its centrality for the artist would prove a vital provocation for poets attempting to clarify where their own dispositions were leading them.

Let us take two portraits of O'Hara as typical of how second-generation New York school artists bring emphatic painterly presence to figurative tasks. O'Hara's famous broken nose was one inducement to painterly freedoms; another was the receding hairline that provided lush fields of play for reflected light. But it was his stance that most excited painters to explore imaginative possibilities within the portrait genre. That combination of

Figure 1. Fairfield Porter (American, 1907–1975), Frank O'Hara, 1957, oil on canvas, 63 7/8 × 45 7/8 in. (162.3 × 116.5 cm). Toledo Museum of Art (Toledo, Ohio), Purchased with funds from the Libbey Endowment, Gift of Edward Drummond Libbey, 1977.31, Photo Credit: Tim Thayer, Oak Park, Michigan.

arrogance and vulnerability, daunting energy and delicate sensibility, ena-bled artists suspicious of abstract expressionist grandeur to bring the same sense of painterly freedoms over to the pleasures of figuration. The figure in Fairfield Porter's 1957 *Frank O'Hara* (Figure 1) has the light yet taut body of an athlete. But there is also a rigidity about the body that distances its physicality and makes a spirit of self-protection seem pervasive. Notice that Porter takes significant expressive risks in composing a body that will

Figure 2. Larry Rivers portrait of Frank O'Hara. Courtesy Tibor de Nagy Gallery, New York. Art © Estate of Larry Rivers/Licensed by VAGA, New York, NY.

not quite assume the standard reclining position of salon paintings. Both O'Hara's thighs seem to refuse the material and psychological support of the couch just as the painting itself seems bound to contextualize its interest in portraiture by citing and disrupting salon tradition. Energy and convention make uneasy adjustments to one another, especially in the strange conjunction of decorative couch and severe, almost minimalist, wall and window. O'Hara sits, or almost sits, at the juncture of multiple visual traditions.

Larry Rivers' 1954 portrait (Figure 2) presents an O'Hara caught up in different kinds of disjunctions that all contribute ultimately to a sense of the power this figure exercised in his friends' lives. There is still the athletic body. But it is subjected to several other dimensions of cultural force. There are the boots, self-conscious signifiers playing with butch sexuality and promising "real" manliness in the contra-posto pose. Then there is his delicately painted body with its frontal vulnerability – the most important symbol of manliness dangling in a mix of aggression and pathos. (This stance is no ordinary contra-posto: it is exaggerated so that manly assertion is inseparable from acute vulnerability. The hands and arms that could defend against vulnerability here assume a quasi-heroic, quasi-distracted and -intellectual stance.) This figure has a kind of inner life, but Rivers seems careful to separate that inner life from any standard psychological predicates or even psychological grammar.[3] The complexity of character derives from how what is portrayed negotiates several contrasting and intersecting styles. There is an abstract painterly harmony in browns that seems to encompass but also to reject the standing figure. And there are free painterly gestures that remind me of strokes by Jasper Johns. Yet the figure is also placed within two competing traditions that promise to secure its realistic impact – one is the tradition of Dutch accurate portraiture and the other is nineteenth-century academic painting as exemplified in, say, Paul Delaroche or William-Adolphe Bougereau. Citation and figuration concur to establish a distinctive blend of care and irony that O'Hara would very much appreciate.

John Ashbery also inspired portraits by his friends, although he had neither a broken nose nor a receding hairline. I want to use a photographic portrait of him in his Chelsea apartment to introduce another aspect of New York School painting in the work of Jane Freilicher (Figure 3). Notice how Freilicher's *A Painting Table* (1954) occupies pride of place over his sofa in the photograph. Ashbery valued this painting for its ability to achieve an anti-photographic realism by means of "the free techniques and feelings of Abstract Expressionism."[4] That allegiance to painterly traditions is captured nicely by her stressing the presence of her palette. Within the painting itself, the brushwork incorporating the outside darkness with the gossamer curtain provides a more subtle mark of Freilicher's fidelity to a kind of abstraction within her realism. More important yet is how she turns realism to the purposes of rendering an event of seeing that, Ashbery notes, pulls against fidelity to the represented objects.[5] The various cans in the painting give very little information but their color: they exist primarily as part of a seeing, or even of a glance, rather than as something permanent that sustains the artist's craft. The objects seem noted more than described. For there is a sense of instant event about the painting, reinforced by the sheer plenitude

February 8, 1975

Figure 3. John Ashbery photographed by Jill Krementz in his apartment on February 8, 1975.
Photograph of John Ashbery © Jill Krementz, all rights reserved.

of the signifiers and the painting's strangely awkward structuring gestures. The vases containing the brushes almost balance the vertical on the left comprised by the window, but they occupy a different plane, and the busy variety contrasts sharply with the static darkness. There are also many diagonals and loops that organize some of the objects. So there seem too many patterns to organize the painting; it exceeds order – another aspect of its sense of submitting to events of seeing if it is to take on any reality at all.

Ashbery's comments on this figurative assemblage bring out how the painter's work becomes the focus for the poet's thematic probing:

> *The Painting Table* is a congeries of conflicting pictorial grammars. The result is a little anthology of ways of seeing, feeling, and painting, with no suggestion

that any one way is better than another.... What is better than anything is the renewed realization that all kinds of things can and must exist side by side at any given moment, and that that is what life and creating are all about.[6]

Now realism itself seems a strange imperative because the painters expand it to deal with the range of feelings elicited by objects. Realism now has to acknowledge and play with the imperative to keep kinds of reality in continuity with one another.

One could approach this fusion of painterly and poetic concerns by tracing the many lyrical appreciations of specific qualities in the first- and second-generation New York School painting by the poets and by recent critics like Kimberly Lamm writing on James Schuyler.[7] But because of my limited space (and limited knowledge) I want to dwell on how O'Hara, Ashbery, and Barbara Guest elaborate the desire to recast surrealism so that it accommodates New York painting and then give their own distinctive twists to how these painters help articulate their own imaginative orientations. This capacity for discursive self-representation was especially important because the invocation of painterly affinities helped enormously in the poets' developing alternatives to the dominant conservative poetics (which I will say more about in a moment) that seemed recipes for success for young writers entering the publishing world during the 1950s.

Let me be more specific. The paintings discussed here and the discourses they generate were part of what it meant to be young and talented in New York City during the early 1950s. The G.I. Bill had opened educational opportunities and transformed schooling – from Kenneth Koch's and O'Hara's being able to attend Harvard to the saxophonist Larry Rivers's deciding to become a painter and having funds to attend classes given by Hans Hoffman. New York would be the arena where such educations could be tested for their capacity to influence high culture, as Abstract Expressionism was already in the process of doing. But such educations also had to be uneasy with any dominant style, in part because they were so intensely aware that history is the dumping ground of styles. Then there was the emergence of The Museum of Modern Art as an institution eager to replace the Grand Tours of wealthy bourgeois by a series of shows documenting painterly achievements from Pierre Bonnard and Henri Matisse to surrealism and Chaim Soutine. Art was in the air – as possibility more than as authority. In fact, New York offered an ideal situation for young artists because many of the European exiles who had been so central to fostering its aura of sophistication were returning home – leaving both a residue of aristocratic ambitions for painting and a vacuum for how those ambitions were to be satisfied.[8] Perhaps it is not surprising in retrospect (although still shocking) that the Central Intelligence Agency would decide to invest in making the city the world center for innovative art.[9]

The situation in poetry was not so promising. While the painter-exiles were leaving, the major modernists remained gray eminences defining what poetry should be. Not surprisingly then, Robert Lowell seemed the most important younger poet in the United States. *Life Studies* was published in 1951 and quickly won from both O'Hara and Ashbery an undying enmity for its morbid heterosexual self-absorption and its apparently self-satisfied alienation from the very qualities of community and inventiveness that poets were experiencing in New York. Where else could poetry go to escape the weight of literary tradition and the demands of the New Criticism for complex artefactuality that Lowell honored even as he sought an expressive freedom within it? Perhaps the only release possible was for the poets to mine the opportunities in the intellectual ferment the painters were creating. The poets were already enmeshed in the painterly world. They only had to channel the energies of their intellectual lives into their work as poets. And they needed luck, which arrived in the guise of Frank O'Hara. As Ashbery remembers it, "The one thing lacking in our privileged little world was the arrival of Frank O'Hara to kind of cobble everything together and tell us what we and they were doing."[10]

Among the poets of the New York School, Barbara Guest was the most explicit on the need to turn to painters in order to create models of space and fluid interconnection that could alter the poets' sense of their own possibilities: in her view, "modern painters" were "the revolutionaries to whom writers turn in the desire to break from the solemnity of the judicious rules of their craft."[11] And we will soon see that in many ways she was the most radical in her use "of some of their methods, especially the method that "lends an idea of space to the poem."[12] But O'Hara and Ashbery wrote more extensively about how the diverse projects of postwar New York painting were all surrealist in spirit and therefore explorations of where modernist art could go if it refused the asceticism of cubism and constructivist abstraction. And they offer brilliant examples of how two very different poetic orientations could anchor themselves in that surrealist spirit. O'Hara's hallmark "I do this, I do that" formulations are most attentive to the freedom of self-making involved in surrealist critiques of representation, while Ashbery loves the ways surrealism composes "a plane where the subconscious and the concrete mingle on equal terms."[13] Surrealism offers enigmatic figures marked by an incompleteness of being for which self-expression is an always present and always inadequate metaphor.

Many critics have remarked on O'Hara's fundamentally painterly style in his commitment to process and in his emphasis on a freedom in structuring details that loosely adapts collage principles.[14] But I am more interested in how, by treating Pollock as an exemplary surrealist, O'Hara manages to adapt Pollock's example to developing a free honesty or experimental individualism in poetry. Artefactuality need not be planned but can become inseparable from the intensity of engaging the self in providing names for what one is experiencing. And then one might adapt this mode of being present to an immensely various set of contents, ranging from the playful camp self-consciousness of Rivers's intricate levels of significance that cannot quite be fused to Freilicher's overripe exploding of realist logic.

Any surrealist art would be attentive to how the unconscious comes into play. But O'Hara saw that Pollock put aside the ultimately realist dream that one could find an imagery by which to portray that level of the mind. The unconscious had to be manifest as a source of energy consistently challenging any version of habit or normativity that promised variants of conventional representation. If one imagined this expression on the model of Pollock's maintaining a dynamic line that refuses subordination to concepts, one could conceive the unconscious not as a separate domain from consciousness but as a structuring of conative energies that can be continuous with the reality constituted by the work's decision. The sense of "revelation" emerges through a course of "stress and conflict" that does not seek meaning or need to honor any kind of memory of what art should look like.[15] The success of the work can be measured only by how we enter directly into the energies provoking the work and the sense that these energies have been exhausted through the work they produce.

We can list briefly the three primary ways in which O'Hara might be seen as continuing Pollock's spirit of innovation. First O'Hara finds his own ways to develop what in Pollock is an "amazing ability to quicken a line by thinning it, to slow it by flooding ... to change, to reinvigorate, to extend, to build up an embarrassment of riches in the mass by drawing alone."[16] And then narrative is possible simply in terms of how the speaker's decisions bring a world into the present tense while emptying it of all external demands that it take particular shapes, as in these lines from "Personal Poem":

> we go eat some fish and some ale it's
> cool but crowded we don't like Lionel Trilling
> we decide, we like Don Allen we don't like
> Henry James so much we like Herman Melville[17]

Second, once one has this power over the line, one must put it to work by manifesting the scope of its presence, and so display the difference this play of force can make in our sense of the world. Pollock's primary instrument for achieving a kind of metaphoric force without metaphor consists in his brilliant use of scale. Scale unites line with a sense of the force of "the painter's body, not of the image of a body, and the setting for the scale, which would include all the referents," so that there could be a union of physical and spiritual reality in a "oneness that has no need for the mediation of metaphor and symbol."[18] In O'Hara, scale becomes the constant presence of the variety of New York City and the poet's capacity to engage an immense range of popular cultural signifiers. Third, what makes this sense of scale believable in O'Hara is his willingness to lay himself on the line so that each line seems to exhaust what is happening in his present and to position himself on the verge of another investment that may go off on a tangent. O'Hara's is a quotidian expressivism in which there emerges all-encompassing honesty and "spiritual clarity" where there can be "no secrets."[19] All the negative force of surrealism's critique of the staging of "art-content" frees in Pollock and O'Hara a "monumental and agonizing ... eradication of conflicting beliefs toward the total engagement of the spirit in the expression of meaning."[20] Here the spirit "can act freely and with unpremeditated knowledge ... in a last effort of recognition which is the justification of being."[21]

Ashbery has a very different focus. He shares O'Hara's negatives: unfreedom is the force of expectation buttressed by what easily becomes a tyrannical and blind insistence on "truth." But Ashbery's version of surrealism turned from a focus on the self to how this style established a tradition of active "unknowing" cultivated by constructing planes of experience where "the subconscious and the concrete mingle on equal terms."[22] The very first essay in *Reported Sightings* claims "that Surrealism has become a part of our daily lives" because of the diverse and unpredictable crossing of levels of being we need to make sense of quotidian experience.[23] This version of surrealism depends on recognizing how proclaimed surrealists like Dali and Ernst present quite limited versions of this new multiplicity because they root their challenge to reason in the hope that they can somehow provide images that capture or reflect unconscious activity. The fuller surrealism would eschew the opposition conscious-unconscious for the multiple strangeness within what seems almost pictorially exemplified by de Chirico, whose "manner and substance form an inseparable whole" constituting "an irreducible, magic substance," "beyond the reach of interesting ideas."[24] Then one can fully appreciate how "such painters as Pollock, Motherwell, Newman, and Rothko" become "more truly surreal" in their later work than in the work obviously influenced by surrealist artists.[25] For that work provides a richer challenge to the authority or reason and a greater willingness to follow imagination for whatever forces it can muster to express states whose immediacy befuddles our typical expectations of what can make sense. All these artists cultivate the all-over picture rather than what it represents so that they produce a "dance of non-discovery" in which every element can fascinate and none is required to matter "more than another."[26] Where Eliot's generation "had to bring the whole history of human thought into play," "today it is possible not to speak in metaphors."[27] When the self in poetry does not have to carry the burden of securing metaphorical interpretation, it becomes free to revel in the many ways objects and situations appear and "accumulate the electrodes of my feelings."[28] And because these feelings seem solicited by what is not self, they are free to agglutinate in the various paths that cross and seem redirected by the neighborhoods objects enter – think again of Freilicher's *The Painting Table*.

The most important feature for Ashbery's sense of surrealism was the work's resistance to any effort to impose a unity that might attribute a distinct purpose to the work. He wanted a sense of pleasure in irreducible difference, like the various ways images make claims on the real in Freilicher or the play of quotation against care in Rivers. That sense of difference cannot be subsumed into structural patterns like those proposed by Saussure. Rather the play of levels of sense and allusion become constitutive. Such an art embraces incompleteness and the coexistence of contrary forces on every level of experience. Hence Ashbery stresses how Fairfield Porter's work shows that there need be "no ideas in art, just objects and materials that combine, like people, in somewhat mysterious ways."[29] Where O'Hara locates freedom in manifesting the energy not to be trapped by memory of his own feelings, Ashbery emphasizes a freedom deriving from how the world's intricate dissociations give ample occasions for almost surrendering to the luscious incompleteness of dream logic.

De Chirico's painting is for Ashbery the best articulation of how the spirit of surrealism fully enters quotidian experience. On the concrete level, de Chirico emphasizes the distinctiveness of objects that come from different worlds yet create a sense that they "had always been meant for each other."[30] But we have to wonder in what world these objects might realize their affinities. The naturalism by which details are rendered is "consistently undermined by devices such as the introduction of multiple vanishing points ... and the placing of highlights where shadows logically ought to be."[31] Then there is the matter of the pervasive mysterious dread that responds to the details but refuses to interpret them as metaphoric or suggest a plausible relation between the general and the particular. It seems as if the painter thinks any feature that promises synthesis into a concrete universal would impose a false intelligibility and threaten the mystery he protects by allowing differences and incompatibilities to establish what formal unity the painting needs. Rather than pursuing the concrete universal, the artist's ideal becomes prolonging "the dance of non-discovery."[32] The aim is to unite "the inexhaustibility of poetry with the concreteness of painting."[33] Poetry and painting in this spirit might even claim ethical significance because they exemplify experiences that suggest that our compulsions to resolve tensions stem less from what the world demands than from how our psyches are trained to displace that very world in pursuit of their own needs. Perhaps it is better simply to accept the tensions differences produce and then imaginatively flesh out the competing options: "It is, fittingly for our late century, a work shot through with oppositions that [R. B.] Kitaj is able to indicate but never quite resolve satisfactorily, which is as it should be."[34]

Guest matters for my story primarily because she was the writer most focused on the specific issue of how poets might absorb within their own craft the interests and possibilities of this spirit of surrealism in painting. Like Ashbery, she wanted to cultivate the force of differences among levels of sense so that the poem would take on a concrete multiplicity of relations, making it very much like a canvas.[35] So our task with her is to follow how she uses painting to develop a structuring visuality for the lyric capable of honoring the irreducibly complex and concrete play of these differences without imposing models of understanding typically derived from the intricate linguistic syntax of which she was also very fond.

Ashbery and Schuyler, for example, emphasize figures for visuality quite different from Guest's emphasis on intricate syntax, ultimately turning against appeals to discursive understanding. So where Schuyler stresses the concreteness of imagistic and tonal details, and Ashbery is fascinated by the instability of cultural codes, Guest seems to emphasize contrasts between writerly and painterly aspects of syntax – the one oriented toward description and argument, the other toward internal balance and subtlety.[36] And in that process she manages verbal echoes of Porter's deformations, Rivers's intricacies of allusiveness that trouble the concrete image, and Freilicher's prolific painterly sense of a real that exceeds the boundaries of conventional empiricism.

This tension between what syntax can enact and what semantics can gather has been central for poets ever since they began emphasizing the nondiscursive event qualities of their images. And it is intensified by the fact that logically, poetry's relation to sound patterns seems to echo its

commitment to images, because both gain power by resisting the understanding. Witness Pound's twin obsessions with the concreteness of the
image and the evocativeness of the musical phrase. So it is not surprising that many poets and critics have formulated accounts of this tension.
Rather than bind myself to any particular poet's story, I will use the most
abstractly formal and synthetic account I know, namely Nelson Goodman's
Languages of Art.

Goodman distinguishes between language as a system depending on discrete structured differences and painting as operating within a syntactic
density where there are always an infinite possible set of differences that
might bring significance to details and relationships. Language divides the
world into differences that make a difference, as stressed in structural linguistics, and differences that are not registered as significant, like differences
in pronunciation or accompanying gestures. For Goodman, language is syntactically articulate but semantically dense. Pictures, on the other hand, are
syntactically and semantically dense.[37] Every difference is in principle divis-
ible into significant further differences.

Goodman exemplifies this difference by contrasting an electrocardiogram
and a Hokusai drawing of Mt. Fujiyama that might be indistinguishable
taken as visual material.[38] But when we read the electrocardiogram, we treat
it as syntactically articulate: the only differences in the picture that matter are the signs that register semantically because of contrast with other
discrete signifying features. In the Hokusai, however, every segment of the
painting can be significant – the shape of the line of the mountain, the shad-
ing of the figure, the textures that gradually rather than discretely modulate
into one another.

This distinction matters for Guest and the other poets because they were
fascinated by possibilities of pushing the differential logic of words as far
as possible toward incorporating the continuous replete space of painterly
composition. One could elaborate that point psychologically in poems like
her "Brown Studio" (1962), which play on a speaker's ability to reconstruct
a scene in such a way that the scene ultimately subsumes agency into the
physical atmosphere it composes. This sense of engagement in the visual
then provides a strange and uncontrollable otherness that at once frightens
and exhilarates the intelligence. It comes to seem that the elaborate syntax itself produces a subject matter extending beyond what our vehicles for
determining meaning can control.

With "Nebraska" (1973), Guest models an even more ambitious crossing of painterly mark and linguistic sign. Here surrealism departs from any
promise of deep psychological truths to stretch the domains of meaning and

reference toward something approaching a sheer physiology, but shaped by imagination. The opening sets the affective logic:

> Climate succumbing continuously as water gathered
> into foam or Nebraska elevated by ships
> withholds what is glorious in its climb like
> a waiter balancing a waterglass while the tray
> slips that was necklace in the arch of bridge[39]

This is not a simple set of images trying to express something ineffable about the psyche. Rather the images are strangely continuous with the intricate flow of syntax, especially given that it is the syntactic powers of "as" and "like" that establish the need for the images. It is as if once syntax can sustain a world that resides between reference to an actual Nebraska and Nebraska as itself a figure, language moves toward the replete space established by conjoined images free to follow their own possibilities of connection. Can we describe climate without images and metaphors? Perhaps Nebraska has to float in order to be free of its conventional, utterly landlocked condition (in every register).

Guest's concluding stanza offers her richest realization of these possible supplements to discursive meaning:

> Hallucinated as Nebraska the swift blue
> appears formerly hid when approached now it
> chides with a tone the prow striking a grim
> atmosphere appealing and intimate as if a verse
> were to water somewhere and hues emerge
> and distance erased a swan concluding bridge
> the sky with her neck possibly brightening
> the machinery as a leaf arches through its yellow
> syllables so Nebraska's throat[40]

The force of this final "so" is especially intriguing. Does it suggest that the preceding figures all express qualities that refer to "Nebraska's throat," or does it project "Nebraska's throat" as one more metaphor in the effort to characterize what is involved in hallucinating a site such as Nebraska? The question is unanswerable. But that does not mean it is not productive. The question allows Nebraska a mode of existence that can give even that state a complex vitality because it is now in effect adorned by the two chains that this poem weaves: one of possible reference and one of the undoing of reference for a continuous set of metaphoric equivalents organized along several axes like proximity of sound, visual analogy, and emotional association. One can say that along one chain the poet tries to keep in the foreground the capacity of language to afford a coherent structure of signs. But that foreground continually recedes because of a corollary pressure to make the word function as mark in what Goodman calls a "syntactically replete surface" where every kind of difference in gradation and texture is available for reflection.

Guest seems to feel Nebraska needs this supplemental semantics because if this topic is to take on significance, it will have to depend on the poet's imaginative abilities to reconfigure the contexts within which we imagine it. One might ask, or perhaps must ask: what has the poem to do with the actual Nebraska? And a writer whose adult life was lived in Berkeley and New York City might answer, "How could poetry be content with the actual Nebraska?" If Nebraska is to be a candidate for a "fair realism," the state may have to become something we do not find on any map or government survey. Nebraska has to be a state of mind, an "Oklahoma" brought up to date from its existence in Rodgers and Hammerstein's musical. And Nebraska best becomes a state of mind if it can be located not just as a renewed object of attention but as a force literally establishing paths for the imagination. To refresh Nebraska one has to turn constantly to metaphors and similes that seem to take on their own logic, or to tease us with possible Nebraskas hidden to the practical mind.

Thus Nebraska can flourish only if we are willing to entertain how the imagination can produce strangely plastic continuities that replace traditional description. It is as if Nebraska's nondescript nature relative to traditional descriptive values heightens the effectiveness of setting two ideals of description against one another. If Nebraska is the object of description, it here evokes a surreal abandon, as if Nebraska could only come alive by letting it hover as a real stimulus for a series of imaginative equivalents. Yet this may not be enough. The "real" Nebraska of our geography classes may so lack engaging details that it exemplifies the kind of worldly phenomenon especially dependent on what our sentences can invent about it beyond our irritable reaching after fact and reasons. If Nebraska is to live for the mind, the description may have to acknowledge its fictiveness so that Nebraska matters because of how it solicits imagined details.

Now I think we are in a position to appreciate why the syntax here is so elaborate and why that elaborateness in Guest and in Ashbery plays roles quite different from the roles such intricacy plays in traditional lyric poetry. In Yeats or in Stevens, for example, elaborate syntax is a measure of the poet's ability to bring complex and ambivalent acts of mind into an order that makes rhetoric an effective supplement to argument. Guest, in contrast, seems to develop almost a pure syntax that emphasizes how much apparent discontinuity language can produce within what could be determinate reference. Or, more generously, we can say that in this poem syntax must establish a formal complexity compensating for the semantic simplicity shaping our typical ideas of Nebraska. Syntax calls attention to what can be produced by the experience of sheer language reveling in its capacities for distinction. Here reality for the moment submits to the law of imagination – which is that there are many laws for the imagination, all equally capable of generating a sense of our power to find satisfaction in the mind for what is disturbingly difficult to love in the real world. Poetry proves an indispensable and instructive guide to post-representational painting.

NOTES

1. Frank O'Hara, *Art Chronicle 1954–1966* (New York: George Braziller, 1975), 17–18.
2. Ibid., 15. Andrew Epstein, in *Beautiful Enemies: Friendship and Postwar American Poetry* (New York: Oxford University Press, 2006), 88, calls this tracking "experimental individualism." In my essay in Diggory ed., I emphasize how Pollock correlates responsibility with existential contingency.
3. Sam Hunter, *Rivers* (New York: Harry N Abrams, 1971), 14 ff., is good on the complex tone in this portrait.
4. John Ashbery, *Reported Sightings: Art Chronicles 1957–1987*, ed. David Bergman (Cambridge, MA: Harvard University Press, 1999), 96.
5. "Lesser artists correct nature in a misguided attempt at heightened realism, forgetting that the real is not only what one sees but also a result of how one sees it – inattentively, inaccurately perhaps, but nevertheless that is how it is coming through to us, and to deny this is to kill the life of the picture" (Ibid., 242).
6. Ibid., 243–44.
7. See, for example, Kimberly Lamm, "'One Lighting the Other Seductively': James Schuyler, Eileen Miles and the Sexuality of Literary Influence," *How 2 Work/ Book*: 1 (no 8), 2002, http://www.asu.edu/pipercwcenter/how2journal/archive/online_archive/v1_8_2002/current/workbook/lamm-essays.htm. Schuyler's own art criticism, collected in *Selected Art Writing*, ed. Simon Pettet (Santa Rosa, CA: Black Sparrow Press, 1998), is a great version of sensitive responsiveness to particulars.
8. Martica Sawin, *Surrealism in Exile and the Beginning of the New York School* (Cambridge, MA: MIT Press, 1995), 413.
9. See Serge Guilbaut, *How New York Stole the Idea of Modern Art* (Chicago: University of Chicago Press, 1985).
10. Ashbery, Reported Sightings, 241.
11. Guest, *Forces of Imagination: Writing on Writing* (Berkeley, CA: Kelsey Street Press, 2003), 51.
12. Ibid., 107.
13. Ashbery, Reported Sightings, 325.
14. There is far too much good criticism on O'Hara than I can cite here. I found David Lehman's *The Last Avant-garde: The Making of the New York School of Poets* (New York: Doubleday, 1998) and William Watkins's *In the Process of Poetry: The New York School and the Avant Garde* (Lewisburg, PA: Bucknell University Press, 2001) most useful for thinking about the poet's relationship to painting.

15. O'Hara, *Art Chronicle*, 14.

16. Ibid., 32. All references to O'Hara's poetry are to *The Collected Poems of Frank O'Hara*, ed. Donald Allen (Berkeley: University of California Press, 1995). O'Hara's specific practices of lineation are worth noting. His early poetry usually emphasized short, mobile lines, a practice he continued throughout his career. Later these were accompanied by more orchestral compositions adapting Whitman's line but modifying the bardic into a conversational seriousness, as in "To the Film Industry in Crisis" (232) and "In Memory of My Feelings" (252–56). Both modes stress enjambment, primarily to display a self always trying to catch up with and invest in the syntax-bending energies of his thinking, as in "Poem (When Your Left Arm Twitches)" (133). The pauses also often establish a sense of vulnerability and caution (or the honesty O'Hara finds in Pollock), modified by a flexibility that can shift quickly to other selves as the psyche rushes to fill in the pronounced pauses. "Joe's Jacket" seems to me O'Hara's richest lineation because he brings the mobility of the short line to the psychological complexity reveling in the capacities of much longer units of expression. Here the enjambments marvelously manage also to turn on words that offer their own sense of substance, even in transit, so that the motion is insistent but slowed by the hovering that tests what is being expressed. Notice in the poem's opening how the "I" that gets expressed takes on the combination of substance and transition afforded the nouns that conclude lines: "Entraining to Southhampton in the parlor with Jap and Vincent, I / see life as a penetrable landscape lit from above / like it was in my Barbizonian kiddy days when automobiles / were owned by the same people for years and the Alfa Romeo was / only a rumor under the leaves beside the viaduct and I / pretending to be adult felt the blue within me and the light up there / no central figure me, I was some sort of cloud or a gust of wind (329)."

17. O'Hara, The Collected Poems, 336.

18. O'Hara, *Art Chronicle*, 34–5.

19. Ibid., 25.

20. Ibid.

21. Ibid., 26.

22. Ashbery, Reported Sightings, 325.

23. Ibid., 4.

24. Ibid., 8.

25. Ibid., 7, also 269.

26. Ibid., 305.

27. Ibid., 82.

28. Ibid.

29. Ibid., 312.

30. Ibid., 404.

31. Ibid., 403.

32. John Ashbery, *Selected Poems* (New York: Penguin, 1986), 67.

33. Ashbery, *Reported Sightings*, 307. This poem, "Clepsydra," goes on to say, "In this way any direction taken was the right one, / Leading first to you, and through you to / Myself that is beyond you and which is the same thing as space, / That is the stammering vehicles that remain unknown, / Eating the sky in all sincerity because the difference / Can never be made up:" (*Selected Poems*, 68–9).

34. Ibid., 303. Watkins, especially 200–23, is helpful on tensions between what he calls "the grammatical and the non-rational poetic text" that includes musical densities for the lyric. Robert Kaufman, in his forthcoming book *Negative Romanticism: Adornian Aesthetics in Keats, Shelley, and Modern Poetry*, is very good on how "musical architecture" in Guest pulls against discursive understanding. And I find the visual artist William Kentridge offering the most powerful contemporary version of this surrealist logic because the production of meaning is constantly occurring on more levels than the conscious mind can follow. This does not mean we need to hypothesize an unconscious but only a disseminating power in art that we have to track, even though there is no possibility of our formulating its power in discursive terms.

35. Guest, *Forces of Imagination*, 107.

36. I should note that this material on Guest repeats much of my essay, "Barbara Guest and the Boys at the Cedar Bar: Some Painterly Uses of Language," *Chicago Review* 53/4 and 54/1 (2008): 82–7. And it is worth noticing, given my title, that relying on syntax was crucial for Guest in part because it could avoid any talk of gender, a topic on which she was very sensitive because of her position as both insider and outsider within the masculine world of the other poets. Making this claim also enables me to avoid Rachel Blau DuPlessis's brilliant account of Guest's relying on Surrealist principles to identify with the subject matter of Picasso's portraits of Dora Maar in "The Gendered Marvelous: Barbara Guest, Surrealism, and Feminist Reception," in *The Blue Studio* (Tuscaloosa: University of Alabama Press, 2006). DuPlessis shows superbly how Guest reconstructs "the interior of a painting" by allowing the painting to "'enter my unconscious' so that it can begin 'to exist spiritually'" (170–1). And she demonstrates how concerns for space can function beyond syntax: "Rather than seeing the nude only via the painter's eye, Guest's poem makes us see the space and symbiosis between painter and model, body and time, viewer and situation. She is working with the negative spaces, the push and pull, the in-betweens" (180).

37. As Catherine Elgin, *Nelson Goodman's Philosophy of Art* (New York: Garland Publishing, 1997) puts it:

> A mosaic pattern or a dot matrix design easily fits into a digital scheme – one whose characters are discrete and determinable. But to construe them as pictures is to read them differently. When we read a computer printout as a picture, we treat the array of grays that compose it as drawn from the full range of possibilities.... When we read a mosaic as a nativity scene, we treat its colors, sizes, and shapes as elements of a dense field of alternatives. Even if the artist was in fact limited in the choices available to him, we read the work as part of a scheme that provides unlimited options. (181)

38. Nelson Goodman, *Languages of Art* (Indianapolis: Bobbs Merrill, 1968), 229.

39. Barbara Guest, *The Collected Poems of Barbara Guest*, ed. Hadley Haden Guest (Middletown, CT: Wesleyan University Press, 2008), 101.

40. Ibid., 102.

FURTHER READING

Altieri, Charles. "Barbara Guest and the Boys at the Cedar Bar: Some Painterly Use of Language." *Chicago Review* 53/4 and 54/1 (2008): 82–7.

"Contingency as Compositional Principle in Fifties Poetics." In Terence Diggory and Steven Paul Miller, eds. *The Scene of My Selves: New Work on New York School Poets*. Orono: National Poetry Foundation, 2001, 359–84.

Ashbery John. *Reported Sightings: Art Chronicles 1957–1987*. Ed. David Bergman. Cambridge, MA: Harvard University Press, 1999.

Clune, Michael. "'Everything We Want': Frank O'Hara and the Aesthetics of Free Choice." *PMLA* 120.1 (January 2005): 181–96.

Diggory, Terence and Stephen Paul Miller, eds. *The Scene of My Selves: New Work on the New York School Poets*. Orono: National Poetry Foundation, 2001.

DuPlessis, Rachel Blau. "The Gendered Marvelous: Barbara Guest, Surrealism, and Feminist Reception." In *The Blue Studio*. Tuscaloosa: University of Alabama Press, 2006, 162–85.

Elgin, Catharine, ed. *Nelson Goodman's Philosophy of Art*. New York: Garland Publishing 1997.

Epstein, Andrew. *Beautiful Enemies: Friendship and Postwar American Poetry*. New York: Oxford University Press, 2006.

Goodman, Nelson. *Languages of Art*. Indianapolis: Bobbs Merrill, 1968.

Guest, Barbara. *Forces of Imagination: Writing on Writing*. Berkeley: Kelsey Street Press, 2003.

Hunter, Sam. *Rivers*. New York: Harry N. Abrams, 1971.

Kaufman, Robert. *Negative Romanticism: Adornian Aesthetics in Keats, Shelley, and Modern Poetry*. (Forthcoming)

Lamm, Kimberly. "One Lighting the Other Seductively": James Schuyler, Eileen Miles and the Sexuality of Literary Influence," *How 2 Work/ Book*: 1 (no. 8), 2002, http://www.asu.edu/pipercwcenter/how2journal/archive/online_archive/v1_8_2002/current/workbook/lamm-essays.htm

Lehman, David. *The Last Avant-garde: The Making of the New York School of Poets*. New York: Doubleday, 1998.

O'Hara, Frank. *Art Chronicle 1954–1966*. New York: Georges Braziller, 1975.

Sawin, Martica. *Surrealism in Exile and the Beginning of the New York School*. Cambridge, MA: MIT Press, 1995.

Schuyler, James. *Selected Art Writings*. Ed. Simon Pettet. Santa Rosa: Black Sparrow Press, 1998.

Watkin, William. *In the Process of Poetry: The New York School and the Avant Garde*. Lewisburg: Bucknell University Press, 2001.

5

MICHAEL DAVIDSON

The San Francisco Renaissance

It is a long way from Astor Place or Kenyon College.[1]

       – Kenneth Rexroth

But the city that we create in our bartalk or in our fuss and fury about each other is in an utterly mixed and mirrored way an image of the city. A return from exile.[2]

       – Jack Spicer

Enabling Fictions

When Jack Kerouac celebrated the birth of the San Francisco Renaissance in his 1958 novel, *The Dharma Bums*, he established one of the most enduring myths by which mid-century literary culture in the Bay Area is known. The inaugural moment, according to Kerouac, was a poetry reading at the Six Gallery in 1955 that featured five young poets – Allen Ginsberg, Michael McClure, Gary Snyder, Philip Whalen, Philip Lamantia – appearing together for the first time:

> Everyone was there. It was a mad night. And I was the one who got things jumping by going around collecting dimes and quarters from the rather stiff audience standing around in the gallery and coming back with three huge gallon jugs of California Burgundy and getting them all piffed so that by eleven o'clock when Alvah Goldbook [Ginsberg] was reading his, wailing his poem "Wail" drunk with arms outspread everybody was yelling, "Go! Go! Go!" (like a jam session and old Rheinhold Cacoethes [Kenneth Rexroth] the father of the Frisco poetry scene was wiping his tears in gladness.[3]

Kerouac's enthusiastic portrait of the event, whose centerpiece was Ginsberg's "Howl," captures the sense of excitement of the occasion and the centrality of the Beat generation in its cultural imaginary.[4] His use of "Renaissance" rather than "school" or "movement" recognizes the diversity of voices heard that evening and testifies, perhaps, to a much longer cultural ferment in the

West for which the term "Renaissance," like the ornate false fronts of San Francisco's Victorian houses and Daniel Burnham's Beaux Arts Civic Center, strikes the appropriate cultural tone.

San Francisco's history of literary innovation (and eccentricity) extends back to the late nineteenth century when writers like Ambrose Bierce, Frank Norris, Bret Harte, and Jack London met in the pages of Harte's magazine, *The Overland Monthly*, or in afternoon soirees in the Oakland Hills. Many features of what would become the San Francisco Renaissance can be seen in this earlier bohemian milieu: the celebration of nature, a vatic, testamentary poetic style, working-class naturalism (in London and Norris), occultism and mysticism, Gothicism merged with a streetwise populism. Postwar writers like Rexroth, Snyder, and William Everson paid homage to this earlier California tradition, seeing it in archetypal terms as an agonistic encounter of eastern metropolitan migrants with the raw edges of Manifest Destiny. The result, as Everson notes, is a "collision between Victorian materialistic complacency (the Genteel Tradition) and unconscious American pantheistic sublimity."[5]

World War II served as a catalyst for a revival of this late Victorian bohemia with an influx of ex-soldiers on the G.I. Bill, factory workers from the war industries, conscientious objectors from the Waldport camp in Oregon, and displaced artists from the East Coast. Writers in San Francisco during the late 1940s and early 1950s found themselves unmoored from the political and internationalist modernism of the Popular Front. The Hitler-Stalin Non-Aggression Pact and the emerging revelations of Stalin's gulag had demoralized much of the left, and the defeat of the Wallace presidential campaign in 1948 cast a pall on postwar political activism. Joseph McCarthy's Senate and subsequent HUAC hearings, along with federal legislation against union organizing and political movements, contributed to the period's disillusion. Many old left intellectuals turned into free-market boosters, supporting American consensus against the threat of Soviet superpower dominance. To achieve such consensus, New York intellectuals like Irving Howe, Clement Greenberg, Daniel Bell, and Delmore Schwartz attempted to cleanse modernism of its more avant-garde features and redefine it through a selective application of T. S. Eliot's criticism. When Rexroth, in my epigraph, speaks of the region's advantageous distance from Astor Place and Kenyon College, he was dismissing New York intellectuals and New Critics in the same breath.

Rexroth characterized the writing of the late 1940s as elegiac, reflecting the loss of a vital activist as well as culturally innovative modernist tradition. His own anarcho-pacifism was reflected in early poems like "The Phoenix and the Tortoise" or "Climbing Milestone," the latter of which pits the rugged western landscape against the resilient proletarian tradition. The combination of elegy and anarcho-pacifist politics can also be seen in the early work of Robert Duncan, Jack Spicer, Everson, and Lamantia, all of whom found themselves on the West Coast during the 1940s and whose poems reflect a sense of loss and existential malaise that belies their relatively young age, anticipating a new personalism that would be the hallmark of the subsequent generation.

In the late 1940s, Duncan, Spicer, and Robin Blaser were students at the University of California, Berkeley, studying medieval history, English literature, and linguistics. In the evenings, the trio, along with other young writers, participated in a series of informal readings, discussion groups, and séances at various Bay Area apartments that combined a love of magic and mysticism with homosexual intrigue and competitiveness. This synthesis can be seen in poems such as Duncan's "Medieval Scenes" and "Venice Poem" or Spicer's "Imaginary Elegies." Their nightly meetings at Duncan's Hearst Street apartment or Throckmorton Manor were the basis for what they half-jokingly called "The Berkeley Renaissance," a movement formed around the study of modernism (Joyce, Pound, Lawrence, H.D.) as a continuation of the romantic tradition. At a moment when the New Criticism was in ascendency at Berkeley, the poetic brotherhood thumbed their collective noses at the English Department and sought to renew the wellsprings of romanticism based not only in the nineteenth century but in pre-Socratic philosophy, Renaissance neo-Platonism, and the Hellenistic mysteries.

There were other formative sites for artistic change brewing in the region. The California School of Fine Arts (later the San Francisco Art Institute) collected a stellar faculty that included painters such as Clyfford Still and Richard Diebenkorn, who worked with the new generation of art students, many benefitting from the G.I. Bill. Among the students was McClure, who came to study with Still but gravitated to poetry once he discovered the poetry scene around Duncan. Spicer, who was teaching at the Art Institute at the time, was instrumental in forming the King UBU Gallery that eventually became the Six Gallery.[6] Collaborations between artists and poets could be seen in a number of new journals appearing at that time (*Goad, Inferno, Golden Goose, Circle, Semina*) as well as in local galleries and art spaces.

Another center for poetry in the early 1950s was the San Francisco State College Poetry Center, then under the directorship of Ruth-Witt Diamant, who hired Duncan in 1956 to serve as her assistant. At a moment when the phenomenon of live poetry reading had been invigorated by the reading tours of Dylan Thomas, the Poetry Center offered an opportunity for locals to hear the work of more established writers such as W. H. Auden, Stephen Spender, Theodore Roethke, and William Carlos Williams, at the same time that it offered a forum for new writers who were beginning to publish in the pages of the *Black Mountain Review, Origin*, and *The Evergreen Review*.[7] It was through the auspices of the Poetry Center that Spicer gave his infamous "Poetry as Magic" workshop at the San Francisco Public Library. Spicer's provocative exercises for the workshop included the requirement to write a spell or evoke magic spirits and to fill out a questionnaire with prompts such as "What insect do you most resemble?" or "Invent a dream in which you appear as a poet."[8]

The arrival of Ginsberg, Kerouac, McClure, Snyder, Whalen, Robert Creeley, Joanne Kyger, Lew Welch, and others in the early 1950s brought a critical mass of young writers to the Bay Area whose readings, small press publications, and nontraditional lifestyles became a magnet for media interest. The term "Beat," popularized by Kerouac in a number of magazine articles, served as a descriptor for a generation that, as Kerouac famously described it in *On the Road*, was "mad to live, mad to talk, mad to be saved … who never yawn or say a commonplace thing, but burn, burn, burn like fabulous yellow roman candles exploding like spiders across the stars."[9] Whether or not individual writers identified with this characterization, the term stuck. *San Francisco Chronicle*'s feature editorialist Herb Caen added the suffix "nik" to Kerouac's term, based on the recently launched Soviet satellite, Sputnik, thus linking the Soviet threat with the local counterculture "Beatnik." Some of the participants reveled in this media attention, appearing on nighttime talk shows and publishing articles in mainstream magazines like *Playboy* and *Esquire*. Kerouac's appearance on the *Steve Allen Show* or the obscenity trial over Ginsberg's "Howl" brought national attention to the Beat movement and established San Francisco as a site of antiestablishment ferment.

The Beat movement – its publications but also its cultivation of lifestyle politics – would exert a powerful influence on any number of new social movements of the 1960s in which music, fashion, political activism, and lifestyle choices would be inextricably connected with aesthetic positions.

Performative Poetics

Although one could define the aesthetics of mid-century writing in the Bay Area as a revival of romanticism, there were many gradations within that term. The elegiac tradition that I have mentioned drew on Blake, Whitman, and Robinson Jeffers. The blank-verse cadences of British writers such as Dylan Thomas and George Barker could be felt in early Duncan, Everson, and Rexroth. Lawrence Ferlinghetti, Bob Kaufman, and Lew Welch worked in a distinctly populist vein, exploiting a Marx Brothers goofiness and cartoon satire. Nature poetry, often modeled on classical Japanese and Chinese poets, was central to the poetics of Snyder, Whalen, Rexroth, and James Koller. A revival of medieval balladry and Elizabethan lyric was reflected in Duncan, Helen Adam, James Broughton, and Madeline Gleason. Surrealism was another particularly important aesthetic vein in the work of Lamantia, Spicer, McClure, and George Hitchcock.

Elsewhere I have defined the unifying threads of these traditions as embodying a performative attitude toward language.[10] By "performative" I mean that poetry, among the San Francisco writers, was expected to "do" as much as "represent," to act on the reader as co-participant in the evolving form. At one level this quality can be seen in the significance of the poetry reading as a central venue for the poem. Local bars, coffeehouses, and apartments became the testing ground for new work in which the page was secondary to oral presentation. Poetry read to jazz accompaniment extended the oral tradition to include collaboration across genres. Another dimension of performativity demanded that poetic language challenge or engage the reader as collaborator. Ginsberg's frontal attack on Cold War–era mind control and sexual repressiveness would be the most obvious example of this tendency. One may find this quality equally in McClure's *Ghost Tantras* written in what he termed "beast language," which utilized an Artaud-like sound poetry and could be witnessed in a Public Television documentary featuring the poet roaring at lions in the San Francisco Zoo. The tradition of Dada performance was continued in Spicer's "Blabbermouth Night," in which poets competed for a prize by uttering spontaneous nonsense syllables.

Blabbermouth Night was symptomatic of the performative character of Spicer's poetics from the outset. In an early statement in the Berkeley magazine *Occident*, Spicer declared: "We must become singers, become entertainers. We must stop sitting on the pot of culture."[11] Drawing on Yeats's theories of poetic dictation, Spicer argued that poetry comes not from emotions recollected in tranquility, but rather from an endistanced outside that enters the poet and creates the poem. The poet's task is not to contain ideas through an objective correlative but to clear the mind in order to let the poem in. Spicer often compared the poet to a radio that receives the poem from beyond. According to Spicer, poetic dictation permits language to achieve an objective quality equivalent to other objects. In his translations of and letters to García Lorca he thematizes this possibility:

> I would like to make poems out of real objects. The lemon to be a lemon that the reader could cut or squeeze or taste–a real lemon like a newspaper in a collage is a real newspaper. I would like the moon in my poems to be a real moon, one which could be suddenly covered with a cloud that has nothing to do with the poem–a moon utterly independent of images. The imagination pictures the

real. I would like to point to the real, disclose it, to make a poem that has no sound in it but the pointing of a finger.[12]

The idea that the poem might provide an analogous linguistic equivalent for objects or spaces leads Spicer to invent poems that the Spanish poet never wrote, rendering them in an English that Lorca never knew. By addressing many of his poems to specific friends, lovers, or imagined enemies, Spicer violated the terms of impersonality that his poetics would seem to support. At the same time, his use of personal address often confused the boundary between poem and reader.

A rather different example of a "performative poetics" would be Helen Adam's theater pieces and ballads. Adam came to the United States from Scotland where, at age sixteen, she was known as the "Elfin Pedlar of Pixy Pool," writing poems in the Scots ballad tradition. When she arrived in San Francisco, she enrolled in Spicer's Magic Workshop, where she encountered Duncan, McClure, Madeleine Gleason, and others. Her haunting, mischievous ballads, modeled on Christina Rossetti, Blake, or Keats, and her full-voiced delivery of them became legendary. Her masque, *San Francisco's Burning*, was performed with many of the local poets participating, and her ballads often featured questing knights, vengeful maidens, witches, and spirit voices based, in some cases, on actual denizens of the San Francisco poetry community. Although forged in a more archaic idiom, her rhymed poems nevertheless addressed contemporary issues such as the nuclear arms race, 1960s youth culture, racism, and the Vietnam War. Her transformations of gothic tropes offer wicked proto-feminist debunkings of male authority in which the nymph or bride, having lured her beloved into her grot, turns into a sorceress. In "I Love my Love," the witch takes the form of the bride's hair that attacks and ultimately smothers the guileless suitor:

The hair rushed in. He struggled and tore, but whenever he tore a tress,
"I love my love with a capital Z," sang the hair of the sorceress.
It swarmed upon him, it swaddled him fast, it muffled his every groan.
Like a golden monster it seized his flesh, and then it sought the bone,
Ha! Ha!
And then it sought the bone.[13]

Although Adam participated actively in many of the events of the San Francisco Renaissance, she is seldom mentioned in accounts of the period, no doubt because of her dedication to unfashionable poetic styles and idioms. But it was precisely her *dedication* to an oral, folkloric tradition and unabashed romanticism that earned her adherents as different in their own way as Duncan, Spicer, and Ginsberg and later poets around St. Mark's Church in New York's lower east side.

Sacramental Matters

If the quality of performance marks the poetics of writers in San Francisco, it also inflects the idiosyncratic mix of religious practices that were shared by many of them. Journalists of the period liked to mock what they took to be the religious eclecticism of Bay Area writers, but a close look shows writers engaged at a fairly serious level. There was a strong tradition of Catholic activism, going back to the Catholic Workers movement absorbed by Rexroth, Lamantia, and Everson, the latter of whom, as Brother Antoninus, became a lay monk in the Dominican order. Ginsberg actively studied Hindu religion and in his later years was a disciple of the Tibetan Buddhist master, Chogyam Trungpa, at the Naropa Institute in Colorado. Whalen was ordained *unsui* (Zen Buddhist monk) in 1973 and became abbot of the Hartford Street Zen Center in San Francisco. Snyder lived in Japan for many years where he was formally trained in Zen Buddhism. Other poets on the scene participated in greater or lesser extent in alternative religious practices – theosophy, Rosicrucianism, cabala – generally at a fairly serious level.

A more important aspect of this sacramentalism would be a mythopoeic imperative in which the "open field" poem permits access to a new ecological or holistic consciousness. Duncan states these ideas most forcefully in *The Opening of the Field*, which opens by describing poetry as a "place of first permission" that yields access to cosmic orders.

> Often I am Permitted to Return to a Meadow
> as if it were a scene made-up by the mind,
> that is not mine, but is a made place,
> that is mine, it is so near to the heart,
> an eternal pasture folded in all thought....[14]

Such lines embody what Charles Altieri characterizes as an "immanent poetics" among postwar poets deriving from early Romantics like Wordsworth for whom poetry embodies (rather than contains) the mind's processes.[15] By "entering" the poem without preconception – a variation on Keats's "negative capability" – the poet is permitted understanding of natural and spiritual orders otherwise hidden from view. In the lines quoted earlier, Duncan remembers a children's dance from his childhood that then enters his adult dreams. The poem's reflection on the pasture in which the dance occurs leads him to "a place of first permission, / everlasting omen of what is."[16]

The pursuit of poetic immanence is also a feature of Gary Snyder's poetry, combining Zen Buddhist meditation practice with an environmentalist, ecological ethos. Central to his work is the need to balance poetic rhythms with respect for nature, meditation, and physical labor. Many of his poems in long sequences like *Myths and Texts* and *Mountains and Rivers without End* reflect this trinity of features through explorations of Native American and East Asian religious traditions, but they are no less evident in individual poems that embody natural supernaturalism. In "A Walk," Snyder describes a period when he worked cutting trails for the U.S. Forest Service. The poem describes a Sunday hike to Benson Lake in the high Sierras. Although the poem poses as a diversion from his hard daily work, it is clear that his "walk" is another kind of labor, one that engages the poet's proprioceptive and perceptive faculties:

> The clear sky. Deer tracks.
> Bad place by a falls, boulders big as houses,
> Lunch tied to belt,
> I stemmed up a crack and almost fell
> But rolled out safe on a ledge
>   and ambled on.[17]

Although metaphysical issues are not mentioned, it is clear that this "walk" is a form of meditation, one attentive to the textures of animal life and geological formations. Where more traditional poets of this period negotiated the doctrinal problems of the incarnation within the frame of institutional religions such as Catholicism, Duncan, Snyder, Ginsberg, and Whalen found spiritual solace in the breath of the individual and the rhythms of natural processes.

Sexual Politics

Sexual politics occupies another significant place in the cultural history of the Bay Region. Following World War II, San Francisco became a sanctuary for homosexuals and lesbians, and although local police conducted regular raids on bars and meeting places, a subterranean culture was very much alive. Gay political activity in the city was focused around well-established homophile groups like the Matachine Society (of which Spicer was a member), the Daughters of Bilitus, and in the 1970s the Alice B. Toklas Democratic Club, whose activism culminated in the election of Harvey Milk to the Board of Supervisors in 1977. Many of the poets associated with the period in question were gay, and their poetry often served as a site for sexual self-expression. Duncan had published an important essay in 1944, "the Homosexual in Society," an early and courageous critique of homophobia but also a warning to other gays against sexual insularity.[18] When John Crowe Ransom read the essay, he reconsidered his previous acceptance of Duncan's poetry in *The Kenyon Review*, deciding in a letter that he now recognized the sexual "advertisement" in the poems that the essay made explicit. Ransom's response to Duncan's essay displays the tensions surrounding the period's new critical advocacy of aesthetic detachment when matters of sexuality are concerned.

Although the San Francisco Renaissance was largely a male province, it had – as the example of Adam, Gleason, Kyger, or Diane di Prima illustrate – a substantial cohort of women writers who lived and worked productively with their male colleagues, publishing poetry, coordinating poetry readings, and performing in poets' theater events. More recently, feminist scholars have rediscovered or revisited lesser-known women writers of the Beat movement who contributed to the scene, including, among others, Joan Vollmer, Carolyn Cassady, Edie Parker Kerouac, Eileen Kaufman, Mary Fabilli, Hettie Jones, Joanna McClure, Janine Pommy Vega, and Brenda Fraser.[19] Moreover, many of these writers challenged stereotypical gender roles by living and creating their art in nontraditional domestic arrangements."[20]

Legacies

The historic San Francisco Renaissance was over by the mid-1960s, but it spawned a number of developments that would endure into the new millennium. The linguistic experimentalism and emphasis on the "outside" of language in Jack Spicer's poetics continued in Language writing, although stripped of Spicer's spiritual and mythological emphases and given a specifically ideological and political component. Duncan's homoerotic romanticism made a solid impact on younger gay writers like Bruce Boone, Aaron Shurin, Robert Gluck, Judy Grahn, and Susan Griffin. In like manner, Duncan's mythopoeic and hermetic lyricism exerted a profound influence on Michael Palmer, Norma Cole, and Nathaniel Mackey. Zen Buddhist meditation practice as a model for composition in Philip Whalen and Gary Snyder continued with Leslie Scalapino, Norman Fischer, Steve Benson, and others connected with the San Francisco Zen Center. The political and urban activism of Rexroth, Ginsberg, di Prima, and others continued in the mobilization of the Filipino community by Al Robles over the proposed demolition of the International Hotel or in the Mission District through the Third World Communications Network (Janice Mirikitani, Ntozake Shange, Jessica Hagedorn, and Victor Hernandez Cruz) and readings at the Glide Church in the Tenderloin. The spirit of Beat performance continues through the evolution of open-mike, stand-up, and slam events that emphasize the immediacy of the poem-as-act and its public performance. And needless to say, the tradition of performing poetry to jazz has given way to a wide range of poetry and music collaborations.

Such lists of shared affinities are ultimately reductive by generalizing a few obvious parallels between generations to the exclusion of significant local variations. Language writing, among its Western practitioners – such as Bob Perelman, Lyn Hejinian, Barrett Watten, Ron Silliman, Carla Harryman, and Rae Armantrout – was much more influenced by the arrival of continental philosophy and Marxist critical theory than it was by Spicer's surrealist debates with Martians. At the same time Robert Duncan and Lyn Hejinian, while appearing worlds apart stylistically, nevertheless share a common aspiration toward the "open text" as a means of keeping, as Hejinian says, "all the elements of the work ... maximally excited."[21] While Robert Hass is indebted to Western writers such as Rexroth, Everson, or Jeffers, he manifests his ecological and environmental concerns through a less bardic and stentorian, considerably more conversational voice. Although Mackey was initially influenced by Robert Duncan's open-ended "Passages" series, his literary genealogy owes a profound debt to African Dogon religion, contemporary free jazz, and African-American cultural traditions. Hence what we might see as a "legacy" of the San Francisco Renaissance is less a set of stylistic or aesthetic principles than a spirit of community, innovation, and political alliances.

Some of this spirit of cross-fertilization and collaboration can be seen in three generations and three collaborative ventures that illustrate the range and variety of creative life in the Bay Region between the late 1960s and the 1990s. The first involves the creation and production of Shange's verse play, *For colored girls who have considered suicide / when the rainbow is enuf* (1974). The play was first performed at the Bacchanal in the East Bay, a collaborative venture with Raymond Sawyer's Afro-American Dance Company and Halifu's The Sprit of Dance. It involved the participation of other poets – Hagedorn and Joanna Griffin – and was inspired by Grahn's *Common Woman Poems* of 1974. In her introduction to the play, Shange credits the role of "women poets, women's readings & a multilingual woman presence" in the poetry movement of the late 1960s with providing inspiration.[22] The controversy over the play's critique of black masculinity launched a nationwide debate within the African-American community over the role of gender in the construction of race, and within the feminist movement over the importance of race and class. What we call second-wave feminism drew much of its inspiration from such collaborative projects that grew out of Bay Area presses, women's studies programs, bars and coffeehouses, and collective art spaces.

The second collaboration involves the example of Language writing whose poetics represents a severe challenge to the expressivist or testamentary styles of the 1950s. The concept of a unitary self manifested through the voice, so central to much mid-century poetry, is sharply rebuked in Robert Grenier's manifesto phrase, "I hate speech" and this challenge is further developed in Ron Silliman's essay "The New Sentence."[23] In their work, the unitary subject gives way to an idea of multiple selves or collective voices constructed in specific social contexts. The open or field poem that Duncan articulated and that empowered an expressivist poetics during the 1960s was supplemented by procedural poems based on complex numbering systems, wordlists, and aleatory events. The collective memoir of the West Coast Language writers, *The Grand Piano* (named after the Haight-Ashbury coffeehouse where many early Language writing events first occurred), is itself an act of cultural recovery rendered through prose sections that respond to the movement's gestation (1975–1980), as well as to the political and social changes of the later Cold War period. In its mission statement, the authors claim that *The Grand Piano* is an "ongoing experiment in collective autobiography by ten writers originally identified with Language writing in San Francisco."[24] Each author responds to every other in a changing sequence over the space of ten volumes. The final result continues the principle of open forms as an exploratory gesture while interpellating the community as the locus of composition. In this respect, the legacy of the San Francisco Renaissance still lives on in forms its original inhabitants might not recognize.

A third group of writers, loosely gathered under the "New Narrative" rubric, has brought queer sexuality and gay politics into conversation – and conflict – with many of the premises of Language writing. Gluck, Bruce Boone, Kevin Killian, Steve Abbott, and Dodie Bellamy, writing in small magazines such as *Jimmy and Lucy's House of K*, *Soup*, and *Mirage*, have developed new forms of prose that combine personal narrative with self-reflexive commentary on the writing as it proceeds. Their work implicitly stands at odds with the nonlinear, paratactic styles of Language writing and explicitly in conflict with what they take to be its avoidance of issues of gender and sexuality. As Kaplan Harris says of the movement, New Narrative "ultimately seeks ... a textual performance that can recognize itself as a cultural construct and simultaneously affirm the political value of a life-changing story."[25] New Narrative writing bridges the several generations and different literary styles of Bay Area writing by combining confessional personal details – often of an explicit sexual character – that we identify with the expressive poetics of the 1950s and a self-critical, self-reflexive metacommentary that we identify with more experimental traditions. The homoerotic concerns of Duncan or Spicer are sustained, albeit with a recognition of new political challenges posed by the AIDS crisis of the mid 1980s and new alliances formed with local minority communities.

What links these three very different collaborative events is less the formal nature of their composition than their shared dedication to a critical and social poetics fusing formal innovation with issues of community and lifestyle. In each case, poetic form is challenged by genre-bending developments in drama, performance, prose, and digital technologies. As we have seen by reference to the long history of Bay Area bohemia, the cultural field of the city has been receptive to such forms of innovation. Jack Spicer's belief that "the city we create in our bartalk … is in an utterly mixed and mirrored way an image of the city" embodies the spirit of debate and discussion that even the most private poem generates. With several generations of writers emerging since the heyday of the San Francisco Renaissance, we can better see the generative result of these debates in an increasingly global environment. A virtual community forged through e-mail, blogs, and digital publications makes the sectarian debates of Spicer's bar world seem an antique form of sociality. And what had been a fierce defense of localism (Spicer insisted that his books not be sold east of the Rocky Mountains) against what he called the "fix" of established culture has become a hemispheric conversation about the work of art in an age of globalization. In this respect, the San Francisco Renaissance fulfilled its early quest for a fusion of romantic expression, community, and politics that had been sidetracked by Cold War consensus. If subsequent generations do not recognize themselves in the mirror of the San Francisco Renaissance, it is perhaps because the movement's organic origins contained the seeds of its transformation into an oppositional culture at large.

NOTES

1. Kenneth Rexroth, "San Francisco Letter," in *The World Outside the Window: The Selected Essays of Kenneth Rexroth*, ed. Bradford Morrow (New York: New Directions, 1987), 57–64, 57.
2. Jack Spicer, *The Heads of the Town up to the Aether*, in *My Vocabulary Did This to Me: The Collected Poetry of Jack Spicer*, ed. Peter Gizzi and Kevin Killian (Middletown, CT: Wesleyan University Press, 2008), 247–314, 306.
3. Jack Kerouac, *The Dharma Bums* (New York: Penguin Books, 1986), 13–14.
4. Another noteworthy occasion at the Six Gallery, Robert Duncan gave a performance of his play, *Faust Foutu*, starring McClure, Spicer, Helen Adam, Ida Hodes, and others – an event that featured, among other highjinks, Duncan stripping naked.
5. William Everson, *Archetype West: The Pacific Coast as a Literary Region* (Berkeley, CA: Oyez, 1976), 50.
6. The King Ubu Gallery was formed by Duncan, Jess (Jess Collins), Spicer, and artists associated with the San Francisco School of Fine Arts. Its proximity to the nearby School and its collaborative administration with painters made it an important venue for exhibitions and openings. For an excellent history of the School and relationships between artists and poets, see Richard Candida Smith, *Utopia and Dissent: Art, Poetry, and Politics in California* (Berkeley: University of California Press, 1995).

7. On the Poetry Center, see Lewis Ellingham and Kevin Killian, eds., *Poet Be Like God: Jack Spicer and the San Francisco Renaissance* (Middletown, CT: Wesleyan University Press, 1998), 52–54.

8. On the Magic Workshop, see Ellingham and Killian, *Poet Be Like God*, 79–84.

9. Jack Kerouac, *On the Road* (New York: Penguin Books, 1976), 5–6.

10. Michael Davidson, *The San Francisco Renaissance: Poetics and Community at Mid-Century* (Cambridge: Cambridge University Press, 1989).

11. Jack Spicer, "The Poet and Poetry – A Symposium," *Occident Magazine* (Fall, 1949), reprinted in *The House That Jack Built: The Collected Lectures of Jack Spicer*, ed. Peter Gizzi (Middletown, CT: Wesleyan University Press, 1998), 228.

12. Jack Spicer, "Dear Lorca," *My Vocabulary Did This to Me*, 133.

13. Helen Adam, "I Love My Love," *A Helen Adam Reader*, ed. Kristin Prevallet (Orono, ME: The National Poetry Foundation, 2008), 67.

14. Robert Duncan, "Often I Am Permitted to Return to a Meadow," *Opening of the Field* (New York: Grove Press, 1960), 7.

15. Charles Altieri, "From Symbolist Thought to Immanence: The Logic of Post-Modernist Poetics," *Boundary* 2.1 (Spring 1973): 605–41.

16. Duncan, "Often I Am Permitted to Return to a Meadow." *Opening of the Field*, 7

17. Gary Snyder, "A Walk," *The Back Country* (New York: New Directions, 1968), 11.

18. Robert Duncan, "The Homosexual in Society," *A Selected Prose*, ed. Robert J. Bertholf (New York: New Directions, 1995), 38–50.

19. On women writers, see Brenda Knight, ed., *Women of the Beat Generation: The Writers, Artists and Muses at the Heart of a Revolution* (Berkeley, CA: Conari Press, 1996). See also Ronna C. Johnson and Nancy M. Grace, eds., *Girls Who Wore Black: Women Writing the Beat Generation* (New Brunswick, NJ: Rutgers University Press, 2002).

20. Elaine Tyler May, *Homeward Bound: American Families in the Cold War Era* (New York: Basic Books, 1988).

21. Lyn Hejinian, "The Rejection of Closure," *The Language of Inquiry* (Berkeley: University of California Press, 2000), 43.

22. Ntozake Shange, *For colored girls who have considered suicide / when the rainbow is enuf* (New York: Scribner Poetry, 1977), ix.

23. Ron Silliman, "Language, Realism, Poetry," *In the American Tree: Language, Realism, Poetry* (Orono, ME: The National Poetry Foundation, 2002). Silliman, "The New Sentence," *The New Sentence* (New York: Roof Books, 1987), 63–93.

24. *The Grand Piano: An Experiment in Collective Autobiography*, Part 9 (Detroit, MI: Mode A, 2009), 222.

25. Kaplan Page Harris, "New Narrative and the Making of Language Poetry," *American Literature* 81.4 (December 2009): 805–32, 806.

FURTHER READING

Damon, Maria. *The Dark End of the Street: Margins in American Vanguard Poetry*. Minneapolis: University of Minnesota Press, 1993.

Davidson, Michael. *The San Francisco Renaissance: Poetics and Community at Mid-Century*. Cambridge: Cambridge University Press, 1989.

Ehrenreich, Barbara. *The Hearts of Men: American Dreams and the Flight from Commitment.* New York: Anchor, 1993.

Everson, William. *Archetype West: The Pacific Coast as a Literary Region.* Berkeley, CA: Oyez, 1976.

Hunt, Tim. *Kerouac's Crooked Road: The Development of a Fiction.* Berkeley: University of California Press, 1996.

Gray, Timothy. *Gary Snyder and the Pacific Rim: Creating Counter Cultural Community.* Iowa City: University of Iowa Press, 2006.

Johnson, Ronna C. and Nancy M. Grace, eds. *Girls Who Wore Black: Women Writing the Beat Generation.* New Brunswick, NJ: Rutgers University Press, 2002.

Knight, Brenda, ed. *Women of the Beat Generation: The Writers, Artists and Muses at the Heart of a Revolution.* Berkeley, CA: Conari Press, 1996.

May, Elaine Tyler. *Homeward Bound: American Families in the Cold War Era.* New York: Basic Books, 1988.

Meltzer, David. *San Francisco Beat: Talking with the Poets.* San Francisco: City Lights, 2001.

Parkinson, Thomas, ed. *Casebook on the Beat.* New York: Crowell, 1961.

Smith, Richard Candida. *Utopia and Dissent: Art, Poetry, and Politics in California* Berkeley: University of California Press, 1995.

Sterritt, David. *Mad to be Saved: The Beats, The '50s, and Film.* Carbondale: University of Illinois Press, 1998.

6

RONNA C. JOHNSON

Three Generations of Beat Poetics

"The requirements for prose and verse are the same, i.e. *blow*."[1]
– Jack Kerouac, letter to Malcolm Cowley, 1955

The Beat generation emerged after World War II in New York City and San Francisco, concurrently with abstract expressionism in painting and bebop jazz. Characterized by Allen Ginsberg as "a group of friends who had worked together on poetry, prose and cultural conscience from the mid-forties until the term became popular nationally in the late fifties,"[2] the Beat movement carried its diverse poetics and composition techniques through three generations into the mid-1960s, forming a coherent and mature identity.[3] Beat's eclecticism absorbed the aesthetics of abstract expressionist painting and bebop jazz, Buddhist ethics and practices, nineteenth-century American Romanticism, and twentieth-century modernism. While Beat Poetry drew from Ezra Pound and William Carlos Williams and the modernist imperative to "make it new," it transcended these forms to construct a new poetics suited to the Atomic Age. And while it owed a debt to Charles Olson's "Projective Verse," it translated Olson's privileging of the breath into the collective space of the performance, anticipating slam and other recent modes of open improvisation.

Beat poetry debuted as contestatory, sexually uninhibited, transgressive writing that built on hybrid forms that challenged the repressive establishment of the Cold War United States. In this respect, the literary movement that came to be known as Beat is not separable from the generation of bohemians who were consciously seeking to divorce themselves from reactionary beliefs and restrictions of mid-twentieth-century American culture. Both came to national attention simultaneously on October 7, 1955, in San Francisco at the Six Gallery poetry reading, an avant-garde literary premiere that officially connected East Coast Beat poets with their West Coast counterparts. Renowned for Ginsberg's first public declamation of "Howl," the event was presided over by Kenneth Rexroth, Anarchist elder poet-statesman of the

San Francisco literary scene, while Jack Kerouac shouted "Go!" from the audience. The reading showcased a range of poetics: Ginsberg's Whitmanian prophecy built on anaphoric strophes; Philip Lamantia's blood surrealism (Lamantia, whose visionary style in his 1946 *Erotic Poems* had impressed the great French surrealist, André Breton, did not read his own work at the Six Gallery, but that of his friend, the late John Hoffman); Michael McClure's anarcho-mysticism; Philip Whalen's Buddhist movements of consciousness; and Gary Snyder's eco-mystical individual revelation. Lawrence Ferlinghetti, publisher of San Francisco's City Lights Books, which had just initiated the Pocket Poets Series with his *Pictures of the Gone World* in 1955, telegraphed Ginsberg after the reading with an allusion to Ralph Waldo Emerson's response to Walt Whitman's *Leaves of Grass*: "I greet you at the beginning of a great career. When do I get the manuscript?" *Howl and Other Poems* (1956) became Number Four in the series.[4] A year later in another landmark moment of Beat writing, the book was seized in San Francisco on charges of obscenity, a case resolved in Judge Clayton W. Horn's 1957 ruling that its vernacular language was not obscene and was speech protected by the First and Fourteenth Amendments of the U.S. Constitution.[5] In spite of this precedent, Beat writing underwent repeated legal attack for its poetics of uncensored language and thought. This history of provocation, suppression, and arrest both characterizes and belies the triumphs of Beat poetry and poetics: the commitment to public readings and performances, which returned poetry to the people from its elitist sequestrations on the page and in the academy; the restoration of demotic and vernacular languages to poetic idiom; the revival of the bardic-strophic tradition – unpracticed in the United States since Whitman – in the litanies of "Howl" and in list poems like Anne Waldman's "Fast Speaking Woman" (1975); the cultivation of visionary high energy and breath-based elongations of the poetic line; the blurring of distinctions between verse and prose forms; the rise of small presses and do-it-yourself publications; and the affirmation of constitutional protections for unfettered speech and composition.

Journal and anthology publications as well as conferences and reading series fostered these gains. Robert Creeley, editor from 1954 to 1957 of the influential *Black Mountain Review*, appointed Ginsberg and Olson guest coeditors of the final issue (No. 7, Autumn 1957), which collected an array of writers who would later become classified and canonized as Beat, San Francisco Renaissance, and Black Mountain poets.[6] This heterogenous avant-garde emerged all the more visibly in Donald Allen's influential 1960 anthology of countercultural verse, *The New American Poetry, 1945–1960*. Declared by Marjorie Perloff to be the "fountainhead of radical American poetics," it was followed by *The Moderns: An Anthology of*

New Writing in America (1963), edited by LeRoi Jones, and *The Poetics of the New American Poetry* (1973), edited by Donald Allen and Warren Tallman.[7] The postwar poetry avant-garde was also supported through a new national poetry circuit, with readings programmed by Elizabeth Kray at the New York YMHA Poetry Center and Ruth Witt-Diamant at the San Francisco Poetry Center, and by two major poetry meetings.[8] The Vancouver Poetry Conference of 1963, hailed by Creeley as a "landmark" assembly, occasioned Denise Levertov's singular contribution to Beat poetics, her proposal to amend Creeley's "now famous formula" that "form is never more than the extension of content" to "form is never more than the *revelation* of content."[9] The correction bends Creeley's spare Black Mountain poetics to the visionary perception and personal disclosure distinctive to Beat writing, although Levertov ultimately eschewed the movement. The Berkeley Poetry Conference of 1965, sponsored by the University of California Extension, united Beat and Black Mountain poets in an academic setting. Olson declaimed from his 1960 masterwork, *The Maximus Poems*, and Snyder presented "Poetry and the Primitive," which urged the "skilled and inspired use of the voice and language to embody rare and powerful states of mind … personal to the singer, but at deep levels common to all who listen," affirming a poetics of energy transmission advanced by Olson and Kerouac.[10] A "flash point of the mimeo revolution," the Berkeley conference also attracted emergent poets, such as Waldman and Lewis Warsh, who met at Robert Duncan's reading and started *Angel Hair* magazine (1966–1969) and press (1966–1978), bringing Beat and New York School poetics into the 1960s counterculture.[11] Waldman also joined Ginsberg in 1974 to found the Jack Kerouac School of Disembodied Poetics at Naropa Institute in Boulder, Colorado, an important poetry proving ground that stands even now as a durable Beat legacy to American poetry.

The Beat generation and the Beat literary movement reached an apotheosis of sorts on January 14, 1967, at the San Francisco Human Be-In, prelude to the Summer of Love. Beat poets presiding at the Be-In included Lenore Kandel, and from the 1955 Six Gallery reading, Ginsberg, Snyder, and McClure. Third-generation Beat poet-musicians Jim Morrison and his band the Doors, mentored by McClure, attended; and the Grateful Dead, inspired by Kerouac, performed. Kandel, the only woman to read from the Be-In stage, personified the Beat transition from 1950s hipster bohemia to 1960s hippie counterculture, with her reading from *The Love Book*. Heterosexual erotica chanted in vernacular sex language from the female lover's point of view, Kandel's poetry merged Beat and San Francisco Renaissance poetics with the Eastern spirituality, sexual ecstasy, and proto-feminism that typified the New Age 1960s.[12] Diane di Prima's contemporaneous *Revolutionary*

Letters evinced the transformation from hipster to hippie poetics by way of left-radical politics and countercultural communitarianism.[13] But *The Love Book* marked a culmination of the 1955 Beat movement advent; as with the suppression of "Howl" a decade earlier, it was seized for obscenity and sent to trial in San Francisco in 1967. Amplifying Ginsberg's proclamation that "[c]ensorship of language is direct censorship of consciousness" and violates the "shape of ... mind," Kandel warned in 1967 of the "murder of the soul" by "[a]ny form of censorship, whether mental, moral, emotional, or physical, whether from the inside or the outside," and of its pernicious "barrier against self-awareness ... and ... revelation."[14]

The distinctive influences of abstract expressionist painting, bebop jazz, and New York hipsterism on Beat poetry emerge in the very terms with which the poets described their own and one another's work. Ginsberg named Kerouac's improvisatory style and rhythmics "spontaneous bop prosody" and "wild neo-bop prosody," resounding with Anatole Broyard's prescient recognition of bebop poetics in the "portentous trochees" and "decapitated cadences" of the hipster's "unnaturally accentual or discontinuous" "stride."[15] Bob Kaufman refers explicitly to jazz in "O-Jazz-O War Memoir: Jazz, Don't Listen to It at Your Own Risk"[16] and invokes it implicitly in the long-form poem, "Second April" (1959),[17] patterned on jazz compositional practices.[18] Translating this zeitgeist to poetic performance, ruth weiss pioneered jazz poetry readings in 1956 at the San Francisco club The Cellar. A widely adapted innovation, the reading format integrated Beat poetics with jazz foundations.[19] Gregory Corso, inspired by Charlie Parker and Miles Davis, evoked bebop's speed in his poetics of "automaticism," "in which the mind accelerates a constant hour of mind-foolery, mind-genius, mind-madness."[20] In the same year, with the publication in 1958 of the fifth book of *Paterson*, William Carlos Williams prized Jackson "Pollock's blobs of paint squeezed out / with design! / pure from the tube. Nothing else / is real."[21] Ted Joans claimed in 1960 that "poetry of this generation is just as abstract expressionist or action-packed as the paintings of the American style."[22] For Joans, improvisation pervaded all art forms: "No. 1: I want my paintings to swing, like good jazz solos"; "No. 22: I never know beforehand what I'm going to paint, I just start wailing."[23] Kerouac's own "action" writing, which he called "wild form," urged a forward propulsion redolent of both the bebop jazz and abstract impressionist modes of improvisation of the period: "write fast, get it all in, or out, up, down, everywhere throw it."[24] Olson likewise advised poets to "keep moving, keep in, speed, the nerves, their speed ... the split second acts, the whole business, keep it moving as fast as you can, citizen."[25] Kandel's "junkie angel" in "Blues for Sister Sally," models the nihilistic vagabond of "the sewers of your cities / from east coast / to west coast/to nowhere."[26] The work's synaesthetic chant – "(holy holy) / holy needle / holy powder / holy vein" – recalls Mezz Mezzrow's hipster "trance" on hearing Bessie Smith's "moanful stories."[27] It also reprises "Footnote to Howl"'s claim that "The typewriter is holy the poem is holy the voice is holy the hearers are holy the ecstasy is holy."[28]

Although Ferlinghetti feared the "death of the creative artist" from "the wiggy nihilism of the Beat hipster," this nihilism was a stereotype, and countered by the prevailing vision of the hipster in Beat literature.[29] Kerouac heard the "rumblings of a new soul" in the hipster's "new language, actually spade (Negro) jargon."[30] What Broyard had termed "jive language" infused the "American idiom" Williams esteemed for having "as much originality as jazz."[31] Bob Kaufman, by contrast, may have appeared to bear out the nihilist stereotype in his credo of "uninvolvement" and "ambition to be completely forgotten," a disengagement fitted to his bouts of addiction, nomadism, and street living, and his surreal yet confrontational political, antiracist, and anti-imperialist poetry.[32] But his "Bagel Shop Jazz" provided an anti-nihilist hipster cartography with its tripartite icons of Jewish intellectual/ethnic "chick"/ Negro hipster.[33] For Kaufman, the hipsterism of Beat poetics lay in improvised spoken riffs rather than written texts. For Joans, the oral form was not simply a mode to be privileged over the written; it was the reliable sign of the presence of a poet: "if you should see a man / walking down a crowded / street / talking / aloud / to himself … run / toward him / for he is a / poet / you have nothing to fear / from the / poet / but the truth."[34] This unrestrained public declamation also describes Kaufman's praxis, which he knew attracted repression and retaliation: "WHEN THE POET PROTESTS THE / DEATH HE SEES AROUND / HIM, / THE DEAD WANT HIM SILENCED, / HE DIES LIKE LORCA DID / …THE POET SHOCKS THOSE AROUND HIM. HE SPEAKS OPENLY OF WHAT AUTHORITY HAS DEEMED UNSPEAKABLE, HE BECOMES THE ENEMY OF AUTHORITY."[35] What appears as hipster disaffection is in fact a revitalized American romanticism, which Kerouac characterized as "wild self-believing individuality."[36]

The aesthetic, social, and political commitments of the new American poetry of the Beat period were often articulated in manifesto form. Kerouac's 1953 "Essentials of Spontaneous Prose" made Olson's influential "Projective Verse" into a foundational statement of Beat poetry.[37] Kerouac, Ginsberg, McClure, Jones, and di Prima, among others, embraced Olson's poetics of "the HEAD, by way of the EAR, to the SYLLABLE / the HEART, by way of the BREATH, to the LINE" in which syllable and line derive from "pressures of breath."[38] Joanne Kyger's visceral response to Olson – "PROJECTIVE VERSE hits me like a whallop. Poetry is true stuff the way he writes of it" – led her to imagine a technology of breath poetics: "composing" by "reading over [a] tape recorder" and "playing back and typing it," so "[t]he breath line would be natural at least."[39] Kerouac built lines by following breath "rhythms of rhetorical exhalation and expostulated statement" and advocated "rhetorical breathing (as jazz musician drawing breath between outblown phrases)" instead of following the Poundian musical phrase or, in jazz parlance, the head of the tune, because, he declared, "Everybody knows it's not the tune that counts but IT!"[40] Thwarting the conscious mind in composition, Ginsberg conceived his 1959 poem "Kaddish" as "chant," "where you actually *use* your body, use your breath," "a physiological thing" that is "less intellectual or verbal."[41] In "Feminafesto," Waldman turns Olson's "projective" poetics to feminist purpose in her call for "a utopian creative field where we are defined by our *energy* not by gender ... [an] extension of [bodily] energy" transmitted by "a radically disruptive and subversive kind of writing [producible] right now" only, or best, by women.[42] Kyger's adaptation of Olson, which she refers to as "projectivity," draws on a liminal state she names "The VERGE," a location of "the only creative / truly creative / moment – when things have not yet condemned them- / selves – by coming alive – to extinction."[43] It is a poetics that casts Olson's body-breath-line progression in female terms, a pre-orgasmic existentialism.

In "How You Sound??" (1959), another manifesto with kindred intentions to those of Olson's "Projective Verse," LeRoi Jones displaces such forebears as Pound with an avant-garde of "recent fellows": "the only 'recognizable tradition' a poet need follow is himself ... (You have to start and finish there ... your own voice ... how you sound)."[44] Kerouac's refusal of a "preconceived idea of what to say" is thus seconded by Jones, who rejects "any preconceived notion or *design* for what the poem *ought* to be."[45] Corso also refuses preconception by building a poetics from "unstandard sounds," in which a "standard flow" of words is "intentionally distracted diversed into my own sound."[46] Free poetic discourse subsumes words by digression in Kerouac, by the "self" in Jones, by "sound" in Corso. The overturning of conventional constraint is clear in Jones's assertion that "There cannot be anything I must *fit* the poem into. Everything must be made to fit into the poem."[47] Kyger, meanwhile, would not "*force* my mind to be clever or *force* / it to poetry.[48] Fidelity to the free mind led Kerouac to his notorious Whitmanian insistence on "*no revisions*": "tap from yourself the song of yourself, *blow! – now! – your* way is your only way ... spontaneous, 'confessional,' interesting, because not 'crafted.' Craft *is* craft."[49] In a further emancipation a decade later, third-generation Beat poet-musician Patti Smith advocates a poetics of inversion and appropriation that subsumes rules through words: "People say beware but I don't care / The words are just rules and regulations to me."[50] Directly influenced by Ginsberg and Corso, Smith rejects linguistic "regulations" for a rock poetry of original verse and found art, as in her 1970 "Gloria," which combines lines of her poem "Oath" ("Jesus died for somebody's sins but not mine") with riffs from the Van Morrison blues-rock classic.

Beat bohemia's interracial and intercultural assumptions would encounter a different line of contention from a second generation of black Beat poets. Ted Joans's hipster poetics is infused, not surprisingly, with a valorization of his race: "No. 21: Being an American is an advantage for me, and being an American Negro is the best damn thing that ever happened to me."[51] At the same time as "being an American Negro" is cause for celebration, however, Joans recognizes the racist repressions of nonstandard English: "No. 35: I don't give a damn what those futher muckers say about my way of talking."[52] But the 1965 assassination of Malcolm X galvanized a refiguration of Beat poetry, as in LeRoi Jones's shift from improvisational poetics in the imagist discourse on "wives, gardens, jobs" of "How You Sound??" to a poetics of political engagement in "State/Meant": "The Black Artist must draw out of his soul the correct image of the world ... how it differs from the deathly grip of White Eyes."[53] Jones's 1964 poem "Black Dada Nihilismus" inscribes the collapse of interracial Beat bohemia with its chants of guerilla-style execution for White hipster "friends": "Come up, black dada / nihilismus. Rape the white girls. Rape / their fathers. Cut the mothers' throats. / Black dada nihilismus, choke my friends / in their bedrooms with their drinks spilling."[54]

Ted Joans's 1971 "Proposition for a Black Power Manifesto" is a long-form list poem about racial justice in a vernacular of swinging strophes and exclamations of Black pride: "The language of this manifesto is written in is black-talk / for black-talk is our own black language ... there is nothing in our black-talk to be ashamed of / we can be proud of our creative expressions and sounds."[55] In response to rising activism against racialized oppression, LeRoi Jones abandoned Beat for Black Arts, and eventually renounced his slave name, renaming himself (Imamu) Amiri Baraka in 1967. Joans responded by leaving the United States for long periods at a time. Kaufman, however, had always already mediated his hipster poetics with Black nationalist politics. In his *Abomunist Manifesto* (1959), the figure of the "Abomunist," appears, as Baraka notes, as "some kind of excluded radical" with "real feelings of being opposed to society," suffering "abominations" of "abominable" America.[56] Or as Kaufman put it himself in his surreal line: "Abomunists spit anti-poetry for poetic reasons / and frink."[57] Kaufman's apostrophe poem, "Benediction" (circa 1960), challenges Ginsberg's "America" with pitiless faux forbearance – "America, I forgive you ... I forgive you / Eating black children, I know your hunger ...

I realize how necessary it was" – and contempt for the fatal prosperity of the American dream – "Everyday your people get more and more. / Cars, television, sickness, death dreams. / You must have been great / Alive" – an attack on the deadly postwar consumer culture condemned by hipsterism and Black nationalism alike.[58]

Beat poetics were not merely inscribed in manifestos and manifesto poems, or even limited to the poetry itself, as di Prima insists in "Rant": "There is no way you can *not* have a poetics / no matter what you do: plumber, baker, teacher / you do it in the consciousness of making / or not making yr world."[59] Or as Kyger put it, "*Everybody* practices magic / whether they know it or not."[60] Di Prima meets Jones's "MY POETRY is whatever I think I am," with a more expansive conception: "there is no part of yourself you can separate out / saying, this is memory, this is sensation / this is the work I care about, this is how I / make a living / it is whole."[61]

Di Prima's democratic poetics fits with a rise in feminism. "I Get My Period, September 1964" and "Brass Furnace Going Out: Song, after an Abortion," for example, are confessions of female fecundity situating poetics in the body with unapologetic literalism and relevance.[62] In "The Quarrel," the poet's antagonism toward male entitlement and the suppression of female art is articulated through a refusal to speak about it ("because it's just so fucking uncool to talk about it"), a sleight of hand of "cool" hipster poetics tuning Dickinson's "say it slant" to avowals of female subjectivity.[63] Later works extend epic treatment to an essentialized concept of the feminine as creative, as in the multivolume *Loba*, centered around the mystical energies of a shamanic she-wolf.[64] Kyger's feminism, by contrast, is diffident, indirect, poeticizing the peculiar omissions and excisions that typify female presence in Western literary canons (including the Beat canon). Her 1996 "Poison Oak for Allen" foregrounds the persistent invisibility of the female poet as a gendered object, dematerialized in the ego of male comrade-poets.[65] Waldman's 1975 "Fast Speaking Woman," another of the Beat movement's long-form list poems, delivers more than thirty pages of vibrating incantatory repetitions of the declarative enunciation "I am," many of which typify claims of second-wave feminism: "I'm a shouting woman / I'm a speech woman / I'm an atmospheric woman / I'm a flesh woman / I'm a flexible woman."[66] Modified intermittently and altered in performance, Waldman's poem exists in a condition of being unfinished that complements its poetics of conversion, whereby the Beat male-centered anaphoria of "best minds" serves a feminist, woman-centered ethos.

Waldman and Janine Pommy Vega, contemporaries in a third generation of Beat poet-musicians that includes Smith, Bob Dylan, Ed Sanders, and Laurie Anderson, express their Beat poetics through 1960s countercultural reconceptualizations of gender. The foregrounded female subject in Vega's first collection, *Poems to Fernando*, refocuses Beat's romantic tendencies with the elegiac speaker who deploys hipster poetics to advance a distinctively female subject.[67] *Poems to Fernando* is formed of dislocation and loss, a mourning distinct from the long-line keening of the poet's mentor Ginsberg, resonating instead, as Maria Damon has suggested, in a "fractured and slightly distorted syntax ... with the verse of Emily Dickinson, H.D., Joanne Kyger, and the early work of Denise Levertov."[68] Vega's is not Kandel's or Ginsberg's synaesthetic chant, but a synaesthesia of emotional disorientation and romantic exuberance, a poetics of the feminine under duress yet in free voice.[69] In a crucial self-enfranchisement, the poet transforms herself from object to subject, migrating from margin to center of Beat poetry, as in this moment from *Poems to Fernando*, where Vega draws a corrective matrilineal line: "this pile of Pot, like grandmother's leavings / the lamplin girl leaves love at the doorsill / every pen / starting; leaking out – / a freak of nature this poem."[70]

Reflecting the movement's location on the cusp of the postmodern, Beat poetics and praxis dissolved distinctions not only between high and mass cultures, academic and vernacular poetic dictions, poetry and prose, memoir and fiction, breath and line, body and mind, but also, as Stephen Prothero has argued, between "matter and spirit, divinity and humanity, the sacred and the profane."[71] Thus as Kerouac told Ted Berrigan, his poetics "applie[d] to prose as well as poetry" in an art of undifferentiated "utterance," and Creeley noted that in Kerouac the "distinction between the two forms [is] ... artificial – they are inseparable."[72] The genre blurring in ruth weiss's case is embodied in her claim that "whatever medium I use ... It is always poetry" even when it is painting, plays, or film.[73] Di Prima's *Dinners and Nightmares* (1961) also demonstrates a postmodern fluidity in a pastiche of deconstructed literary forms joining plays, journals, dreams, conversations, interior monologues, free verse, and lists into a single poetic discourse.[74] Waldman realizes an even more fully postmodern Beat style and poetics in her late work as when she assumes in "Feminafesto" a stance she described as transcending gender: "I'd like here to declare an enlightened poetics, an androgynous poetics, a poetics defined by your primal energy not by a heterosexist world ... a poetics of transformation beyond gender."[75]

The most visible institutional legacy of the Beat movement, the Naropa University (originally Naropa Institute), combines the Beat movement's spontaneous composition techniques and poetics with a spiritual dimension of Buddhist meditation practices, another vital facet of Beat poetics. The link in Beat poetics among uncensored mind and language, the breath as the basis of the line, the courting of "unstandard sounds" (to recall Corso), and the creative energy of the meditative process is apparent in poetics fostered by Buddhist study and practice. In her poetry performances, Waldman assimilates her Eastern attentions: "The pivotal word for me, in terms of how I relate Buddhist practice to my practice of writing, is 'energy.'"[76] Kerouac celebrated the "new American poetry" as "a kind of new-old Zen Lunacy poetry, writing whatever comes into your head as it comes, poetry returned to its origin, in the bardic child, truly ORAL."[77] Whalen's "Since You Ask Me" (1959) expresses a Buddhist-inflected method of mind-writing: "[t]his poetry is a picture or graph of a mind moving, which is a world body being here and now which is history … and you."[78] Kyger practices a kindred poetics, using the page, like Whalen's "picture or graph," "for scoring each movement of mind / breath."[79] Ginsberg made his poetics of charting the mind a now famous mantra: "Mind is shapely, art is shapely. Meaning mind practiced in spontaneity forms its own image."[80]

Ultimately, Beat evolutions of breath-line poetics encompass an abstract experimental dimension, epitomized for Ginsberg in Corso, who "gets the pure abstract poetry, the inside sound of language alone."[81] Michael McClure's abstract poetics – "no logic but sequence of feelings"– resists boundary differentiation, circumventing intellect by unbridled language, fusing Beat poetics and "Projective Verse" by transcending Olson's "poetry of the intellect and physiology" with "writing of the Emotions, intellect and physiology. The direct emotional statement from the body (from the organs and from the energy of movements)."[82] Corso refused to bind sound to sense, Kerouac to differentiate verse and prose, di Prima to segregate poetics from living, and McClure to distinguish animal self from intellect: "There is no separation between body and mind."[83] Abstract, borderless literary forms and cultural liminalities suggest Beat poetry's postmodern liberation – expressive and discursive, social and political – from arbitrary formal confines, a liberation described perhaps most succinctly in McClure's "THERE ARE NO CATEGORIES!!!"[84] McClure's "beast language," a neo-Projective Verse of pure guttural breath-sounds, permits an obliteration of sense by breath akin to Kerouac's poetics in "Sea," a "dictated" record of Pacific surf sounds appended to *Big Sur* (1962) and inspired by Joyce's *Finnegans Wake*.[85] The fusion of breath-based lines to sound in these McClure and Kerouac texts render the body a vibrating chamber in a project as close to singing as the unspoken word on the page might get. Bob Dylan iterates these poetics to fruition in the sung projection of the line and its propulsive musical accompaniment, as in "Stuck Inside of Mobile with the Memphis Blues Again" (1966), where the leering moan "Awww Mama, can this really be the end?" is an unalloyed abstract sound that overcomes an intended denotative sense.[86] Or as Ginsberg puts it, referring to "Like A Rolling Stone" (1965), but effectively summarizing three generations of Beat poetics, "Dylan puts his whole lung in one vowel: 'How does it FEEL' … the whole body into it," epitomizing a physiological vocalization that is the "expression of the whole body, 'single body, single mind.'"[87]

NOTES

1. Jack Kerouac, *Selected Letters: 1940–1956*, ed. Ann Charters (New York: Viking, 1995), 516.
2. Allen Ginsberg, *Deliberate Prose: Selected Essays 1952–1995*, ed. Bill Morgan (New York: Harper Collins, 2000), 237.
3. See Ronna C. Johnson and Nancy M. Grace, "Visions and Revisions of the Beat Generation," in *Girls Who Wore Black: Women Writing the Beat Generation*, ed. Ronna C. Johnson and Nancy M. Grace (New Brunswick, NJ: Rutgers University Press, 2002), 12–17.
4. Allen Ginsberg, *Howl and Other Poems* (San Francisco: City Lights, 1956).
5. Allen Ginsberg, *Howl: Original Draft Facsimile*, ed. Barry Miles (New York: Harper Perennial, 1995), 173–74.
6. *The Black Mountain Review* 7 (Autumn 1957).
7. Donald Allen, ed., *The New American Poetry, 1945–1960* (New York: Grove, 1960); LeRoi Jones, ed., *The Moderns: An Anthology of New Writing in America* (New York: Corinth Books, 1963); Donald Allen and Warren Tallman, eds., *The Poetics of the New American Poetry* (New York: Grove, 1973). Other key anthologies include Donald Hall, Robert Pack, and Louis Simpson's *New Poets of England and America* (New York: Meridian, 1957), often cited as the impetus for Allen's *New American Poetry* and as the primary adversary in the so-called anthology wars that are often credited with the foundation of a general divide in American poetry between "mainstream" (represented by the poets in Hall et al.) and "avant-garde" (represented by those in Allen); and Donald Allen and George F. Butterick, eds., *The Postmoderns: The New American Poetry Revisited* (1966; New York: Grove, 1982). Marjorie Perloff's remark occurs in "Whose New American Poetry? Anthologizing in the Nineties," *Diacritics* 26.3/4 (Autumn/Winter 1996): 104–23, 104.
8. See Michael Davidson, *The San Francisco Renaissance: Poetics and Community at Mid-Century* (New York: Cambridge University Press, 1989), as well as Chapter 5 of this volume.
9. Denise Levertov, "An Admonition, 1964," in Allen and Tallman, eds., *Poetics of the New American Poetry*, 310.
10. Gary Snyder, "Poetry and the Primitive," in Allen and Tallman, eds., *Poetics of the New American Poetry*, 395.
11. Steven Clay and Rodney Phillips, *A Secret Location on the Lower East Side* (New York: New York Public Library/Granary, 1998), 27, 177–79.
12. Ronna C. Johnson, "Lenore Kandel's *The Love Book*: Psychedelic Poetics, Cosmic Erotica, and Sexual Politics in the Midsixties Counterculture," in *Reconstructing the Beats*, ed. Jennie Skerl (New York: Palgrave/St. Martin's Press, 2004), 89–104.

13. Diane di Prima, *Revolutionary Letters* (San Francisco: City Lights, 1971).

14. Ginsberg, *Deliberate Prose*, 144; Kandel is cited in Allen and Tallman, *Poetics of the New American Poetry*, 344, 451.

15. Ginsberg, *Howl and Other Poems*, "Dedication"; Ginsberg, *Deliberate Prose*, 242; Anatole Broyard, "A Portrait of the Hipster" (1948), cited in *Beat Down to Your Soul: What Was the Beat Generation?*, ed. Ann Charters (New York: Viking, 2001), 45–6.

16. Bob Kaufman, *Cranial Guitar* (Minneapolis, MN: Coffee House Press, 1996), 94.

17. Bob Kaufman, *Solitudes Crowded with Loneliness* (New York: New Directions, 1965), 65–74.

18. Maria Damon, "Bob Kaufman," in *The Encyclopedia of Beat Literature*, ed. Kurt Hemmer (New York: Facts on File, 2007), 173.

19. Nancy M. Grace, "Single Out: Interview with ruth weiss," in Nancy M. Grace and Ronna C. Johnson, *Breaking the Rule of Cool* (Jackson: University Press of Mississippi, 2004), 55–80. See also, Nancy M. Grace, "ruth wiess's *DESERT JOURNAL*: A Modern-Beat-Pomo Performance," in Skerl, *Reconstructing the Beats*, 57–72.

20. Gregory Corso, *Gasoline* (San Francisco: City Lights, 1958), 9–10.

21. William Carlos Williams, *Paterson: Book Five* (New York: New Directions, 1963), 213.

22. Ted Joans, "Tape Recording at the Five Spot," in *The Beats*, ed. Seymour Krim (Greenwich, CT: Faucet, 1960), 211–13.

23. Ibid., 211–12.

24. Kerouac, *Selected Letters*, 371, 521 (1955).

25. Charles Olson, *Collected Prose*, eds. Donald Allen and Benjamin Friedlander (Berkeley: University of California Press, 1997), 240.

26. Lenore Kandel, *Word Alchemy* (New York: Grove, 1967), 61–2.

27. Ibid, 61; Mezz Mezzrow and Bernard Wolfe, *Really the Blues* (1946; New York: Citadel Press, 1990), 53.

28. Ginsberg, *Howl*, 27. For the connection between Kandel and Ginsberg, see Ronna C. Johnson in Skerl, *Reconstructing the Beats*, 92.

29. Ferlinghetti, cited in Hemmer, *Encyclopedia*, 230.

30. Jack Kerouac, "The Origins of the Beat Generation," in *Viking Critical Library Edition* of On the Road, ed. Scott Donaldson (New York: Viking, 1979), 361–62.

31. Broyard, "Portrait," 44; Williams, *Paterson*, 225.

32. Cited in Raymond Foye, "Editor's Note" to Bob Kaufman, *The Ancient Rain: Poems 1956–1978* (New York: New Directions, 1981), ix.

33. Kaufman, *Cranial Guitar*, 107–108; see also Maria Damon, *Postliterary America: From Bagel Shop Jazz to Micropoetries* (Iowa City: University of Iowa Press, 2011).

34. Ted Joans, "The Truth," *Teducation: Selected Poems 1949–1999* (Minneapolis, MN: Coffee House Press, 1999), 228.

35. Kaufman, *Cranial Guitar*, 131.

36. Kerouac, "Origins," in Donaldson, *Viking Critical*, 361.

37. Kerouac, "Essentials of Spontaneous Prose" in Donaldson, *Viking Critical*, 531–33; Olson's "Projective Verse," in Allen, *New American Poetry*, 386–96.

38. Olson, ibid., 388.

39. Joanne Kyger, *Strange Big Moon: Japan and India Journals: 1960–1964* (Berkeley, CA: North Atlantic Books, 2000), 60, 62.

40. Kerouac, "Essentials," in Donaldson, *Viking Critical,* 531; Kerouac, *On the Road,* in Donaldson, *Viking Critical,* 206.

41. Allen Ginsberg, "First Thought, Best Thought," in *Composed on the Tongue,* ed. Donald Allen (Bolinas, CA: Grey Fox, 1980), 106.

42. Anne Waldman, "Feminafesto," in *Kill or Cure* (New York: Penguin, 1994), 114–15.

43. Joanne Kyger, *As Ever: Selected Poems,* ed. Michael Rothenberg (New York: Penguin, 2002), xv; Kyger, *Strange Big Moon,* 254.

44. LeRoi Jones, "How You Sound??" in Allen, *New American Poetry,* 425.

45. Kerouac, "Essentials," in Donaldson, *Viking Critical,* 531–33. Jones, "How You Sound??" in Allen, *New American Poetry,* 425.

46. Corso, *Gasoline,* 10.

47. Jones, "How You Sound??" in Allen, *New American Poetry,* 424.

48. Kyger, *Strange Big Moon,* 258.

49. Kerouac, "Essentials," in Donaldson, *Viking Critical,* 531–33.

50. Patti Smith, "Oath" (1970) in *Complete* (New York: Doubleday, 1998), 8–9.

51. Joans, "Tape Recording," in Krim, *The Beats,* 212.

52. Ibid., 213.

53. Jones, "How You Sound??" in Allen, *New American Poetry,* 424; Jones, "State/Meant," in Allen and Tallman, *Poetics,* 383.

54. LeRoi Jones, *The Dead Lecturer* (New York: Grove, 1964), 63.

55. Ted Joans, "Proposition for a Black Power Manifesto," in *A Black Manifesto for Jazz in Poetry and Prose* (London: Calder and Boyars, 1971), 11.

56. Quoted in Kaufman, *Cranial Guitar,* 11.

57. Kaufman, Ibid., 117.

58. Ibid, 105.

59. Diane di Prima, *Pieces of a Song: Selected Poems* (San Francisco: City Lights, 1990), 159–61.

60. Joanne Kyger, "Morning Mess," in *About Now: Collected Poems* (Orono, ME: National Poetry Foundation, 2007), 328.

61. Jones, "How You Sound?" in Allen, *New American Poetry,* 424; di Prima, "Rant," *Pieces,* 159.

62. Di Prima, *Pieces,* 161.

63. Diane di Prima, "The Quarrel" (1961), in Richard Peabody, ed., *A Different Beat: Writings by Women of the Beat Generation* (London: Serpent's Tail, 1997), 46, 73–4.

64. Diane di Prima, *Loba* (New York: Penguin, 1998).

65. Kyger, *About Now,* 618.

66. Anne Waldman, *Fast Speaking Woman: Chants & Essays* (1975; San Francisco: City Lights Books, 1996), 3.

67. Janine Pommy Vega, *Poems to Fernando* (San Francisco: City Lights, 1968).

68. Maria Damon, "Revelations of Companionate Love; or, The Hurts of Women: Janine Pommy Vega's *Poems to Fernando,*" in Johnson and Grace, *Girls,* 213–14.

69. Damon, "Revelations," *Girls,* 210; and Grace and Johnson, *Breaking,* 233.

70. Vega, *Poems to Fernando,* 43.

71. Stephen Prothero, "Introduction," *Big Sky Mind: Buddhism and the Beat Generation,* ed. Carole Tomkinson (New York: Riverhead Books, 1995), 20.

72. Ted Berrigan, "The Art of Fiction XLI: Jack Kerouac," in Donaldson, *Viking Critical*, 538–72; Kerouac, "Essentials," in Donaldson, *Viking Critical*, 531–33; Robert Creeley, "Introduction," Jack Kerouac, *Pomes All Sizes* (New York: Penguin, 1995), iv.

73. Cited in Grace, "ruth weiss," *Reconstructing the Beats*, 60.

74. Di Prima, *Dinners and Nightmares* (San Francisco: Last Gasp, 2003).

75. Waldman, *Kill or Cure*, 145.

76. Anne Waldman, "Poetry as Siddhi," *Vow to Poetry* (Minneapolis, MN: Coffee House, 2001), 172.

77. Jack Kerouac, "The Origins of Joy in Poetry," *Scattered Poems* (San Francisco: City Lights, 1971), n.p.

78. Allen, *New American Poetry*, 420.

79. Kyger, *As Ever*, xv.

80. Ginsberg, *Deliberate Prose*, 230.

81. Corso, *Gasoline*, 7.

82. Allen and Tallman, *Poetics*, 422–23.

83. Michael McClure, *Scratching the Beat Surface* (San Francisco: North Point Press, 1982), 44–5.

84. Michael McClure, "Peyote Poem III," *The Portable Beat Reader*, ed. Ann Charters (New York: Viking, 1992), 272.

85. Jack Kerouac, *Big Sur* (New York: Farrar, Strauss & Cudahy, 1962), 219–41.

86. Bob Dylan, *Lyrics 1962–1985* (1973; New York: Knopf, 1985), 228–29.

87. Allen, *Composed on the Tongue*, 106–07.

FURTHER READING

Belgrad, Daniel. *The Culture of Spontaneity: Improvisation and the Arts in Postwar America*. Chicago: University of Chicago Press, 1998.

Davidson, Michael. *The San Francisco Renaissance: Poetics and Community at Mid-Century*. New York: Cambridge University Press, 1989.

Grace, Nancy M. and Ronna C. Johnson, *Breaking the Rule of Cool: Interviewing and Reading Women Beat Writers*. Jackson: University Press of Mississippi, 2004.

Hemmer, Kurt. *The Encyclopedia of Beat Literature*. New York: Facts on File, 2007.

Hrebeniak, Michael. *Action Writing: Jack Kerouac's Wild Form*. Carbondale: Southern Illinois University Press, 2006.

Johnson, Ronna C. and Nancy M. Grace, eds. *Girls Who Wore Black: Women Writing the Beat Generation*. New Brunswick, NJ: Rutgers University Press, 2002.

Mohr, Bill. *HOLD-OUTS: The Los Angeles Poetry Renaissance, 1948–1992*. Iowa City: University of Iowa Press, 2011.

Skerl, Jennie, ed. *Reconstructing the Beats*. New York: Palgrave/St. Martin's Press, 2004.

Tomkinson, Carole, ed. *Big Sky Mind: Buddhism and the Beat Generation*. New York: Riverhead Books, 1995.

Trigilio, Tony. *Allen Ginsberg's Buddhist Poetics*. Carbondale: Southern Illinois University, 2007.

7

MARGO NATALIE CRAWFORD

The Poetics of Chant and Inner/Outer Space: The Black Arts Movement

> if you had heard her
> chanting as she ironed
> you would understand form and line
> and discipline and order and
> america.[1]

> – Lucille Clifton, "study the masters"

In the short story "Northern Iowa: Short Story and Poetry" (2007), Amiri Baraka, the most acclaimed poet of the 1960s and early 1970s Black Arts movement, revels in African Americans' use of free verse: "Verse is a turn, simply. Like a wheel, it has regular changes.... Except what we *want* is *vers libre* – free verse. Never having been that, *free*, we want it badly. For black people, *freedom* is our aesthetic and our ideology. *Free Jazz, Freedom Suite, Tell Freedom, Oh, Freedom!* And on!"[2] As free verse abounds during this cultural movement, the artists give poetry a new sound and appearance that is as radical as the political and cultural revolution it heralded. In its embrace of free verse, the sound of Black Arts poetry fully matches what Houston A. Baker names "deformation of mastery." As Baker explains, a continuum exists between *mastery of form* (African American writers' skillful use of the dominant forms, the "master's tools") and the *deformation of mastery* (African American writers' use of these tools in a manner that changes the dominant forms themselves and destroys the master's house).[3] As a hip hop chant has put it: "The roof, the roof, the roof is on fire / We don't need no water / Let the motherfucker burn."[4]

The soundtrack of the Black Arts movement was jazz, soul, rhythm and blues, and the spoken word that paved the way for hip hop. According to the poet and music critic A. B. Spellman, most Black Arts poets secretly wanted to be jazz musicians.[5] The musical sound Black Arts poetry captures, often through the play with homophony and non-semantic sounds, bears out that claim. Take Amiri Baraka's emblematic lines, in "It's Nation Time" (1970):

> It's nation time eye ime
> It's nation ti eye ime
> Chant with bells and drums
> It's nation time[6]

Black Arts poetic jazz was the difference, in Baraka's words, between know-ing how to play an instrument and knowing how to utilize that instrument. During both his Beat movement identity as LeRoi Jones and his Black Arts move away from the "slave name," Baraka constantly wrestled with the difference between being well trained ("mastering the form," in Baker's terms) and well prepared to innovate ("deform the mastery"). For Baraka, the difference innovation makes is also the difference that comes from intu-ition or instinct: "Knowing how to play an instrument is the barest super-ficiality if one is thinking about becoming a musician. It is the ideas that one utilizes *instinctively* that determine the degree of profundity any artist reaches."[7]

As words became their musical instruments, many Black Arts poets dis-covered that making a poem work on the page was the "barest superfici-ality." The poems had to work on the page and in the complicated streets. Creative power is not just a matter of reaching inside, to one's "instinct" – it is also a matter of reaching out, from the realm of inner consciousness to the outer realm of collective action. Thus an in-between space between song and word (often referred to as "spoken word") was created as the poets discovered the power of chant.

In his aptly titled *Black Chant* (1997), Aldon Lynn Nielsen looks at African American poetry in the liminal period immediately before the Black Arts movement to explain what really happens when poets translate jazz music into jazz poetry, and he distinguishes between the "composed" and the "improvised" in jazz poetry. The "improvised" are the parts of many jazz poems that must be performed in order to be fully audible. The "composed" are the parts that, on the page, appear to be less experimental and less of an attempt to capture orality within the limits of written form. Nielsen argues that African American jazz poems defy the difference between the composed and the improvised. Black Arts poetry, in particular, explodes this imagined difference between the oral and the written. The terms "spoken word" and "performance poetry" are often used interchangeably to describe the more populist forms of contemporary American poetry. During the Black Arts movement, poets embraced the rhythm of chant as the standard sound of poetry. Jayne Cortez, for example, confesses, "I guess it's a speak-chant type thing."[8] The back cover of Woodie King's anthology *Black Spirits* (1972) announced the poems' ties to performance: "Many of the poems in this book as read by their authors are available on the Black Forum record label, LP456, entitled Black Spirits."⁹

Among the "speak-chant" techniques of Black Arts poetry is frequent explosion of words that is controlled by the use of anaphora – the repetition of a first word, in each line of a stanza, as a means of translating a verbal chant into the space of precision and controlled musical notes. In the second stanza in the following passage from the poem "Gwendolyn Brooks," by Haki Madhubuti, the word "black," at the beginning of each line, provides the form (the foundation) for the open form of the words that follow.

> black so black we can't even see you black on black in
> black by black technically black mantanblack winter
> black coolblack 360degreesblack coalblack midnight
> black black when it's convenient rustyblack moonblack
> black starblack summerblack electronblack spaceman
> black shoeshineblack jimshoeblack underwearblack ugly
> black auntjimammablack, uncleben'srice black williebest
> black blackisbeautifulblack i justdiscoveredblack negro
> black unsubstanceblack.¹⁰

Baker's dialectic of mastery of form and deformation of mastery takes the shape, in this poem, of the fixing of the word "black," followed by the twisting and turning of that word, and then the continued return, after the line breaks, to the fixed word "black." The words "& with black came poets" depict poetry as the vehicle that opens up the word "black" into the nuances and subtleties of what A. B. Spellman identified as Black Arts poetry's "Negritudinous surreal dream."¹¹ The surreality in this poem consists in the play between blackness and the abstraction of blackness ("black unstubstanceblack"), tied to the all-encompassing refrain "black," as each line circles back to the repeated first word.

As the chant begins to define the sound of Black Arts poetry, many poets deploy this anaphoric technique, where the repeated first word links the irregular lines and makes the word a type of mantra, a sound that can create a spiritual or psychological transformation. If "black" is the mantra in Madhubuti's "Gwendolyn Brooks, in Larry Neal's poem "The Narrative of the Black Magicians," it is the word "form":

> O Ancestor faces form on film our minds
> form our contours out of deep wailing saxes.
> form in the voice our would-be leaders.
> form child.
> form in the rush of war.
> form child.
> form in the sun's explosion.¹²

When "form" becomes the mantra of the chant form itself, we see an emphasis on becoming, as in the ontological sense invited in "Gwendolyn Brooks" with the repetition of "black," but we also see all the more clearly its aesthetic sense, delivering a poetics of becoming.

Neal knows the rules and knows how to break them too. His use of the period, at the end of each line, followed by the lower case first letter in the word "form," stages the breaking of the rules as the breaking of each line of the chant to create a slower and still more urgent chant than the faster, louder chant of "Gwendolyn Brooks." There is also a difference of tone, which in these two poems is the difference between the chants that make an audience move collectively as they nod, clap, smile, or raise the Black Power fist, and the chants that make a listener want to close her eyes even as she stands in the midst of the crowd listening to Black Arts poetry being performed next to one of the outdoor murals, at a bookstore reading, or in a community center. Neal's chant that leads to the closed eyes produces, in the reader or listener, a stillness to receive and create. The rush of motion, followed by the repetitive pause produced by the word "black," in Madhubuti's chant, by contrast, constantly threatens at the end of each line to not return to the framing word "black." The layering of "black" ("double black," "blackblack," "blackisbeautifulblack,") constantly threatens to create new words, strange spellings, and new graphic use of the white space on the page.

The chants that made the audience *move* shared a great connection, during this social movement, to poems that literally moved across the page. These poems signal the second step of the Black Arts poetics of chant. After the mantras of "Black" and "form" had been fully galvanized, the poets, remaining in the state of en(chant)ment, deformed the visual norms of poems. This deformation was staged in the many poems with very irregular line lengths and, often, the breaking of lines; first a few indentations form the left margin, and then, with each new break, closer and closer to the right margin, the edge of the page, before returning to a line that begins in the left margin, only to move back to the edge of the page in the next lines. In the poem "friends i am like you tied," A. B. Spellman connects this move to the "far end of the page" to the freedom of "moving on down the line." A few lines after the self-reflection, "a.b. break something action i've / acted who mans the far end of the i?," he performs the move to the "far end": "moving on down the line you now we" (*Black Fire*, 248–249).

Chanting was an aesthetics of linkage ("you" becoming "we") as well as breakage. The role of breakage is underscored in Nikki Giovanni's iconic chant that shapes the break of the line into the missing question mark and the need to kill a dominant ideology. In the poem "The True Import of Present Dialogue, Black vs. Negro" (1968), Giovanni questions the usefulness of a chant if it does not lead to concrete, revolutionary action. Her mantra is "can," as opposed to Neal's "form" and Madhubuti's "Black." She chants:

> Can you kill
> Can you kill
> Can a nigger kill
> Can a nigger kill a honkie
> Can a nigger kill the Man
> Can you kill nigger[13]

The constrained lack of indented lines in this inquisitive chant is itself a form of resistance to constraint. When compared to the poems that have the multiple indented lines (where *black* words move across *white* space), this chant begs to break out of the controlled form. Indeed the speaker asks, later in the poem, "Can you cut it off." The call for aesthetic warfare, figured in this section of the poem as the call for the cutting off of a "blond head," is staged as a rage that cannot be contained by the even left margins. When compared to the poems that move more dramatically across the page, Giovanni's chant becomes the meta-poem that explains why "killing," aesthetic warfare, must attack the visual default settings of poetry.

Amus Mor, one of the most under-recognized trailblazers of the movement, captures the shift from controlled chant to playing on the page to the deformation of the stanza. Spanning eight pages, his "Poem to the Hip Generation" (1972) has jagged-edged margins on the left and the right until the final two short stanzas, which have justified margins on the left and a tight compactness that the other open stanzas lack. The beginning stanza introduces David ("he was David" are the last words) by visualizing the "first steps" of both David and "the nation" (*Black Spirits*, 134). As the first three lines following the opening line are indented, successively, closer and closer to the right margin, the birth of David slowly unfolds. This birth is tied to the biblical creation story, an "electric storm," urban roof tops, soup lines, kitchenettes, and a "nation's first step." This birth is the birth of David's jazz; we learn, in the fourth stanza, that David enters the "academy / of Lester the president." The visual steps in the first lines of the poem thus present David's own "first step" toward jazz:

> david dug genesis
> did not dream
> heard the electric storm
> that was his intro (134)

The word "dug" is the spectacular vernacular that captures David's love of the biblical story. There is something about the biblical language that makes David begin to move over the roof tops and gain a new self-image. He does not move into the self-enclosure of dreams but rather an open space that feels like "an electric storm," the tumultuous wind that you can only feel on the roof tops that are so close to the electricity lines spanning across the city.

The word "dug" also captures David's digging (his questioning), throughout the poem, echoed in the repeated words "who are we / where are we going / what are we here for." Mor makes the digging much more than the creation of a metaphysical hole when he ends the poem with answers to these questions: "we are the hipmen / ... where are we going / into the sky / ... why were we sent here / only to love." Just as Sun Ra's response to the Black Power call and response "What time is it? Nation Time" was to declare "It's Planet Time" (the name of his 1973 album), Mor, in this poem, makes the move to outer space, "going / into the sky," the birth of the black nation. The opening stanza's "first steps of nation" are rewritten in the final stanzas as the first steps into outer space. In this closing part of the poem when Mor makes hipness, outer space, and love the answer to the cosmic questions about identity, action, and the future, his lines are no longer literally moving across the page with the uneven left margin. In this final stanza, with its left-justified lines, the poet pauses to breathe deeply and rest after the long jazz riff performed throughout the poem. The return to the normative stanza shape is a return to the controlled Black Arts chant after the play with the enchantment of Black Arts outer space.

The "poetics of outer space" and "the poetics of inner space" clarify many aspects of Black Arts poetry. Gaston Bachelard's use of the term "poetics of space" undergirds my use of these two terms. Just as Bachelard theorizes about the intertwining of the inner and the outer, Black Arts poetics collapses the boundaries between the inner space of black consciousness and the outer space of activism and collectives. The movement placed great emphasis on the role of poetry in public spaces (hence the painting of poetry on outdoor murals, such as the painting of Baraka's "SOS" on *The Wall of Respect* [1967] and Nelson Steven's *I am a Black Woman* mural [1973], which includes the painting of Mari Evan's poem). The movement also emphasized the creation of "Black space" within oppressive, dominating white space. The "Black space" of the poet's page and the "Black space" of communities attempting to find space for self-determination were rendered directly in Broadside Press's 1966 reproduction of Gwendolyn Brooks's 1960 poem "We Real Cool" (Figure 4).[14] The words in the poem are white against a black background and capture the inner world of the seven young "pool players" at "the Golden Shovel." The broadside format, moreover,

Figure 4. Reproduction of Gwendolyn Brooks broadside, "We Real Cool."
Courtesy of the Library of Congress. Reprinted by Consent of Brooks Permissions.

suggests an alternative place of pedagogy, a *black*board: a space defined by
an aesthetic that differs fundamentally from the dominant *school* of poetry
that this social movement labels "white." During the Black Power movement, many Black liberation community elementary schools were created.
Madhubuti was the founder of one of these alternative schools, the Institute
of Positive Education. The visual interpretation of "We Real Cool" is not
only tied to the indoor space of the alternative (black-oriented) classroom;
the image also evokes the public art of graffiti. Brooks herself identifies this

poem with the public "accessibility" cultivated in Black Arts poetry: "My aim, in my next future, to write poems that will somehow successfully 'call' (see Baraka's 'SOS') all black people: black people in taverns, black people in alleys, black people in gutters, schools, offices, factories, prisons, the consulate: I wish to reach black people in pulpits, black people in mines, on farms, on thrones."[14] "We Real Cool" is a pre-Black Arts poem that "calls" black people in this wide open space. The line "We left school" hails this outer space. The inner space of the young men, their defiant self-image, can only exist outside of the dominant "school."

Brooks wrote "We Real Cool" before she became a vital member of the Black Arts movement and a mentor figure for many younger Black Arts poets. As opposed to many of the young poets who rejected the use of sonnets and other "closed" forms of poetry that they viewed as white forms, Brooks, during and after the Black Arts movement, continued to write poems that neither took up the typical Black Arts chant rhythm, the common experimentation with line indentation and the visual form of the poem, nor dwelt in any easily recognizable African American vernacular. Nonetheless, Brooks, after what she herself describes as her "conversion" during the Black Arts movement, consciously and complexly situates her post-1967 conversion poetry in the "Mecca" of the movement. Her poem, "In The Mecca" (1968), places Black Arts poets in the very center of her meditation on searching and being lost in structures (actual buildings as well as poetic structures). The poem tells a story about the lost child "Pepita" in a building that is now part of the "Black Belt" ghetto but used to be an elegant upper-class residence. The diction in the poem, best described as "King's English," becomes, for Brooks, as fluid as the street vernacular of "We Real Cool." Throughout "In the Mecca," the search for the lost child is inseparable from the speaker's movement through linguistic and material space. The Mecca is the master's house (the ornate building that formerly had upper-class white residents) that is now, on the surface, simply an African American slum. As the speaker searches for the lost child, the speaker finds an exquisite language that captures that which is in between the ornate and the ordinary. For example, a description of Mrs. Sallie, the missing child's mother, plays with essence and fragmentation: "Our prudent partridge. / A fragmentary attar and armed coma. / A fugitive attar and a district hymn."[15] The image of the "prudent partridge" conveys the way that this mother has been made to "perch" with such careful balance, even though she has the whimsical spirit that yearns to wander. She is the mother searching for her child who has never been able to get lost in the whimsical aspects of life. Perched like the partridge, she has never allowed herself to sing outside the regimented bars of those "district hymn[s]."

The chewy language voiced throughout "In the Mecca" starkly opposes the character of the aspiring poet Alfred ("Alfred is un- / talented. Knows."), who makes the art such a stale, highbrow performance. As Alfred quotes Leopold Senghor, he makes the 1930s and 1940s Négritude movement itself into a type of cultural capital. His posturing makes the speaker think of Senghor the President of Senegal, not Senghor the poet who wanted to own his own words instead of using the colonizing toys. After squeezing herself around Alfred's toxic art of imitation and his attempt to take up too much space (he "who might have been a poet-king"), Brooks calls directly for "Don Lee," who wants a "new art and anthem":

> Don Lee wants
> a new nation
> under nothing;
> a physical light that waxes; he does not want to
> be exorcised, adjoining and revered;
> he does not like a local garniture
> nor any impish onus in the vogue;
> is not candlelit
> but stands out in the auspices of fire
> and rock and jungle-flail;
> wants
> new art and anthem; will
> want a new music screaming in the sun. (423–424)

"Don Lee" is also the "slave name" that is discarded, in 1973, when its bearer renames himself "Haki Madhubuti." The words in the spiritual "Amazing Grace" – "I was lost but now I'm found" – capture the way that the speaker feels when she meets Don Lee in the midst of the Mecca. In this "lost but now I'm found" poetic narrative, Brooks uses the precision of the iambic meter to set up her steady pace through the "black Mecca" literally created by "white flight," the term sociologists use to describe the quick exit, in segregated communities, by white residents once a neighborhood begins to turn "black." The "waxing" Brooks ties to Don Lee signals that her formalist poetics and the Black Arts free verse meet in the open space created when she, Don Lee, and the other Black Arts poets she mentored find a black aesthetic that is the outer space of a community's interior (not the internalization of the outer that makes Alfred, the false poet, keep choosing the wrong words).

The poetics of the Black Arts movement often staged the "perfect" words as the words that can hail ideal (black) readers and make them want to enter into an individual and collective consciousness-raising movement. In the iconic poem "SOS" (1966), Baraka makes the call for blackness sound like the frantic words in a walkie-talkie.

> Calling black people
> Calling all black people, man woman child
> Wherever you are, calling you, urgent, come in
> Black People, come in, wherever you are, urgent, calling
> you, calling all black people
> calling all black people, come in, black people, come
> on in.[16]

The speaker must talk quickly and loudly in order to be heard over the static of this two-way radio transmission. The beauty of the poem is its ability to evoke the static without needing any direct representation of this noise. The repetition of the words "calling" and "urgent" and the sparse language show that the speaker knows that he must avoid any unnecessary words to ensure delivery of the message, in spite of the static and necessarily poor reception. The poet's precise craft becomes inseparable from the crafting of the counter-ideology, the message aiming to destroy the static (the constant interference created by the dominant aesthetic and power structure). Remember the "electric storm," in Amus Mor's poem "Poem to the Hip Generation," where the electrical interference makes David, the jazz poet, begin to run across the roof tops. Baraka, in "SOS," aims for that same flight as he calls for an inward motion ("come / on in"). The move inward (to a black consciousness that makes "Black" mean both community and the deconditioned individual mind) is, for Baraka, a vexed and difficult journey, but also if the ideal (black) readers pause to begin to think about being free, a very *natural* move. The journey inward is not an easy move to a comforting essence, one of the assumptions made when the Black Arts movement is too quickly packaged as a flawed first step, a type of identity politics that did not understand the limits of essentialized (contained) blackness. When "SOS" is painted on *The Wall of Respect*, the outdoor mural, the words "come / on in" literally gain the brick wall texture of "come / on out." On the page, the poem invites the walkie-talkie response – that which in our twenty-first-century African American vernacular takes the shape of "Holla back." The final words "come / on in" are a call for the response that the painted poem exemplifies. The pull inward, in Black Arts poetry, is also a push outward.

For women of the Black Arts movement, hollering back was not always the delivery of the kind of chant that celebrated the calls of the male poets and the performed black male identities that occupied so much space during this social movement. For Nikki Giovanni, Mari Evans, Carolyn Rodgers,

Sonia Sanchez, Johari Amini, Julia Fields, and many other women poets, the space of the in-between became very useful as they, in the words of Brooks, "civilized a space / wherein to play their violin with grace." [17] Julia Fields's "I Loves a Wig" (1975) is a persona poem that assumes the point of view of a working-class African American woman who views the movement as bourgeois and critiques its assumption that wearing a wig signals self-hatred. The poem counters the depiction of internalization in Baraka's "An Agony. As Now." (1964) – "I am inside someone / who hates me. I look / out from his eyes." [18] These women poets testify that black women's liberation was not tied to a necessity of purging (instead of internalization), but rather finding words to express black women's hunger during this Black Power movement: black women's need to *consume*, and not just participate in black male poets' acts of purging.

In Nikki Giovanni's poem, "Of Liberation," the purging process is explicitly rendered without any recognition, by the speaker, of the need to purge sexism: "The sisters need to make flags / (there are no nations without a flag)." [19] This normative gender role-playing is performed only after a step-by-step purging of whiteness: "Everything comes in steps / Negative step one: get the white out of your hair / Negative step two: get the white out of your mind / Negative step three: get the white out of your parties / Negative step four: get the white out of your meetings" (46). The speaker in this poem pauses, immediately before this stanza, to emphasize her lack of any desire to criticize black men: "It has been pointed out: 'The last bastion of white supremacy / is in the Black man's mind' / (Note – this is not a criticism of brothers)" (46). Purging, in other words, privileges a male-oriented audience. As the woman speaker colludes in her own oppression (women flag makers versus male nation-builders), she revels in the Black Arts purging, but the final words are "Listen to your own Black hearts" (49). This move inward, after the speaker's strident listing of the problems and plan of action, changes the tone of the poem, as the speaker gestures toward a very subtle recognition, at the end of this performance, that the inner space of black women's trauma and oppression has been effaced in this masculinist understanding of Black liberation.

The latent hunger, signaled in the reference to "your own Black hearts," is brought to the surface when Audre Lorde, in "Naturally," a poem that is both a part of the movement and critical of the movement, calls for "black bread." [20] Lorde's Black Arts poetics of inner and outer space is very compelling because she herself balanced on the edge between being a credentialed Black Arts poet – by virtue of publishing with Broadside Press, one of the two most influential Black Arts presses – and a poet whose work, while deeply informed by, never fully participated in the poetics of this social movement.²¹ The speaker in this poem, with sighs and sarcasm spurred by real frustration, questions the movement's mantras, "Black is Beautiful," "Black Pride," and "Natural Black Beauty." Contrasting the outer space of cities and capitalism with the limited spatial dimension of the body, the poem's closing stanzas question the effectiveness of the Black Arts and Black Power movements' use of body politics: "And who trembles nightly / With the fear of their lily cities being swallowed / By a summer ocean of naturally woolly hair?" (18). This social movement reveled in the ferociousness of the Afro and other natural hair styles, but Lorde likens this bodily aesthetic warfare to "a summer ocean" that really does not pose any threat to the real sites of power (the "lily [white] cities"). In the final stanza, through a focus on cans of "Natural Hair Spray," "made and marketed in Watts," Lorde depicts the commodification of this bodily warfare. As opposed to the celebration of purging in Giovanni's "Of Liberation," Lorde's image of Watts laborers spending money on products they have themselves produced rewrites Black Arts purging as a useless "spray" that can never "swallow" the "lily cities." The poem's closing proposition, "Proud beautiful Black women / Could better make and use / black bread," calls for a different internalization, a "swallow[ing]" that would fight against the cultural consumption of blackness, by both capitalism and the Black Power movement, and begin to look for a type of consciousness-raising less invested in bodily signs of aesthetics and more invested in black currency ("bread" being a slang reference to money).

The poetics of inner and outer space gains a diasporic reach in the work of Keorapetse "Willie" Kgositsile, a South African exile who gains a central role in the Black Arts poetry movement with poems shaped around the broken boundaries between African American and African space. There is a call and response between Brooks's poetry and Kgositsile's. Brooks, in the introduction to Kgositsile's *My Name is Afrika* (1971), offers a poem entitled "To Keorapetse Kgositsile" in which she proclaims "MY NAME IS AFRIKA"! / – Well, every fella's a Foreign Country. / This Foreign Country speaks to You."²² Kgositsile's "Exile" (1975) cites Brooks' poem "Kitchenette Building" (1945), but whereas Brooks's poem ends with an image of the shared bathrooms in kitchenette buildings and the lack of enough "lukewarm water," Kgositsile, in his response, begins with the terror of the water during the Middle Passage: "And the ocean, my brother knows, is not our friend."²³ After this invocation of the Middle Passage, Kgositsile moves, in the next stanza, to the need for a "community alarm" that would resound throughout the "oceans," signalling a "wake up" call that would be local and cosmopolitan. Recalling Brooks's words, "We are things of dry hours and the involuntary plan," the oceanic "community alarm" becomes that which would awaken those who have been "grayed" by the "involuntary plan."[24] Kgositsile depicts this "plan" as colonialism when he writes, "Did you say independence?" and "Lumumba, do you hear us?" (49). Brooks depicts this "plan" as the shackles that continue, post-slavery and post–Great Migration, to reduce African Americans, in the urban landscape, to "things." As Kgositsile responds to Brooks's poem, he insists on the intersections between the plan of the Middle Passage, the "Black Belt" neighborhoods in Chicago, and colonialism in Africa. Kgositsile's reshaping of "Kitchenette Building" into "Exile" demonstrates his desire to add a diasporic dimension to Black Arts poetry even as he appreciates the local specificity of this poetry. Just as Brooks sets up a phenomenology of space and sound as she wonders if "giddy sounds" like "Dream" can survive in the oppressive structure of the kitchenette buildings, Kgositsile, in the penultimate stanza in "Exile," sets up a phenomenology of space and sound: "I stand among my silences / in search of a song to lean on" (49). Kgositsile's poetics of inner and outer space "leans on" Black Arts sounds as he creates a transnational sound.

This diasporic extension in Black Arts poetry was yet another way in which simple understandings of form were deformed in the poetics of this vital social movement. Once we gain an appreciation of the interplay, in this poetry, between inner and outer space, we see the poets' keen awareness of the spatial dimensions of a poem – a poem could work on the street, on the page, and across an ocean. The use of music and performance enabled this poetry to circulate widely among people who were not usually reading poetry or buying poetry books. The slim broadside poetry volumes were sold at public gatherings and community poetry readings. Standard single-page poetry broadsides enabled this grassroots poetry to become entirely portable, as captured in Haki Madhubuti's tribute to Gwendolyn Brooks: "pee wee used to carry one of her poems around in his back pocket."[25] Cultural movements such as the Black Arts movement rely on an everyday type of collaboration between community leaders, writers, organizers, visual artists, event participants, and audience members. This organic collaboration lies fully in the zone of *process* as opposed to the *object* that we tend to fetishize as texts. To what extent are literary and cultural movements inevitably reconstructed and remembered as textual objects as opposed to process-oriented, anti-object collaborations? Black Arts poetry foregrounds process (the repetition in chant) and never hides the seams of the text (the edges between the inner and the outer). "Sound for sounding" are the words Amiri Baraka uses, in his preface to Larry Neal's poetry volume *Black Boogaloo* (1969), as a means of explaining sound as process as opposed to sound as object. Before ending the preface with the question "What does boogaloo mean?," Baraka counsels, "Post 'literary' because we are men who write.... Literary sound like somethin' else ... sound like it ain't sound. And sound is what we deal in ... in the real world ... sound for sounding."[26]

NOTES

1. Lucille Clifton, *Blessing the Boats: New and Selected Poems 1988–2000* (Rochester, NY: BOA Editions, Ltd., 2000), 25.
2. Amiri Baraka, *Tales of the Out & the Gone* (New York: Akashic Books, 2007), 133.
3. Houston A. Baker, Jr., *Modernism and the Harlem Renaissance* (Chicago: University of Chicago Press, 1987), xvi.
4. The chant circulates widely but it was introduced in the rap single "The Roof Is on Fire" by Rockmaster Scott and The Dynamic Three (Jersey City, NJ: Reality Records, 1984).
5. A. B. Spellman, personal interview, Washington DC, April 10, 2007.
6. Amiri Baraka, *The LeRoi Jones/Amiri Baraka Reader*, ed. William J. Harris (New York: Thunder's Mouth Press, 1991), 242.
7. LeRoi Jones, "The Jazz Avant-Garde," *Black Music* (1968; New York: Da Capo Press, 1998), 71.
8. Graham Lock and David Murray, eds., *Thriving on a Riff: Jazz and Blues Influences in African American Literature and Film* (Oxford: Oxford University Press, 2009), 128.
9. Woodie King, *Black Spirits: A Festival of New Poets in America* (New York: Vintage Books, 1972).
10. Don L. Lee (Haki Madhubuti), *Directionscore: Selected and New Poems* (Detroit, MI: Broadside Press, 1971), 88.
11. A. B. Spellman, "Big Bushy Afros," *International Review of African American Art* 15.1 (1998), 53.
12. LeRoi Jones and Larry Neal, eds., *Black Fire: An Anthology of Afro-American Writing* (New York: William Morrow & Company, 1968), 314.
13. Nikki Giovanni, *Black Feeling Black Talk/Black Judgment* (New York: Harper Perennial, 1971), 19.
14. This broadside is reproduced in James D. Sullivan, *On the Walls and in the Streets: American Poetry Broadsides from the 1960s* (Urbana & Chicago: University of Illinois Press, 1997), 37.
15. Gwendolyn Brooks, *Blacks* (Chicago: Third World Press, 1987), 407.
16. Baraka, *Jones/Baraka Reader*, 218.
17. Gwendolyn Brooks, *Annie Allen* (1949; Westport, CT: Greenwood Press, 1971), 38.
18. Baraka, *Jones/Baraka Reader*, 52–3.
19. Giovanni, *Black Feeling*, 48.
20. "Naturally" first appeared in 1970, in the Black Power movement's most groundbreaking feminist anthology, *The Black Woman: An Anthology*, ed. Toni Cade Bambara (New York: Mentor, 1970), 18.
21. Third World Press (Chicago, Illinois) is the second, founded during the Black Arts movement and still thriving.
22. Keorapetse Kgositsile, *My Name Is Afrika* (New York: Doubleday, 1971), 15.

23. Keorapetse Kgositsile, *If I Could Sing: Selected Poems* (Roggebaai, South Africa: Kwela, 2002), 49.
24. Brooks, *Blacks*, 20.
25. Don L. Lee [Haki Mudubhuti], *Don't Cry, Scream* (Chicago: Broadside Press, 1969), 17.
26. Larry Neal, *Black Boogaloo: Notes on Black Liberation* (San Francisco: Journal of Black Poetry Press, 1969), i.

FURTHER READING

Baker, Houston A. *Afro-American Poetics: Revisions of Harlem and the Black Aesthetic.* Madison: University of Wisconsin Press, 1988.

Benston, Kimberly. *Performing Blackness: Enactments of African-American Modernism.* New York: Routledge, 2000.

Clarke, Cheryl. *"After Mecca": Women Poets and the Black Arts Movement.* New Brunswick, NJ: Rutgers University Press, 2005.

Collins, Lisa Gail and Margo Natalie Crawford, eds. *New Thoughts on the Black Arts Movement.* New Brunswick, N.J: Rutgers University Press, 2006.

Gayle, Addison, ed. *The Black Aesthetic.* Garden City, NY: Doubleday, 1971.

Harper, Phillip Brian. "Nationalism and Social Division in Black Arts Poetry of the 1960s" in *Critical Inquiry* 19 (Winter 1993).

Jones, Meta DuEwa. *The Muse Is Music: Jazz Poetry from the Harlem Renaissance to Spoken Word.* Chicago: University of Illinois Press, 2011.

Jordan, Jennifer. "Cultural Nationalism in the 1960s: Politics and Poetry." In *Race, Politics, and Culture: Critical Essays on the Radicalism of the 1960s.* Ed. Adolph Reed, Jr. Westport, CT: Greenwood Press, 1986, 29–60.

Smethurst, James L. *The Black Arts Movement: Literary Nationalism in the 1960s.* Chapel Hill: University of North Carolina Press, 2005.

8

LISA SEWELL

Feminist Poetries

Since the 1970s, the number of women writing, publishing, and receiving recognition for their poetry has increased exponentially, an "extraordinary tide" that corresponds to the advent of the women's liberation movement, the "second wave" of twentieth-century feminism.[1] Influenced and inspired by the Civil Rights, anti-Viet Nam war, and "free love" movements during the 1960s, the women's liberation movement is thought to have officially begun in 1963, when Betty Friedan published *The Feminine Mystique,* and the Presidential Commission on the Status of Women released its report on gender inequality. Freidan's widely read book exposed "the problem that has no name," exploring the costs for middle-class women of seeking fulfillment primarily through their husbands and children.[2] The Commission's report also opened women's and men's eyes to the gender discrimination that informed all aspects of American life, and eventually led to the formation of the National Organization for Women (NOW), with Friedan as one of the founding members.

During this period, many women poets began writing about experiences, injustices, and issues that disproportionately affect women – pregnancy and childbirth, child rearing, female sexuality, domestic violence and sexual abuse – but this chapter will focus on writers whose work can be identified explicitly as feminist, who see themselves as participating in a project that arises out of a "concern with women's political struggles and the place of literary expression in women's lives."[3] Although they are all engaged in a critique of patriarchy and of women's historical exclusion from the literary canon, there is little consensus among them about how best to articulate and enact a feminist position in poetry. For the sake of providing a discursive framework, I have divided feminist poetry into three provisional categories. The first describes both radical and mainstream feminist poets whose work engages the voice-centered lyric of much of the poetry of this period, but focuses on revising and revaluing cultural understandings of the feminine and enacting a direct critique of masculinist values. The second group, multicultural feminist poets, also rely on expressive language and are concerned with gender, but their work foregrounds differences, embracing a poetics of multiplicity – what Gloria Anzaldúa has called a *"mestiza consciousness"* – and criticizing the heterosexist, classist, and racist blind spots of mainstream feminism.[4] The third group, experimental feminist poets who have been influenced by the poststructuralist critique of subjectivity and language, endeavor to create a poetry that interrogates the patriarchal structures and assumptions that are embedded in language itself, rejecting dominant modes of expression and calling attention to the artifice of all textual constructions.

The Mainstream Lyric

The feminist poetry that initially gained recognition during the 1970s and 1980s drew on modes of expression and ideologies that informed contemporaneous movements such as confessional poetry, the Beats, and the Black Arts movement. Declaring that the "personal is political," this mode of feminist poetry self-consciously melds private, individual experience with public concerns, blending "the subjective and collective."[5] Many of the ideas that became central to this mode of feminist poetry were articulated by Adrienne Rich in her widely anthologized 1971 essay, "When We Dead Awaken: Writing as Re-vision." In an early articulation of what Elaine Showalter would later term gynocriticism, Rich calls for "a radical critique of literature, feminist in its impulse" that would recognize and resist the ways the dominant literary tradition has constructed a particular version of femininity.[6] But more importantly for feminist poetry, she calls for the exploration of "a whole new psychic geography" and the discovery of a language and images that could map and build that new consciousness.[7] Using her own development as a poet as her example, Rich analyzes the self-repression into which she was indoctrinated during the 1950s and 1960s and charts her slow emergence into consciousness. She describes her decision to give up the protective "asbestos gloves" of traditional form and feminine decorum in order to access the potentially corrosive material that might arise from an honest exploration of her experiences as a woman, mother, and wife.[8] Rich proposes an alternate tradition in which women would no longer write "for" men, or with men in mind, but would "speak to and of women in … poems, out of a newly released courage to name, to love each other, to share risk and grief and celebration."[9] She also valorizes the connections that might form between women, emphasizing collaboration instead of the solipsistic "I" of post-Romanticism.

Muriel Rukeyser, who began writing in the 1930s under the influence of Modernism, had long been engaged in the kind of revisioning work Rich calls for in her essay. The feminist note in Rukeyser's work grew more pronounced as second-wave feminism took hold, but as early as the 1950s, she was writing poems that would become touchstones for feminist poetry and for the women's movement. Even poems from Rukeyser's first book, *Theory of Flight* (1935), portray a burgeoning feminist consciousness, although the voice is more decorous and restrained than in later work. In the long title poem, Rukeyser appropriates the airplane, making it an instrument for "political, sexual, and poetic liberation," in contrast to the masculinity and militarism it represented at the time.[10] Through the activity of the airplane, "sky, earth, and their meeting place" are blurred and merged; all of space becomes "one punctuated flowing."[11]

Rukeyser also began pointedly questioning the roles women were required to play quite early in her career, in poems like "More of a Corpse than a Woman," from *U.S. 1* (1938), and "Anne Burlak," from *A Turning Wind* (1939), in which she celebrates the leader of the National Textile Workers' Union: "Let her be seen, a voice on a platform, heard / as a city is heard."[12] But it is in *The Speed of Darkness* (1968) that Rukeyser abandons formal and rhetorical restraint, engaging a looser line in language that is distinctly unpoetic, though full of urgency. "The Poem as Mask," which champions true self-expression – "There is no mountain, there is no god, there is memory / of my torn life, myself split open" – became iconic of feminist poetics through its place as the epigraph to *No More Masks!*, one of the first popular anthologies dedicated to women's poetry.[13] She also wrote directly and without shame about women's bodies and sexuality, depicting menstruation, orgasm, pregnancy, and childbirth. In the title poem, she writes:

> Whoever despises the clitoris despises the penis
> Whoever despises the penis despises the cunt
> Whoever despises the cunt despises the life of the child[14]

Using anaphora to convey the power of her convictions and to create a physical, indefatigable energy, Rukeyser insists on the giving value of the sexual body and reclaims the derogatory term "cunt" from its misogynistic context.

In her poem "Kathe Kollwitz," Rukeyser asks, "What would happen if one woman told the truth about her life? / The world would split open," and a whole generation of poets responded.[15] Adrienne Rich, who played an important role in bringing Rukeyser's work to the attention of writers and critics, was probably the most central figure in further establishing and defining the contours of this feminist aesthetic. Rich began publishing her poetry in the 1950s. W. H. Auden chose her first book, *A Change of World* (1951), for the Yale Younger Poets prize and praised her poems for their "detachment from the self and its emotions."[16] But over the next thirty years, Rich would move away from detachment, restraint, and decorum in her efforts to find a form and a language for her developing feminist consciousness and create an aesthetic in which "the woman in the poem and the woman writing the poem become the same person."[17]

Diving into the Wreck: Poems 1971–73 and *The Dream of a Common Language: Poems 1974–77* mark a sea-change in Rich's work. In language that is clear, direct, and passionate, Rich conducts an analysis of women's oppression, writing poems that recover and discover women's histories, celebrate women's self-determination, and explore female sexuality and desire. In "Rape," she indicts a culture in which "father" and "cop" perpetuate the victimization of women: "You have to confess / to him that you are guilty of the crime / of having been forced."[18] Poems like "For a Sister," "Translations," "Power," and "Paula Becker to Clara Westhoff" focus on ordinary and extraordinary women whose lives have been insufficiently recorded or recognized. In the revelatory title poem of *Diving Into the Wreck*, Rich appropriates the masculinized activity of deep sea diving to describe the difficult work of reimagining human life outside the strictures of patriarchy, and of the need to reclaim history – "the wreck and not the story of the wreck / the thing itself and not the myth"[19] – for those whose stories have been erased.

The poems in these collections also reflect Rich's coming out as a lesbian, elucidating the theory of a lesbian continuum developed in her important essay, "Compulsory Heterosexuality and Lesbian Existence," and articulating a feminine sexuality that is not defined by masculine desire.[20] In poems like "Phantasia for Elvira Shatayev," which like "Diving into the Wreck" appropriates a masculinized activity (mountain climbing), Rich posits an ideal of sisterhood and an alternative, intuitive mode of communication and communion that can be shared by women. Although the poem describes a failed women's climbing expedition of Lenin Peak in 1974, Rich uses their attempt as an inspiration and example of what might be possible if women work together. In "Twenty-one Love Poems," a series of poems that echoes but diverges from the traditional sonnet sequence, Rich establishes a precedent for describing emotional and sexual love between two women. In later works, like *An Atlas of the Difficult World* (1991) and *Dark Fields of the Republic* (1995), Rich develops a broader critique of patriarchy that recognizes the ways men and women from all classes, ethnicities, and regions suffer under its strictures.

Much of the feminist poetry that garnered attention during the 1970s and 1980s emphasizes the interconnections between social and personal lives in language that can articulate and claim an authentic self for women even as it appropriates forms and figures from poetic texts and traditions identified with male authorship. We can find examples in Judy Grahn's revisionary feminist epics, "The Queen of Wands" and "The Queen of Swords," in which she retells *The Odyssey* and reimagines the story of Helen of Troy, or Alicia Ostriker's poems about female biblical figures and her own experiences with breast cancer. Carolyn Kizer, Maxine Kumin, and Marilyn Hacker exemplify feminist poets who resist the assumption that working in traditional meters and forms keeps the poet from accessing volatile materials. Hacker has been very outspoken in insisting that the dominant literary tradition belongs to women and can be appropriated and reclaimed by them. Hacker's *Love, Death, and the Changing of the Seasons* (1986) is a sonnet sequence that recounts a love affair between a female teacher and her younger, female student. Immersing herself in the tradition of the sonnet sequence, Hacker celebrates, critiques, and revises its assumptions, themes, conventions and tropes, self-consciously resisting the objectification of women that seems to inhere in the form. Her beloved, Rachel, is depicted as both subject and object, writing her own poems and, once the two become lovers, participating in sexual activity as a desiring and active partner – and Hacker uses both crass and lyrical language to describe that sexuality. In one poem, she tells her beloved, Rachel, exactly what she wants: "First, I want to make you come in my hand / while I watch you and kiss you."[21] Whereas the beloved in the traditional sonnet sequence is silent, in the poem "What You Might Answer," Hacker imagines what Rachel, her beloved, might say in response to Hacker's romanticization of her: "Nobody needs her Frye boots cast in bronze. / I don't like crowds and now I'm feeling crowded."[22] By including many poems that depict the unremarkable, quotidian lives of the couple – including sonnets about cooking and clothes shopping – Hacker renders the lesbian love affair unexceptional. At the same time, she graphically and aggressively depicts lesbian desire and sexuality in order to celebrate and foreground that difference, arguing for unconventional understandings of gender and sexuality in a supremely conventional form.

Feminist Poets and Identity Politics

Influenced by, but distinct from, poets like Rich, Hacker, Grahn, and Ostriker, women poets of color began to formulate their own aesthetic during the early 1980s, demonstrating a commitment to gender equity but also articulating their communities' ongoing experiences of sexism, racism, and poverty – experiences that were not fully recognized or addressed by the largely white, middle-class women's liberation movement. While their work focuses on personal experience and uses direct language, their focus and the direction of their anger are quite distinct. Critical of the assumptions about shared experiences that inform mainstream feminist poetry, their work describes an acute awareness of fluid and conflicting identity categories, emphasizing differences of class, race, ethnicity, and sexuality and describing a "differential consciousness ... a new kind of subjectivity developed under conditions of multiple oppression."[23] As Chela Sandoval explains, "differential consciousness permits the practitioner to choose tactical positions, that is, to self-consciously break and reform ties to ideology."[24] Instead of articulating or revealing a previously unknown feminine identity, multicultural feminist poets weave "between and among" various oppositional ideologies and political strategies.[25]

Sonia Sanchez, Audre Lorde, and June Jordan are all African-American feminist poets whose writing is rooted in a Black Arts aesthetic that rejects the hegemony of the dominant literary tradition and treats poetry as a means of constructive political activism. The "differential consciousness" they develop embraces multiple positions: their work indicts sexism and homophobia within the African-American community and the racism of white, mainstream feminism. Like Rich, Audre Lorde is known as much for her essays and activism as for her poetry. In her poetry and in her life, she embraced the multiple, sometimes incompatible, identity positions she occupied. She conceived of herself as a "Sister Outsider" (the title of her essay collection), positioning herself simultaneously inside (a sister, connected by blood) and outside the feminist, gay, and African-American communities to which she belonged. As Rudolph Byrd suggests, the term "illustrates the ways in which Lorde reclaimed and transformed overlapping, discredited, and marginalized identities – black, lesbian, feminist – into a powerful, radical and progressive standpoint."[26] Her poems express outrage at racism and sexism, delineating the violence that can exist in both private and public lives, and describing the difficulties of childbirth and raising children, the struggle for voice, and the dishonesty of silence. "Sister Outsider" also vividly depicts the sexism and homophobia Lorde experienced within the African-American community.

In *The Black Unicorn* (1978), Lorde fully articulates her sense of her own multiplicity, of inhabiting numerous and sometimes conflicting identities: black woman, mother, daughter, lesbian, feminist. "From the House of Yemanja" describes her sense of inheriting a doubleness from her mother, having had it "cooked" into her: "My mother had two faces and a frying pot / where she cooked up her daughters / into girls."[27] In this collection,

Lorde laments the history of the black diaspora, reclaiming African mythology and calling on female African gods for wisdom, strength, and endurance. In "A Woman Speaks," the "not white" female speaker is a god or spirit whose magic "is unwritten" but powerful, and who can cross boundaries between new and old, male and female: "beware my smile" she warns, "I am treacherous with old magic / and the moon's new fury."[28] Other poems also insist on the mutablility of identity and situate this sense of "both/and" in an African-American matriarchal tradition.

This insistence on vital differences within unity also characterizes the writings of other feminist poets of color. Latina writers Cherríe Moraga and Gloria Anzaldúa explore gender oppression and feminine sexuality, rewriting myths of female empowerment, and indicting the homophobia and misogyny within the Chicano community as well as the racism of the wider culture. Their influential anthology, *This Bridge Called My Back: Writings by Radical Women of Color* (1982), explores the alienation from mainstream feminism experienced by women writers of color. In their introduction, Moraga and Anzaldúa explain their desire to "express to all women – especially to white middle-class women – the experiences which divide us as feminists."[29] The anthology is ethnically, racially, and generically mixed, including personal memoirs, didactic essays, letters, and poetry by women of color from many backgrounds. Moraga and Anzaldúa emphasize that the feminism of the writers included in the anthology is rooted not only in gender oppression, but in their cultural backgrounds: "our feminist politic emerges from the roots of both of our cultural oppression and heritage."[30]

Anzaldúa articulates the specific multiplicities that inform her thinking and her writing in "*La conciencia de la mestiza.*" In this important essay, she foregrounds the power of the imagination to overcome incompatible world views and the possibility of developing a new "consciousness of the Borderlands," which involves the recognition of "cultural collisions," the development of "tolerance for contradictions, a tolerance for ambiguity," and the breakdown of the "subject/object duality" that undergirds Western thought and culture.[31] Enacting the celebration of multiplicity, Anzaldúa's and Moraga's work is linguistically and formally hybrid, moving between Spanish and English and incorporating discursive writing, fables, and poems. Even in the introduction to her landmark work, *Loving In the War Years*, Moraga establishes that the text will be multiple: "Este libro covers a span of seven years of writing."[32] *Loving In the War Years* includes Moraga's much anthologized essay, "La Güera" (the fair-skinned girl or woman), in which she explores the legacy of being from a mixed-race family. In vivid, emotional language, Moraga describes the consciousness that results from occupying multiple positions of oppression and confronting the internalized racism, classism, and homophobia that exists "not only outside [her] skin, but inside [her] skin."[33]

The idea of multiple selves and conflicting oppressions also informs the work of American Indian feminist poets like Joy Harjo, Linda Hogan, and Leslie Marmon Silko. But American Indian belief systems create a differential consciousness in their work that is distinct from that of other feminist poets of color. Harjo has said that she is "woman identified," but her feminist identity does not fit easily into American Indian belief systems, which value community over the individual, blur the boundaries between waking and dreaming, and take an alinear approach to time. As Kim Whitehead has pointed out, "the roots of feminism in Western ideas of individual rights and freedoms and its tendency to emphasize a vision that deals with only one half of the community makes it in many ways an alien concept in tribal settings."[34] Harjo draws on an oral tradition of communal songs, chants, and prayers, and includes references to stories and mythic figures from her native heritage: Harjo's father was Creek and her mother part French and part Cherokee; Harjo herself is an enrolled member of the Muscogee Creek tribe. The decimation of American Indian tribes and culture in the United States gives the preservation of tribal myths and histories within the writings of these poets a real urgency. The poem "Remember" is a chant in which Harjo calls on readers and on herself to remember their connection to the natural world and to family, but also to "the plants, trees, animal life who all have their / tribes, their families, their histories, too. Talk to them, / listen to them. They are alive poems."[35]

Harjo and the other multicultural feminist poets I have been discussing attempt to enact a differential consciousness that can oppose the reductiveness and exclusivity they encounter in mainstream feminist poetry. But for the most part, despite some experimentation with form, their feminism is inscribed primarily through content and "revisionary" perspectives: language is treated as transparent, and it is clear that they believe direct expression can best accomplish their transformative goals. By the 1980s, scholars and critics like Sandra Gilbert, Suzanne Juhasz, and Alicia Ostriker were developing rubrics for situating and legitimizing this alternative tradition. Ostriker's *Stealing the Language: The Emergence of Women's Poetry in America*, one of the most influential critical volumes that appeared during this period, reflects the belief, shared by many other feminist critics and poets writing at the time, that women's poetry can "illuminate the condition of women and therefore of humanity in an unprecedented way" – making the unknown visible, making what was once unintelligible legible.[36] Ostriker argues that women's poetry "exists in much the same way that 'American poetry' exists," and she traces an aesthetic that relies largely on the kind of direct expression that is characteristic of poets like Rich, Hacker, Lorde, Moraga, and Harjo.

The Critique of Language and Subjectivity

Not all feminist poets or feminist critics agree that direct, representational language can provide this illumination or that there is an authentic femininity that can be made legible. During this same period, a diverse group of women poets were developing an oppositional feminist poetics that not only resisted male-generated images of the feminine, but disrupted normative ideas about language and subjectivity, questioning the legitimacy of all forms of definition, including that of an essential femininity, distorted or otherwise. Often fragmented and disjunctive, the work of these experimental feminist poets is characterized by digression, interruption, and narrative discontinuity, often blurring the boundaries between poetry and theory, lyric and narrative, and imaginative and critical writing. By shifting the boundaries of the poem to include its most material features, thus opening it up to "the world and particularly to the reader," these works involve the reader in the production of meaning and also call attention to the poem's construction.[37]

In ":RE:THINKING:LITERARY:FEMINISM," Joan Retallack calls the kinds of poetry that Ostriker valorizes a "picture theory of women's liberation," one that depends on mimesis, drawing "images from life to present them as (like) replicas in the text."[38] Retallack sees such poetries as limited because the imperative for accessibility ends up requiring "reverent uses of the very constructions that contain the injustice. To depict may be to trigger an image in the mind's eye/I, but does it reconfigure the grounds for major conceptual change?"[39] Retallack argues that poetry that uses direct, clear language, even when depicting female experiences that had previously been devalued or suppressed, confirms a "centered, unitary," and ultimately masculinist definition of subjectivity.[40] Instead of images of the female – empowered or otherwise – Retallack calls for "enactments of the feminine" that trouble assumptions about gender and subjectivity and also disrupt grammar and syntax, treating language as a dynamic system.[41]

Kathleen Fraser and Rachel Blau DuPlessis have long been producing the kind of "joyful, troublesome, gender/genre exploding" poetry Retallack envisions in her essay.[42] Fraser has written of her initial excitement in the 1970s about the possibilities the women's movement created for young poets like herself: "Finally, one imagined, there would be a warm room where the multiple styles of women's minds and bodies and poetics languages could flower."[43] But she found that her own poetic impulses, which tended toward the disjunctive and "troublesome," did not find a home in the journals – *Conditions*, *Sinister Wisdom* or *13th Moon* – that were championing women's poetry. Instead of treating it "as a place of self-expression, for giving a true account, for venting rage," Fraser wanted her poetry to express her experience of feminine "multiplicity and fragmentation" structurally, and she worked to link grammar, syntax, and formal qualities to the female body and female subjectivity.[44] Fraser's subject matter in *In Defiance of the Rains* (1969), her earliest linguistically and formally innovative work, is often just as focused on feminine experience as that of her more expressive contemporaries. But as Linda Kinnahan suggests, by using mixed typography and the white space of the page, Fraser engages "the lyrical without following familiar and constraining scripts of voice, emotion and self."[45] The poems structurally reflect the interruption, digression, and cyclicity that inhere in pregnancy and child rearing.

In addition to contributing her own work to what she called "The Tradition of Marginality," Fraser was central to the founding of the journal *HOW(ever)*, which published six volumes between 1983 and 1992 and became a groundbreaking venue for experimental women poets and feminist inquiry. Fraser worked with a number of editors – Beverly Dahlen, Frances Jeffer, Susan Gevirtz, Carolyn Burke, and Rachel Blau DuPlessis – who shared her feelings of alienation from both the mainstream feminist community and the seemingly male-dominated experimental writing community known as the "Language school." DuPlessis has also contributed to the field of experimental feminist poetry and poetics, both as an explicator and practitioner. In *The Pink Guitar: Writing as Feminist Practice* (1990), DuPlessis explores the question of a "woman's aesthetic" and delineates strategies that she and others have used to "depoeticize: reject normal claims of beauty. Smoothness. Finish. Fitness. Decoration. Moving sentiment. Uplift."[46] Moving between feminist theory, poetics, and literary history, the essays that make up *The Pink Guitar* resist the logical structures and linear trajectory expected of literary criticism. The chapters/essays incorporate quotations from other artists and writers without any introduction or contextualization; Duplessis follows a principle of juxtaposition and contingency instead of incorporation and elucidation. In all of her writings, DuPlessis emphasizes rupture. Paragraphs may begin mid-sentence, and connections between paragraphs are often associative instead of strictly logical: "I struggle to break into the sentences that of course I am capable of writing smoothly. I want to distance. To rupture. Why? In part because of the gender contexts in which these words have lived, of which they taste."[47]

The Pink Guitar includes chapters on other experimental feminist poets, but like Rich in "When We Dead Awaken," DuPlessis uses her own poetry to demonstrate what a poetry of feminine rupture might look like. In the essay "Otherhow," she explains that in her poem, "Writing," she "put words on the margin [to] try to break into the lyric center with many simultaneous writings occupying the same page space. I overwrite or interleave typeset lines of writing with my own handwriting, not trying to obliterate or neutralize, but to – to what? To erode some attitude toward reading and writing."[48] "Writing" can be understood as the predecessor to her canto-like, serial, epic poem, *Drafts*, which she has been working on since 1986.[49] Written over the course of twenty-two years, *Drafts 1–38: Toll* (2001) and *Drafts 39–57, Pledge with Draft unnumbered: Précis* (2004) challenge the masculine privilege of the epic and exemplify the specifically feminist project of her work. Instead of a narrative chronicle that can overturn central Western texts like the *Iliad* and the *Odyssey*, DuPlessis writes a (post)modernist epic that contrasts with modernist-era masculinist works like Ezra Pound's Cantos and T. S. Eliot's "The Waste Land." She appropriates their formal innovations and self-consciously incorporates a "feminist consciousness of language and its capacity to shape identity and experience."[50]

Even though it is ordered chronologically, *Drafts* accrues a web of interrelated and self-reflexive meanings. DuPlessis shifts fluidly between registers and tones, moving from personal anecdote to social commentary, incorporating phrases, fragments, repetitions, and gaps, splicing in snippets from other texts. There is no narrative thread or single speaker, but the focus on feminine identity is clear from the very first cantos: "Draft 1: It" establishes the non-neutrality of "it," and the inadequacies of pronouns to depict identity; "Draft 2: She" explores gendered language and the embedded meanings within words. In these poems, DuPlessis also makes use of the page to signal ideas that cannot be expressed in grammar, syntax, and semantics alone. In "Draft 5: Gap," dark rectangles block out parts of the poem, evoking the censor's pen and the self-censorship women perpetuate in order to make themselves acceptable or appealing. *Drafts* is an ongoing, open-ended project; the title underscores the non-mastery of her ambitions, and the provisional, feminized "and/or" position DuPlessis valorizes.

A number of experimental feminist poets – Rae Armantrout, Lyn Hejinian, Carla Harryman, and Leslie Scalapino – were part of the West Coast Language writing movement of the 1970s and 1980s. During this period, Language writing was widely perceived as a male prerogative and masculine terrain, and women "tended to [be] represent[ed] … as secondary participants or … passive benefactors."[51] In "Feminist Poetics and the Meaning of Clarity," Armantrout explores this question, recounting her response to being asked (by Language poet Charles Bernstein), "Why don't women do language-oriented writing?"[52] Armantrout writes that her initial response "was that, as an oppressed group, women have a more urgent need to describe the conditions of their lives."[53] But she comes to question this assumption, asking "whether the nature of women's oppression can be best expressed in the poem that ... 'looks conventional.'"[54] Following Lacan's formulation that women are positioned outside the symbolic order, Armantrout suggests that if this *lack* of access to meaning making is one of the conditions of women's existence, then transparent language and conventional narrative may not in fact be the best form for describing those conditions: As outsiders, women might, in fact, be well positioned to appreciate the constructedness of identity, and therefore to challenge the contemporary poetic convention of the unified voice.[55] Providing examples from the "open" poetry of Lyn Hejinian and Lorine Neidecker, Armantrout argues that such work is "dynamic" and "contrapuntal" and achieves a more accurate picture of the contradictions and self-divisions that inform feminine identity and women's lives.[56]

Although Language writers like Armantrout, Hejinian, and Harryman employ similar techniques of rupture and disjunction, their work must be differentiated from that of DuPlessis and Fraser. Rather than asserting that there is such a thing as a feminine form or that language or form itself is somehow gendered, their work explores "the relations among knowledge, language and gender."[57] In her essay "La Faustienne," Hejinian compares Geothe's Faust's ways of "acquiring knowledge" with those of Scheherazade, who knows by "making."[58] Hejinian suggests that Faust's pursuit of knowledge is linked to colonialism, sexism, and the abuse of power, whereas Scheherazade pursues "knowing," an activity that is generative and saves a life. As Megan Simpson has suggested, the "Faustienne" (note the feminization of the adjective) quest to make and produce knowing, as opposed to acquiring knowledge, is the driving impulse in Hejinian's writing from early works like *Writing as an Aid to Memory* (1978), with its title that suggests that writing produces memory and knowledge, to more recent works like *Happily* (2000) and *A Border Comedy* (2001).

My Life, Hejinian's widely read, unconventional "autobiography," appears to have the hallmarks of "women's writing," announcing its relationship to interiority with its title. While it includes some content that can be understood as "personal," however, *My Life* does not present an intimate narrative of Hejinian's life. Each section mixes descriptive sentences with aphorisms and philosophical observations, shifting without logic from the past to the present and back again. The unit of construction is the sentence, but within sections, the sentences do not build into linear narratives:

> A moment yellow, just as four years later, when my father returned home from the war, the moment of greeting him, as he stood at the bottom of the

stairs, younger, thinner than when he had left, was purple – though moments are no longer so colored. Somewhere, in the background, rooms share a pattern of small roses. Pretty is as pretty does. In certain families, the meaning of necessity is at one with the sentiment of prenecessity. The better things were gathered in a pen.[59]

Hejinian uses parataxis to create gaps in logic, and phrases repeat from section to section, their meanings altered by a new context. Instead of a clear narrative of a life, *My Life* creates a sense of what is involved in the production of consciousness. As Simpson notes, "when writing explores the gaps and uncertainty in meaning and representation that mark the limits of language, as Hejinian's writing does through description, the world is not so much discovered as called into being."[60]

Susan Howe's work is experimental and distinctly feminist, although it is also distinct from Language writing. Howe's primary interest is in history: personal, geographical, colonial, and literary. Even more than DuPlessis and Fraser, Howe uses typography and the white page to foreground the visual, sonic, and material qualities of language. Her poems are word collages that call attention to the gaps between histories and ideologies and within language. Howe's most readily identifiable works like "Thorow" and "A Bibliography of the King's Book, or Eikon Basilike" emphasize the visual and material aspects of language: lines of the poems criss-cross horizontally, vertically, and at various angles, frustrating readerly expectations of a place to begin reading, or a place to end. While the sentence functions as the unit of exploration for Hejinian, for Howe, each page in a work operates as a unit, in the same way that the stanza might work in more conventional poetry. This excerpt from *The Secret History of the Dividing Line* (1979), which in part is a meditation on William Byrd's published survey of the border between Virginia and North Carolina in 1728, can provide some sense of the way Howe treats language as material:

> sh dispel iris sh snow sward wide ha
> forest 1 boundary manic a land sh
> whit thing : target cadence marked on
> O about both or don't INDICATION Americ
> sh woof subdued toward foliage free sh [61]

Erasures, elisions, and effacements have taken place: parts of words and of phrases are missing. Boundaries, marks, and indicators are evoked, as is a particular place, "Americ" – even though something has been cut off or out. The repetition of "sh" suggests both comfort and silencing, as well as an abbreviated feminine pronoun. DuPlessis has suggested that the evocation of silence in Howe's work is "a trope for an anti-authoritarian practice. The foregrounding of otherness. The critique of centers, hierarchies, authorities. The suspicion of dominant meaning."[62]

Part of Howe's project is to "recover the varied female, feminine and feminized voices of the past, to render audible what she refers to … as the 'silenced factions' from their 'destiny of calamitous silence' to which traditional historiography has banished them."[63] As she writes in the prologue to *The Europe of Trusts* (1990), "I wish I could tenderly lift, from the dark side of history, voices that are anonymous, slighted – inarticulate."[64] Many of those voices are feminine, and in *The Liberties* (1980), included in *The Europe of Trusts*, Howe conducts an extensive interrogation of the suppression of the feminine from social and literary histories, and within patriarchal language, alluding to a number of female figures "in various states of exile and silence."[65] Her primary focus is on the effaced history of Hester (Esther) Johnson, whom Jonathan Swift referred to as "Stella," and who for twenty-eight years was central to Swift's life and yet never had an official role in his world. As Lynn Keller explains, "Her near-erasure from the historical record and her thwarted self-definition typify what Howe sees as the situation of women in history."[66] The poem collages together snippets from texts that are connected, however tangentially, to Stella's existence, but instead of constructing yet another portrait that also obfuscates the person of Esther Johnson, Howe reconstructs "some of the processes by which Stella's 'real' identity was erased from history."[67] Howe's project of revision and recovery also extends to her invaluable critical studies, *The Birth Mark* (1993) and *My Emily Dickinson* (1985). The latter examines Dickinson's life and work in the context of the constrictions under which she wrote, presenting her as a subversive figure who has been fetishized and marginalized by a predominantly male literary establishment.

Howe's deformation and use of other texts to call attention to the gaps in history, particularly in relationship to women, has influenced a new generation of feminist poets who use similar techniques with quite different effects, including a number of poets of color. Harryette Mullen's *Muse and Drudge* (1995), M. Nourbese Philips's *Zong!* (2008), and Theresa Hak Kyung Cha's *DICTÉE* (1982) are just a handful of books that engage a disjunctive aesthetic to explore issues of racial identity and colonialism as they intersect with gender oppression.

In the late 1980s and early 1990s, a number of critical studies were published that identify and delineate the parameters of feminist poetry in more complex terms. Jan Montefiore, Kim Whitehead, and Liz Yorke, for example, engage in psychoanalytic and poststructuralist theories to suggest that feminist poetry is polyvocal and presents a complex vision of gendered identity. But they keep their focus on poets like Rich, Lorde, Sylvia Plath, and other "expressive" writers, ignoring or overlooking more experimental, avant-garde feminist poets. More recently, beginning with Ann Vickery's *Leaving Lines of Gender: A Feminist Genealogy of Language Writing* (2000), scholars like Elisabeth Frost, Linda Kinnahan, and Megan Simpson have begun to chart the evolution of this tradition of experimental feminist poets. On the one hand, the interrogations of language and subjectivity continue to seem problematic for feminist poets who find the challenges of innovative and experimental work too opaque to engender change or speak to all women. On the other, for experimental feminist poets, poetry that treats language as transparent seems too essentialist and naïve about its own constructions to effect change. As recent anthologies of women's poetry that have brought together poetry from both sides of the divide demonstrate, the effect of these conflicts around representation has been, paradoxically, not a narrower but a more inclusive and more varied body of work that can reasonably be identified as feminist.

NOTES

1. Alicia Ostriker, *Stealing the Language: The Emergence of Women's Poetry in America* (Boston: Beacon Press, 1986), 7.
2. The phrase is the title of the first chapter of Betty Friedan's, *The Feminine Mystique* (New York: W. W. Norton, 1983).
3. Kim Whitehead, *The Feminist Poetry Movement* (Jackson: University Press of Mississippi, 1996), xiii.
4. Gloria Anzaldúa, "*La conciencia de la Mestiza*: Towards a New Consciousness," *Writing the Body: Female Embodiment and Feminist Theory*, eds. K. Conboy, N. Medina, and S. Stanbury (New York: Columbia University Press, 1997), 236.
5. Whitehead, 37.
6. Adrienne Rich, *On Lies, Secrets and Silence: Selected Prose 1966–1978* (New York: W. W. Norton, 1979), 35.
7. Ibid.
8. Ibid., 40.
9. Ibid., 49.
10. Lexi Rudnitsky, "Planes, Politics, and Protofeminist Poetics: Muriel Rukeyser's 'Theory of Flight' and *The Middle of the Air*," *Tulsa Studies in Women's Literature* 27.2 (Fall 2008), 240.
11. Muriel Rukeyser, *A Muriel Rukeyser Reader*, ed. Jan Heller (New York: W. W. Norton, 1994), 12.
12. Ibid., 61.
13. Ibid., 213. See also Florence Howe and Ellen Bass, *No More Masks! An Anthology of Poems by Women* (Garden City, NY: Anchor Press, 1973), 1.
14. Rukeyser, 228.
15. Ibid., 217.
16. Rich, *A Change of World: Poems*, with a foreword by W. H. Auden (Hartford, CT: Yale University Press 1951), 8.

17. Rich, *On Lies, Secrets and Silence*, 47.
18. Rich, *Diving into the Wreck: Poems 1971–1972* (New York: W. W. Norton, 1973), 44.
19. Ibid., 23.
20. This essay was originally collected in Adrienne Rich, *Blood Bread and Poetry: Selected Prose 1979–1985* (New York: W. W. Norton, 1985).
21. Marilyn Hacker, *Love, Death, and the Changing of the Seasons* (New York: Norton, 1986), 21.
22. Ibid., 35.
23. Paula M. L. Moya, "Chicana Feminism and Postmodernist Theory," *Signs* 26.2 (Winter 2001), 461.
24. Chela Sandoval, "U.S. Third World Feminism: The Theory and Method of Oppositional Consciousness in the Postmodern World," *Genders* 10 (Spring 1991), 5.
25. Ibid., 13–14.
26. Rudolph Byrd, "Introduction," *I Am Your Sister: Collected and Unpublished Writings of Audre Lorde*, eds. Rudolph P. Byrd, Johnnetta Betsch Cole, and Beverly Guy-Sheftall (Oxford: Oxford University Press, 2009), 5.
27. Audre Lorde, *The Collected Poems of Audre Lorde* (New York: W. W. Norton, 1997), 233.
28. Ibid., 234.
29. Cherríe Moraga and Gloria Anzaldúa, eds., *This Bridge Called My Back: Writing by Radical Women of Color* (New York: Kitchen Table: Women of Color Press, 1983), xxiii.
30. Ibid., xxiv.
31. Anzaldúa, p. 235.
32. Moraga, *Loving in the War Years: Lo Que Nunca Paso por Sus Labios* (Cambridge, MA: South End Press, 2000), i.
33. Moraga and Anzaldúa, 30.
34. Whitehead, 156.
35. Joy Harjo, *She Had Some Horses: Poems* (New York: W. W. Norton, 1983), 40.
36. Ostriker, 13.
37. Lyn Hejinian, *The Language of Inquiry* (Berkeley: University of California Press, 2000), 43.
38. Joan Retallack, *The Poethical Wager* (Berkeley: University of California Press, 2003), 115.
39. Ibid., 118.
40. Ibid., 117.
41. Ibid., 122.
42. Ibid., 118.
43. Kathleen Fraser, *Translating the Unspeakable: Essays by Kathleen Fraser* (Tuscaloosa: University of Alabama Press, 2000), 31.
44. Ibid., 33.
45. Linda A. Kinnahan, *Lyric Interventions: Feminism Experimental Poetry and Contemporary Discourse* (Iowa City: University of Iowa Press, 2004), 65.
46. Rachel Blau DuPlessis, *The Pink Guitar: Writing as Feminist Practice* (New York and London: Routledge, 1990), 144.
47. Ibid.

48. Ibid., 148.
49. See "Knit and knot and gloam and glare," in *Jacket* for a discussion of the relationship between "Writing" and *Drafts*, http://jacketmagazine.com/35/r-duplessis-rb-durgin.shtml
50. Kinnahan, 19.
51. Ann Vickery, *Leaving Lines of Gender: A Feminist Genealogy of Language Writing* (Hanover, ME and London: Wesleyan University Press, 2000), 12.
52. Rae Armantrout, "Feminist Poetics and the Meaning of Clarity," *An Anthology of New Poetics*, ed. Christopher Beach (Tuscaloosa: University of Alabama Press, 1998), 287.
53. Ibid.
54. Ibid.
55. Ibid., 288.
56. Ibid., 290.
57. Megan Simpson, *Poetic Epistemologies: Gender and Knowing in Women's Language Oriented Writing* (Albany: State University of New York Press, 2000), ix.
58. Hejinian, *The Language of Inquiry*, 252.
59. Lyn Hejinian, *My Life* (Los Angeles: Sun & Moon Press, 1987), 7.
60. Simpson, 26.
61. Susan Howe, *Frame Structures: Early Poems, 1974–1979* (New York: New Directions, 1996), 122.
62. DuPlessis, 133.
63. Simpson, 6.
64. Susan Howe, *The Europe of Trusts* (New York: New Directions, 1990), 14.
65. Rachel Tzivia Back, *Led By Language: The Poetry and Poetics of Susan Howe* (Tuscaloosa: University of Alabama Press, 2002), 70.
66. Lynn Keller, *Forms of Expansion: Recent Long Poems by Women* (Chicago: University of Chicago Press, 1997), 197.
67. Ibid., 198.

FURTHER READING

DuPlessis, Rachel Blau. *The Pink Guitar: Writing as Feminist Practice*. New York and London: Routledge, 1990.

Fraser, Kathleen. *Translating the Unspeakable: Essays by Katheleen Fraser*. Tuscaloosa: University of Alabama Press, 2000.

Frost, Elisabeth. *The Feminist Avant-Garde in American Poetry*. Iowa City: University of Iowa Press, 2003.

Hinton, Laura and Cynthia Hogue, eds. *We Who Love to Be Astonished: Experimental Women's Writing and Performance Poetics*. Tuscaloosa: University of Alabama Press, 2001.

Howe, Susan. *My Emily Dickinson*. New York: New Directions, 2007.

Keller, Lynn. *Forms of Expansion: Recent Long Poems by Women*. Chicago: University of Chicago Press, 1997.

Kinnahan, Linda, A. *Lyric Interventions: Feminism Experimental Poetry and Contemporary Discourse*. Iowa City: University of Iowa Press, 2004.

Middlebrook, Diane and Marilyn Yalom, eds. *Coming to Light: American Women Poets in the Twentieth Century*. Ann Arbor: University of Michigan Press, 1985.

Lorde, Audre. *Sister Outsider Essays and Speeches*. Berkeley, CA: Crossing Press, 2007.

Montefiore, Jan. *Feminism and Poetry: Language, Experience, Identity in Women's Writing*. San Francisco: HarperCollins, 1994.

Moraga, Cherríe and Gloria Anzaldúa, eds. *This Bridge Called My Back: Writing by Radical Women of Color*. New York: Kitchen Table: Women of Color Press, 1983.

O'Reilly, Andrea, ed. *From Motherhood to Mothering: The Legacy of Adrienne Rich's Of Woman Born*. Albany: State University of New York Press, 2004.

Ostriker, Alicia. *Stealing the Language: The Emergence of Women's Poetry in America*. Boston: Beacon Press, 1986.

Rankine, Claudia and Juliana Spahr, eds. *American Women Poets in the 21st Century: Where Lyric Meets Language*. Middletown, CT: Wesleyan University Press, 2002.

Retallack, Joan. *The Poethical Wager*. Berkeley: University of California Press, 2003.

Rich, Adrienne. *Blood Bread and Poetry: Selected Prose 1979–1985*. New York: W. W. Norton, 1985.

Rukeyser, Muriel. *A Muriel Rukeyser Reader*. Ed. Jan Heller. New York: W. W. Norton, 1994.

Whitehead, Kim. *The Feminist Poetry Movement*. Jackson: University Press of Mississippi, 1996.

9

NICK SELBY

Ecopoetries in America

Robert Frost's reading at John F. Kennedy's Presidential Inauguration on January 20, 1961 illustrates that in both political and poetic terms, occasions and environments matter. Frost, then nearly eighty-seven and America's unofficial poet laureate, found that the snow glare and sunshine on this cold bright day made it impossible for him to read the typescript of the poem he had written for the event. Instead he recited from memory 'The Gift Outright,' originally written in 1942. The poem depicts a sort of homespun wisdom in America's relation to, and uses of, the environment – the land – it inhabits; its rhetoric of expansive freedom, of America's mission into the wilderness, and of self-possession echoes the rhetoric of hope surrounding the occasion of Kennedy's presidency. But underlying the optimistic rhetoric we find an ambivalent defensiveness in the speaker's tracing of the relations between land, poem, and America:

> The land was ours before we were the land's.
> She was our land more than a hundred years
> Before we were her people. She was ours
> In Massachusetts, in Virginia,
> But we were England's, still colonials,
> Possessing what we still were unpossessed by,
> Possessed by what we now no more possessed.[1]

There are distinct ideological pressures felt here in the relationship set up between poetic power, as witnessed in the power of this poem as a lyric utterance, and the politics of power that are played out in myths of the land as the determinant of American identity (perhaps ironically mirrored in the pressure of the sun's glare upon Frost's poetic performance, as though the pressure of the natural world cannot help but define the poetic moment). Indeed, the questions with which Frost's poem confronts us serve well to begin a definition of what an environmental poetry ("ecopoetry," or even an "ecopoetics") in America would be. Just what sort of "possession" of the land can (or should) a poem envisage and enact? Why, or indeed how, can we read a poetics of the land as peculiarly American? At what points do the "environments" of poems and politics coincide? How might a poem be seen as an ecological intervention? What is the relation between the metaphorical and the "real" world of nature?

Two more questions that are implicitly posed by Frost's poem are also at the heart of this chapter's attempts to examine the environmentally oriented writing that has come to be called ecopoetry and to make an argument about some of its current directions and preoccupations in the United States. First is the question of how ecopoetry arises as a response to a perceived crisis in the modern, indeed postmodern, world. For many ecologically minded critics in the United States, the publication of Rachel Carson's *Silent Spring* in 1962 is the first articulation of a crisis, of an awareness of incipient and insidious ecological disaster. But in postmodern literary theories emerging at the same moment, the crisis was textual, one of representation in which a relativism with respect to values led to a profound disdain for precisely the sorts of grand narratives (such as global disaster) on which ecological awareness seemed to be predicated. The question then becomes, are ecopoetry and postmodernism inimical (with the former asserting, ultimately, that the earth we inhabit is always already a reality we ignore at our peril, and the latter asserting that even something so seemingly solid as the land we inhabit is, ultimately, an ideological construct)? This leads to a second question: how might a poem, or a reading of a poem, be ethically responsive to (and responsible for) the environment from which it emerges?

This chapter argues that to read poetry in a post-pastoral age (as Terry Gifford has called it) requires a delicately poised ethics of close reading, of response and responsibility to the local conditions of the poem.[2] If ecopoetry in America has a particular poetic and ethical force, this is because of its ability to draw on a poetic tradition in which questions of pastoral versus urban space, of ideas versus things, of open field composition, of suspicion about the role of metaphor within a culture that privileges metaphors of space, identity, and settlement, haunt the Emersonian proposition that America's very nature is poetic, that "America is a poem in our eyes."[3]

It is the contention of this chapter that as ecopoetry has developed in America, it has, increasingly, made play of the apparent gap between reading the world ecologically and reading the world as a poem. William Rueckert, in a 1978 essay that first used the term "ecocriticism" and that defines many of the issues with which ecocriticism continues to be concerned, emphasizes not only the interrelation between human and nonhuman nature, but that between two areas of intellectual endeavor: ecology and literary study. Ecopoetics depends on what Rueckert calls "the first law of ecology," namely that "Everything is connected to everything else."[4] More recently, Cheryll Glotfelty has noted that "ecocriticism takes an earth-centred approach to literary studies [... and] takes as its subject the interconnections between nature and culture."[5] Such descriptions are useful precisely because they see ecopoetics – and thus ecopoetry – not as a narrowly defined genre, but as a set of various practices and concerns, as an exploration (rather than definition) of the interrelated environments of poem and world. For Lawrence Buell, the question of environment is paramount: it is both the "measure" of an ecopoetics and – interestingly – "a discourse."[6] In making this point, Buell invokes Angus Fletcher's notion of the "environment-poem," one that "does not merely suggest or indicate an environment as part of its thematic meaning, but actually gets the reader to enter into the poem as if it were the reader's environment of living."[7] For Buell and Fletcher, both poem and world are discursive environments, dependent on each other for the meanings we read into them. And key to this understanding of the poem as environment is the "as if" in Fletcher's formulation. It is only through figurative and referential means that our lived environment can be experienced, much less understood, as such. Poetry is thus a structure of active engagement with reading as an environmentally conscious act. In this model, ecopoetry resists the tempting proposition of transcendence, where poem gestures to a reality somewhere outside the realm of the poem. Rather, ecopoetry lays bare the contingency between poem and world; both are environments in which we live.

As we shall see, Ecopoetries in America have – especially through an investment in lyric modes – sought to explore such contingencies and interdependencies. Given that conceptions of land, nature, and wilderness – and with them senses of place, space, and the pastoral – all feature in the development of an American imaginary, one that we have already witnessed at play in Frost's "The Gift Outright," it is not surprising that Frost is often seen as a starting point for considering what an American ecopoetry might look like. For J. Scott Bryson, Frost (along with Robinson Jeffers, Wallace Stevens, Marianne Moore, and William Carlos Williams) is the writer of "a new form of nature poetry" that is "antiromantic" in intention and thus heralds a new strain of ecological awareness in American poetry. Important both to a reading of Frost and to the history of ecopoetry in America more generally is the distinction that Kent C. Ryden makes when he seeks to recognize Frost not simply as a "nature poet," whose work focuses on a "separate and pristine natural world," but as one whose work is keenly engaged with "the social and cultural aspects of nature in New England."[8] The difference between seeing Frost as a "nature poet" and seeing him as an "ecopoet" (although Ryden does not explicitly name him as such) is instructive precisely because it declares that ecological awareness is about engagement with the Natural world, about a way of being in the world that is not merely passive spectatorship. Robert Faggen has claimed that one of Frost's most famous "nature poems," "The Oven Bird," "remains one of the greatest poems of the tension between the human and natural world."[9] Indeed this is clearly a poem that arises from Frost's keen environmental engagement, its speaker listening to, and meditating upon, "a singer everyone has heard." Finally, however, the hearing of the bird's song – the poem's own reading of that song and rendering of it as lyrical – delivers an anthropocentric world view. Though the bird's call may deliciously, and punningly, "[make] the solid tree trunks sound again," the poem's sense of loss, nostalgia, and diminished possibilities in the world sound out its debt to pastoral traditions in which the human finds itself alienated in nature."[10] The poem's final lines make much of this tension, framing it as the gap between words and things: "The question that he frames in all but words / Is what to make of a diminished thing."[11] This question, then, effectively renders nature unreadable, no longer "pristine" and resolutely "separate." In the face of such diminishment, the poet is left to wonder.

Frost's vision of nature as mysterious, ultimately unknowable, has roots in the work of the nineteenth-century philosopher Ralph Waldo Emerson and is thus grounded in particular ways of reading the land that have shaped American thought. Perhaps the most famous moment in Emerson's writings is the passage in "Nature" where he declares himself a "transparent eyeball ... part or particle of God."[12] This moment of transcendence, however, is raised upon a refusal to take into account the very land he occupies. Boston Common, reduced to a "bare ground," in Emerson's transcendental revelation, signals the profound disengagement in American thought between the human and the nonhuman, culture and nature, in which the very ground Americans inhabit is rendered as sublimely unapproachable, mysteriously other. That what Harold Bloom has described as "the most American passage that will ever be written" depends on such a refusal to read the land has profound implications for the development of an American ecopoetics, especially given the national cultural investment in ideas of America as the land of opportunity, a new world.[13]

In the poetry of Wendell Berry and W. S. Merwin we encounter two related and equally strenuous, but ultimately very different, attempts to read against this tradition of environmental disengagement in American thought. Both Berry and Merwin offer, therefore, two possible ecopoetic ways out of the impulse toward the pastoral that haunts Frost's work. For Berry this takes the form of a poetic investigation of "reverence" for nature, whereas for Merwin a troubled investigation of problems of "reference" in nature, and in the poem, is at the heart of his ecopoetics.

Berry epitomizes the ecopoet as traditionalist. He is a "poet-farmer" whose work stems from a profound reverence for the natural world. His poetry is powerfully rooted in a sense of place (his Kentucky farm) and in his Christian faith. Reverence for nature underpins his ecopoetics not – contra Emerson's transcendent refusal to read the land – to make the earth mysterious, unreadable, but rather to engage it fully so as to redeem it. The poem "The Morning's News" (which appeared in Berry's 1970 collection, *Farming: A Notebook*) opens with bitter disillusionment about humankind's "cold violence," which has made them "lonely / among the creatures."[14] The initial occasion of the poem is despair at American involvement in Vietnam, but it is Berry's poetic reengagement with the world immediately at hand (through his son, whose eyes are "so open to the world," and his "sloping fields now turning / green") that proves redemptive:

> Another morning comes with its strange cure.
> The earth is news. Though the river floods
> and the spring is cold, my heart goes on,
> faithful to a mystery in a cloud,
> and the summer's garden continues its descent
> through me, toward the ground.[15]

Because of Berry's insistence that poetry is not autonomous from nature, this "strange cure" does not represent a turning away from the political or an abjuring of poetic responsibility. Rather, Berry's ecopoetics effects this "cure" in the realization that, as Berry notes elsewhere, "nothing exists for its own sake, but for a harmony greater than itself, which includes it."[16] What this interdependency allows for in Berry's poetry, as William Cronon has observed, is "the task of making a home in nature," of redeeming nature and wildness through culture.[17]

In another poem, "The Clearing," making a home of the land is imaged through the "clearing" of a derelict farm and the everyday tasks of farming. Berry's work – as both farmer and poet – is to "clear" a space in which we might dwell soundly, ecologically, and with an awareness of nature as a web of relations that extends among animals, humans, land, and poem. For Berry – as though in a rebuke to Emerson – it is poetic vision that allows us to see the ground more clearly and not to read nature romantically, simply as an index of human desires. Such "vision must have severity / at its edge: / against neglect," we are told, with the hard edge of the poetic lines matching that of the axe that clears a space beneath the overgrown brush, a clearing for culture: "Vision reaches the ground / under sumac and thorn, /

under the honeysuckle, / … It sees clear pasture, / clover and grass, on the worn / hillside."[18] This poem argues that the proper uses of the land embed humans in nature ("Against nature, nature / will serve well enough"), not because humans work against nature, but because they work – inescapably – within it. The task of poet and farmer is thus to sustain an interdependent cycle of life: "Feed the lives that feed / lives."[19] Through its figures of clearing the ground, working the land, and feeding livestock, the poem establishes what Berry describes as "Nature's measure" – that is, "a conscious and careful recognition of the interdependence between ourselves and nature that in fact has always existed and, if we are to live, must always exist."[20]

Dana Phillips has written of Berry that "because he is a farmer [he] offers specifics for the treatment of postmodern conditions" in his poetics of "'reproductivity,' or of nature's "use-value."[21] But the charge may be made that Berry's reverence for nature as our "measure," as that solid reality on which we finally ground ourselves, fails to account for one of the key conditions of postmodernity, namely that all supposed realities are fundamentally "textual," which usually is intended to mean without any reliable truth-value. Indeed, Phillips's description of ecopoetics as a "treatment" for the postmodern condition is often reframed as the charge that ecopoetry and ecocriticism are hostile to postmodern thinking, and in precisely these terms. The most vocal ecocritic to voice this sort of view is Jonathan Bate. However, Bate's skepticism about postmodern relativism surrenders his terms of analysis and his definition of ecopoetry to a rather foggy set of mystifications, based on an erroneous division. "Ecopoetics," he writes, "reawakens the pre-scientific magic of naming…. Postmodernity proclaims that all marks are textmarks; ecopoetics proposes that we must hold fast to the possibility that certain textmarks called poems can bring back to our memory humankind's ancient knowledge that without landmarks we are lost."[22] Just what such "ancient knowledge" might be, or why (or even how) ecopoetry should avoid the pressing concerns of the "troubled present," as Dana Phillips has called it, is never explained.[23] More temperately, Greg Garrard urges the need to "distinguish between postmodernist theory, which is mainly inimical to ecocriticism, and postmodern ecology, which will increasingly become its scientific reference point."[24] The poetry of W. S. Merwin can be seen as an index of this postmodern turn in American ecopoetry. Instead of the sort for reverence for nature we encounter in Berry's poetry, Merwin's poetry engages the postmodern through an investigation of reference and of the troubled nature of the relationship between word and world. Merwin's poetry recognizes that, as Richard Kerridge puts it, "The real, material ecological crisis … is also a cultural crisis, a crisis of representation."[25]

Central to the sense of crisis in Merwin's poetry is his apprehension of incipient ecological disaster. Writing in 1958, he depicts the crisis in terms of the threat to the planet's survival posed by nuclear destruction. For Merwin, the threat of nuclear destruction is specifically ecological because it makes clear both the gap between humans and nonhuman nature, and the hubris of human dominion over nature:

> [T]he other animals [i.e., nonhumans] are not aware that tomorrow they may be blasted to nothing ... I go on the assumption that there is some link between a society's threat to destroy itself with its own inventions, and that same society's possibly ungovernable commitment to industrial expansion and population increase ... and which threaten more and more of the wild life of the globe.[26]

While this argument about ecological crisis calls, of course, for a closer human understanding of nature, it is also significantly troubled by how a poem may actually come to represent either such a crisis or such a closer understanding of nature, given that a poem itself may be one of those human "inventions" linked to our destructive hubris. The poem "For a Coming Extinction" (from *The Lice*, 1967) draws out these pressures. From the outset, the poem's ecological commitment is ironically heard through its speaker's assumed superiority over nature (or more specifically, over a whale about to be slaughtered, and which the poem addresses):

> Gray whale
> Now that we are sending you to The End
> That great god
> Tell him
> That we who follow you invented forgiveness
> And forgive nothing[27]

The poem here knows – in the phrase "we who follow you," and in ways we presume its speaker does not – that to follow the whale to its destruction, to hunt it, is inevitably to bring about our own destruction. Yet, to recognize this is also to reinscribe our own destruction as the poem's dramatic and ethical center; it is to read the whale as a metaphor for human annihilation, with its poetic wake "Leaving behind it the future / Dead / and ours."[28] Merwin's ecopoetics is textured by such ambivalence because it recognizes that language both mediates and frustrates interaction between humans and nature: "I [the human speaker] write as though you [the whale] could understand / And I could say it."[29]

By recognizing the complicated relationship between writing, saying, and understanding in any poetic examination of ecological disaster, Merwin develops an ecopoetry that is commensurate with postmodern conditions in America. His is therefore a poetry of resistance, as Charles Altieri has noted, but it also points out new directions in American ecopoetry through its explicit attention to its own acts of reference to the material world.[30] Its self-conscious marking of the gap between word and world and its detailing of "the intimate ways in which language and landscape are intertwined" argue for an identification in American ecopoetry of the major strains and pressures with which postwar American poetry has had to deal.[31] This is felt in a poem such as "Losing a Language," in which the extinction of species and the limits of language are seen to coincide:

> ...many of the things the words were about
> no longer exist
>
> the noun for standing in mist by a haunted tree
> the verb for I
>
> ...
>
> this is what the words were made
> to prophesy
>
> here are the extinct feathers
> here is the rain we saw[32]

Both textmark and landmark, the ecopoem (like, indeed, much postwar American poetry) is troubled by the relationship of the poem to the "things" of the world, and asks what is the "here" that we occupy. No longer does it seem sufficient to declare (following Emerson and Walt Whitman) that America itself is a poem; rather, an ecopoem must necessarily examine the grounds of such a declaration: under what terms, it asks, is a poem's speaking subject active (a "verb for I") within a poetic landscape ("in mist by a haunted tree")?

The work of Gary Snyder is central to any discussion of American ecopoetry, largely because it asks precisely this sort of question. His poetry too is haunted by a sense of ecological crisis, of the damage done to nature by human intervention. *Turtle Island*, his Pulitzer Prize-winning collection of 1974, contains his most vehemently ecological poems, poems of outrage at nuclear power, environmental destruction, and the rapacity of American capitalism. And in an earlier collection, *Myths & Texts* (1960), systems of logging in ancient China and in contemporary America are poetically brought together in an assertion of the long historical continuity of human destruction of the land we occupy. Because of logging, the poem asserts, "the [Ancient Chinese] hills slipped into the Yellow Sea," and "All America [is] hung on a hook / & burned by men, in their own praise."[33] Unsurprisingly, Snyder has been described as "the most ecologically self-conscious of twentieth-century poets" and as "the poet laureate of deep ecology."[34] The tendency has been to read Snyder's poetry – largely because of his Buddhist beliefs – as untroubled by the gap between landscape and poem, world and word, and to see its profound environmental awareness as stemming from a sense of a visionary interconnectedness of all life.[35] While such a sense is undeniable, Snyder's work, I believe, is crucial to the development of American ecopoetry precisely because of its attention to the troublesome relationship between a poetics of reverence and one of reference. On the one hand, Snyder is acutely aware of his place as part of nature. The introductory note to *Turtle Island* makes this point: "Each living being is a swirl in the flow, a formal turbulence, a 'song.'"[36] A poem, then, is a part of such a flow, a song of reverence. On the other hand, however, Snyder's poetry is deeply troubled by a conceptual gap – "turbulence" perhaps – that opens up between the landscape of the poem and the actual land it works over.

The title poem of Snyder's first published collection, *Riprap* (1958), exposes this dichotomy between poem and land, mind and things. The poem was written while Snyder was working in the mountains of the American Northwest and describes the making of a cobble-path up a mountain. The poem's detailed attention to place, environment, and the work of human hands on the land asserts a sense of universal connectedness while also realizing that words are not rocks, and that physical labor in the mountains is a metaphor for the work of a poem: "Lay down these words / Before your mind like rocks. / placed solid, by hands / In choice of place, set / Before the body of the mind."[37] What I am suggesting is that Snyder's importance as *the* exemplary American ecopoet lies in his poetry's ability both to assert reverence for nature and to express skepticism about a poem's referentiality with respect to nature. This is crisply encapsulated in the poem "Straits of Malacca 24 Oct 1957," in which three poetic versions of the same event – the intervention, and passing, of the human (in the form of a ship) over a natural scene – demonstrate how a struggle to get nature right, to read ecologically, might best issue from a poetics of linguistic indeterminacy:

> *a.*
>
> soft rain on the
> gray ocean, a tern
> still glides low over
>
> whitecaps
> after the ship is gone
>
> *b.*
>
> Soft rain on
>   gray sea
> a tern

>   glides brushing
>   waves
>   The ship's silent
>   wake
>
>
>   c.
>
>   *Fog of rain on*
>   water
>   Tern glides
>   Over waves,
>   the
>   wake[38]

The "here" of this poem is marked irrevocably by the signs of human intervention. As an ecopoem it is both an idea and a thing; an event and the recording of an event. So, despite its apparent simplicity and visionary clarity, it recognizes that poem and world are complexly interwoven. It suggests that to read poetically is to read ecologically. And this realization, in turn, might be read back into the development of American poetry and poetics in the twentieth century. The end of "Riprap" announces that "all change, in thoughts, / As well as things." If the specific echo here is of William Carlos Williams's famous dictum "no ideas but in things," it also recalls what is perhaps the defining struggle of modern American poetics, namely to find an accommodation between the poem and the world of things.

I am suggesting, therefore, that American ecopoetry – with its conscious struggle to make articulate the relationship between the United States as a nation and as a poetic landscape – is perhaps more intimately connected to the wider history and development of American poetry and poetics in the twentieth century than has usually been assumed or argued. In moving toward a conclusion, then, I want to test this assertion by looking briefly at some more examples of ecopoetry in America so as to suggest some of the trajectories in which it has moved away from the sort of naïve pastoralism embedded in romantic conceptions of the American land, and has thus sought to reengage questions of lyric agency and ethical responsibility.

Lorine Niedecker's poetics are rigorously ecological. Her poetry is evocative of porous landscapes, based in and of her life at Black Hawk Island, Wisconsin, and traces the metaphorical margins between poem, water, land, and twentieth-century experience. Indeed, Harriet Tarlo has described Niedecker's poetry as envisioning a "radical philosophy of reciprocity."[39] For Niedecker, perhaps above all others, the place of the poet is in a continually engaged, yet risky and edgy, textual encounter in which poem and land respond mutually as metaphors of each other. Her poetry thus provides an ecological critique of the relationship between ideas and things:

> A monster owl
> out on the fence
> flew away. What
> is it the sign
> of? The sign of
> an owl.[40]

Niedecker's ecopetics provides a way of formulating a poetic response to the world "out" there that is, on the one hand, witty, hard-edged, and clear in its depiction of a world of things and, on the other hand, alive with feeling for the losses and delicate interrelations of an environmental aesthetics. "Paean to Place," Niedecker's masterpiece, demonstrates how the poetic music of a place constitutes its essential element. Niedecker's assured sense of the sound made by this poem is evident in the rich music of its hauntingly sparse opening:

> Fish
>   fowl
>   flood
>   Water lily mud
> My life[41]

First published in *My Life by Water* (1970), "Paean to Place" is a meditative sequence about Black Hawk Island. Throughout this poem, ideas of place and the local compose a delicate counterpoint with themes of history, family, and writing and – most dazzlingly – with a consideration of the ethical reach of our place in the universe, how "In us an impulse tests / the unknown."[42]

If Niedecker's poetic testing of the unknown is one measure of the development of an ecopoetics in America, so too is Charles Olson's rather more grandiose exploration of American space, place, and inhabitation. Olson's sense of the poetic "here" in the *Maximus Poems* is woven out of a distinctly "American / braid" where, as he notes, "SPACE [is] the central fact to man born in America."[43] Such an awareness is felt in his acute sense of being alienated from the land – mythic, poetic, and actual – on which he lived. It is such a sense that animates much of the tortured energies and exploratory poetics of *The Maximus Poems*, especially its earlier sections. In "Maximus, to himself," Olson declares, "But even at my trade, at it, I stood estranged / from that which was most familiar."[44] As an archetypal – mythic even – ecopoet, Olson registers a bitter recognition of the alienating forces of market capitalism and of an economic system with a vested interest in maintaining the gap between humans and the world within which they labor. His response to this recognition is the poetics of the "open" text, where poet and poem (and, by extension, the reader) are conceived of as operating in the same "field" of energies, breathing – as it were – together. For Olson, the poem is not a metaphor of the world, marking its own distance from the things it describes, but merely one sector of a complexly interwoven phenomenological universe.

Olson's "open field" poetics is a decisive and vital component in later developments in ecopoetry in America. This can be seen most vividly in A. R. Ammons's environmentally charged work, in which the poet's body, poem, and environment act out a continuous exchange. "Corsons Inlet," for example, starts as "a walk over the dunes" but soon develops into a meditation on how poetic and real environments intersect "like a stream through the geography of my work."[45] However, it is in the later long poem, *Garbage* (1993), that Ammons offers a challenging, new ecopoetic direction. Rather than natural abundance and open landscapes providing the ground for his ecopoetic investigation of contemporary America, it is America's clutter, its waste, what it rejects (rather than the wilderness of space it celebrates), that becomes the matter of this poem:

> garbage has to be the poem of our time because
> garbage is spiritual, believable enough
>
> to get our attention, getting in the way, piling
> up, stinking, turning books brownish and
>
> creamy white: what else deflects us from the
> errors of our illusory ways, not a temptation
>
> to trashlessness, that is too far off, and,
> anyway, unimaginable, unrealistic:[46]

Here in the very decay we produce is a figure for the ecopoem's self-conscious investigation of the ways in which textual and natural environments interrelate. For Ammons, the interwoven nature of the word, world, and text and of our uses – and experiencing – of the environment we inhabit is witnessed at the level of the poem's syntax. *Garbage* is one continuous sentence, more than 120 pages long. Ammon's use of the colon to separate thought from thought, or delineate the poem's internal spaces, leads to a sense of the poem and the landscape it traverses as being involved together in a process of continual interfolding wherein poetic, bodily, and philosophical experiences are constantly measured against one another. The poem's ecological point is to demonstrate that the "errors of our illusory ways" stem from our reluctance (or even inability) to read the world around us as though it were poetic and thus demanding of proper "attention."[47]

My final example, Lisa Jarnot's "Tell Me Poem" (2003), is – like Ammons's *Garbage* – a poem that derives from experience of an urban (rather than rural, or pastoral) experience. Its setting is conspicuously American, yet it demands a reciprocity between ancient and contemporary scenes, between internal and external landscapes. Its poetics is one of interaction, response, and responsibility in the face of a world in which our knowledge of that world seems circumscribed. It is, in short, a new kind of ecopoem:

> Tell me why you don't
> want to know about the
> snake cults in ancient
> greece and then tell me
> why someone started all
> the tin foil on fire on
> avenue b and then tell
> me the story about osgood
> and ferocious the giant
> squirrels.[48]

If, in Emerson's terms "America is a poem in our eyes, its ample geography dazzles the imagination," Jarnot's lyric project here demands an ethics of responsibility that goes beyond a traditional vision of American poetics. The dazzle of burning tinfoil here instigates an ecopoetics that seeks to read beneath America's dazzling geographies, and that reaches for the real ground that the American poem might occupy.

NOTES

1. Robert Frost, *The Poetry of Robert Frost*, ed. Edward Connery Lathem (London: Jonathan Cape, 1977), 348.
2. Terry Gifford, "Gary Snyder and the Post-Pastoral," in J. Scott Bryson, ed., *Ecopoetry: A Critical Introduction* (Salt Lake City: University of Utah Press, 2002), 77–87.
3. Ralph Waldo Emerson, "The Poet," in Sherman Paul, ed., *Emerson's Essays* (London: J. M. Dent, 1980), 224.
4. William Rueckert, "Literature and Ecology: An Experiment in Ecocriticism," in Cheryll Glotfelty and Harold Fromm, eds., *The Ecocriticism Reader: Landmarks in Literary Ecology* (Athens and London: University of Georgia Press, 1996), 105–23, 108.
5. Cheryll Glotfelty, "Introduction," in Glotfelty and Fromm, *Ecocriticism Reader*, xviii–xix.
6. Lawrence Buell, *The Future of Environmental Criticism: Environmental Crisis and Literary Imagination* (Malden, MA and Oxford: Blackwell, 2005), 50.
7. Buell, *Future*, 50. The passage quoted is from Angus Fletcher, *A New Theory for American Poetry: Democracy, the Environment and the Future of Imagination* (Cambridge, MA and London: Harvard University Press, 2004), 122.

8. J. Scott Bryson, "Introduction," in Bryson, *Ecopoetry*, 2; and Kent C. Ryden, "Robert Frost, the New England Environment, and the Discourse of Objects," in Karla Armbruster and Kathleen R. Wallace, eds., *Beyond Nature Writing: Expanding the Boundaries of Ecocriticism* (Charlottesville and London: University Press of Virginia, 2001), 297–311, 299.

9. Robert Faggen, "Frost and the Questions of Pastoral," in Faggen, ed., *The Cambridge Companion to Robert Frost* (Cambridge: Cambridge University Press, 2001), 49–74, 60.

10. Frost, *Poetry*, 119–20.

11. Ibid.

12. Ralph Waldo Emerson, "Nature" (1836), in Paul Lauter, ed., *The Heath Anthology of American Literature*, Second Edition, Volume One (Lexington, KY: D. C. Heath & Co., 1994), 1504.

13. Harold Bloom, *Agon: Towards a Theory of Revisionism* (Oxford: Oxford University Press, 1982), 180.

14. Wendell Berry, *Collected Poems* (San Francisco: North Point Press, 1985), 109.

15. Ibid., 110.

16. Wendell Berry, "Notes: Unspecializing Poetry," in *Standing on Earth: Selected Essays* (Ipswich, CT: Golgonooza Press, 1991), 141.

17. William Cronon, "The Trouble with Wilderness; or, Getting Back to the Wrong Nature," in Cronon, ed., *Uncommon Ground: Rethinking the Human Place in Nature* (New York and London: W. W. Norton, 1996), 69–90, 89.

18. Berry, *Collected Poems*, 180–81.

19. Ibid., 182, 184.

20. Wendell Berry, "Taking Nature's Measure," cited in Dana Phillips, "Is Nature Necessary?" in Glotfelty and Fromm, *Ecocriticism Reader*, 221.

21. Ibid., 220.

22. Jonathan Bate, *The Song of the Earth* (London: Picador, 2000), 175.

23. Dana Phillips, "Ecocriticism, Ecopoetics, and Creed Outworn." *New Formations* 64 (Spring 2008): 37–50 is a powerful counterargument to Bate's. In defining his position against Bate, he notes "neither ecocriticism nor ecopoetics will flourish so long as they continue to value the ever-receding and now-mythical past more than the real but troubled present, to say nothing of the possibly very grim future" (50).

24. Greg Garrard, *Ecocriticism* (London and New York: Routledge, 2004), 14.

25. Richard Kerridge, "Introduction," in Richard Kerridge and Neil Sammells, eds., *Writing the Environment: Ecocriticism and Literature* (London and New York: Zed Books, 1998), 1–9, 4.

26. W. S. Merwin, "On Ecology," in Ed Folsom and Cary Nelson, eds., *Regions of Memory: Uncollected Prose, 1949–82* (Urbana and Chicago: University of Illinois Press, 1987), 204.

27. W. S. Merwin, *Selected Poems* (Tarset: Bloodaxe Books, 2007), 58.

28. Ibid., 8.

29. Ibid.

30. Charles Altieri, "Situating Merwin's Poetry since 1970," in Cary Nelson and Ed Folsom, eds., *W. S. Merwin: Essays on the Poetry* (Urbana and Chicago: University of Illinois Press, 1987), 159–97, 184.

31. The quotation is from Christopher MacGowan, *Twentieth-Century American Poetry* (Malden, MA and Oxford: Blackwell, 2004), 138.

32. Merwin, *Selected Poems*, 120.

33. Gary Snyder, *Myths & Texts* (1960; rpt. New York: New Directions, 1978), 3–4.

34. Bate, *Song*, 246; Garrard, *Ecocriticism*, 20.

35. For a discussion of the implications of this way of reading Snyder, see Nick Selby, "'Coming back to oneself / coming back to the land': Gary Snyder's Poetics," in John Tallmadge and Henry Harrington, eds., *Reading under the Sign of Nature: New Essays in Ecocriticism* (Salt Lake City: University of Utah Press, 2000), 179–97.

36. Gary Snyder, *Turtle Island* (New York: New Directions, 1974), n.p.

37. Gary Snyder, *Riprap and Cold Mountain Poems* (San Francisco: North Point Press, 1965), 32.

38. Gary Snyder, *Left out in the Rain: New Poems 1947–1985* (San Francisco: North Point Press, 1986), 76.

39. Harriet Tarlo, "Lorine Niedecker On and Off the Margins: A Radical Poetics out of Objectivism," in Vicki Bertram, ed., *Kicking Daffodils: Twentieth-Century Women Poets* (Edinburgh: Edinburgh University Press, 1997), 191–209, 204.

40. Lorine Niedecker, *Collected Works*, ed. Jenny Penberthy (Berkeley, Los Angeles, and London: University of California Press, 2002), 103.

41. Ibid., 261.

42. Ibid., 267.

43. Charles Olson, *Call Me Ishmael* (New York: Reynal & Hitchcock, 1947), 15.

44. Charles Olson, *The Maximus Poems*, ed. George F. Butterick (Berkeley and London: University of California Press, 1983), 56.

45. A. R. Ammons, *Collected Poems 1951–1971* (New York: W. W. Norton, 1972), 148, 149.

46. A. R. Ammons, *Garbage* (New York: W. W. Norton, 1993), 8.

47. Ibid.

48. Lisa Jarnot, *Ring of Fire* (Cambridge: Salt, 2003), 8.

FURTHER READING

Armbruster, Karla and Kathleen R. Wallace, eds. *Beyond Nature Writing: Expanding the Boundaries of Ecocriticism*. Charlottesville and London: University Press of Virginia, 2001.

Bate, Jonathan. *The Song of the Earth*. London: Picador, 2000.

Bryson, J. Scott, ed. *Ecopoetry: A Critical Introduction*. Salt Lake City: University of Utah Press, 2002.

Bryson, J. Scott, *The West Side of Any Mountain: Place, Space and Ecopoetry*. Iowa City: University of Iowa Press, 2005.

Buell, Lawrence. *The Future of Environmental Criticism: Environmental Crisis and Literary Imagination*. Malden, MA and Oxford: Blackwell, 2005).

Cronon, William, ed. *Uncommon Ground: Rethinking the Human Place in Nature*. New York and London: W. W. Norton, 1996.

Fletcher, Angus. *A New Theory for American Poetry: Democracy, the Environment and the Future of Imagination* (Cambridge, MA and London: Harvard University Press, 2004).

Garrard, Greg. *Ecocriticism*. London and New York: Routledge, 2004.

Gatta, John. *Making Nature Sacred: Literature, Religion, and the Environment in America from the Puritans to the Present*. Oxford and New York: Oxford University Press, 2004.

Gifford, Terry. *Green Voices: Understanding Contemporary Nature Poetry*. Manchester: Manchester University Press, 1995.

Gilcrest, David W. *Greening the Lyre: Environmental Poetics and Ethics*. Reno: University of Nevada Press, 2002.

Glotfelty, Cheryll and Harold Fromm, eds. *The Ecocriticism Reader: Landmarks in Literary Ecology*. Athens and London: University of Georgia Press, 1996.

Kerridge, Richard and Neil Sammells, eds. *Writing the Environment: Ecocriticism and Literature*. London and New York: Zed Books, 1998.

Nash, Roderick Frazier. *Wilderness and the American Mind*. Fourth edition. New Haven, CT and London: Yale University Press, 2001.

Phillips, Dana. *The Truth of Ecology: Nature, Culture, and Literature in America*. Oxford and New York: Oxford University Press, 2003.

"Ecocriticism, Ecopoetics, and Creed Outworn." *New Formations* 64 (Spring 2008): 37–50.

Scigaj, Leonard M. *Sustainable Poetry: Four American Ecopoets*. Lexington: The University Press of Kentucky, 1999.

Tallmadge, John and Henry Harrington, eds. *Reading under the Sign of Nature: New Essays in Ecocriticism*. Salt Lake City: University of Utah Press, 2000.

10

STEVE MCCAFFERY

Language Writing

"Why go on reading Language poetry?" asks Stephen Fredman in 1983, suggesting a cultural finality after its first decade of formulation.[1] Similarly, Marjorie Perloff, a long-time ardent supporter of Language writing, has more recently questioned its currency. Quoting short passages from writers as diverse as Bruce Andrews, Diane Ward, and Peter Inman, she assesses them collectively as written in "a period style" sharing "specific features."[2] This chapter tries to answer these questions toward its end but opens with a different interrogation – "What is Language writing?" – and in deference to the aforementioned two skeptical claims, it is written partly in the present and partly in past tenses. (The switch will be deliberately indiscriminate.) I have further chosen to address the topic of "Language writing" rather than "Language poetry" as the more accurate term for a key feature in this movement's formulation, which involved not only a consensual denial of the difference between poetry and theory, but also a deliberate erosion of the fixed partitions between prose and poetic genres.

By the late 1970s, the term Language (or L=A=N=G=U=A=G=E) Poetry came to identify a loose collection of writers whose different approaches to style and form must be admitted, but whose unanimity condensed around a shared belief that language was not a neutral conduit for ideas or feelings but an active agent (through its applications and manifestations) in the social construction of being and the real. A common tenet united them: the need to de-idealize language, revisit the very notion of communication by rethinking the relation of the latter to textual materiality and production, and envision new political possibilities for poetry. This chapter focuses on the foundational theorizations of this writing, and pays less attention (for reasons made clear later) to the vast range of poetic output.

Language writing did not originate by way of a collective manifesto; what is certain, however, is that during the 1970s, what subsequently became labeled "Language" poems began to appear and disseminate through an autonomous infrastructure of small magazines, talk series, workshops, residencies, and readings (primarily, but not entirely, within the Bay Area).[3] The Tasahara Bakery, the Grand Piano, 80 Langton Street (San Francisco), Saint Marks Poetry Project, The Ear Inn (New York), and A Space (Toronto) were some of the venues, and *Doones*, *This*, *Tottels*, *Hills*, *Big Deal*, *Toothpick*, *100 Posters*, and *Miam* were a few of the magazines.

Many of the early attempts to formulate an alternative to the "New American Poetry" (embalmed inside the pages of Donald Allen's historic 1960 anthology) emerged through the latter half of the 1970s from epistolary correspondence, a vibrant series of public talks and discussion groups, and arguments over drinks in bars and restaurants, which supplemented printed material and helped foster community.[4] The correspondence among three foundational theorists (Charles Bernstein, Steve McCaffery, and Ron Silliman) at the time reveals a mutual searching for conceptual frameworks in contemporary continental theory and especially Structuralism.[5] A lone declaration registers its anecdotal origin: the now-legendary 1971 words of poet Robert Grenier "I HATE SPEECH," which appeared in the first issue of Barrett Watten's magazine *This*.[6] Another important inaugural document is Silliman's short "Preface and Notes" to "The Dwelling Place: 9 Poets," which appeared in the ethnopoetics journal *Alcheringa*.[7] Significantly Silliman does not announce the launch of any new movement in 1975 but rather a *tendency* among diverse young writers: "Called variously 'language centered,' 'minimal,' 'non-referential formalism,' 'diminished referentiality,' 'structuralist.' Not a *group* but a *tendency*."[8] Silliman's notes make clear that the "tendency" is to facture a poetry of diminished rather than non-reference. As he correctly points out, words cannot be non-referential owing to the fact that words always "originate in interactions with the world."[9] Prototypical Language writing thus sought a reduction of the referential vector, not its absolute negation. Silliman situates this tendency in a rich genealogy that embraces then-current continental and Marxist theory (Lacan, Barthes, Rossi-Landi, Voloshinov, Bakhtin, Derrida), the European avant-garde (the Russian Futurists and concrete poetry), senior American poets (Robert Creeley and Larry Eigner), and preliterate, oral cultures. It is here too that public mention is first made of the Balinese Ramayana Monkey Chant called *Ketjak*, a name that Silliman will later adopt for the earliest published example of what he termed the "New Sentence."[10]

In this respect Silliman's groundbreaking work on the social origins of referentiality outlined in his 1980 essay, "Disappearance of the Word, Appearance of the World," is a salient, recuperative move back to a language of the gestural and linguistically "meaningless" identified with poetical economies before techno-capitalism's hegemonic triumph.[11] Silliman cites a translation of a sweatbath poem of the North American Fox tribe and the early-sixteenth-century poet John Skelton as marking the diachronic and cultural diversity of the gestural in poetry. The Dadaist poet Tristan Tzara provides another convenient precedent here in his own ethnographic researches into African languages. (It was sometimes Tzara's practice to mix authentic African song into his so-called *chants nègre* that he performed alongside sound poems at the Cabaret Voltaire in Zurich.) Silliman, however, stands somewhat alone in this cultural mapping, and the direction taken in subsequent Language theory neither embraces nor develops the central tenet of ethnopoetries (announced in 1970 in *Alcheringa's* first issue): to stage and demonstrate the surprising affinities within translated tribal poetries to twentieth-century avant-garde practices. The subsequent foundational theorizing of Language writing largely marks a departure from ethnopoetic affinities (grammatical distortion, nonsense, the powerful materiality of words, minimalist texts), to formal linguistic disruption (including many of the pre-capitalist so-called gestural elements), to a broadly based Marxist critique of language. Form thus becomes politicized, and a critico-political stance emerges as the mandatory designator of a necessary and urgent poetics.

L=A=N=G=U=A=G=E became the name of a movement more by accident than merit. Launched in 1978 under the joint editorship of Bruce Andrews and Charles Bernstein, the journal of that name found itself propelled into academic debate in 1984 with an abridged version, *The L=A=N=G=U=A=G=E Book*, which facilitated the rapid domestication of Language writing inside the academy.[12] After its publication, difficult texts became teachable, and "Language Poetry" found itself added to the curriculum of contemporary and twentieth-century American poetry. Here it may prove useful to revisit its initial manifestation. *L=A=N=G=U=A=G=E* was set up to be a journal not of primary creative texts but theoretical conjectures and statements *about* poems and poetics. Short jottings were favored over extended theoretical proclamations moving toward a forum of shared ideas (the editors' call to readers to supply a list of nonpoetic texts that they have found influential or significant being one example).[13] Of equal importance to understanding and encountering the first three decades of Language writing is the journal *Poetics*, coedited by Lyn Hejnian and Barrett Watten from 1981 to 1999, which assumes the role of critical mouthpiece after the termination of *L=A=N=G=U=A=G=E* in 1981.

The theoretical demarcations of Language writing were further consolidated in the mid-1980s and throughout the 1990s with the publication of essay collections and monographs by major practitioners, including Andrews, Bernstein, Hejinian, McCaffery, Perelman, Silliman, and Watten, as well as important critical volumes on these same writers.[14] Starting in the mid-1980s, Language writing also gathered momentum and academic endorsement from established and emergent scholars like Lee Bartlett, George Hartley, Jerome McGann, and Marjorie Perloff.[15] And from 1986 to 1994, a trio of important anthologies appeared that served both to gather tendencies and expand the reader base: *In the American Tree*, edited by Silliman (1986), *"Language" Poetries*, edited by Douglas Messerli (1987), and *The Art of Practice: Forty-Five Contemporary Poets*, edited by Dennis Barone and Peter Ganick (1994).[16]

The full impact of the anthologies is uncertain; however, in the case of *In the American Tree*, I believe one effect is. What initially appeared as a recurring critique of late capitalist discourse among a range of writers finally emerged as an identifiable movement constructed along stridently national lines. Silliman's is a hugely important (and epoch-defining) anthology, yet it excluded British and Canadian writers "for reasons of space and clarity."[17] What "clarity" means here is left unexplained, but the gesture in these exclusions (and in the allusion to William Carlos Williams's *In the American Grain* in the title) is clear: Silliman is interested in a national construction via an American narrative and debate. Whether *In the American Tree* consolidates a facet of American cultural history or amputates an international potential (a world as opposed to a national poetic revolution) remains a moot point. Certainly, parallel manifestations of linguistic critiques, poems of similar stylistic and formal affinities, were being produced in the United Kingdom and Canada at this time, but in England no substantial ancillary theorizing occurs. British poet Allen Fisher's long poem *Place* is in part a bold revisioning of Charles Olson's poetics of place via a theory of quantum communication. The foregrounding of the material nature of the sign was probably carried to its extreme in the destructive writings of Bob Cobbing and others in his London-based Writer's Forum, and to its most erudite and obscure in the poetry of J. H. Prynne. Veronica Forrest-Thomson introduced the radical work of the Parisian Tel Quel group into contemporary poetic parlance, but her tragic death in 1975 prevented the possibility of any truly trans-Atlantic alliance.[18] It is left to further research whether an international Language writing movement was or still is tenable.

In the United States, Language writing quickly revealed its oppositional stance to several major literary proclivities: 1) the consecration of the individual voice (linguistically marked by the axis of the "I" understood as a marker of self-plenitude, "truth," and "sincerity") in the ego-chamber of the confessional lyric stance that had been entrenched via the poetry of Sylvia Plath, Robert Lowell, John Berryman, Louise Glück, and Jorie Graham in a multiplicity of MFA programs and those poems that populate the pages of such venues as the *American Poetry Review* and the *The New Yorker*; 2) the ego-cosmological syntax that Robert Duncan expounded in "Towards an Open Universe" and the processual, physiological, and predominantly speech-based poetics grounded on organic models of the poem that had gained momentum through the 1920s via the early Williams, to culminate in Olson's valorization of breath and syllable in his important 1950 pamphlet "Projective Verse" and Denise Levertov's theorizing of the poem as organic form;[19] and 3) the so-called poetry of accommodation: Jerome McGann invoked the term to describe a prevailing poetry of social disaffection that failed to advance into an area of meaningful linguistic critique. All of these tendencies assumed unquestioningly a governing instrumental logic whereby the poem could appear to function as the unproblematic, unmediated transmission of experience or emotion from the writer to the reader.[20] Language writing resisted these familiar poetic tendencies with texts based on nonorganic matrices, and a socio-poetics that confronted the inescapable mediation of all discursive production of both self and experience. It is perhaps Ron Silliman more than any other Language writer who has emphasized this ineluctable mediation of the self through language: "The words are never our own. Rather, they are our own usages of a determinate coding passed down to us like all the other products of civilization, organized into a single, capitalist, world economy."[21]

British critic Geoff Ward is correct to claim that the work of Language writers proffers "a standing rebuke to the prevailing mediocrity of America's cultural output during the Reagan and Bush administrations."[22] Language writing's primary engagements then are discursive and ideological (if the two are indeed separable): the broad fate of language under supply-side monopoly capitalism, where exchange and seriality order the governing logic, and an ideological horizon entrenches speech, sincerity, narrative, referentiality, and representation as the unquestionable desiderata of linguistic function. Its critical-political method is certainly not that of orthodox social protest (outrage at American imperial policy, for instance, the common rhetoric of defiance, verbal solidarity with the downtrodden, etc). Poems of emotionally charged disaffection enjoy a rich genealogy and ultimately resolve into a lyric attenuation that at its base seeks to clarify a single subject position.

Without doubt the most vexed issue among practitioners in the first decade of Language writing is that of referentiality (understood as a sociohistorical outcome of reference) and narrative (held to be the dominant literary paradigm of the commodity-centered ideology of contemporary capitalism). The latter, understood as a destination outside linguistic constructions, commits language as such to the simple role of a conduit, a projectile carrier that "falls away" when the desired extralinguistic destination (plot) is reached. McCaffery and Silliman especially teased out these implications by way of a broadly Marxist critique of narrative as unavoidably commoditizing linguistic signs as well as erasing the mode of the production within writing. Narrative reference was considered less a path out of language into a real or fictive world than an active pathology within the sociocultural sphere, remarking the quintessential commodity fetish. The critique of referentiality was forged against the backdrop of Vietnam and Watergate. (In Canada it was first against the historical tapestry of Canada's involvement with supplying napalm to aid in that war, then against the trauma of the "October Crisis" of 1970.)[23] This critique of referentiality is not inaugurated by Language theorists; it develops from misgivings articulated by an earlier generation of poets. In his 1966 poem, "Wichita Vortex Sutra," Allen Ginsberg claims accusingly that "The War is language" and worked in that poem to expose the mythic foundation of "common reference" that choked the products issuing as news and comment from the "language factory" of journalism.[24] Ginsberg's comments themselves echo early Dada sentiments around the insidious perplication of language and war. In March 1915, Hugo Kersten and Emil Szittya, the two editors of the literary newspaper *Der Mistral*, launched a frontal attack, not on the military conflict of World War I itself, but on the linguistic structures of the bourgeois institutions – religion, law, politics, and the news industry – that collectively comprised a "grammar of war." Poems were included in the March issue that deliberately undermined grammatical and syntactic norms. (The choice is telling: there are calligrammes by Apollinaire and examples of Marinetti's *parole in libertà*, or words in freedom).[25]

Two years after Silliman published "Preface and Notes" to "The Dwelling Place," the concept of "diminished reference" would drop away, and he would move toward a distinction between "non-referential" and "post-referential" writing in order to advocate the latter.[26] In a letter to McCaffery dated November 8, 1976, Silliman articulates a still unknown "post-referentiality" onto collective practice: "non-referentiality: this is simply the attempt to void commodity language by specific context, a negation: thesis-antithesis. what is needed is the *next* step: a future synthesis to a post-serial collective language, a language of the group not the series. I'm for post-referentiality, even tho I don't today really have a full grasp as yet as to what it might wld be."[27]

One might ask where precisely is the class struggle located in Language writing, and we find the answer in the sociopolitical ramifications of readership: "[A Language-centered poem] ... is the first step (and only that) of the return of the poem to the people. It is a politicized poem not a 'political poem' (which is a counter-tendency occurring within the commodity fetish). It tells you these words are empty until you fill them with your presence, reading them, being them."[28] The recognition of the reader function as an issue of ideological contestation rather than an unproblematically "given" structural coordinate within a semiotic system thus remains a primary insight that catalyzed the early primary Language texts of all its foundational practitioners.

Hejinian offers a definitive formulation of this recognition as the "open text" in her 1983 essay, "The Rejection of Closure": "The open text, by definition, is open to the world and particularly to the reader. It invites participation, rejects the authority of the writer over the reader and thus, by analogy, the authority implicit in other (social, economic, cultural) hierarchies."[29] The notion of the open text, with space left for productive intervention on the reader's part, developed through a pattern of Marxist thinking (rather than through either Umberto Eco's theories of the open work or Jauss's and Iser's theories of reader response).[30] In Hejinian's words, the open text "resists the cultural tendencies that seek to identify and fix material and turn it into a product; that is, it resists reduction and commodification."[31] An emancipation was desired from the historically determined passivity of reading understood as the consumption of a commoditized language object. Andrews and Bernstein jointly call in their preface to *The L=A=N=G=U=A=G=E Book* for "a repossession of the linguistic sign through close attention to, and active participation in, its production."[32] This should not be construed as a broad call to neologism (although it does cast the transrational linguistic distortions and truncations of poets David Melnick and Peter Inman in a novel light), but rather a refusal to treat reading as a predominantly consumptive act.[33] Where its earlier generation questioned the ideology of predetermined form (concretized in Robert Creeley's well-known assertion that "form is merely an extension of content"), Language writing questions the sociology of predetermined methods of reading and insists on the fundamental politicality of the reader-writer relation.[34]

Jochen Schulte-Sasse, in his introduction to Peter Bürger's *Theory of the Avant-Garde*, explains the intervention into the sociopolitics of readership effected by the open text in a sentiment (if not a vocabulary) that allows us to situate Language writing within a directly classic (i.e., Bürgerian) genealogy of the avant-garde: "The avant-garde saw that the organic unity of the bourgeois institution of art left art impotent to intervene in social life, and thus developed a different concept of the work of art. Its concept of art sees a chance to reintegrate art into social praxis if artists would create unclosed, individual segments of art that open themselves to supplementary response."[35] If not an entire reintegration of "art into social praxis," Language writing creates works designed to integrate the reader into a semantically creative praxis. The *konstellationen* of Eugen Gomringer (formulated in the late 1950s) offers an antecedent to this productive integration, either unknown to or at least not commentated on by foundational Language theorists. In his 1968 preface to *The Book of Hours and Constellations*, titled "verse to constellation: aim & form of a new poetry," Gomringer writes: "the constellation is a system, it is also a playground with definite boundaries. the poet sets it all up. he designs the play-ground as a field-of-force & suggests its possible workings. the reader, the new reader, accepts in the spirit of play, then plays with it."[36] The stress, of course, falls on the ludic, not the political.

On the strategic point of readership McCaffery stands as a lone revisionist. His "Writing as a General Economy" attempts to theorize a poetics developed from the ideas of Georges Bataille (1897–1962), especially his theory of the two economies: a restricted economy of calculation, cautious investment, driven by profit, and a general economy of indifferent, profitless expenditure – an economy, I might add, that characterizes several pre-capitalist formations.[37] Bataille provided a useful way to think of poems as economies, rather than forms or structures, circulations of sound pulses, rhythmic materialities, and pressures. Bataille also opened a way to expand on Silliman's early call for a gestural poetics modeled on pre-capitalist patterns of culture and economy. McCaffery's theory inverts the model of production outlined by Silliman and attempts to revision the indeterminacies of the open "Language" texts not as sites for productive engagement (which McCaffery considered at that time a capitulation back to capitalist paradigms), but rather as a semantic locus in which to experience the risk of a loss of meaning. The reader, thereby, is neither returned to the role of a passive consumer of narrative and description, nor emancipated in productive engagement, but thrust into affect and then reflection.

The call to post-referentiality hardly met with unanimous assent. In a 1980 editorial note to *L=A=N=G=U=A=G=E*, Andrews and Bernstein appear keen to absent themselves from "The Politics of the Referent" and any consequential binding:

> The tendencies in writing McCaffery is talking about under such headings as "language-centered" are as open to the entrapments of stylistic fixation as any other tendency in recent poetry.... In this context, the idea that writing could be stripped of reference is as troubling and confusing a view as the assumption that the primary function of words, one-on-one, to an already constituted world of "things." Rather, reference, like the body itself is a given dimension of language.[38]

It is clear that the advancement of a precise revolution in poetics was not the governing mandate for *L=A=N=G=U=A=G=E*; the desire was to offer ideas toward a wide range of alternative styles and forms.

The issue of referentiality and the referent did not sustain interest beyond the last half-decade of the 1970s, and through the 1980s the polymodal tended to dominate the majority of Language writing. Rather than abolishing traditional styles, it incorporates a multiplicity of them via discursive collage. As Bernstein notes, "There is a willingness to use, within the space of a text, a multiplicity of such different discourses [i.e., politics, autobiography, fiction, philosophy, common sense, song ...]."[39] For Bernstein at least, the Language *tendency* is an inclination to syncretic formations as opposed to absolute discursive constructions, to a re-territorialization and re-amalgamation of, for example, philosophical, personal, and political elements. Indeed, the range of stylistic modes in Language writing (readily sampled in the previously mentioned anthologies) reveals a multiplicity so stunning as to counter any claim to a unitary poetic. From the "Fired Reading" method of Alan Davies and Nick Piombino, to the New Sentence as practiced primarily by Hejinian, Watten, Silliman, and Carla Harryman to the rich thesaurus of "experiments" itemized by Bernadette Mayer, to the atavistic neo-zaum (or transrational) texts of Inman and homophonic translations of Melnick, to the mixed and intermedia performances of Andrews and Sally Silvers and the transcribed improvised utterances of Steve Benson, through the material ruptures of Susan Howe and the semantically unsettling early poems of Michael Palmer, it is impossible to tender a total or adequate assessment, let alone offer a clear definition. Certainly, they demonstrate that non- and post-referential aspirations did not win the day. In this respect Andrew Ross's 1989 interview with Andrews and Bernstein proves revealing. In it they offer a "definition" of Language writing as something that resists definition (unwittingly echoing Friedrich Schlegel's definition of Romanticism). The coeditorial *telos* of $L=A=N=G=U=A=G=E$ is contemporary eclectic, offering in its pages a "diverse body of radical, or radial eccentricities."[40] The refusal to support a post-referential writing, the resistance to an institutionalizing discourse, and the concomitant embrace of heterogeneity is one of the most important contributions of the Language legacy to contemporary literature. This centripetal dissemination rather than centrifugal condensation into *definiens* and *definiendum* stands in broad concurrence with Bakhtin's theory of diversity, that "heteroglossial" cultural topography that began to emerge in Anglophone regions in the 1960s.

Within this vortex, however, two commonalities are apparent among Language writers: a privileging of the material text over the representational function and textual opacity over transparency. Language poems have become notorious for their designed opacity and strategic unworkability within normative readerly expectations, for their indeterminate pronoun relations, catachresis, a preference for parataxis (goodbye John Milton!)

and non-syllogistic articulations (what Gilles Deleuze and Felix Guattari term "disjunctive syntheses") over grammatical and clausal subordination (hypotaxis), and extreme disjunction. Emancipated writing of this kind frequently becomes the *event* of writing and that way approximates the kind of intransitive signifying practice that Roland Barthes called for.[41]

In Silliman's words, Language writing involves "taking a stance toward language, the activity of composition and reality, which will call forth strategies and structures that are both generative and unconcealing of their constructedness."[42] It is a stance shared by John Cage and Jackson Mac Low in their systematic chance compositions and by the majority of rule-constrained literature of Oulipo.[43] Language writing's extreme disjunction is perhaps best seen in the early work of Andrews. The poems release a festive expenditure of phrases as social material free of narrative and representational imperatives. It is Andrews's work that is most consonant with Bataille's theory of sacrifice and general economy – a festive expenditure of signs. Indeed, it is his work that lends itself most cogently to a poetics of symbolic action.

Arguably the most significant formal innovation within Language writing is the New Sentence. Jointly conceived by Watten and Silliman (to be subsequently adopted by many Bay Area Language poets including Hejinian and Harryman), it is exclusively a production of the Bay Area poets. Watten's testimonial in Part 7 of *The Grand Piano* allows us to date the precise birth of the New Sentence to June 1, 1974: "The next day – Saturday – Ron began *Ketjak*, a work to which we may continue to refer."[44] Silliman's essay "The New Sentence" outlines its pattern and primary significances. Admittedly inspired by structural linguistics, it proposes a radical reconception of the basic unit of poetry (the sentence instead of the word) and its spatial organization (the paragraph rather than the line or stanza).[45] But it is not just a matter of turning from traditional measures of poetry to those of prose. Repudiating the pattern of syllogistic logic, the New Sentence organizes sentences paratactically and without any clear relation to higher integrations.[46] "This is a sentence if it is an event," claims Gertrude Stein in 1931, and Silliman's formulations are certainly in concurrence with Stein's "eventist" treatment of the sentence.[47] At the same time, the utilization of the New Sentence as a generative form whose structure remains transparent in order to expose the precise mode of textual production aligns it to the tradition of Russian Formalism and Silliman's own investment in counter-fetishistic nonnarrative. But what exactly the New Sentence is remains a moot point between its two inventors. Where Silliman places it in a double historical tradition of the sentence as such and of the prose poem, Watten presents it as a cultural project, providing "an argument of othering ... in which objects of dissociation are argued in from outside."[48] Watten presents a convincing case for not situating the New Sentence within formal criteria and literary history, but rather within a cultural topology.

In retrospect, many of the more ambitious proclamations of Language writing savor of a rhetoric of self-empowerment: "Our analysis [is] of the capitalist order as a whole and of the place that alternative forms of writing and reading might occupy in its transformation. It is our sense that the project of poetry does not involve turning language into a commodity for consumption; instead, it involves repossessing the sign through close attention to, and active participation in, its production."[49] Others appear intransigently absolute, such as the following strained synthesis of poetry, language, and economics: "A grammatical critique can be mobilized by presenting language as opaque and resistant to reinvestment. A language centered writing, for instance, and zero-semantic sound poetry, diminishes the profit rate and lowers investment drives just as productive need is increased."[50]

The style and tone, however, are understandable against the backdrop of the felt urgencies of the time. A rethinking of the possible relations of poetry to language, politics, and revolution through paradigms other than representation were sadly lacking before the theories of Language writing. It is beyond dispute that Language writing collectively initiated radical writing practices implemented through a series of strategic collapses, most preeminently those of the unitary subject, the singular writer, and the clear partition between genres.

NOTES

1. Stephen Fredman, *Poets' Prose: The Crisis in American Verse* (Cambridge: Cambridge University Press, 1983), 152.
2. Marjorie Perloff, "The Pleasures of Déjà Dit: Citation, Intertext and Ekphrasis in Recent Experimental Poetry," in *The Consequence of Innovation: 21st Century Poetics*, ed. Craig Dworkin (New York: Roof Books, 2008), 255–300.
3. Much information on the San Francisco Bay Area scene from 1975 to 1980 can be gleaned from the ten-volume *Grand Piano: An Experiment in Collective Autobiography* (Detroit, MI: Mode A, 2006–2010).
4. Donald Allen, ed., *The New American Poetry, 1945–1960* (New York: Grove Press, 1960).
5. "Steve McCaffery, Ron Silliman & Charles Bernstein. Correspondence: May 1976–December 1977," edited and chosen by Steve McCaffery in *Line. A Journal of Contemporary Writing and Its Modernist Sources* 5 (Spring 1985): 59–89.
6. Robert Grenier, "On Speech," *This* 1 (Winter 1971), 86–7.
7. Ron Silliman, ed., "The Dwelling Place," *Alcheringa* 2 (1975): 104–20.
8. Ibid., 104.
9. Ibid., 118.

10. Ron Silliman, *The New Sentence* (New York: Roof Books, 1987).

11. Ibid.

12. Charles Bernstein and Bruce Andrews, eds., *The L=A=N=G=U=A=G=E Book* (Carbondale and Edwardsville: Southern Illinois University Press, 1984).

13. In issue No. 3, June 1978. For a full discussion of the implications of the book's impact, see Barrett Watten, *The Constructivist Moment: From Material Text to Cultural Poetics* (Middletown, CT: Wesleyan University Press, 2003), especially Chapter 2, "The Secret History of the Equals Sign," 45–102.

14. Important collections and monographs by Language writers include: Barrett Watten, *Total Syntax* (Carbondale: Southern Illinois University Press, 1984); Bob Perelman, *Writing Talks* (Carbondale: Southern Illinois University Press, 1985); Charles Bernstein, *Content's Dream: Essays 1975–1984* (Los Angeles, CA: Sun and Moon Press, 1986); Steve McCaffery, *North of Intention: Critical Writings, 1973–1986* (New York: Roof Books, 1986); Bruce Andrews, *Paradise & Method: Poetics & Practice* (Evanston: Northwestern University Press, 1996); Perelman, *The Marginalization of Poetry: Language Writing and Literary History* (Princeton, NJ: Princeton University Press, 1996), and Lyn Hejinian, *The Language of Inquiry* (Berkeley: University of California Press, 2000). For major examples of early volumes devoted to these writers, see the eighth issue of Rod Smith's magazine *Aerial*, devoted to the work of Barrett Watten (1995), followed by an issue of the Santa Cruz-based magazine *Quarry West* on *Ron Silliman and The Alphabet* (1998), followed in turn by *Aerial 9*, devoted to the work of Bruce Andrews (1999). All three were substantial volumes, with the Watten issue extending to more than 300 pages, the Andrews to a little short of the same figure (285), and the Silliman (in *Quarry West*'s larger format) to 194 pages.

15. Marjorie Perloff, "The Word as Such: L=A=N=G=U=A=G=E Poetry in the Eighties," *American Poetry Review* 13 (May/June 1984): 15–22; Lee Bartlett, "What Is Language Poetry?" *Critical Inquiry* 12.4 (Summer 1986): 741–52; Jerome McGann, "Contemporary Poetry, Alternate Routes" in *Politics and Poetic Value*, ed. Robert von Hallberg (Chicago: University of Chicago Press, 1987), 253–76; George Harley, *Textual Politics and the Language Poets* (Bloomington: Indiana University Press, 1989)

16. Silliman, ed., *In the American Tree* (Orono: National Poetry Foundation, University of Main at Orono, 1986); Douglas Messerli, ed., *"Language" Poetries: An Anthology* (New York: New Directions, 1987); Dennis Barone and Peter Ganick, eds., *The Art of Practice: Forty-Five Contemporary Poets* (Elmwood, CT: Potes & Poets Press 1994).

17. Silliman, *In the American Tree*, xx.

18. It is worth mentioning, however, that Forrest-Thomson's *Poetic Artifice: A Theory of Twentieth-Century Poetry* (New York: St. Martin's Press, 1978) was seminal material for one major American Language text, Charles Bernstein's 1987 "Artifice and Absorption," collected in Bernstein, *A Poetics* (Cambridge, MA: Harvard University Press, 1992).

19. Robert Duncan, "Towards an Open Universe," in *A Selected Prose*, ed. Robert J. Berthoff (New York: New Directions, 1995); Denise Levertov, "Some Notes on Organic Form," *Poetry* 106.6 (September, 1965): 420–25; Charles Olson, *Collected Prose*, ed. by Donald Allen and Benjamin Friedlander (Berkeley and Los Angeles: University of California Press, 1997).

20. McGann, "Contemporary Poetry, Alternate Routes."
21. Ron Silliman, "*IF BY 'WRITING' WE MEAN LITERATURE (if by 'literature'
    we mean poetry (if ...))....*" in *The L=A=N=G=U=A=G=E Book*, 167.
22. Geoff Ward, *Language Poetry and the Avant-garde* (British Association for
    American Studies. Keele: University of Keele, 1993), 16.
23. The October Crisis involved the twin kidnappings of James Cross (British dip-
    lomat) and Pierre Laporte (Québec cabinet minister) by the *Front de libération
    du Québec* (FLQ). Laporte was later murdered, and fears of terrorist activities
    precipitated the then-Prime Minister Pierre Eliot Trudeau to reinvoke the highly
    controversial 1914 War Measures Act.
24. Allen Ginsberg, *Collected Poems 1947–1997* (New York: HarperCollins, 2006),
    401.
25. For full details, see Matthew S. Witkovsky, "Chronology" in *Dada: Zurich,
    Hannover, Cologne, New York, Paris* (Washington, DC: Distributed Art
    Publishers, 2005).
26. Silliman, "For Open Letter," in *Open Letter* 3.7 (Summer 1977): 89–93.
27. "Steve McCaffery, Ron Silliman & Charles Bernstein Correspondence: May
    1976–December 1977," in *Line* 5 (Spring, 1985): 59–89, 65.
28. Silliman, "For Open Letter," 93.
29. Hejinian, *The Language of Inquiry*, 43.
30. Umberto Eco, *The Open Work*, tr. Anna Cancogni (Cambridge, MA: Harvard
    University Press, 1989); Wolfgang Iser, *The Act of reading: A Theory of Aesthetic
    Response* (Baltimore: The Johns Hopkins University Press, 1980).
31. Hejinian, *The Language of Inquiry*, 43.
32. Andrews and Bernstein, *The L=A=N=G=U=A=G=E Book*, x.
33. David Melnick in his *PCOET* (San Francisco: G.A.W.K., 1975) and Peter Inman
    in *Ocker* (Berkeley, CA: Tuumba Press, 1982) both resuscitate the Russian avant-
    gardist practice of *zaum* or transrational language.
34. Olson quotes the remark *Collected Prose*, 138.
35. Jochen Schulte-Sasse, "Foreword: Theory of Modernism versus Theory of the
    Avant-Garde," in Peter Bürger, *Theory of the Avant-Garde*, tr. Michael Shaw
    (1974; Minneapolis: University of Minnesota Press, 1984), xxxix.
36. Eugen Gomringer, *The Book of Hours and Constellations. Poems by Eugen
    Gomringer presented by Jerome Rothenberg* (New York: Something Else Press,
    1968), xxx. Gomringer's poems in this fashion first appeared through German
    imprints in 1960.
37. McCaffery, "Writing as a General Economy" in *Artifice and Indeterminacy: An
    Anthology of New Poetics*, ed. Christopher Beach (Tuscaloosa: University of
    Alabama Press, 1998), 201–21.
38. L=A=N=G=U=A=G=E Supplement Number One (June 1980), cover. In this
    repudiation of the referential model, Language writing inherits a predecessor
    earlier than Stein and the Russian Futurists. It is Swinburne who first unleashes
    a tsunami of linguistic material on the *res-verba* détante, and it is only the mel-
    opoeic violence and propensity to anaphora in his poetry that occludes this
    genealogy.
39. Bernstein, Introduction to "A Language Sampler," *Paris Review* 86 (Fall 1982), 75.
40. Interview with Andrew Ross in Ross ed., "Reinventing Community: A Symposium
    on/with Language Poets," *Minnesota Review* 32 (1989): 27–50, 28.

41. Roland Barthes, "To Write: An Intransitive Verb?" in *The Structuralist Controversy: The Languages of Criticism and the Sciences of Man*, ed. Richard Macksey and Eugenio Donato (Baltimore: Johns Hopkins University Press, 1972), 134–56.

42. "Interview," conducted by Tom Beckett, in *The Difficulties: Ron Silliman Issue*, 2.2 (1985), 34–46, 34.

43. Acronym for "Ouvroir des littératures potentielles," which stood for both the writers and the practices of the loose international collective that produced such works as Georges Perec's *La Disparition* (a long prose work in French written without the use of the letter "e") or, more recently, Christian Bök's *Eunoia* (a volume of poetry divided into sections, each organized by a single vowel letter and consisting of poems whose words have no other vowels but the designated one).

44. *The Grand Piano* 7, 106.

45. The best account of Structuralism's influence on Language writing is Silliman's *The New Sentence*. See especially 73–76. The eponymous essay was originally published in *Talks: Hills 6/7* (1980): 190–217.

46. Silliman, *The New Sentence*, 91.

47. Gertrude Stein, *How to Write* (Paris: Plain Editions, 1931), 144.

48. *The Grand Piano* 7, 107.

49. Andrews and Bernstein, *The L=A=N=G=U=A=G=E Book*, x.

50. McCaffery, "From the Notebooks," ibid., 160.

FURTHER READING

Critical TextsAndrews, Bruce. *Paradise & Method: Poetry & Praxis*. Evanston, IL: Northwestern University Press, 1996.

Bartlett, Lee. "What Is Language Poetry?" *Critical Inquiry* 12.4 (Summer 1986): 741–52.

Beach, Christopher (ed.). *Artifice and Indeterminacy: An Anthology of New Poetics*. Tuscaloosa: University of Alabama Press, 1998.

Benson, Steve, Carla Harryman, Lyn Hejinian, Bob Perelman, Ron Silliman, and Barrett Watten. "Aesthetic Tendency and the Politics of Poetry: A Manifesto." *Social Text* 19/20 (Autumn 1988): 261–75.

Bernstein, Charles. *A Poetics*. Cambridge, MA: Harvard University Press, 1991.

Dworkin, Craig. *Reading the Illegible*. Evanston, IL: Northwestern University Press, 2003.

Fredman, Stephen. *Poet's Prose: The Crisis in American Verse*, 2nd ed. Cambridge: Cambridge University Press, 1990.

Hartley, George. *Textual Politics and the Language Poets*. Bloomington: Indiana University Press, 1989.

Ma, Ming-Qian. *Poetry as Re-Reading: American Avant-Garde Poetry and the Poetics of Counter-Method*. Evanston, IL: Northwestern University Press, 2008.

McGann, Jerome. *The Point Is to Change It: Poetry and Criticism in the Continuing Present*. Tuscaloosa: University of Alabama Press, 2007.

Reinfeld, Linda. *Language Poetry: Writing as Rescue*. Baton Rouge: Louisiana State University Press, 1992.

Poetry AnthologiesBarone, Dennis and Peter Gannick, eds. *The Art of Practice. 45 Contemporary Poets.* Elmwood, CT: Potes & Poets Press, 1994.

Silliman, Ron, ed. *In the American Tree*, 2nd ed. Orono, ME: National Poetry Foundation, 2002.

Sloan, Mary Margaret, ed. *Moving Borders. Three Decades of Innovative Writing by Women.* Jersey City, NJ: Talisman House, 1998.

11

HANK LAZER

American Poetry and Its Institutions

> The fact is that virtually all poetry is now under some kind of institutional
> supervision.[1]
>
>   – Jed Rasula
>
> … and the crisis for poetry, for the aesthetic,
> is to create a space for poetry again and again.[2]
>   – Charles Bernstein

The direct economic value of a poem is miniscule, if not zero or negative. As James Sherry, poet and publisher of Roof Books, once remarked, the easiest way to reduce the value of a blank piece of paper is to begin to write a poem on it. While poetry is produced in great quantity and is studied by a huge number of creative writers, it does not sell enough to be a worthwhile pursuit in and of itself. One might expect the reigning ideology to be consistent with Henry David Thoreau's observations in the "Economy" chapter of *Walden*: "avoid all trade and barter."[3] Thoreau tells the anecdote of a strolling Indian who unsuccessfully attempted to sell his woven baskets. Thoreau indicates that he "too had woven a kind of basket of delicate texture," perhaps punning on the textuality of his delicately woven (and, in terms of sales, very unsuccessful) books. But unlike the Indian, he "studies rather how to avoid the necessity of selling them."[4] I remember Gary Snyder many years ago (in the mid-1970s) when he visited Virginia suggested starting a creative writing program that, in addition to writing workshops, offered occupational training such as auto repair or nursing so that the poet would not have to attempt to sell his "woven baskets" or be restricted to teaching others how to weave. "[T]rade," Thoreau concluded, "curses every thing it handles; and though you trade in messages from heaven, the whole curse of trade attaches to the business."[5]

The paradox for American poetry is that this business (which is often characterized as *not* being a business) has little to do with the sale of the commodity itself. Ron Silliman begins his essay, "The Political Economy of

Poetry," with the assertion that "Poems both are and are not commodities."[6] No one in the United States makes a living directly from the sale of his or her poetry, although popular poets such as Billy Collins and Maya Angelou may come close. Generally speaking, one could not sell enough poems to *The New Yorker* and *Poetry* to stay above the poverty line. But the publication of poems (especially books of poems, and most especially award-winning books of poems) certifies one as a possible recipient of the more significant forms of income: academic employment; honoraria for workshops, lectures, and readings; and prizes.[7] Most books of poetry sell well fewer than 1,000 copies, and poets rarely receive substantial royalties and advances for their work, but there clearly is an income to be made from poetry's more lucrative ancillary activities.

Poets & Writers, Inc., a key communication and certification channel for writers, contains "the most comprehensive listing of literary grants and awards, deadlines, and prize winners available in print."[8] Poets & Writers lists more than 9,100 certified authors and claims, with "each issue reach[ing] more than 80,000 writers," to "address issues of importance to creative writers, from finding an agent to promoting one's book."[9] Which raises the further question: how is the aspiring poet to gain access to these professional (and professionalizing) pathways?

Without answering the question, we can note what may be the most astonishing aspect of the contemporary institutionalization of American poetry: that in spite of the nearly worthless nature of the business's principal commodity, the poem, there has been an extraordinary, extensive hyper-professionalization of the business. The vantage of the current century has served to make this hyper-professionalization all the more visible, as evident in some prominent recent efforts to trace the history of creative writing in the United States.[10] Studying poetry's institutional developments since 1945 wanders implicitly into questions such as who or what is this poetry for, and increasingly leads into a densely forested terrain of overdetermination and teeming productivity – a terra incognita that is not subject to a credible description, overview, or analysis. My own range of consideration will, of necessity, be limited, with most of my attention being devoted to creative writing programs, the changing nature of publishing, the recent effects of poetry's digitalization, and an overarching consideration of poetry as a business.

When we attempt an overview of American poetry and its primary institutional locations and professionalizing habits post 1945, an obvious first place to look is graduate programs in creative writing. Most striking is their remarkable proliferation since 1936, when the Iowa Writers' Workshop became the first program to offer a graduate degree in creative writing.

After 1945, a number of high-profile universities would follow suit, including Johns Hopkins (1947), Stanford (1947), and Cornell (1948). And the growth has been exponential: between 1975 and 2010, according to the Association of Writers and Writing Programs (AWP), the total number of creative writing programs has exploded from 79 to 852.[11] But the story here is not simply one of continuing to track the growing number of programs and graduates. We also see today an increasingly diverse range of creative writing programs, from "low residency" to "traditional" MA and MFA programs to PhD programs with a "creative" dissertation option and an emphasis on scholarly and theoretical development. In the AWP's description of its membership, programs and institutions figure as prominently as the people participating in them: "Since 1967, AWP has supported writers and writing programs around the world. We now provide services to over 34,000 writers, 500 member colleges and universities, and 100 writers' conferences and centers."[12] AWP's self-professed mission is "to foster literary achievement, to advance the art of writing as essential to a good education, and to serve the makers, teachers, students, and readers of contemporary writing."[13]

In a daring and data-rich endeavor, Seth Abramson in the November/December 2009 issue of *Poets & Writers* published a ranking of MFA programs in creative writing, including a Top 50, in an effort to assist potential students in making an informed choice about the strengths and weaknesses of particular programs. Abramson spent three years gathering the data. The top five institutions in the poetry category were Iowa, Virginia, Michigan, UMass-Amherst, and Texas. As one might imagine, these rankings generated considerable protest from the AWP.[14] One element of that protest was the failure of the survey to include low residency programs, which are growing in number. In fact, a number of major universities, through their extension programs and divisions of continuing studies, now offer low residency or online programs and courses in creative writing.

If the workshop is the centerpiece for programs in creative writing, then one should not be surprised at the proliferation of free-standing writing workshops, often with a smattering of "celebrity" poets as instructors, often at very attractive locations, thus mixing vacation with "study" or travel/fun with "learning." For example, The 2009 Key West Literary Seminar touted eight present and former poet laureates (Billy Collins, Rita Dove, Yusef Komunyakaa, Maxine Kumin, Paul Muldoon, Kay Ryan, Mark Strand, and Richard Wilbur). Looking at the ads in the May/Summer 2009 issue of *The Writer's Chronicle* (published by the AWP), if you were interested in attending a writing workshop, your choices ranged from Boulder, Colorado, Deer Isle, Maine, and Portland, Oregon, to Paris, Tuscany, and Assisi; from

Middlebury, Vermont, Bainbridge Island, Washington, and Jackson Hole, Wyoming, to Costa Rica, Ghana, Paris, and Mali; from Taos and Santa Fe to Key West, Gettysburg, Toronto, Pont-Aven, and Iowa City.

A sampling of one relatively new "vacation" workshop – US Poets in Mexico (Mérida, Yucatán, México, first held in January 2009) – gives you a sense of this particular market niche.[15] The testimonials of attendees show us how easily the poetry workshop can be fitted to the Club Med cruise vacation model. One attendee savored "the friendliness of all those who attended, students and staff; the late night dinners and drinks; the helpfulness, the encouragement, the new ideas and new viewpoints" and concluded: "USPiM now tops my list of inspirational settings for poets who want to learn, have fun, and experience a beautiful city." Another praises the atmosphere as "absolutely collegial – not a hint of hierarchy," and indicates "there is a 100% chance of my return participation." Another participant concludes: "Through the afternoon Spanish lessons and the wordplay in workshops my language skills expanded, in a magic-realist landscape (art institute housed in a deco train station, bomb-bright colors of the heladería, rioting jackdaws, cumbias in the street and a world beat disco).... I returned home with enough assignments, reading suggestions and inspiration to last years, as well as an extended community of poet friends. I'll return to a USPiM workshop asap."

While it is easy to mock these testimonials (why not add massages, meditation, and optional exercise trainers too?), one could just as easily ask, why not? Why shouldn't the workshop be located in a wonderful travel destination, and why shouldn't a pleasant collegiality be part of the customer or workshop attendee's experience? The student, after all, is a paying *customer*; programs depend on enrollment and income in order to remain viable, and there is increasing competition for these customers. In such a market economy, customer satisfaction drives the business; without it, the business comes to an end.

In the context of this business of training writers, one might ask about the burgeoning creative writing workshop and degree program industry: What is it doing? Why? For whom? To create what? Have these institutions produced an improved product? Is American poetry decidedly "better" as a result of seventy years of rapidly proliferating creative writing programs? Is there, as one might assume, a much greater readership for poetry as a result of these programs? Is there a greater sense of poetry's relevance to American culture generally? While programs in creative writing, like nearly all academic degree-granting programs, are subject to review and evaluation, these larger questions are almost impossible to answer, nor would it be smart to venture answers to these questions by pinning the answer (or, in the language of assessment, the outcomes) to a single source such as the writing programs.

Let's look, then, at the *product* issuing from the creative writing programs (as well as from the many poets not associated with such programs). Let's consider what is taking place with the publication of books of poetry. Craig Dworkin has gathered some very valuable snapshot information about the current state of poetry book publication in the United States:

> Poets House (New York), which aspires to acquire every book of poetry published in America, excluding vanity press publications, has shelved over 20,000 volumes from between the years 1990 and 2006. According to Bowker, the leading data provider to the publishing industry (the same company that assigns ISBN numbers), there were 37,450 poetry and drama titles between 1993 and 2006. Considering only books published during the last year [2006]: Poets House catalogued 1,971 titles with a 2006 copyright; Bowker registered 5,486 new titles under the category of poetry; and Amazon lists 9,444 poetry titles with that publication date for sale. (8)[16]

As Dworkin points out,

> The typical print run for a book of small press poetry, somewhere between 200 to 1,000 copies, is almost always optimistic, determined more by volume breaks in production costs ... than by any realistically projected sales. Only a very small handful of those poetry books, somewhere less than half of one percent of one percent, will ever sell more than a thousand copies, or go into a second printing.[17]

But print-on-demand and small-batch printing over the past few years have radically altered this process. I'm not sure that it makes much sense any longer (in poetry) to think about a "first edition" or an initial press run or a second printing. Publishers such as Salt and BlazeVOX have been leaders in the small-batch print-on-demand model, which allows a publisher to create many titles per year. Although there is a set-up cost, there is only a minimal cost of actually publishing and storing the books (which do not occur until there is a buyer for the volume).

While many of the traditional venues for poetry publication have faced increasing financial constraints, their diminishing output has clearly not diminished the number of titles published. The boundary lines between "vanity" presses, self-publication, online publication, print-on-demand, and refereed publication have grown quite blurred. Friends still publish friends (think of the early publishing history of modernist poetry and the Objectivists, to name a couple of examples), with many poets establishing their own presses for precisely this purpose. But online publication or available-for-free online chapbooks and books have changed the landscape for poetry publication in ways that may preempt the sciences' movement to a system of free, open access. Publishers such as Lulu are proliferating, making it very easy for anyone to have a very affordable and user-friendly way to get a book published.[18]

One can hear a chorus of laments: if anyone's book can get published, how do we know what's any good? Or, linked to strictures of professionalization, how can we determine the worth (for tenure and promotion considerations and for merit-based pay increases) of Professor X's book of poems and/or online journal publications? Shall we still rely on sciences-inspired standards: acceptance/rejection rates; citations; number of reviews; and the dream of "objectivity." which values blindly refereed submission processes, to help us determine how to "credit" Professor X's output? Indeed, the value of "outside" evaluations (is there such a thing in the intensely networked world of poetry?) is further compromised insofar as well-considered negative reviews are a rarity, as are "objective" or balanced letters of recommendation and evaluation.

This somewhat anarchic, decentralized economy takes a lot of work to produce. To achieve the myriad fiefdoms of American poetry, a poetry ecosystem of nearly infinite variety and difference without a discernible epicenter, is no small accomplishment. It takes a peculiar mix of tenacity, idealism, and absurd labor for such an enterprise to be built. One might think of the development of American poetry as mirroring or rhyming with the ascendancy of the personal computer. In the early days of the computer, what was envisioned and expected was the rise of more sophisticated mainframe computers. Instead, the decentralized world of the personal computer won out. Or, to employ a more philosophical description from Emmanuel Levinas: "infinity is produced by withstanding the invasion of a totality."[19]

A counterpoint to my somewhat utopian vision of a thousand flowers blooming is to lament the lack of central authority and to bemoan the collective poetry culture's inability to reinstitute a highly selective poetry canon. From such a perspective, one could argue for a history of American poetry that focused on "major figures" and "major works," so that the lineage of Eliot, Pound, Stevens, and Frost, extending to Robert Lowell, would have a new successor, a recognized consensus "major" poet. But something went wrong – profoundly wrong (and thus profoundly *right*) – in the cultural machinery that produces "major U.S. poets." Through the homogenizing effects of the rapidly proliferating creative writing programs and, via the personal computer, the radically democratized means of production rather inadvertently short-circuited the hero-promotion system and centralization of production and recognition. Even though there still are institutions that pretend to a centralized form of recognition – the appointment of a poet laureate, major awards like the Pulitzer and MacArthur – increasingly these acts of recognition result in skepticism – who? really? you're kidding![20]

A slightly different perspective – other than polarities of praising a mystifying, anarchic multiplicity or a longing for a renewed central set of judgments – is voiced by Charles Bernstein, who suggests that:

> the question for American poetry – and it has been a question for a long time – is what are the terms of the common? Emerson imagines an America that is in process, where the commonness is an aspiration, not something that is a given social fact. Langston Hughes says we are a "people in transition." The "point" is not to hurry through this *going* because we never arrive. *Get used to it!*"[21]

Bernstein worries "that harmony would be too close to homogeneity."[22] While the preoccupation (or occupation via degree programs, workshops, and professionalization) with the plainspoken, readily understandable, personally expressive, and recognizable individualistic voice may push American poetry in the direction of homogeneity, the genre itself and its disparate practitioners prove highly resistant to any nonproliferation treaty. If Shelley imagined all poets as working on one great poem, perhaps the American poetry domain, taken collectively, is working on a poetry of infinite difference – as many poems as "we" are – produced by a nearly infinite variety of social communities (and individuals). Perhaps all "we" have in common is that we write poetry (and perhaps that we like to purchase notebooks).[23] Or, as the website has transformed the concept of the anthology – no longer a problem of choosing which poems to include, given that the available space is infinite – so too has our "one great poem" become an infinitely large, all inclusive poem-website (and thus an unreadable and unknowable infinitely inclusive hypertext).

With so many academic programs teaching students how to write and, implicitly or explicitly, how to read poetry, one might assume that we have developed an increasingly sophisticated readership-writership, and that the writing has improved. Truly, however, there is significant debate about whether writing is a craft that can be taught.[24] The competition in writing, most especially in poetry, lacks anything resembling the precision of a high jump or shot-put competition or a time for the 100-meter freestyle. Often, the value of a poem or body of work is not known for quite some time, and even then, the worth and pertinence of the work continue to undergo massive change depending on the cultural/historical context of the reading moment. Are there, then, other ways to approach the value of poetry-as-product, other than asking if the product is getting better?

In the fall of 1984, I directed a poetry symposium, What Is a Poet?, at the University of Alabama. I deliberately selected participants who represented an aesthetic range; my other premeditated act was to put together a panel of poets *and* critics to see if a productive dialog might be possible. The participants included Charles Bernstein (taking part in only his second academic conference), Denise Levertov, Charles Altieri, David Ignatow, Helen Vendler, Gerald Stern, Marjorie Perloff, Louis Simpson, and Kenneth Burke (in one of his final conferences). In the context of the mid-1980s and the overall humanities culture of the time, with the ascendancy of critical theory in English departments and with a growing rift between creative writers and the "critical" faculty, such a conference led to walkouts, accusations, angry statements, and a highly charged environment for critical exchange.[25] Similarly, in my research and data for poetry reading series in the late 1980s, there were rather clear lines of demarcation and de facto lists of who could and could not read in various sponsored creative writing reading series.[26]

Today, the tale being told is principally one of progress, tolerance, and hybridity: a superficial sense that intense polarizations are a thing of the past and that now student writers (and their encompassing creative writing programs with their institutional extensions – reading series, visiting faculty positions, journals, anthologies) can freely try any style and experiment with any aesthetics without fear of reprisal. As the story might go, the old days – when to read critical theory or to demonstrate an active interest in Language writing entailed affiliations that in most creative writing programs would doom a student-writer to ostracism – have given way to an inclusive, democratic openness. Bob Perelman and Lyn Hejinian have taught (on a visiting basis) at Iowa. "Avant-garde" magazines such as *Fence* and "traditional" ones such as *Poetry* alike publish *all* kinds of poetry. And the major anthologies of the day, such as *American Women Poets of the Twenty-First Century: Where Lyric Meets Language* (2002) and *American Hybrid: A Norton Anthology of New Poetry* (2009), now include the work of "innovative" poets such as Hejinian, Rae Armantrout, Norma Cole, Mei-Mei Berssenbrugge, Susan Howe, Harryette Mullen, Rod Smith, or Keith Waldrop, alongside the work of "traditional" poets such as Lucie Brock-Broido, Robert Hass, Albert Goldbarth, Lynn Emanuel, or Alice Fulton.

But the tale of happy hybridity obscures more conflicted information. An *extended* residence in a new mode of composition (or an out-of-favor one) involves learning, commitment, and risk. The hybridity now being proposed as a resolution to earlier oppositions depends on a lack of historical context and a nearly complete lack of risk, as the student-writer produces his or her weekly assigned "Language" or aleatory poem. In fact, it may not be possible to "try on" a fundamentally oppositional poetics/aesthetics once the context of oppositionality has vanished or become hugely diminished. More fundamentally, the underlying anxieties – that appeared in a polarized manner in the 1980s over the flashpoints of philosophy, theory, and Language writing (and that were very much at the heart of the tensions manifested in my 1984 What Is a Poet? symposium) – are really not at all settled. For the most part, what have been learned over the past twenty-five years are superficial politeness and superficial tolerance.

Behind the mainstream/experimental divide for which hybridity has emerged as the solution, an antipathy toward Language writing still abides in the institutions of American poetry, rightly identified by Rasula with an underriding current of anti-intellectualism:

> The real dirty word in the American poetry clubhouse is *intellectual*. The fitful absorption of modernism into Anglo-American letters was prelude to a lurking and easily revived anti-intellectualism. Resentful accusations of "difficulty" in poetry, commonly associated with modernism, usually mean that the reader (critic) doesn't want poetry to think.[27]

Rasula, I think, is correct in locating the flashpoint in an uneasy accommodation of modernism's radical experimentation and ambition, impulses that are not well suited to the poem-by-poem, line-by-line methodology of most creative writing workshops. As one of those dreaded European theorist suggests, "Poetry is not a kind of art of thought, but thinking is its element as space is that of the plastic arts and time is that of music."[28] The freedom, depth, play, emotion, aesthetics, and centrality of that thinking, as in early modernist poetry, remain the prime disturbers of the hive of creative writing. Unbridled thinking makes for a dissonant buzz.[29]

National Endowment for the Arts (NEA) data on the readership for serious literature, which shows a steady decline in readers of poetry, has gotten considerable national and international news coverage and thus, for some, passes as a fundamental truth. That tale of woe is underscored by the popularity of arguments – such as "Can Poetry Matter?" by Dana Gioia, who was director of the NEA when these studies were undertaken – which bemoan the marginalized or near-terminal state of poetry, with Gioia and others assigning much of the blame to difficult (as opposed to "accessible") poetry.

But there is some important countervailing information to consider, which suggests a more optimistic perspective on our transitional generation as we exit the prolonged era of the book:

Alphabetic writing in books remains the dominant medium for poetry in our time, as it has over the past many hundreds of years; but there was poetry and poetics before the invention of the alphabet, just as new poetries and new poetics will emerge from our post-alphabetic environment of digital and electronic language reproduction. Indeed, the *how*, as well as the archive of poetry, is more likely to be found on the web than in books.[30]

Charles Bernstein suggests that the new digital technology "is not reproducing but producing new possibilities for both the art of poetry and the archive of poetry," and thus he is interested in "the implications of mp3 files for poetry, since we are now witnessing a transvaluation in poetry from the printed book to the sound file of an individual poem."[31] To put it quite simply, the readership of poetry is migrating (and rather rapidly). The NEA's gloomy data stems, in part, from looking in the wrong place (or too narrowly defined a place) to locate engagement with poetry in the United States.

To examine this transition from book to media file, consider a 2006 snapshot from data and observations in "Poetry Off the Books: The Internet is where poetry proliferates," by Craig Morgan Teicher. His article approaches the issue from a market perspective, beginning with an observation: "Ever at the cutting edge, poetry may have finally found its ideal medium, one in which money, at least, is hardly a factor: the Internet."[32] This is how Teicher's section entitled "Webzines Go Legit" begins:

> Foremost among poetry's homes on the Web are the increasing numbers of high-quality online literary magazines that have sprung up in recent years. New editors not wanting or unable to finance expensive print journals have designed engaging Web sites featuring new poems, book reviews and links to other poetry-related sites. These magazines are publishing a wide range of poetry, from Pulitzer Prize winners to up-and-coming poets still in M.F.A. programs. Unlike print journals, they are not hindered by the problem of distribution – anyone with access to the Internet can read them. Of course, poetry publishers count on their poets publishing individual poems to bring readers to their books, and the Internet opens a whole new avenue for getting readers' attention.[33]

Teicher's analysis is intriguing on several counts. First, he makes the Internet poetry magazine sound like AA minor league baseball – a place where poets can demonstrate their hitting ability while trying to make it to the big leagues (which, of course, is the trade house book). And the wide range of poets begins with the farm league MFA-ers (is any other route imaginable to the big leagues?). From a publisher's viewpoint, the Internet creates a great opportunity for free advertising of the poem-book-product. In fact, Teicher points out that astute print publishers scout the digital scene for up-and-coming prospects. What I find most interesting is the attempt to recuperate a hierarchy of prestige for poetry publishing in an admittedly deregulated, egalitarian, and anarchic environment. For Teicher, part of the governing perspective is to remain focused on the narrow funnel that extends from the limited domain of the trade-published book.

Teicher cites Australian poet John Tranter's e-journal *Jacket* as a model for newer publications. *Jacket*, from its inception in 1997 to April 2006, had more than 500,000 visits.[34] *Octopus Magazine*, founded in 2003, makes the case for the economic dynamics of Web-based magazine publishing most dramatically. A print magazine may cost several thousand dollars per year to publish. By contrast, the editors of *Octopus* maintain the site for "less than $100 per year." "Since its inception, *Octopus* has published almost 200 poets [as of April 2006]," and "the site averages between 200 and 250 visits per day."[35]

An even more eye-catching data point – one that flies in the face of the NEA tale of poetry woe – comes from newly emerging online resources such as The Academy of American Poets site, the Poetry Foundation, and PennSound. *Poetry Daily* (www.poems.com), which reprints poems from print journals and new books, averages between 40,000 and 50,000 daily visits, and links send readers to Amazon.com where they can buy featured books.[36]

Teicher also traces the rise of the poetry blog, which he suggests took "firm hold around 2003." He points to Ron Silliman's blog in particular, which launched in 2002 and, until Silliman's migration to Twitter in 2011, remained one of the most frequently visited. In 2005, Silliman's blog hit the 500,000 visitor mark, and in 2006 it was averaging "over 1,100 daily visits."[37] Teicher quotes Silliman, who observes, "I've had over 616,000 visitors to my Web log. Not bad for a guy who has never had a book that sold more than 4,000 copies."[38]

Where are we headed in the twenty-first century? If Teicher's 2006 data do not convince you that the NEA is looking in the wrong place for readers, consider some 2009 numbers for PennSound: 20 million mp3 downloads per year; more than 50,000 downloads per day on average. I cite these data as reliable information, knowing full well that plenty of Web stats are inflated (as a second or less on a Web page often counts as a "visit" or "hit").[39] The 20 million figure reports only mp3 files of poetry readings and talks that a user has actually downloaded or streamed. PennSound, with its especially rich recordings (video and audio) by innovative poets, calls into question the assumption that challenging, innovative poetry is the most marginalized and least attended to of all.

My own effort to get some sense of American poetry and its current institutions convinces me that, in Levinas's terms, we are choosing and developing infinity rather than totality, even as many institutions try to rein in, deny, recuperate, absorb, or ignore the rapidly changing and infinitely diverse terrain for American poetry. There remain significant flashpoints (particularly linked to competition for resources and recognition), and many of these above-ground and below-ground tensions strike me as continuations of the uneasy (or perhaps never to be completed) absorption of the radical innovation that is the ongoing legacy of modernism. Most intriguing is poetry's migration from its long-term residence in the printed book into the digital horizon. Most inspiring is the vitality, variety, and accessibility of American poetry today.

NOTES

1. Jed Rasula, "Innovation and 'Improbable Evidence,'" in *The Consequence of Innovation: 21st Century Poetics*, edited by Craig Dworkin (New York: Roof Books, 2008), 59–92, 83.
2. Charles Bernstein, "The Task of Poetics, the Fate of Innovation, and the Aesthetics of Criticism," Ibid., 37–57, 41.
3. Henry David Thoreau, *Walden* (Princeton: Princeton University Press, 1989), 64.
4. Ibid., 19.
5. Ibid., 70. The most notorious and most reported instance of a major award being made to a poetry organization was Ruth Lilly's bequest of approximately $100 million to *Poetry* in 2002.
6. Ron Silliman, *The New Sentence* (1977; New York: Roof Books, 1987), 20.
7. Beyond the Pulitzer, the Bollingen Prize, an NEA Fellowship, and the Guggenheim Fellowship, there are now "mega-prizes" such as the MacArthur Fellowship (also known as the genius award) with significant financial awards. The MacArthur, for example, provides a "no strings attached" $500,000 award over a period of five years. To date, thirty-six poets have been awarded a MacArthur. There are also an ever-increasing number of smaller prizes.
8. As noted on the organization's Web site, "Poets & Writers, Inc. is the primary source of information, support, and guidance for creative writers. Founded in 1970, it is the nation's largest nonprofit literary organization serving poets, fiction writers, and creative nonfiction writers." http://www.pw.org/about-us (accessed July 18, 2011). A recent gift solicitation from the organization claims: "Last year more than 100,000 writers took advantage of our Web site and magazine, where they found information on where they might publish their work, shared insights on everything from literary agents to MFA programs, read inspiring profiles of established authors, and took advantage of the most reliable listing of writing contests available in print or online. Also, close to 1,000 writers received a total of over $200,000 from P&W to teach workshops or give readings in senior centers, prisons, libraries and other venues, which more than 95,000 individuals attended." Message to the author, December 15, 2009, Email.
9. http://www.pw.org/about-us/about_poets_amp_writers (accessed July 18, 2011).

10. See D. G. Myers, *When Elephants Teach: Creative Writing Since 1880* (1996; Chicago and London: The University of Chicago Press, 2006) and Mark McGurl, *The Program Era: Postwar Fiction and the Rise of Creative Writing* (Cambridge, MA: Harvard University Press, 2009).

11. http://www.awpwriter.org/aboutawp/index.htm (accessed July 21, 2011).

12. http://www.awpwriter.org/membership/index.htm (accessed July 21, 2011).

13. http://www.awpwriter.org/aboutawp/ (accessed July 21, 2011).

14. Seth Abramson, "The Top 50 MFA Programs in the United States" *Poets & Writers Magazine* 37.6 (November–December 2009): 81–91. The *Poets & Writers* Web site offers an updated listing and article: http://www.pw.org/content/top_fifty_mfa_programs_united_states_comprehensive_guide (accessed July 21, 2011). See also the exchange of letters between Matt Burriesci, Acting Executive Director of the AWP, and Seth Abramson in "Rank and Foul," *Poets & Writers Magazine* 38.1 (January–February 2010): 11–13.

15. U.S. Poets in Mexico, e-mail advertisement sent to author, November 21, 2009.

16. Craig Dworkin, "Seja Marginal," in *The Consequence of Innovation*, 8. (Editor's note: It is not easy to produce comparable relative figures for poetry publication between 1945 and the present. But two different bodies of data yield results that give some idea of the dramatic increase in volumes published. The online catalog of the Library of Congress for "poetry" or "poems" in the United States yields 132 results for 1945 and 199 for 1947. The same search yields 928 results for 2005 and 976 for 2007. Publication of the *Bowker Annual of Library and Book Trade Information* dates from 1961. For comparison to the 2006 *Bowker Annual* figure cited by Dworkin, the 1969 *Annual* lists 104 new titles in "Poetry, Drama" for 1967 and 116 for 1968 [New York and London: R.R. Bowker Company, 1969, 36]).

17. Ibid., 15–16.

18. Poetry publishing exists at an intriguing, conflicted crossroads. The University of California Press on July 15, 2011, announced that it was suspending indefinitely publication of its poetry series. (See http://chronicle.com/blogs/pageview/u-of-calif-press-to-suspend-acclaimed-poetry-series/29142 [accessed August 7, 2011]). On May 19, 2011, Amazon announced that e-book sales surpassed the *combined* sales of hardcovers and paperbacks (see: Emma Bazilian's article in *Adweek*, May 20, 2011 – www.adweek.com/news/technology/e-book-sales-pass-print-amazon-131839 [accessed August 7, 2011]). A countervailing news item from July 10, 2011: independent publisher BlazeVOX goes Kindle, with thirty initial poetry titles (priced from $0.99 to $2.99), and by July 30 BlazeVOX announced fifty-five titles (e-mails to author).

19. Emmanuel Levinas, *Totality and Infinity: An Essay in Exteriority*, tr. Alphonso Lingis (1979; Boston: Kluwer Academic, 1991), 104.

20. For an intriguing critique of Pulitzer Prize selections, see Ron Silliman's blog for November 23 and 26, 2009, www.ronsilliman.blogspot.com (accessed July 20, 2011).

21. Bernstein, "Task," 38.

22. Ibid.

23. Hank Lazer, "Notes on Notable Notebooks: Their Role in Writing Poetry," *First Draft*, Vol. 16, No. 1 (Fall 2009): 8–9, 15.

24. See Louis Menand's essay, "Show or Tell: Should Creative Writing Be Taught?" *The New Yorker*, June 8 and 15, 2009: 106–112. Menand questions the premise that "creative writing is something that can be taught" and quotes the University of Iowa Writers' Workshop Web site: "We continue to look for the most promising talent in the country in our conviction that writing cannot be taught but that writers can be encouraged"; http://www.uiowa.edu/~iww/about.htm (accessed July 20, 2011).

25. See http://writing.upenn.edu/library/What-Is-a-Poet/ (accessed July 20, 2011) for photos of the symposium, a brief essay on the twenty-fifth anniversary of the symposium, and a panel discussion transcript. See also Joel Brouwer's blog for the Poetry Foundation, http://www.poetryfoundation.org/harriet/2009/07/what-is-a-poet/#more-4298 (accessed July 20, 2011), which generated heated responses.

26. Hank Lazer, "Poetry Readings and the Contemporary Canon," *Opposing Poetries: Volume One: Issues and Institutions* (Evanston, IL: Northwestern University Press, 1996), 47–54.

27. Rasula, "Innovation," 73.

28. Franz Rosenzweig, *The Star of Redemption* (Madison: University of Wisconsin Press, 2005), 263.

29. To understand the intensity of resistance, turf defense, and opposition below the calm surface of professed openness and accepting hybridity, see "Advice for Graduating MFA Students in Writing: The Words and the Bees" (*The Writer's Chronicle*, Vol. 28, No. 5 [May/Summer 2006]: 1–8) by D. W. Fenza, Executive Director of AWP. Fenza attacks poets and critics such as Charles Bernstein and Marjorie Perloff, calling them "morally repugnant" and accusing them of abusing books and authors and torturing "the poor mother tongue."

30. Bernstein, "Task," 39.

31. Ibid, 45.

32. Craig Morgan Teicher, "Poetry Off the Books: The Internet Is Where Poetry Poliferates," *Publishers Weekly* 253.15 (April 10, 2006): 22–25, 22.

33. Ibid.

34. Ibid. (*Jacket* morphed into *Jacket2* [http://jacket2.org/] with PennSound and Kelly Writers House.)

35. Ibid., 23.

36. Ibid., 25.

37. Teicher, "Poetry Off the Books," 25.

38. Ibid., 22.

39. Charles Bernstein and Alan Filreis, e-mail to the author, November 9–11, 2009.

FURTHER READING

Dworkin, Craig, ed. *The Consequence of Innovation: 21st Century Poetics*. New York: Roof Books, 2008.

Harbach, Chad. "MFA Vs. NYC." *N + 1* 10 (Fall 2010): 1–12.

Lazer, Hank. *Opposing Poetries: Volume One: Issues and Institutions*. Evanston, IL: Northwestern University Press, 1996.

Menand, Louis. "Show or Tell: Should Creative Writing Be Taught?" *The New Yorker*, June 8 and 15, 2009: 106–112.

Myers, D. G. *When Elephants Teach: Creative Writing Since 1880*. 1996; Chicago and London: The University of Chicago Press, 2006.

Teicher, Craig Morgan. "Poetry Off the Books: The Internet is Where Poetry Poliferates," *Publishers Weekly* 253.15 (April 10, 2006): 22–25.

12

CHRISTINA PUGH

The Contemporary "Mainstream" Lyric

In American poetry today, "mainstream" lyric is the school that has no name. Perhaps more precisely, it is the school that is not a school. Given that its practitioners include poets as diverse as Jorie Graham, Frank Bidart, and Rita Dove, the "mainstream" lyric is irreducible to a demographic identity, a set of precise aesthetic goals, or a settled-on technique. Thus the difficulty of defining the lyric "mainstream" lies precisely in the latter's naturalization: like ideology, we feel it to be both everywhere and nowhere. Although its position can appear culturally safeguarded – by institutions like the Poetry Foundation and by presses such as Graywolf and Ecco – the "mainstream" lyric, unlike the Language writing that critiques it, thrives on a certain benign neglect when it comes to the question of self-definition.[1]

We may thus be tempted to define the "mainstream" by all that it is not, much in the manner that Alice Fulton describes Emily Dickinson's poetry: "Dickinson defines subtle states by saying what they are *not,* possibly because no word exists for the emotional realm she's creating."[2] Indeed, given that to write "mainstream" is ostensibly to write with the grain rather than against it – or to swim with rather than against the current of tradition – "mainstream" poetics is monolithic only in the eyes of those who oppose it on aesthetic or political grounds. Language poet Lyn Hejinian, for example, famously critiques the "simpleminded model of subjectivity and authority" that is enacted by the "romantic, unitary, expressive self" in "mainstream" lyric and its predecessors.[3] For Hejinian and other Language writers, "mainstream" tradition is the intellectual product of a mainstreamed America, regardless of the politics that its practitioners may personally espouse: a way of writing, in other words, that connotes capitalist individualism rather than a set of collective goals.[4]

Thus an arguably capacious range of poetic voices appears "mainstreamed," in the sociological sense, only to those who approach it with the same disregard for difference that afflicted William Carlos Williams's judgment of the sonnet as "a form which does not admit of the slightest structural change in its composition."[5] At the same time, the "mainstream's" deeply conservative, sometimes reverential stance toward literary history does make for an almost autonomic affinity between poets, which often involves the propagation of long-standing lyric values such as emotional texture, musicality, and linguistic sheering or density. Although we are far from Pindar, and from the oral poetry that W. R. Johnson celebrates in *The Idea of Lyric*, many "mainstream" poets identify with the work of predecessors ranging from the time of John Donne and before.[6]

Contemporary poets are not, however, simply "mouth[ing] other poets," in Sylvia Plath's terms.[7] We can often find colloquial notes in "mainstream" diction, which can be corralled into lyric musicality of a potentially jazzy stripe: in *Black Zodiac*, for example, Charles Wright names "winter's vocabulary, downsized and distanced," thus transforming corporate slang into postindustrial lyricism.[8] The challenge that C. Day Lewis perceived as central to the poetic endeavors of Wordsworth, Dickinson, and Hardy remains a viable goal, then, for Wright and others: "The singing line could be broadened by an alliance with the speaking line: it was, and still is, a fascinating technical problem – how to incorporate some of the roughness, flexibility and down-to-earthness of common idiom into a lyrical texture."[9] "Lyrical texture" is key here: the "mainstream" poem strives toward a musicality that is at once topical, idiosyncratic, and linguistically pleasurable. Indeed, a poet like Wright is often more interested in imbuing colloquial language with the pleasure of *melopoeia* than in sharpening it to perform explicit political or ideological critique.

Despite their differences in voice, form, and technique, then, "mainstream" poets maintain a preservationist rather than iconoclastic relationship to canonical literary history. In this way, T. S. Eliot's "Tradition and the Individual Talent" becomes more than a delimited paean to high modernism; it also suggests a synchronic aesthetic stance that can be viscerally espoused by contemporary "mainstream" poets themselves:

> [T]he historical sense involves a perception, not only of the pastness of the past, but of its presence; the historical sense compels a man to write not merely with his own generation in his bones, but with a feeling that the whole of the literature of Europe from Homer and within it the whole of the literature of his own country has a simultaneous existence and composes a simultaneous order.[10]

To be sure, the limitations of Eliot's viewpoint have been well noted; he constructs an arguably elitist and exclusionary "Western tradition" to which "mainstream" poets need not be limited. Yet the sense of geologic time – often a sharpened sensibility in these poets – and the role of intertextuality remain indispensible to understanding the work that is inspired by contemporary poets' literary and intellectual forebears. Such projects range from Jorie Graham's homage to Western philosophers in *Materialism*, to retellings of the *Odyssey* in Louise Glück's *Meadowlands*, Thom Gunn's *Moly*, and Derek Walcott's *Omeros*; from Carl Phillips's rethinking of Donne's Holy Sonnets in his "Blue Castrato" series in *From the Devotions*, to Lucie Brock-Broido's reinscription and reinterpretation of Dickinson's "master letters" in her book of the same title – and the list goes on.[11] To "make it new" today is, ultimately, to keep making it old, even if the precise cadence of these contemporary voices may seem unimaginable before the last couple of decades. Such is the conundrum and the lifeblood of the "mainstream."

How might the preceding list address Hejinian's critique of the lyric "I" as commensurate with a "unitary, expressive self"? Certainly, its intensive intertextuality would seem to preclude straightforward self-expression as we usually understand it. But more importantly, even a cursory reading through literary history (Shakespeare, Donne, Milton, Keats) reveals that the lyric "I" – or the poetic speaker – has never been unitary or, by extension, "expressive" of anything unitary. As we'll see, the best "mainstream" poets are those who took neither the confessional ethos (and its ostensibly referential relation to "selfhood") nor Language critiques of that ethos to heart, but who instead have drawn from a much longer tradition in which the lyric "I" – while not always scrambling or refracting syntax, as in more experimental work – has long been understood to be fictional, rhetorical, and multivalent. "Mainstream" poetics is therefore more than allusive; it also seeks to replicate the most complex speaker-constructions found over the course of literary history.

Indeed, this strand of speaker-construction is nothing new; it is traceable from Donne to Dickinson to Berryman.[12] In the last twenty-five years, we can find it as readily in the formal poems of Thom Gunn as in the dispersed yet indexical Graham: "How the invisible / roils. I see it from here and then / I see it from here."[13] Now, as in the past, the lyric's "I" is not only incommensurable with the expression of a *biographical* self, but its rhetorical and fictional speaker – whether or not it is posited as an explicit "I" – may not be commensurate with a self at all, at least insofar as the term implies a strong degree of referentiality.[14]

However, given that the positing of an "I" is often materially central to a lyric poem's unfolding, we should consider more deeply what the best lyric poetry – contemporary and otherwise – offers as an alternative to Hejinian's notion of self-expression. We usually understand the latter as an untroubled one-to-one correspondence between biographical experience and artistic representation, but Roland Barthes provides a different context for the word "expression," one whose Latin derivation suggests instead the process of photography: "...'imago lucis opera expressa'; which is to say: image revealed, 'extracted,' 'mounted,' 'expressed' (like the juice of a lemon) by the action of light."[15]

In quoting Barthes here, my intention is not to suggest that poems should have the documentary capacities of certain photographs, but instead to emphasize the etymological association of "expression" with the *technical* properties of extraction and condensation within representation. Thus what the photo does with light, the poem accomplishes with prosody and technique as the agents that "express," or "chemically" enlighten, empirical or nonempirical material into representation; that the poet is, in turn, the agent of technique remains unproblematic in this context.

Ultimately, this line of thinking recalls M. H. Abrams's discussion of the lyric "I" and its historical paradoxes:

> Although the lyric is uttered in the first person, the "I" in the poem need not be the poet who wrote it. In some lyrics, such as John Milton's sonnet "When I consider how my light is spent" and Samuel Taylor Coleridge's "Frost at Midnight," the references to the known circumstances of the author's life make it clear that we are to read the poem as a personal expression. Even in such personal lyrics, however, both the character and utterance of the speaker may be shaped by the author in a way that is conducive to the desired artistic effect.[16]

Abrams's first sentence suggests the time-honored dramatic monologue or persona poem, in which a historical persona or created character is made to speak; such "mainstream" poets as Bidart and Ai are still profitably engaging this lyric subgenre. Yet the final point of this passage is even more instructive for our purposes: while material in poems may surely be taken from actual "experience" – after all, even at this moment of Flarf and Google-induced poetry, persons are still the ones doing the writing – such experience must be subordinate to, and transformed by, poetic structure.[17] "Personal expression" is therefore not commensurate with what Abrams calls the "personal lyric" (pace Abrams himself). More recently, Mark Strand has articulated this distinction from the poet's perspective: "[W]hen I use 'I,' I'm not reporting on anything that I do. I draw on events and feelings that I've lived through; but I don't feel that I am being autobiographical. The 'I' is a convention."[18]

For many contemporary American poets, the "direct line" to such convention is the work of their nineteenth-century forebears Dickinson and Whitman, both creators of variously outsized, imminently rhetorical poetic "I"'s. To understand this, one only need juxtapose Dickinson's "It would have starved a gnat / To live so small as I" with the countervailing, sometimes exclamatory grandiosity of "Title Divine! Is mine!".[19] Or recall Whitman's "referential" self-constructions that are transparently identifiable as bombastic rhetorical fictions ("Walt Whitman, a kosmos, of Manhattan the son").[20] The actualization of such speakers, who contain more multitudes than any empirical self could reasonably support, is dependent on the readerly imagination described by Jonathan Culler: "Any speaker whom the reader fills in or imagines will be a poetic construct."[21]

Indeed, to see the poem as reflection (of the poet's person) rather than artifact is the province and pitfall of the beginner. It is therefore unsurprising that our most successful "mainstream" poets are less concerned with putting the self into poetry – or with the labor of keeping it out – than with transforming strands of intellectual and emotional material into grist for poetic form; as Glück says, "first, *I love it.* / Then, *I can use it.*"[22] Clearly, poetry sometimes *is* associated with self-expression and truth-telling in our culture; but this belief is a function of the fallacy that Glück has defined as "our failure to separate poetry which *sounds like* honest speech from honest speech" (emphasis mine).[23]

As Glück shows in "Against Sincerity," it is poetic form and lineation – not reducible to rhyme and meter, but often vestigially dependent on it – that has always enabled the poet to separate the work from the "self," thereby creating a permeable boundary between the personal and the impersonal, the personal and the universal. Mutlu Konuk Blasing describes the results of such "formalization": "The poet's personal memories and associations in the mother tongue are formalized and thus socialized as a generic discourse of a virtual 'I,' so that other speakers with other, different, memories and associations can recognize their 'own truths' as socialized/individuated subjects in language."[24] For Blasing as for Abrams, then, even traceable "personal" material in poems must yield to the depersonalizing effect that poetic form, in its protean possibilities, confers on it. The movement from the internal self of the poet to the externalized structure of the poem – from the biographical "I" to what catches the eye and reverberates in the ear – is always imminently technical and, to a certain degree, alchemical (recall Barthes's notion of photographic "expression").

I would argue that the so-called confessional poem of the mid-twentieth century offers a vivid instance of the kind of "virtual 'I'" that Blasing describes; nevertheless, Confessionalism has become a virtual byword for ignoring the very formalization that makes the "I" virtual rather than autobiographical. The "confessional" label was a misnomer, in other words, at least insofar as it implied a direct confession of life events. Adam Kirsch notes that "in confession, [criticism] found a bad metaphor for what the most gifted of these poets were doing. The motive for confession is penitential or therapeutic ... but the [confessional] poets ... always approached their writing as artists, and their primary motive was aesthetic."[25] The nature of the work arguably opened the door to new and more daring representations in poetry, but the confessional poets were not writing memoir as we understand that popular genre today. The "confessional" Plath, for example, often wrapped her poems in metonymies and metaphors of a distinctly mythological cast.[26] And the "confessional" Bishop was able to excise her lesbian identity so assiduously from her published poems that they were still being decoded long after her death.[27] As we can see from the sometimes-dramatic contrast between their personal writings and their published poems, neither Plath nor Bishop established – or more importantly, cared to establish – a continuous identity between poetry and biographical life. On the contrary, the torrid emotional urgency of *Ariel*, combined with its patently fictional constructions of Plath's "self," is precisely what any poet has license to create.[28]

Partially for these reasons, our best "mainstream" poets have remained largely unconcerned by the misunderstandings surrounding the confessional work of the previous generation. In "Self-Portrait as Apollo and Daphne," for example, Graham re-constellates Plath's personae by de-individuating the titular "self" into a pair of characters from Greek mythology.[29] Graham's further contribution is to inhabit the always-incipient phenomenology of characters who remain arrested within the webs of their determining storylines:

> the shards caught here and there – *what did you do*
> *before?* or *will you forgive me?* or *say*
> *that you'll love me for*
>
> *ever and ever*
> (is it a squeal of brakes is it a birthcry?)
> (let x equal forever he whispered let y let y....)[30]

Here, Graham's hypothetical "shards" of lovers' speech remain unanchored to any character: they are attributed neither to Daphne nor to Apollo. What we see instead is not only self-portraiture as self-splitting, but the further lyric reduction of these parenthetically "split" figures: that is, their "characterization" is subordinate to the magnified role of inchoate narrative event. By extension, the titular "self" may be neither unique nor unitary; Graham suggests that selves are not limited to fleshly entities, but are instead parceled out among the scores of our inherited cultural mythologies – which, while "mathematically" unsparing, remain elliptical in what they reveal of their own divisions and equations ("let y let y....").

Graham's career trajectory is instructive for what it suggests about the role of "mainstream" lyric criticism in assigning poetic value. Although her synecdochal relationship to contemporary lyric may seem unassailable today, such positioning was not a foregone conclusion. Indeed, the very breadth of poets to whom Graham is compared suggests other critical and generic possibilities for her body of work. While Helen Vendler places Graham's long lines in a lineage ranging from Hopkins to Whitman to Stevens, Catherine Sona Karagueuzian notes that she is often compared to the Language writers.[31]

Indeed, Graham's poetry in *The End of Beauty* and after can seem to enact a very particular tenor of indeterminacy that was promulgated by the Language writers. Yet it was Vendler's "siring" of Graham in the lyric family tree – as shown in the very subtitle of her book *The Breaking of Style: Hopkins, Heaney, Graham* – that proved definitive for the poet's critical placement. One could claim that Vendler's influential role in "making" a lyric poet is similar to the ideological process that Virginia Jackson describes in *Dickinson's Misery*: "...history has made the lyric in its image."[32] Even though I would not go as far as Jackson does here – I do believe that Graham's poetry is fundamentally lyric – Graham's reception points to the ways that criticism can fasten a potentially hybrid poetic body of work under the aegis of "mainstream" values.

Perhaps there is no greater contemporary paean to these values, and to the incommensurable tenors of the lyric voice, than Glück's *The Wild Iris*.[33] Here, the poet personifies flower species and a dimly Judaic God figure in poems that are interspersed with others containing a more recognizably human voice – one, indeed, that is modeled on the figure of Glück herself. But these loosely autobiographical poems cannot simply be taken at face value. They are integral to the book's larger, polyphonic project of exploring what Steven Knapp calls both "the nature of personified agency, and ... the contrast between such agency and the lives of our ordinary selves."[34] It is within this lacuna that the book's power resides. And given that Barbara Johnson describes apostrophe as "almost synonymous with the lyric voice," there is a sense in which Glück is also anatomizing the lyric genre as such.[35]

By overlaying personification, apostrophe, and prosopopoeia in these various figures, Glück creates a chorus of monologues – voices that can speak, but never listen or reply: "Certainly / you don't look at us, don't listen to us," says the choral voice of "Field Flowers" to an unnamed human figure.[36] By creating a heteroglossic populace that nonetheless cannot achieve dialogue, *The Wild Iris* explores the constitutive, insistent nature of monologism in the lyric, which we see with some clarity in the book's title poem:

> You who do not remember
> passage from the other world,
> I tell you I could speak again: whatever
> returns from oblivion returns
> to find a voice:
>
> from the center of my life came
> a great fountain, deep blue
> shadows on azure seawater.[37]

Figured metaphorically as a fountain's water, the liquid voice of the iris is inflective of the monologic voice as such, much as the "deep blue / shadows on azure seawater" cast blue on blue: here, shadow is the result of gradation rather than contrast (or, in painterly terms, *chiaroscuro*).[38] Voice is therefore a subtler superimposition, not a dark shadow cast in sun by the self's limbs and lineaments. By extension, a speaking flower "finds a voice" by likening that voice to a shadowed fountain of which its own petals remain tenor. While this is, in a sense, an extremely self-reflexive moment, it is also a figure that is worlds away from "finding a voice" in the workshop setting (which relies on the dictum, "Write what you know").

Indeed, some of Glück's flowers claim to have no knowledge at all, thus divorcing lyric speech from preconceived ideation: "The great thing / is not having / a mind," muses a red poppy in a poem of the same name.[39] Because many of Glück's flower voices speak at the very moment of their rebirth in the spring, the wild iris's "oblivion" is always the near shore of the speeches they make. To be sure, the human figures in the book are afflicted by their own oblivions, persistently calling to an "unreachable father"[40] rather than listening to the flowers' questions and injunctions. In this sense, *The Wild Iris* is nothing but a book of address, less upholding Roman Jakobson's conative function than dramatizing its necessary failure if tested as a communicative device.[41] As Glück creates apostrophe as a system of incommensurate – and perpetually missed – signals between the human and the imaginary, or lyrically derived, divine, her work also recalls Johnson's characterization of Gwendolyn Brooks's "The Mother" as a similar reconfiguration of the trope: "...the grammatical I/thou starting point of traditional apostrophe has been replaced by a structure in which the speaker is simultaneously eclipsed, alienated, and confused with the addressee."[42]

To lean so heavily on the trope of personification, especially at the end of the twentieth century, was admittedly a risk, considering that Wordsworth himself was trying to rid poetry of such abstractions back in his "Preface to

Lyrical Ballads." But *The Wild Iris* received the Pulitzer Prize in 1993, which suggests that certain lyric tropes should not be dismissed as outmoded if they are employed with both lucidity and passionate investment. Indeed, there is a sense in which Glück's resurrection of "perennials" is also the perennial and salutary resurrection of personification and apostrophe in the lyric. To claim this, however, is not to say that such resurrection can impart anything like a Christian born-again life: Glück's god is an indifferent one, and the human figures in the book are often melancholic and ineffectual.

Glück's sequence shows the inefficacy – of human experience as a single catalyst for, or determinant of, art. It is in this spirit that we may read Carl Phillips's similar assessment of George Herbert's poetry: "Herbert's poems … are an honest and, to a large extent, self-interested inquiry into questions whose answers did not entirely accord with personal experience."[43] One could add that the very insufficiency of empirical experience is the breeding ground for poetic trope. It also inaugurates the move toward impersonality that Sharon Cameron has described in Emerson's "Experience," when "the most painfully intense property of a particular personal experience – dissociation ('it does not touch me') – migrates so that it is recognizable as the property of *all* experience independent of particularity."[44] This is the crux of Glück's disparately invested – and arguably dissociated – voices in *The Wild Iris*.

Such elusive "experience independent of particularity" also characterizes the work of Thom Gunn, whose fixed poetic forms serve to trouble the boundaries of what we might call the empirical self.[45] In *The Man with Night Sweats*, Gunn elegizes his friends, gay men who died of AIDS in the late 1980s, thus beginning with a personal relationship to an historic epidemic.[46] But through their very use of poetic form, his elegies also enact a salubrious dispersal of the self into the plural other – into friendship inflected with *agape*, with sexuality, and often synonymous with the culture of the gay community in the late twentieth century:

> Contact of friend led to another friend,
> Supple entwinement through the living mass
> Which for all that I knew might have no end,
> Image of an unlimited embrace.
> [...]
> But death – Their deaths have made me less defined:
> It was their pulsing presence made me clear.[47]

Gunn's heroic quatrains and pluralization of elegy readily invoke Gray's "Elegy Written in a Country Churchyard." Moreover, he describes *contact* as both the progress of the virus ("Contact of friend led to another friend") and the deferring of self into relationship not with a single other, but with multiple others (the sexualized "living mass"), which could be infinitely extended in a variant of the mathematical sublime. Surprisingly, it is the pluralized mass – inevitably both the "pulsing" crowd and the infectious growth – that confers boundaries upon the individualized speaker who fully enters it. Whereas Peter Sacks notes that the elegy traditionally works to "place the dead, and death itself, at some cleared distance from the living," Gunn's speaker finds his own contours "clear[ed]" only through the "pulsing presence" of the living mass itself; his very elegy, even in its formal strictures, has rendered him "less defined."[48]

As Mark Jarman and David Mason note, the New Formalists – a group younger than Gunn's generation – have employed fixed forms to promulgate "a valued civility, putting a premium not only on technique, but also on a larger cultural vision that restores harmony and balance to the arts."[49] In contrast, however, Gunn's project is more in line with what we have been discussing as "mainstream" lyric values that are not determined by a single formal choice. Indeed, I have been suggesting that the contemporary lyric succeeds not to the degree that it is "civil," but to the degree that it "suffices," in Stevens's terms, to create a complexity of speaker or linked speakers who are not commensurate with – or limited by – empirical "selves."[50]

In this light, let's consider Gunn's use of trimeter to describe the direst of medical conditions, a choice that recalls Dickinson's use of the ballad meter to enclose extreme emotional straits:

> He still found breath, and yet
> It was an obscure knack.
> I shall not soon forget
> The angle of his head,
> Arrested and reared back
> On the crisp field of bed,
>
> Back from what he could neither
> Accept, as one opposed,
> Nor as a lifelong breather
> Consentingly let go,
> The tube his mouth enclosed
> In an astonished O.[51]

The deceptive gaiety of the three-beat line articulates something between a rock and an existential hard place: to continue to be (comically) defined as a "lifelong breather" like the rest of us, a dying patient cannot reject the breathing tube that he also concomitantly "oppos[es]." As a result of this philosophic and physiological impasse, his mouth must continuously shape – but not say – the open O of apostrophe, which has now become both a vessel for breath and an occlusion of voice. In this sense, "found breath" constitutes the very vestige of life as medically enforced silence.

Thus the ruefully "obscure knack" of aided breathing brings up difficult, if now quite familiar, questions about a dying person's agency with respect to his own death: this terrain is the very limit of "selfhood" and what necessarily troubles its definition. How can we usefully define "consent"? When, in fact, does one stop being a "self" who can provide it? Yet when figured as trimeter rhyme in the poem, these weighty questions have become inexplicably, dolefully "light." As in the lines above, the speaker himself is implicitly redefined through his formal construction – importantly, not just his empirical "witnessing" – of this particular life in a deeply moving, yet also somehow humorous, manner. It is in this sense that "found breath" may be read otherwise: in contrast to "finding a voice" in "The Wild Iris," the phrase is commensurate with "mainstream" lyric's discovery of a form – in this case, a very old folk-meter – to reconsider and to redress the long process of dying: an ancient theme whose metonymies are, for Gunn, ineluctably current.

As we have seen, "mainstream" lyric is nothing if not literarily conservative. But the degree to which literary tradition is itself conservative remains, at the very least, debatable. Despite their differences, Graham, Glück, and Gunn are clearly steeped in a poetics that not only provides pleasure, but also, in Johnson's words, is "capable of conserving and inscribing messages the radicality of which may not yet have been explored."[52] This is not to imbue "mainstream" poetry with a radicalism that it does not have, but instead to articulate that varieties of linguistic music, or the positing of a lyric "I," do not preclude complexity or new knowledge. In the last two decades or so, the work of these and other "mainstream" poets has revealed precisely that.

NOTES

1. This is not to claim that "mainstream" poets are uninterested in contemplating their art within the confines of the essay or other extended prose. But their books of essays – such as Louise Glück's *Proofs and Theories* (New York, Ecco, 1995), James Longenbach's *The Resistance to Poetry* (Chicago: University of Chicago Press, 2004), and Carl Phillips's *Coin of the Realm: Essays on Art and the Life of Poetry* (St. Paul, MN: Graywolf Press, 2004), to name a few – are more likely to place the contemporary lyric in a historical context than to pinpoint what characterizes today's "mainstream" lyric as such.
2. Alice Fulton, *Feeling as a Foreign Language* (St. Paul, MN: Graywolf, 1999), 145.
3. Lyn Hejinian, *The Language of Inquiry* (Berkeley: University of California Press 2000), 329.
4. The degree to which such (sometimes celebrated) atomism is either inculcated or counter-indicated by the workshop environment, or indeed the "poetry world" as such, would be material for another essay.

5. Willliam Carlos Williams, "The Poem as a Field of Action," *Twentieth-Century American Poetics*, ed. Dana Gioia, David Mason, and Meg Schoerke (Boston: McGraw-Hill, 2004), 57. Even the change from the Petrarchan to the Shakespearean sonnet form proves Williams's contention to be untrue.

6. W. R Johnson, *The Idea of Lyric: Lyric Modes in Ancient and Modern Poetry* (Berkeley: University of California Press, 1983).

7. Sylvia Plath, *The Unabridged Journals of Sylvia Plath 1950–1962*, ed. Karen V. Kukil (New York: Anchor Books, 2000), 92.

8. Charles Wright, *Black Zodiac* (New York: Farrar, Strauss, and Giroux, 1997), 46.

9. C. Day Lewis, *The Lyric Impulse* (Cambridge, MA: Harvard University Press, 1965), 17.

10. T. S. Eliot, "Tradition and the Individual Talent," *Critical Theory Since Plato*, ed. Hazard Adams (New York: Harcourt, 1971), 112.

11. Jorie Graham, *Materialism: Poems* (Hopewell, NJ: Ecco Press, 1993); Louise Glück, *Meadowlands* (Hopewell, NJ: Ecco Pres, 1996); Thom Gunn, *Moly* (London: Faber & Faber, 1971); Derek Walcott, *Omeros* (New York: Farrar, Stauss, Giroux, 1990); Carl Phillips, *From the Devotions: Poems* (St. Paul, MN: Graywolf Press, 1998); Lucie Brock-Broido, *The Master Letters: Poems* (New York: A. A. Knopf, 1995).

12. Along these lines, Glück notes that "Berryman began to sound like Berryman when he invented Mr. Bones, and so was able to project two ideas simultaneously" (*Proofs* 44). But the invention's purpose is not a "true" representation of Berryman's self; instead, its goal is the creation of "distinctive voice" (44), as separable from empirical or understandable selfhood.

13. Graham, *Materialism*, 4.

14. Even Paul Allen Miller, who argues in *Lyric Texts and Lyric Consciousness* (New York: Routledge, 1994) that the poetry collection is the birth of "lyric consciousness" (1), ultimately refuses to reduce that consciousness either to straightforward psychology or to the creation of "selfhood" in the work: "This ego is not the historical Catullus, but rather is a function of the reader's engagement with the collection" (74–75).

15. Roland Barthes, *Camera Lucida: Reflections on Photography*, tr. Richard Howard (New York: Hill and Wang, 1982), 81.

16. M. H. Abrams, *A Glossary of Literary Terms*, 6th ed. (New York: Harcourt, 1993), 108.

17. For an extended discussion on the nature of this transfer, see Veronica Forrest-Thomson, *Poetic Artifice: A Theory of Twentieth-Century Poetry* (New York: St. Martin's Press, 1978). For another account of how poetic form transforms Milton's (clearly biographical) experience of blindness in his famous sonnet, see Glück's "Against Sincerity" (*Proofs* 37–41).

18. Lenny Emmanuel, "Mark Strand and Lenny Emmanuel at the Trestle," *Antioch Review* 67.1 (2009): 54.

19. Emily Dickinson, *The Complete Poems of Emily Dickinson*, ed. Thomas Johnson (Boston: Little Brown, 1960), 301–302, 487.

20. Walt Whitman, *Leaves of Grass and Selected Prose* (London: Everyman, 1993), 47.

21. Jonathan Culler, *Structuralist Poetics: Structuralism, Linguistics, and the Study of Literature* (Ithaca, NY: Cornell University Press, 1975), 166.

22. Louise Glück, *Vita Nova* (Hopewell, NJ: Ecco Press, 1999), 29.

23. Louise Glück, *Proofs and Theories: Essays on Poetry* (Hopewell, NJ: Ecco Press, 1994), 35.

24. Mutlu Konuk Blasing, *Lyric Poetry: The Pain and the Pleasure of Words* (Princeton, NJ: Princeton University Press, 2007), 45.

25. Adam Kirsch, *The Wounded Surgeon: Confession and Transformation in Six American Poets* (New York: W. W. Norton, 2005), x.

26. Sylvia Plath, *The Collected Poems of Sylvia Plath*, ed. Ted Hughes (New York: HarperPerennial, 2008).

27. See, for example, Marilyn May Lombardi, *The Body and the Song: Elizabeth Bishop's Poetics* (Carbondale: Southern Illinois University Press, 1995).

28. Nevertheless, as Jacqueline Rose discusses in *The Haunting of Sylvia Plath* (Cambridge, MA: Harvard University Press, 1993), some of Plath's most frequently anthologized poems (e.g., "Daddy") have been castigated precisely because they misrepresented the "facts" of Plath's biography.

29. Jorie Graham, *The End of Beauty* (New York: Ecco Press, 1987).

30. Graham, *The End of Beauty*, 32.

31. See Helen Vendler, *The Breaking of Style: Hopkins, Heaney, Graham* (Cambridge, MA: Harvard University Press, 1995) 71–96; and Catherine Sona Karagueuzian, *"No Image There and the Gaze Remains": The Visual in the Work of Jorie Graham* (New York: Routledge, 2005), 16. (Note: this is actually not Karagueuzian's perspective. Rather than arguing for Graham's categorization as a Language writer, she is simply noting this aspect of Graham's reception.)

32. Virginia Jackson, *Dickinson's Misery: A Theory of Lyric Reading* (Princeton, NJ: Princeton University Press, 2005), 15.

33. Louise Glück, *The Wild Iris* (Hopewell, NJ: Ecco, 1992).

34. Steven Knapp, *Personification and the Sublime: Milton to Coleridge* (Cambridge, MA: Harvard University Press, 1985), 3.

35. Barbara Johnson, *A World of Difference* (Baltimore: The Johns Hopkins University Press, 1987) 185.

36. Glück, *Wild Iris*, 28.

37. Ibid., 1.

38. Johnson also shows that in Mallarme's "L'Azure," the signifier *azure* is a sign not only of poetry-as-such – "a sign that what one is reading is a poem" (*World of Difference* 120) – but also "an explicit version of the ways in which a text is never its own contemporary, cannot constitute a self-contained whole" (Ibid.,121).

39. Glück, *Wild Iris*, 29.

40. Ibid., 3.

41. Roman Jakobson, *Language in Literature* (Cambridge, MA: Belknap, 1987), 67–8.

42. Johnson, *World of Difference*, 189.

43. Phillips, *The Coin of the Realm*, 49.

44. Sharon Cameron, *Impersonality: Seven Essays* (Chicago: University of Chicago Press, 2007), xvii.

45. Though born in Great Britain in 1929, Gunn lived in San Francisco for fifty years – from 1954 until his death in 2004 – thus qualifying, for some, as an American poet even though he never became an American citizen. His inclusion in such anthologies as *The Best American Poetry 1998* suggests that at least

some in the American poetry establishment were more than willing to claim him as their own.

46. Thom Gunn, *The Man with Night Sweats* (New York: Farrar Strauss Giroux, 1992).
47. Ibid., 80.
48. Peter Sacks, *The English Elegy: Studies in the Genre from Spencer to Yeats* (Baltimore: The Johns Hopkins University Press, 1985), 19.
49. Mark Jarman and David Mason, eds., *Rebel Angels: 25 Poets of the New Formalism* (Ashland, OR: Story Line Press, 1996), xviii–xix.
50. Wallace Stevens, *The Collected Poems* (New York: Vintage, 1982), 239.
51. Gunn, *Man with Night Sweats*, 66.
52. Johnson, *World of Difference*, 31.

FURTHER READING

Blasing, Mutlu Konuk. *Lyric Poetry: The Pain and the Pleasure of Words*. Princeton, NJ: Princeton University Press, 2007.

Cameron, Sharon. *Impersonality: Seven Essays*. Chicago: University of Chicago Press, 2007.

   Lyric Time: Dickinson and the Limits of Genre. Baltimore: The Johns Hopkins University Press, 1979.

Culler, Jonathan. *Structuralist Poetics: Structuralism, Linguistics, and the Study of Literature*. Ithaca, NY: Cornell University Press, 1975.

Forrest-Thomson, Veronica. *Poetic Artifice: A Theory of Twentieth-Century Poetry*. Manchester: Manchester University Press, 1978.

Fulton, Alice. *Feeling as a Foreign Language*. St. Paul, MN: Graywolf Press, 1999.

Glück, Louise. *Proofs and Theories: Essays on Poetry*. Hopewell, NJ: Ecco Press, 1994.

Hejinian, Lyn. *The Language of Inquiry*. Berkeley: University of California Press, 2000.

Jackson, Virginia. *Dickinson's Misery: A Theory of Lyric Reading*. Princeton, NJ: Princeton University Press, 2005.

Johnson, Barbara. *A World of Difference*. Baltimore: The Johns Hopkins University Press, 1987.

Kirsch, Adam. *The Wounded Surgeon: Confession and Transformation in Six American Poets*. New York: W. W. Norton, 2005.

Knapp, Steven. *Personification and the Sublime: Milton to Coleridge*. Cambridge, MA: Harvard University Press, 1985.

Lewis, C. Day. *The Lyric Impulse*. Cambridge, MA: Harvard University Press, 1965.

Longenbach, James. *The Resistance to Poetry*. Chicago: University of Chicago Press, 2004.

Miller, Paul Allen. *Lyric Texts and Lyric Consciousness: The Birth of a Genre from Archaic Greece to Augustan Rome*. New York: Routledge, 1994.

Vendler, Helen. *The Breaking of Style: Hopkins, Heaney, Graham*. Cambridge, MA: Harvard University Press, 1995

13

OREN IZENBERG

Poems in and out of School: Allen Grossman and Susan Howe

It is one of the great commonplaces in the history of the theory of art that poetry exists to delight and instruct. Yet if the delight of poetry was once seen as "the first light-giver to ignorance," a privileged vehicle and pre-requisite for the preservation and transmission of other "tougher" forms of knowledge,[1] then our present moment regards the pedagogical imperative in art more suspiciously: as a dulling of our pleasures, as a descent from art's higher calling, or as laying bare its bullying or "palpable design" upon us.[2] The terms of art for poetry's traditional pedagogical genres and modes – sententious, moral, rhetorical, satiric – have been transformed into terms of abuse by generations of critics moved by the Romantics' "abhorrence" for the didactic (Shelley), their preference for power over knowledge (Hazlitt), for "the tigers of wrath" over "the horses of instruction" (Blake).[3] To these, the twentieth century added still another epithet, perhaps the most damning of all, this one meant to suggest both the diminishment of art's vitality under the contemporary conditions of its practice and the dire constriction of its audience when the institutional scene of instruction becomes poetry's all in all: "academic."

As an insult, "academic poet" has always had more punch than precision. At present, as in the 1940s and 1950s when it came into wide use, the label is intended to identify a staid "mainstream," against which more authentic, daring, or experimental writers may rebel. It is affixed to poets who were trained in and/or make a living in the university (but how many poets does that exclude?), and poets whose classical erudition, habits of allusion, or fondness for and facility with traditional poetic forms are judged to come at the cost of artistic originality or some vital relation to experience (a judg-ment that manages always to exempt favored writers like Louis Zukofsky, with his Catullus, his sestinas, and canzones).[4] But for the poets I discuss in this chapter, Allen Grossman and Susan Howe, the term has a more com-plicated freight – one that says less about their alliances and affiliations as artists, and more about their highly deliberated conception of how, and in what context, art acquires its particular value for contemporary culture.[5]

The epic labors of aesthetic and civilizational assemblage and reconstruction that characterize high Modernist poetry represent a qualified return to poetry's didactic project. The footnotes to T. S. Eliot's "The Waste Land" are more than a mere printer's contrivance padding out the text to marketable length; they are an integral part of Eliot's ambition to counter "the decay of a common belief and a common culture" with its own phantasmatic image of a unified Christian civilization."[6] And yet despite Eliot's concession to the medieval university's role in cultivating or sustaining "The Mind of Europe," it was crucial to him not to be seen aping the modern university's *methods*.[7] Thus we are treated to the spectacle of our paradigmatic scholar-poet dismissing his own annotations as "a remarkable exposition of bogus scholarship."[8] Likewise for Ezra Pound, eternal ABD: from the "New Method of Scholarship" proposed at the outset of *I Gather the Limbs of Osiris*, to the crank's syllabus assigned in *ABC Of Reading*, to the enthusiastic and influential embrace of Fenollosa's fantasies about a pictographic Chinese language, Pound's critical essays forward judicious insight, artistically generative misunderstandings, and arrant nonsense with the same strident authority.[9] Although Pound denigrated the academic study of literature taking place in "[i]nstitutions for the obstruction of learning," he also maintained that literature ought to be regarded as itself an institution of knowledge, as a science in its own right: "The arts give us a great percentage of the lasting and unassailable data regarding the nature of man, of immaterial man, of man considered as a thinking and sentient creature."[10] Indeed, it is the sense that artistic pedagogy allows for the crystallization of insight from "Luminous Detail" rather than from the slog of accumulated multitudinous fact that distinguishes the "Ezuversity" from the university: "It's all rubbish to pretend that art isn't *didactic. A revelation* is always *didactic.*"[11]

Modernist poetry's ambivalent relation to didacticism, and particularly to its contested association with the account of the knowledge system cultivated and reproduced by the modern university, continued into the next generations of postmodernists.[12] Charles Olson was a practitioner of "the scholar's art"[13] – historian, cultural geographer, "archeologist of morning" – who came to view Black Mountain College as a potential seedbed for his alternative vision of the polis and its possibilities for human action, but only by imagining a university in which instruction in the arts might replace virtually any other curriculum: "painting, music, dance, writing, architecture, pots, cloth, wood, theatre, printing, sculpture & photography.... No academics."[14] Allen Ginsberg the ecstatic poet was held in on both sides by somewhat more buttoned down selves – the "fair haired boy in academic

Columbia" he had been, and the Distinguished Professor at Brooklyn College he would become – the poet who would publish *Howl: Original Draft Facsimile, Transcript & Variant Versions, Fully Annotated by Author, with Contemporaneous Correspondence, Account of First Public Reading, Legal Skirmishes, Precursor Texts & Bibliography* with barely a trace of Eliotic irony.[15] If the contemporary poet lives in a world in which it is not possible to be genuinely or permanently "expelled from the academies for crazy" – a world in which the academies, like "Howl's" Moloch, embody the condition of knowledge itself, its economy of reason and unreason, its structures of hierarchy, its sanctioned forms of agency – then the artist's inescapable relation to them must at least be marked by an imagined sense of unbelonging and constant passage that Ginsberg illuminates with the glow of internal difference: "who passed through universities with radiant cool eyes hallucinating Arkansas and Blake-light tragedy among the scholars of war[.]"[16]

Both Grossman and Howe inherit the plight of the scholar-poet in its full complexity. Grossman has been justly associated with the highest of high modernists for the unapologetic grandeur of his style and for his sense of art's civilizational importance. His work is conspicuously learned; its range of reference spans the whole scope of the Western literary and intellectual tradition: classical, biblical and philosophical (from "The Sands of Paran" in 1953 to "Descartes Loneliness" in 2007). Howe is no less a poet of ambition and allusion. In her many books since the 1970s, she has taken deeply to heart Pound's example of the "poem containing history," even though her histories, like her sources, are most often American. Emily Dickinson, Jonathan Edwards, Ralph Waldo Emerson, Henry David Thoreau, and Wallace Stevens are among her canonical touchstones, but her main cultural agenda is anti-canonical: to "tenderly lift from the dark side of history, voices that are anonymous, slighted – inarticulate"[17] and to propose the paradoxical and revelatory centrality of apparently marginal figures like Mary Rowlandson ("The mother of us all"[18]), Charles Sanders Pierce ("There always was and always will be a secret affinity between symbolic logic and poetry"),[19] or the obscure utopian Christian sect of the Labadists.[20]

But if Grossman and Howe are direct inheritors of modernist-scale ambition for the continuation, restoration, or redirection of culture, they are also postmodern by default and by design. Most straightforwardly and most trivially, they are postmodern in the stylistic sense. Grossman may write in close proximity to traditional meters and genres, but his poetry encompasses a riot of voices and levels of discourse, and his diction swings from high to low and back again in the space of a single apostrophe: "O kid! if you ever get this *epistola* come and see me...."[21] Howe is a poet of pastiche and assemblage. She uses a narrower range of tones (neither humor nor extremes of passion are given much voice in her work); instead, feeling emerges mysteriously from the texture of her formal experimentation, as she warps the decorum of syntax and of the printed page, layers language atop language in a palimpsest of texts, and, increasingly, blurs the boundary between a book to be read and an object to be beheld.

More significantly, both poets are postmoderns in the now-canonical sense that they bring to bear a reflective "incredulity toward metanarratives," the universalizing frames we use to legitimate knowledge, whether technical, providential, or historical.[22] For Grossman, poetry has an obligation of "sedition" against the naturalized authority of civilizational constructions; it "opposes the satisfaction of supposing that thinking is innocent"; or, as he puts it in more exhortative form, "DO NOT BE CONTENT WITH AN IMAGINARY GOD."[23] Howe's attention to the categorical human work of naming and placing under the aegis of "God and Grammar" seeks to dislodge "a positivist efficiency" that "appropriates primal indeterminacy" and replace it with a consciousness of wandering and error ("Stumbling phenomenology / Infinite miscalculation of history").[24]

Finally, they are postmodern too in the sense of residing fully and without alternative within an "administered world."[25] Both poets have spent the majority of their writing lives as renowned and influential teachers deeply identified with research universities.[26] Allen Grossman taught for more than fifty years, first at Brandeis and then, after 1991, in the English Department at The Johns Hopkins University. Susan Howe taught at the University at Buffalo, the State University of New York, from 1989 until 2006, and cofounded the Buffalo Poetics Program, perhaps the most influential incubator for U.S. experimental writing in the past quarter-century. They have taught generations of poets and scholars without spawning stylistic imitators. If their influence is as much a function of their strength as teachers as their greatness as poets, it is because their pedagogy is not primarily formal – a workshop pedagogy pitting "craft" against creativity-stifling theory – but rather intellectual and conceptual. Both poets write critical texts that partake of the theoretical discourse of their moment in recognizable (though sometimes idiosyncratic) ways. Grossman's *Summa Lyrica* is a "primer of speculative poetics" that considers – in numbered fashion recalling Aquinas or Wittgenstein – "some of the commonplaces by means of which poetry and poetic purposes are accounted for in the West … [placing] individual analyses the context of the whole subject matter."[27] His survey of "the whole" contains such expected features as "Line," "Metaphor," or "The Traditional Unity of the Poem"; it also contains less familiar "commonplaces" that draw the language of scholarship closer to that of poetry:

"Eve," "Majesty," and "Orphic Machines." Susan Howe has published two books (*My Emily Dickinson* and *The Birth-mark: Unsettling the Wilderness in American Literary History*) that hew closely to the decorum of professional literary criticism – its arguments with literary history and textual scholarship – although here too, straightforward critical prose is shot through with lyrical interludes and gnomic aphorisms.

What makes these poet-scholars so distinctive is the force with which they have *linked* these latter two versions of postmodernism: a skepticism about the cultural project that they nonetheless continue to assume as their vocation, and an embrace of the institutional site they occupy as both ground and horizon of poetic practice and a generative site of the values they pursue in art. For Pound, "The lecturer is a man who must talk for an hour."[28] For Allen Grossman, the pedagogue in his poem "The Lecture" is the very figure of the poetic task:

> Place a man in the center, and he becomes
> The man who has prepared for a lifetime
> To answer, and now is ready.[29]

For Howe, the woman on the margin replaces the man in the center, but the terrain is substantially the same. Howe stands "[a]t the threshold of academicism and poetry," wielding the "passionate morality" of the poet-scholar.[30] To call these poets "academic" is not to arraign them for the putatively dulling effects that the academic study of literature has on the making of poems, but rather to identify a crucial aspect of their art in deliberation about and struggle with the question of what will count as knowledge; a question in which the university is centrally implicated, and for which, therefore, the forms and protocols of professional scholarship are a troubling figure. For both Grossman and Howe, traditional poetic questions of wisdom and freedom are experienced as a direct negotiation with the academic institution. And ostensibly "academic" questions – questions of how to secure and allocate access to materials, how to sort common knowledge from esoteric reference, of what it is to teach, or what there is to teach – have migrated from discourse around or about the work of art into the form of the work itself.

In W. B. Yeats's great poem, "Among School Children," the poet finds himself in a "long schoolroom" that stands at the crossroads between the literal and the figurative. Yeats, "[a] sixty year old smiling public man," moves through an actual institution: St. Otteran's in Waterford, the Montessori school that served as a model for a poet-senator tasked to consider of what sort of education might best suit the children of a newly independent Ireland.[31] He moves also through the long schoolroom of his own experience, conscious of his own life's lessons in disappointment and loss. The public and private questions that arise for Yeats in the poem are the same. What kind of education could create a future different than the unmanageable and violent present? What can anyone learn that would justify or redeem the thwarted expectations that are the inevitable consequence of individual life, "the uncertainty of setting forth?" As if in answer to the crucial question posed by the children's stare: what must we know? Yeats offers a figure of reconciliation that celebrates an ecstatic failure of knowledge – the inability to distinguish one thing from another. "How can we know the dancer from the dance?"

Nearly seventy years later, Grossman finds himself confronted by similarly wondering children in "The Great Work Farm Elegy":

> One says, "Old man!" You lectured in my dreams,
> And uttered words I did not understand. Either
> You did not speak clearly, as often you do not;
> Or I did not pay attention. (Often I don't.) So!
> We have come to give you another chance. Explain
> Again what you said in my dream. What did you
> Say? What did you mean? What?"[32]

For Grossman, the poet's primary task is not to present a powerful image or dream of compensation, not to offer consolation in the form of a question that is ungainsayable because unanswerable; it is, rather, to awaken from the dream's unclear instruction and to undertake on behalf of the reader a massive – indeed a total – project of explanation. (" – *I will explain*.").[33] A didactic task on this scale has ontological, epistemic, and ethical implications: it demands conceiving of the world in such a way that fundamental principles can be clarified; it requires the theorization of a ground of authority to speak of them, to judge of value, and to dispense praise and blame.[34]

In "Flax: A Ballad of Schools and Dreams," the pedagogical question posed for the poet by the existence of the school and the vulnerability of its charges is given more substance and more urgent voice:

> And I have heard at the same distance the children singing
> In the school room: "In heaven's name," they sing. "Can you, perhaps,
> Impart to me some power to enable me to bear this force
> Emerging from my heart?"[35]

On Grossman's account, poetry, if it is to have any value, must contribute to our capacity to bear conditions of being that are as inescapable and as unresponsive to choice as the force of feeling in one's own heart – "to obtain for everybody one kind of success at the limits of the autonomy of the will."[36] Among those limits are mortality, the solitude of the mind's private experience, the violence of history, and the blankness of a bare object world. Such limits can be made bearable only when they are made meaningful, taken up as part of a set or structure of shared understandings by means of what Grossman understands as "representation."

This capacious category of representation subsumes not only poetry ("the artistic form of communicative action"), but every conceivable ordering of experience. Thus, Grossman acknowledges, "I have never – for whatever reason – made a distinction between the schoolroom of the poetic principle and the schoolroom of the life-forms of the civilization in general."[37] Politics (addressed to "the staggeringly primitive question as to which human beings were persons"[38]), conceptions of divinity ("the principle of generality that produces the intelligibility of the world and its communicability"[39]), and indeed consciousness itself (what Kant calls our fundamental categories of "orientation in thinking"[40]) are all representations in Grossman's sense; all are among the means for "the maintenance of the intelligibility of the human world by symbols."[41] Our entry into some particular historical order of representations is what Grossman means by "education": "All education involves an expensive exchange of instinctual life for symbolic life, an exchange that in the case of literary education is facilitated by an appeal to the senses *(aut prodesse aut delelctare)*. Instinct is personal, and symbol is social being."[42]

In lyric, the *trope* of this exchange of being for meaning is "immortality" (the first commonplace in the *Summa Lyrica*).[43] Its preeminent *genre* is elegy, in which the individual's private grief for the particular beloved is "translated" into sharable grief,

> ...announcing the fame
> Of tears, calling out the terms
> In a clear way, translating to the long
> Dim human avenue.[44]

In poetic form, the entire drama of representation is crystallized by the artifice of poetic language, and most particularly by the imposition of the order of line, which mounts punctual utterance within a timeless pattern, and which, for all that it is non-mimetic of content, nonetheless sketches "a picture of the world's history from Genesis (opening) to Revelation (terminal closure")[45] But for the reader of Grossman's poetry, perhaps the most compelling and instructive drama of generalization is that of the construction and justification of the poetic speaker itself.

Any reader of Grossman's poetry will note the strangeness of the poet's voice, its weird elevation and relentless archaism even in the midst of low comedy. "The Woman on the Bridge Over the Chicago River" is typical in the way it submerges its few moments of recognizable geography or straightforwardly human protagonists within an intentionally abstract landscape ("Dim human avenue").[46] The corollary to that tonal, formal, or dictional archaism is the poetry's tendency to tip always from autobiography toward myth, so that various guises of the self – "Mind," "Poet," "Philosopher," or "Jew" – are more likely to lie at the center of the poem's action than is the natural or even the social person. In Grossman's poetry, the speaker may have a life, a story, and a situation; over the course of many poems, we learn that he grew up in Minnesota, son of a Chevrolet dealer father named Louis and a mother named Beatrice. In age, he suffers pains in his body, or torments of love and grief. But the speaker of these poems is also freighted with the knowledge that comes from having refracted virtually the entire symbolic culture of the West through his own person. "The idea of 'archaism,'" Grossman writes in *Summa Lyrica*, "associates poetry with the power of prior life.... The middle ground of strong life does not belong to the iconology of the poem."[47] Thus, Father Louis in death becomes "Father Dust," imparting lessons in an Odyssean underworld. Mother Beatrice, who (perhaps) ran a lending library in Minneapolis, shares her name with the Dantean beloved; she demands a justifying story, as Dante's Beatrice demands a journey. In the extended "Romance" of *The Philosopher's Window*, a life narrative is parceled out between the personae of a "sulphur-headed Antipodean parrot" who sails a ship to the end of thought and an aged philosopher with a toothache who observes the damage. In *Sweet Youth*, early and late incarnations of the poet encounter each other as types, and in their encounter consider the universal task of human making "that compels he inevitability of the school."[48] Like blind Homer or inspired Virgil, Grossman's poet is an instrument played by another, who must surrender natural, instinctual life in order to speak.[49]

Even the most seemingly "ordinary" poems in Grossman's oeuvre – poems that approach the observational realism of a poet like Robert Lowell – attest in the end to the universality of representation and to the fundamental difference of Grossman's *poetic* realism. The late poem "Wash Day," for example, is unusual for being pinned to a date and location that seems to mark the action as irreplaceably particular, resolutely unmythic: "July, 1947, Gibbon, Minn."[50] And it is full of the sort of detail whose value seems to arise as much from the sheer pleasures of sonic and imagistic facticity as from the celebration of ordinary labor. Here, now, soap is

> Not store-bought,
> But stone hard pig fat
> and lye mixed with

> oatmeal in a pail.
> Then hacked with a knife
> into Lux-like flakes.[51]

Grossman's "blue-enameled kitchen / stove" fueled by "corncobs / gnawed clean by pigs" might have leapt from the pages of an Elizabeth Bishop catalog.[52] And yet such carefully rendered detail, for all its manifest warmth, is "too cold to be true." Whatever conception of "truth" on offer here, it is not Grossman's late embrace of the sufficiency of experience.

As the poem draws to a close, its conception of significant knowledge veers dramatically into another register:

> At noon, the naked truth descends
> Offering her stunning breasts.
> *Also* here comes the prophet
> Amos, with something in hand.
> In fact, a basket of summer fruit.
> Ch 8, vss. 1,2. (Check it out.)[53]

What do we find when we do "check it out"?

> [1]Thus hath the Lord GOD shewed unto me: and behold a basket of summer fruit. [2]And he said, Amos, what seest thou? And I said, A basket of summer fruit. Then said the LORD unto me, The end is come upon my people of Israel; I will not again pass by them any more.[54]

In the light of our education, whether newly acquired or reacquired, the beautiful profusion of detail has turned to dust. What had presented itself to the eye as sheer bounty – the "summer fruit" of individual experience – can descend as truth only in the light of our shared or sharable cultural narratives of significance. The fact that this particular narrative of significance is punitive (announcing, as it does, the imminent withdrawal of God's protection, and the certainty of Israel's destruction) is neither Grossman's critique, nor his endorsement, of a biblical morality. It is, rather, a function of his ongoing diagnosis of the general and tragic structure of representation: the "bitter logic" that mounts every construction on a destruction, every inclusion on exclusions, that purchases the symbolic at the cost of the organic and secures the narratability of the world at the price of our full participation in it.[55]

Not every allusion in Grossman's poetry is so easy to track down as this one, nor is it always obvious that we are intended or assumed to "check it out." But all of his poetry carries the *charge* of allusiveness, the urgent sense that there is something to know if only one knew where to look it up. Thus the ending of the remarkable Holocaust sonnet sequence, "Flora's ABC,"

presents a series of speech prohibitions, along with a set of mysterious pre-
ferred locutions:

> do not be content to say 'YAHWEH LORD.'
> Say rather, 'Her father was butcher in Luxembourg."
> Do not be content to say, 'Lady's Bedstraw'.
> Say, 'Her virginity.' Do not say, '*Creator spiritus*
> *Veni*.' Say 'Windflower' or, maybe, 'Anemone.'[56]

But, looking it up, we learn that each and every item in the primer of this
poem teaches a version of the same story, whether it is story of a senseless
devotion to an imaginary God who oversees the destruction of bodies and
demands endless praise for his spiritual gifts, or the story of Adonis, whose
youth and beauty can be preserved only by being destroyed and transformed
into a recurrent floral emblem of transience. In this poem, and in Grossman's
poetry in general, the problem of poetic allusiveness reproduces the existential problem of representation (its "bitter logic") as a problem of form
(its "difficulty"). Reading these poems, we trade our pleasure in surfaces for
our knowledge of meanings; encountering these particular and troubling
meanings, we reenact the punitive and privative character of all education in
representation, the "expensive exchange of instinctual life for symbolic life."

In Susan Howe's poems, too, the forms and institutions of knowledge
appear both as enabling conditions and as antagonists. Stephen Collis has
usefully and justly described Howe's project of collage and juxtaposition of
archival materials as "anarcho-scholastic": the poems are scholarly in their
workings through and over textual origins of American mythologies, and for
their keen observations of material particularities of archival work; they are
"anarchic" for their hostility to the way that entrenched histories become
exclusionary myths, and the way that institutional structures of archival
preservation constrain the possibilities of critical interpretation.[57] Collis
characterizes Howe's collaged, open, nonlinear texts as a form of creative
scholarship "deeply critical … of 'authorized' versions of history."[58] But if
there is a signature feature of Howe's many scholarly and poetic forays into
the tradition she calls "antinomian," it is the way she blurs all forms of dissent (theological, intellectual, political, gendered) with her own *intellectual*
dissent, in a series of rhymes that echo across her work: Howe's experience
of being shut out of the stacks at Harvard's Widener Library as a teenager
in the 1950s[59] with Emily Dickinson who "built a new poetic form from her
fractured sense of being eternally on intellectual borders"[60]; *Pierce-Arrow's*
elaborate description of Howe's discomfort in a frigid microform room in
the basement of the Sterling library at Yale[61] with its account of Pierce's
own discomfort within the philosophical establishment he transformed with

the anomalous force of his invention; Howe's creative wandering through Melville's marginalia (themselves compiled by an obsessional graduate student)[62] with the habits of mind afflicting the paradoxically central minor poet James Clarence Mangan:

> Instead of classifying
> he browsed and dreamed
> he didn't even browse
> regularly[63]

Such parallels underwrite in Howe's poetry an elaborate allegory of freedom, and yet, even by her own account, it is a curious sort of freedom only achievable – or legible – within institutions: "I have trespassed into the disciplines of American Studies and Textual Criticism through my need to fathom what wildness and absolute freedom is the nature of expression."[64] It is perhaps an inevitable consequence of this paradox of what she elsewhere calls "library nature" ("true wilderness is like true gold; it will bear the trial of Dewey Decimal") that the moments in her poetry that seem both closest and furthest away from "absolute freedom" are the moments that threaten to break with representation altogether.[65] This is vividly clear in the final page in the poetic sequence "Fragment of the Wedding Dress of Sarah Pierpont Edwards," where with a thin shard of nearly illegible text running vertically along the center of the page, Howe brings the poem as close as she can to being a natural object of experience that also (and for that reason) resembles an aperture that would conduct us from our life on the page into some uncounted place.[66]

If Allen Grossman's broad account of representation provides the theoretical engine that renders theoretically explicit Howe's performative insistence on the relation of the structure of discourse (and its institutions) to social structure, it is his account of its bitter logic that explains how such a narrow poem can give rise to such breadth of feeling. Howe instructs us with the force of her desire for a different kind of poetry; one that might rend the fabric of representations and open onto a new freedom. And yet the text remains; a ghostly, punitive presence demanding our attention, education, and fidelity. What Grossman teaches is that there is no different kind of poetry; the difference of poetry – its particular realism – lies in its devotion to instructing us in the necessary conditions of representation. "Such is the logic of the poetic principle. Nothing New."[67]

NOTES

1. Sir Philip Sidney, "The Defence of Poesy," in *Sir Philip Sidney: The Major Works*, ed. Katherine Duncan-Jones (Oxford: Oxford University Press, 1989), 212–14.

2. John Keats, *Letters of John Keats,* ed. Robert Gittings (Oxford: Oxford University Press, 1975), 224.

3. For a rich account of the transactions between the development of English verse and the practice of humanistic education, see Jeffrey Dolven, *Scenes of Instruction in Renaissance Romance* (Chicago: University of Chicago Press, 2008). On Romanticism's deep ambivalence toward didactic poetry, see David Duff, "Antididacticism as a Contested Principle in Romantic Aesthetics," *Eighteenth-Century Life* 25.2 (Spring 2001).

4. The term was certainly in circulation in the early decades of the twentieth century. Applied to Gray or Landor, Longfellow or Tennyson, it tended to be a mild rebuke by dons to poets sharing a certain donnish sensibility. When it becomes a weapon used in the game of literary distinction by the players themselves, the epithet acquires a sharper edge, as in Guy Davenport's takedown of Robert Lowell's 1967 appearance on the cover of *Time* as American poetry's laureate representative: "He is a thoughtful, serious, melancholy academic poet; if he is representative of anything beyond himself, it is of a broody school of professor-poets whose quiet, meticulous verse is perhaps the lineal and long-winded descendent of the cross-stitch sampler," *The Geography of the Imagination* (Jaffrey, NH: David R. Godine, 1997), 133.

5. These alliances and affiliations are multiple and complex. By Grossman's own account, Robert Lowell "exercised great authority in the long schoolroom of poetic practice at the time I set to work." Yet the earliest critical essay he has preserved takes up the work of Allen Ginsberg, who embodies for Grossman another crucial (and problematic) poetic affiliation with Jewish poetry in America: "the poetry of a *terminal cultural situation.*" See Grossman, *The Long Schoolroom: Lessons in the Bitter Logic of the Poetic Principle* (Ann Arbor: The University of Michigan Press, 1997), 130, 153. Susan Howe, for her part, is most often associated with Language writing of the 1970s and 1980s, although the affiliation has always been more situational than aesthetic or ideological. As with Grossman, Howe's affiliation with a powerful aesthetic tendency runs up against an ambivalent identitarian commitment, in her case, to the dissident role of the woman poet in a patriarchal culture. See Elisabeth Anne Frost, "'Unsettling America': Susan Howe and the Antinomian Tradition," in *The Feminist Avant-Garde in American Poetry* (Iowa City: University of Iowa Press, 2003), 105–135.

6. "After all," Joseph Brodsky wrote of Montale, "a footnote is where civilization survives"; *Less Than One: Selected Essays* (New York: Farrar Strauss Giroux, 1986), 99. Lawrence Rainey gives the definitive account of Eliot's process of composition of and reconciliation to the notes to "The Waste Land" in his *Revisiting The Waste Land* (New Haven, CT: Yale University Press, 2004), 37–9.

7. T. S. Eliot, "Tradition and the Individual Talent," in The Waste Land *and Other Writings,* intro. Mary Karr (New York: Random House, 2001), 102.

8. Eliot's faint praise of Matthew Arnold's poetry as "academic poetry in the best sense; the best fruit which can issue from the promise shown by the prize-poem" is also relevant here. See *The Use of Poetry and the Use of Criticism* (Cambridge, MA: Harvard University Press, 1964), 105.

9. For a thorough and compelling account of Eliot's and Pound's conflicted transactions with professional academic life, see Gail McDonald, *Learning to Be Modern* (Oxford: Clarendon Press, 1993). On the conflicted relation between Modernist

poetics and the research culture of the modern university, see Robert Crawford, *The Modern Poet: Poetry, Academia and Knowledge since the 1750s* (Oxford: Oxford University Press, 2001), 170–222.

10. Ezra Pound, *Literary Essays of Ezra Pound*, ed. T. S. Eliot (New York: New Directions, 1968), 15, 42.

11. Ezra Pound, *The Selected Letters of Ezra Pound 1907–1941*, ed. D. D. Paige (New York: New Directions, 1971), 180.

12. My sense of this "knowledge system" has been informed by the powerful empirical and conceptual work of David J. Frank and Jay Gabler in *Reconstructing the University: Worldwide Shifts in Academia in the 20th Century* (Palo Alto, CA: Stanford University Press), 2006.

13. Robert von Hallberg, *Charles Olson: The Scholar's Art* (Cambridge, MA: Harvard University Press, 1978).

14. Letter to Robert Creeley, cited in Mary Emma Harris, *The Arts at Black Mountain College* (Cambridge, MA: MIT Press, 2002), 175.

15. Allen Ginsberg, *The Letters of Allen Ginsberg*, ed. Bill Morgan (Philadelphia: Da Capo Press, 2008), 131.

16. Allen Ginsberg, *Howl and Other Poems* (San Francisco: City Lights, 1956), 9.

17. Susan Howe, *The Europe of Trusts* (New York: New Directions, 1990), 14.

18. Susan Howe, *The Birth-Mark: Unsettling the Wilderness in American Literary History* (Hanover, NH: Wesleyan University Press, 1993), 167.

19. Susan Howe, *Pierce Arrow* (New York: New Directions, 1999), ix.

20. Susan Howe, *Souls of the Labadie Tract* (New York: New Directions, 2007).

21. Allen Grossman, *How to Do Things With Tears* (New York: New Directions, 2001), 26.

22. Jean-François Lyotard, *The Postmodern Condition* (Minneapolis: University of Minnesota Press, 1984), 4.

23. Grossman, *How to Do Things with Tears*, 94, xi.

24. Susan Howe, "Thorow," in *Singularities* (Hanover, NH: University Press of New England, 1990), 41, 17.

25. Theodor W. Adorno, *Aesthetic Theory*, eds. Gretel Adorno and Rolf Tiedemann, trans. Robert Hullot-Kentor (Minneapolis: University of Minnesota Press, 1997), 56.

26. The idea that postmodern literature is in large part defined by the inescapable horizon of the university is explored at length (albeit in the context of fiction rather than poetry) in Mark Mcgurl, The *Program Era*: Postwar Fiction and the Rise of Creative Writing (Cambridge, MA: Harvard University Press, 2009).

27. Allen Grossman and Mark Halliday, *The Sighted Singer: Two Works on Poetry for Readers and Writers* (Baltimore: The Johns Hopkins University Press, 1992), 206–207.

28. Ezra Pound, *ABC of Reading* (New York: New Directions, 1960), 83.

29. Allen Grossman, *The Ether Dome and Other Poems: New and Selected 1979–1991* (New York: New Directions: 1991), 91.

30. Susan Howe, "Where Should the Commander Be?" *Writing* 19 (November 1987): 6.

31. William Butler Yeats, *The Collected Poems of W. B. Yeats*, ed. Richard J. Finneran (New York: Simon & Schuster, 1996), 215.

32. Allen Grossman, *The Philosopher's Window and Other Poems* (New York: New Directions, 1995), 4.

33. Ibid.
34. See "Whoever Builds": "Whoever builds puts himself in service to materials / And becomes subject to the laws of materials. / .... Do not dissemble / The true state of affairs *which is known!*" Ibid., 85. See also "To the sighted singer, in a / Passionate laboring house. Praise! // But / To the blind singers among sleepy harvesters, – / Everlasting shame...." "Of the Great House," in *The Ether Dome*, 101.
35. Grossman, *The Ether Dome*, 21.
36. Grossman, *The Sighted Singer*, 209.
37. Grossman, *True Love*, 15.
38. Grossman, *The Long Schoolroom*, 59.
39. Grossman, *True Love*, 120.
40. See "Poetry and Enlightenment (Kant on Orientation, Whitman on the Brooklyn Ferry, and Celan on the Meridian)," in Grossman, *True Love*, 1–14.
41. Ibid., 7.
42. Ibid., 164.
43. Grossman, *The Sighted Singer*, 209.
44. Grossman, *The Ether Dome*, 62.
45. Grossman, *The Sighted Singer*, 315.
46. Allen Grossman, *The Woman on the Bridge over the Chicago River: A Book of Poems* (New York: New Directions, 1979), 3.
47. Grossman, *The Sighted Singer*, 221.
48. Allen Grossman, *Sweet Youth: Poems by a Young Man and an Old Man Old and New 1953–2001* (New York: New Directions, 2002), xi.
49. The *ars poetica* of this sacrificial account of the poetic vocation occurs in "The Piano Player Explains Himself," in *The Ether Dome*, 3.
50. Allen Grossman, *Descartes' Loneliness* (New York: New Directions, 2007), 6.
51. Ibid.
52. Ibid.
53. Ibid., 8.
54. Amos 8: 1–2 (KJV).
55. Grossman, *True Love*, 39–70.
56. Grossman, *How to Do Things with Tears*, 68.
57. Stephen Collis, *Through Words of Others: Susan Howe and Anarcho-Scholasticism* (Victoria, BC: ELS Editions, 2006).
58. Ibid., 10–11.
59. Howe, *The Birth Mark*, 18.
60. Susan Howe, *My Emily Dickinson* (Berkeley, CA: North Atlantic Books, 1985), 21.
61. Howe, *Pierce-Arrow*, 5.
62. Susan Howe, "Melville's Marginalia," in *The Nonconformist's Memorial: Poems* (New York: New Directions, 1993), 83–150.
63. Howe, "Melville's Marginalia," ibid., 136.
64. Howe, *The Birth-Mark*, 2.
65. Howe, *Souls of the Labadie Tract*, 19.
66. Ibid., 125. For a compelling account of the implications of Howe's commitment to the poem as object of experience, see Walter Benn Michaels, *The Shape of the Signifier: 1967 to the End of History* (Princeton, NJ: Princeton University Press, 2004), 1–15.
67. Grossman, *The Long Schoolroom*, 213.

FURTHER READING

Back, Rachel Tzvia. *Led by Language: The Poetry and Poetics of Susan Howe*. Tuscaloosa: University of Alabama Press, 2002.

Campbell, Sarah, ed. *I Have Imagined A Center//Wilder Than This Region*. Buffalo, NY: Cuneiform Press, 2007.

Crawford, Robert. *The Modern Poet: Poetry, Academia and Knowledge since the 1750s*. Oxford: Oxford University Press, 2001.

Frost, Elizabeth Anne. "Unsettling America: Susan Howe and the Antinomian Tradition." *The Feminist Avant-Garde in American Poetry*. Iowa City: University of Iowa Press, 2003, 105–135.

Morris, Daniel, ed. *Poetry's Poet: Essays on the Poetry, Pedagogy, and Poetics of Allen Grossman*. Orono, ME: National Poetry Foundation, 2004.

14

MICHAEL W. CLUNE

Rap, Hip Hop, Spoken Word

John Stuart Mill's celebrated definition of lyric poetry as speech that is "overheard" would seem ill-suited to some of the most vital and popular recent forms of American poetry – forms that exist primarily as spoken performance and only derivatively as text.[1] Former U.S. Poet Laureate Billy Collins, for example, introduces a print and audio anthology of performance poetries with the observation that in performance, "poet and audience are bodily exposed to one another and take on the visibility they mutually lack in the silent transaction of the page."[2] If we add to this the observation that rap and hip hop are primarily black forms, then an awareness of the postwar history of the politics of recognition would seem to affirm both Collins's explicit equation of orality with visibility and his implicit equation of visibility with freedom.

But things are not entirely as they seem. In the following I will show how the relationship Mill prizes in the lyric text – where author and reader are invisibly joined – is sought by some forms of postwar poetic performance, even as it is rejected by others. The identification of oral poetry with theatrical visibility is not a neutral description of rap, hip hop, and spoken word, but a divisive question. Indeed, the three forms my title joins are perhaps better divided into two groups based on typical responses to this question. One group – containing much spoken word poetry, most early rap, and some "underground" hip hop – values the emergence of poetry into visibility. The other group contains most rap produced between the mid-1990s and the present, and values invisibility. In what follows, I focus on the second group. I concentrate on rap in part because it has been so consistently misinterpreted according to a model appropriate to the first group. This has led to rap being understood as a peripheral, even degraded version of performance poetry. I want to reverse the usual approach. My

This chapter is partially adapted from my consideration of rap in *American Literature and the Free Market, 1945–2000* (Cambridge: Cambridge University Press, 2010).

hope is that by listening closely to rap's rejection of visibility, we will see the more familiar features of hip hop and spoken word in a new light. I begin by exploring basic features of the rap lyric, features that I then show driving the complex structures of the rap performance.

By the mid-1990s, popular American rap had attained a stable form that persists, though subject to a continuous process of refinement and simplification, practically unchanged in its central features. This form, sometimes described by critics as rap's "formula," essentially consists of two elements: the description of the speaker's money and the development of a violently antagonistic relation between the speaker and a general, unnamed "you." Consider the following examples. "I'll rip your torso, I live the fast life / Come through in the Porsche slow."[3] "I'd rather bust you and let the cops find you / While I be dippin' in the Range [Rover] all jeweled / like Liberace."[4] "I know you better not open your mouth when I ride by / And I know you see this Lexus GS on shine."[5]

This brief catalog of the juxtaposition of money with a threatening stance toward "you" could be multiplied by the lyrics from virtually any popular rap album released over the past fifteen years. Indeed, the "street credibility" or "authenticity" widely recognized as essential for a rapper's commercial success is largely a function of her adherence to the form.[6] The ubiquity of this form means that an earlier distinction between "gangster" and other subgenres of rap has become largely irrelevant.[7] Raps about money without even a gestural threat directed at "you," or raps threatening "you" without any reference to "my" money, practically disappear after 1995. The two elements of the rap form are integrally related, in that the opposition between the "I" and the generalized "you" provides the context in which the meaning of the money is established. The rap form constitutes an interpretation of money. The dynamics of rap's interpretation of money in turn depend on rap's interpretation of blackness.

Rap interprets money in terms of a relation between "I" and "you." Specifically, money makes me *invisible* to you. If, in the examples quoted earlier, the desire to eliminate you is adjacent to the reference to my money, the figure of "bling-bling" conjoins the desire and the money in a single figure. The immense popularity of "bling-bling" in rap over the past ten years indicates its success in integrating both elements of the form. Popularized by the Hot Boys' 1999 hit of the same name, the term is onomatopoeia for the cartoon sound effect made by sparkles of light on a gem or precious metal. Bling is a visual form of money, a fact emphasized by such elements in the original song as the sample of the chimes of the cartoon convention in the chorus, and the references to "diamonds that'll bling-blind ya."[8] The literally thousands of other raps that take up the term also stress its visuality. From Nelly's "I like the way the light hit the ice and glare," to B.G's "it's dark in the room, I hold up my watch / and it's light," "bling" always indicates light shining from the rapper's gold chain, platinum watch, diamonds ("ice"), or Bentley.[9]

Money-as-light shining from my wrist, neck, or car, bling-bling makes me invisible to you. The light reflecting off my money doesn't compel your recognition of my status, wealth, or fame. It doesn't force you to notice me. It *blinds* you, making such recognition impossible. "It's my turn to shine / Fifty karats or better on my wrist and they all blind."[10] "Folks say take that chain off boy ya blindin' me."[11] "You're blinded by the ice / While I release the confrontation."[12] "The light projects off ice and flashes / Blinds your broke asses."[13] The speaker's shining money prevents the other from taking the subject as the object of her gaze. In case there should be any doubt as to the source of this power, rap insists that fake platinum, however shiny, won't blind. Fake bling produces not blindness, but questions: "Is that platinum, or is it only sterling?"[14] To blind you, the chain, watch, diamond, or Bentley has to be real, it has to be *money*. "Hundred thou' for the bracelet/ Foolish, ain't I? / The chain'll strain your eye."[15]

If the antagonism between the first and second person defines the interpersonal relation in rap, my invisibility to you constitutes the master form of that relation. This theme reaches maximal condensation in the ubiquitous phrase, "you can't see me." "You can't see Snoop D O double G."[16] "Stares of a million pairs of eyes / And you'll never realize / You can't see me."[17] "I'm invisible, invisible / Open your eyes vato, you can't see me."[18] "Get your binoculars on / And just try to see me."[19] Finally, such titles as 50 Cent's "You Are Not Like Me" and Clipse's "I'm Not You," demonstrate at the most elementary level the formal *asymmetry* between the first and second person.[20] I can see you but you can't see me.

This asymmetry is absolute and general; it isn't contingent on any feature or attribute of the other. A line from Prodigy's 2000 hit "Y.B.E." pares this down to the essentials: "You couldn't understand my life if you lived it."[21] It doesn't matter who or what you are, we could even be substantively identical, but *you* are not like *me*. This opposition between me and you is more radical than a simple conflict between subject positions. The point is that there is a subject only in the "I" position: *you* are not a subject. This formal asymmetry, and the mechanism that produces it, suggests a *different* vision of human relations, rather than the empty "nihilism" projected onto rap by those critics who recognize its hostility toward the other.[22] After all, a basic mediator of human relationality is what establishes this asymmetry. "You're blinded by the ice." Money restricts subjectivity to me. What could this mean?

We can begin to approach this question by observing how different this dynamic is from what it looks like to most critics. Paul Gilroy, for example, reads rappers' reference to gold and platinum as part of the "complex symbolism of wealth and status in black popular culture."[23] Similarly, Kelefa Sanneh writes that Jay-Z, with "his big-money rhymes and real-life wealth," is "a man obsessed with status."[24] Adam Krims accounts for the popularity of the "crime-boss persona" in rap, which conjoins the display of money with an antagonistic stance toward the second person, by arguing that this conjunction constitutes the "perfect nexus" of "conspicuous consumption."[25] Tricia Rose argues that the rap aesthetic is a model of "status formation."[26] And in his influential sociological study of the inner city, Elijah Anderson sees in rap the reflection of a street culture where expensive jewels are "status symbols," tools by which the individual "manag[es] his self-image, which is shaped by what he thinks others are thinking of him."[27] Whatever relevance these descriptions might have to "black culture," "real life wealth," or inner-city consumption, they fail to address the specific question posed by "big money rhymes." What kind of diamonds can "bling-blind ya?"

Nothing could be more foreign to the concept of the "status symbol," which depends on your recognition of me, than the fiction that money makes me invisible to you. In fact, one might usefully approach the social relation crystallized in bling by thinking of the rapper's Bentley or diamond as the *exact opposite* of the status symbol, the reverse of conspicuous consumption. Money is good because it removes the other from the construction of subjectivity: "you can't see me." When I say that this is the *exact* opposite of conspicuous consumption, I mean to say something precise about the relation of money, subjectivity, and collectivity in rap.

Thorstein Veblen coined the term "conspicuous consumption" in the early twentieth century to describe how people continually make relative "distinctions of superiority and inferiority" among themselves on the basis of their displayed wealth.[28] Conspicuous consumption involves three essential elements: me, you, and an index of social value. Money, the form of general social value, enables me to conflate the empirical "you" with the social group. *My relation to "you" is at the same time a relation to society as a whole.* Thus the invidious comparison with the other, whether an anonymous stranger or a close friend, becomes the scene of subject formation, of my interpellation into the social world. The status established by such an invidious comparison is not subject either to my or to your idiosyncratic interpretation or revision, but receives, through money, a general social sanction. When I drive by you in my new car, the empirical you "stands in" for the generalized social other to establish "me" and my place, and I function in the same way for you. Although my subjectivity depends on your recognition of me, this recognition is not personal, but is standardized by the mediation of money. To become a subject, I identify with the object reflected in your eyes as you look at me. Insofar as my reflection is mediated by money, the object I identify with is placed in a social hierarchy.

The idea of conspicuous consumption, or the "status symbol," depends on a strong sense of the mutuality of subject formation. "I" becomes a subject only by becoming an object to "you" and vice versa. The sense that I become a subject only through the recognition of the other takes on a strongly normative and ethical meaning in such otherwise different writers as Martha Nussbaum and Homi Bhabha. Charles Taylor, to take another example, premises his influential study of the "Politics of Recognition" on the claim that "due recognition is not just a courtesy we owe people. It is a vital human need."[29] The political "demand for recognition" has "been made explicit ... by the spread of the idea that we are formed by recognition."[30] This pervasive belief in the mutuality of subject formation underlies Elijah Anderson's reference to the role of conspicuous consumption in creating the rapper's "self-image, which is shaped by what he thinks others are thinking of him."[31] The first person is parasitic upon the second person, dependent on the other's mirroring gaze.

We are now in a position to understand the alternative sense of self and society that underlies the display of money in rap. This display is not simply different from conspicuous consumption; it is its opposite. Through this inversion, a strategy of appropriation, of status played out between different subjects, becomes the fantasy of a radically transformed subjectivity. "What kinda nigga / Got diamonds that'll bling-blind ya?" Who am I? Blinded by my money, you can't see me, you can't recognize me, you can't make me an object. If by conspicuous consumption I become a subject by becoming an object to another subject, rap money makes me a subject by making your subjectivity irrelevant. This disables the symmetrical me/you relation of conspicuous consumption. I don't see myself from your perspective. The light shining from my money blanks out your gaze. "I" don't depend on "you."

The rap form grounds its interpretation of economic value in this asymmetry. By imagining a different way of constructing the first person, rap imagines the second person to be vestigial, disposable. If conspicuous consumption is like a stick-up, compelling your recognition of my higher status, bling-bling is like murder. This identification of money and violence is not simply a metaphor; it is part of rap's formal structure. "My watch talks for me, my whip [car] talks for me / My gun talks for me / BLAM! What up homie?"[32] The money does the same thing the gun does: it closes your eyes. Whether the blinding light from the platinum watch or the bullet from the chrome gun hits "you" first, the function of the money/gun is to end "my" formal dependence on "you." "You," the generalized social other, is replaced by "me," as a generalized social subject. In conspicuous consumption, society stands in the place of the "you," assessing my money, judging, and placing me as a subject. In rap the collective drops the form of "you" and takes the form of "me." Humanity stands in *my* place and you are nowhere. The access to collective power that money grants is not routed through the gaze of the other, but becomes directly available to me. Through the alchemy of rap money, the collective shines from the "I," and the human world itself is experienced as an intense, amplified subjectivity. We can describe the fictional money produced by rap performance according to the following formula: rap money is economic value in which the crucial element that renders it visible and makes it a technology of recognition has been removed.

We have seen how this works in the figure of "bling-bling." We find another, especially vivid instance of the use of aesthetic form to remove economic form from intersubjectivity in the widespread practice of putting tinted windows on expensive cars. This practice is associated with rap, and rap lyrics frequently reference it. "I represent homies with the money fly guys with gems / drive with the tints that be thirty five percent."[33] "5 percent tint so you can't see up in my window."[34] The value of the kinds of cars celebrated by rap is entirely a function of their actual monetary value. When in 2003 Mercedes's new car, the Maybach, became the most expensive production car in the world, it promptly became the most stylish car in rap, instantly proliferating in countless lyrics. What is the relevant feature of a Maybach? Its economic value. So what is the aesthetic element? The aesthetic element consists of adding tinted windows to cars in order to prevent you from seeing the driver. When I'm driving my actual expensive car down the street, "you can't see me."

When we understand this basic operation of the rap form, we clear an approach to the question of blackness in rap. If the rap form interprets money, it also interprets blackness, and this latter interpretation constitutes the primary resource of the first. Rap and its associated aesthetic practices transform the meaning and value of blackness. The antagonism between rappers and the values of the civil rights generation that preceded them – a set of values still visible in both early rap and contemporary spoken word poetry – is rooted in this transformation. We can express this tension with a simple question: What can it mean for a black artist to proclaim "you can't see me," and to present invisibility not as a condition to be overcome through art, but as a project to be realized through art?

If an earlier generation of black writers and artists sought to defeat their social invisibility, rappers seek to defeat their social visibility. Blackness as invisibility, as a condition signifying the total absence of social recognition, a complete negation of the social world, was understood by writers of the early postwar period as a condition of total deprivation. In a world where whiteness enabled access to full intersubjectivity, black individuals didn't "show up." This was understood to be a structural feature, beyond any given individual's racist or antiracist beliefs. Thus in Ralph Ellison's *Invisible Man*, even the most well meaning white characters remain in crucial respects unable to see the protagonist, encountering instead a blank space onto which they project their expectations. If blackness is invisibility, and invisibility is exclusion from society, then the struggle is to make blackness recognizable, to transform it from a site of total social negativity to a positive site of identity.

Rap revalues black invisibility. This revaluation is made possible by the sense of a new form of value. If collective value can only be obtained through intersubjective recognition, then invisibility is pure deprivation. But if there is a route to collective value that does not pass through intersubjectivity, but that depends on evading intersubjectivity completely, then a position totally exterior to the social world becomes a unique resource. Just as tinted windows on a Bentley remove it from intersubjective status games, blackness-as-invisibility removes money from the social world. With the addition of money to black invisibility, that invisibility ceases to mean deprivation and becomes an impossibly dense concentration of collective value.

The new value of invisibility constitutes the essential horizon for understanding how black invisibility operates here. But most critics, popular and academic, ignore the dynamics of the form and evaluate rap in terms of how well it facilitates the positive recognition of blackness, how it positions blackness as an identity within the social field. Thus for Timothy Brennan rap is an "aural museum" of African-American culture erected to "codify, protect, and exalt the black traditions."[35] Houston Baker celebrates "positive sites of rap" as "raps designed to teach black children their own specific history."[36] These critics imagine that rap exists to mark the subject for display, to make the subject into a certain kind of object to be recognized by another subject.

Let's try to think about a blackness that is not an identity in the social world. "I'm invisible, invisible / You can't see me."[37] For both Ellison and rap's critics, invisibility is pure loss. But rap, by fusing black invisibility with money, transforms it into pure plenitude. In rap, blackness is invisibility, and the color of money is black. This fusion transforms both of the terms. Money leaves the regime of recognition, and invisibility escapes deprivation. The black rapper in the Bentley with tinted windows is unrecognizable, but his invisibility is not Ellison's abyss. Rap's black money defines a space outside intersubjectivity, a space suffused with collective power. In the development of this form, the interpretation of money and the interpretation of blackness evolved together. The historical experience of racially coded invisibility provided a powerful context for realizing a new relation to money. The black voice asking what kind of diamonds will "bling-blind you" on the radio constructs a form of collective value outside the social world. As we shall see, the inventiveness of one generation of black artists in evading invisibility is matched by the inventiveness of another generation in summoning it.

The radically free "I" of the rap lyric invites the audience to inhabit a non-relative subjectivity. "I give niggas what they came to see / A reflection of oneself how they aim to be."[38] But by acknowledging this orientation toward an audience, by presenting the first person as a space the audience can occupy, rap risks reproducing at the level of the performance the very relation it cancels at the level of lyrical form. In other words, there is a basic tension between the rapper/audience relation of the performance and the formal I/you relation of the lyric. Rap excludes "you" qua generalized social other even as it solicits "you" qua audience.

The asocial rap "I" becomes a subject without first becoming an object, without entering intersubjectivity. The mutually constitutive relation between me and you is obviated by bling, which directly invests me with a collective subjectivity. The paradox is that the relation between the first and second person nullified by the rap lyric is reinstated by the rap performance. This paradox constantly threatens to undermine rap's project. Not infrequently, the hidden tension erupts and destroys the careers of rappers who fail to resolve it, and thus can no longer convincingly execute the rap form. While the history of black invisibility constitutes an important resource for rap, this invisible blackness must itself ultimately be realized in performance, and this performance risks the possibility that, like many of rap's academic critics, an audience will interpret "you can't see me" as "please look at me." This dilemma is not resolvable in principle, but it can be overcome, for a time, in practice. I take Michael Fried's analysis of the techniques employed by modern painters to establish the fiction of the beholder's absence before the canvas as a useful model for understanding the dynamics of the rap performance.[39] In rap, formal strategies for "keeping it real," for successfully sublimating the relation to the audience, are proposed and worn out in rapid succession, constituting the other side of the relatively stable features of the lyrical form examined earlier. Indeed, the flux and variation of these secondary formal features guarantees the integrity of the primary features.

The purpose of the rap performance is to hold the "I" open to the audience as a space of identification, but this very openness depends on the "I"'s performative repression of its relation to its audience. Presenting it as an object of identification for an audience wastes the radical integrity of an "I" that becomes a subject without becoming an object. One particularly seductive way of resolving this tension between rap's orientation to the two referents of "you," the generalized social "you" and the empirical "you" of the audience, is for the rapper to treat them identically. The animus directed toward the formal second person thus overlaps with a theatrical hostility to the audience. In such cases, the audience becomes a virtual stand-in for the formal, lyrical "you." Much of the gestural repertoire of the rap performance of the mid-1990s, especially the tendency of the rapper to point threateningly at the audience when referring to "you," reflects this approach.

But this strategy has very clearly defined limits and constantly risks highlighting the very solicitation of the audience that it seeks to efface. The invisibility accomplished in the lyric by the "blinding" of the second person, for example, can obviously not be effected in relation to the audience. Notorious B.I.G.'s contemptuous dismissal of other rappers, "niggas is actors, niggas deserve oscars," refers to the risk run by the rapper who issues threats to the audience he can never fulfill.[40] "I see you in your videos ... holding a gun, [but you] ain't gonna bust [shoot]."[41] The rapper who presents a theatrically aggressive stance toward the audience simply highlights his ultimate dependence on the audience.

Rappers' appreciation of the dimensions of this tension has led to the current pervasive sense that the rap form can only be successfully executed by someone who is *not* a rapper. Thus the ascendant performance conceit is that there is no performance going on. This strategy is explicitly thematized in lyrics, instantiated by the physical stance of the rapper in videos, and by the rapper's verbal delivery, or "flow." The stance presents an alternative to that of the rapper who treats the audience in the same way as the formal "you" and ends up manifesting a debilitating *awareness* of the audience through her theatrical and implausible aggression. Now everything tends to establish the fiction that the rapper standing before the audience is unaware of its presence. This oblique, unacknowledged relation minimizes the tension between the performance and the projection of rap's fundamental fiction, the nonrelative social subject constructed by the rap lyric.

Numerous factors contribute to the success and popularity of this, at first sight quite dubious, strategy. For example, rap's defiant allegiance to the simple elements of its lyrical form, the interpretation of money in the context of an intense hostility to the other, itself strenuously resists the performance values of variety and innovation constantly pushed on it by its critics. The widespread adoption of this strategy also enables the form to mark a vivid and decisive break with earlier forms of rap. Consider the following verses by Rakim, one of the most influential rappers of the mid-1980s. "I just put your mind on pause / and I beat you when you compare my rhyme with yours;" "The scene of a crime every night at the show / The rhyme fiend on the mic that you know."[42] Rakim's lyrics foreground his talents as a rapper, brag about his power over an audience, and challenge other rappers. This stance, characteristic of early rap from Grandmaster Flash to Run DMC, and still apparent in many forms of spoken word and hip hop, is mistakenly believed by many critics to characterize contemporary rap.[43] Thus Timothy Brennan writes that rap's fundamental metaphor is that "words and minds are guns, and winning the talent clash [with a rival rapper] is 'killing the other.'"[44] This sense that the violence directed at the other is a metaphor for the rap performance pervades most rap through the late 1980s.

By the mid-1990s, this dynamic has been reversed. Now the performance, if referenced at all, becomes a metaphor for the violence directed at the other. Jay-Z warns "you" that he's not trying to overcome you with his rap skills: "Here's the shock of your life / The gun not the mic."[45] Some slam and spoken word poets have adopted similar strategies, albeit with a striking difference. Michael R. Brown, for example, declares in "The Ice Worm," "I'm not much of a performer ... I'm from the old school, where poets named things."[46] Brown's confession enlists the audience in his attempt to move oral poetry from theater to an "old" model of poetic speech as naming. The chorus of a popular rap by Big Pun is more typical of rap in its hostility to the audience. "Whatcha gonna do when Pun comes / Knocking at your front door / and wants war / Holy shit! He ain't a rapper he'll kill you."[47] The frame of a performance cannot contain the aggression toward the second person, and Pun underlines this conceit by the abrupt abandonment of the rhyme in the last line. My desire to kill, blind, and cancel "you" is absolutely not a metaphor for rapping, and the strongest way of putting this is to declare, "I'm not a rapper."[48] "Thought I told y'all / I'm not a rapper."[49] "I'll kill you ants with a sledgehammer, I overdo it / So you won't confuse it with just rap music."[50] "If you think I'm just a rapper / You got me fucked up."[51] "You're just a rapper."[52] The attempt to resolve the tension between the formal "you" of the rap lyric and the "you" of the audience thus has the unexpected effect of turning the once-celebrated figure of the rapper into rap's ritualized object of scorn.

One of the most effective ways for a rapper to show that he isn't a rapper is to demonstrate that he isn't very good at rapping. Kelefa Sanneh, in his article on Jay-Z, writes that in his later records, Jay-Z "has simplified his intricate rhyme style: his lyrics have become less tightly constructed, and less descriptive."[53] In an interview, Jay-Z provides the following extraordinary metaphor for his choice to move away from the verbal virtuosity displayed in his early raps. "In his early days, [Michael] Jordan was rocking a cradle, cranking it, all crazy, but he wasn't winning championships.... And then, later in his career, he just had a fadeaway jumpshot, and they won six titles. Which was the better Jordan?"[54] Sanneh, while admitting that Jay-Z's change in style has contributed to his immense popularity, argues that the rapper has forsaken the "artistic ambition" of his earlier career. "No one wants to watch a man make jump shots forever."[55]

But verbal virtuosity doesn't correspond to "artistic ambition" here. Like most critics, Sanneh projects alien aesthetic values onto rap. Jay-Z's decision to simplify his rap style is produced by the immanent contradiction between the performer/audience relation and the me/you relation. By drawing attention to his spectacular style, Jay-Z, like the early Jordan, wasn't "winning championships." His technical skill came at the expense of his success in executing the rap form. Sanneh betrays a fundamental confusion about rap. The essence of post-1980s rap is its interpretation of money. The persistence of the rap "formula" is only an enigma if one imagines that something else, like an "intricate rhyme style," is essential. Not only is verbal virtuosity essentially irrelevant to rap's core values; in certain cases, as with Jay-Z, it can even be opposed to it. Rap's primary formal feature, the conjunction of the reference to money with an antagonism to the second person, is threatened by Jay-Z's conspicuous status as a performer.

Thus the fiction that Jay-Z is not a performer proves essential to making his raps believable. If Jay-Z's early rap foregrounds its status as a special, artistic form of language, his later work masquerades as plain speech. As Krims writes, rap's "enunciation and delivery [are now] closer to those of spoken language, with little sense often projected of any underlying metric pulse."[56] This "spoken" style, muting the stresses and rhymes, de-emphasizing line breaks, provides a vivid contrast to the heavily stressed, "sing-song" style of such early rappers as Too Short and Run DMC.

Recall Billy Collins's observation, cited at the outset of this essay, that orality in the new performance poetries equals theatrical visibility. Collins means only to point out what seems to him the obvious difference between poetry read and poetry heard. But in the fiction so elaborately constructed by rappers, orality does not equal visibility. I'm not a rapper, Jay-Z or Pun rap, I'm just talking, and you're just overhearing me. J. S. Mill would have little trouble putting a name to this complex performance of overheard speech. Rap is the form of contemporary poetry most urgently attuned to the possibilities of the lyric relation.

NOTES

1. The derivative character of the lyric text is most marked in rap; rappers rarely provide authorized texts of their raps. For Mill's view of poetry as overheard

speech, see "Thoughts on Poetry and its Varieties," in *Autobiography and Literary Essays, Vol. 1 of The Collected Works of John Stuart Mill* (Toronto: University of Toronto Press, 1981).

2. Billy Collins, "Introduction," *The Spoken Word Revolution*, ed. Mark Eleveld (Naperville, IL: Sourcebooks, 2003), 4.

3. Black Rob, "Whoa," *Life Story* (Bad Boy 73026, 2000).

4. Mobb Deep, "Eye for an Eye," *The Infamous* (Loud 66480, 1995).

5. B.G., "I Know," *Checkmate* (Cash Money 860909, 2000).

6. I will use "he" and "she" interchangeably. This practice reflects the gender symmetry that characterizes the rap form. While male rappers are disproportionately represented in my examples, as they continue to be in rap generally, the elements of the rap form I examine here are also available to the increasing number of female artists such as Lil' Kim and Foxy Brown.

7. Critics have been predicting the imminent exhaustion of rap's lyrical focus on money and violence since the mid-1990s, during which time it has only become more pervasive. (See especially Timothy Brennan, "Off the Gangsta Tip" *Critical Inquiry* 20 [Summer 1994]: 663–93; and Robin Kelley, "Kickin' Reality, Kickin' Ballistics: Gangsta Rap and Postindustrial Los Angeles," in *Droppin' Science* ed. William Eric Perkins [Philadelphia: Temple University Press, 1996].) By 2001, Kelefa Sanneh can write, regretfully, that "'gangsta rap' is no longer a useful term; over the past ten years, it has come to denote any rapper who talks about gunplay in the first person, and this includes almost every one" ("Gettin Paid," *The New Yorker* [August 20, 2001], 68). By 2009, there were definite signs that the form had begun to weaken, although, given its past resilience, I hesitate to choose an end-date.

8. B.G., "Bling Bling," *Chopper City in the Ghetto* (Cash Money 53265, 1999).

9. Nelly, "Ride With Me," *Country Grammar* (Uptown 1577413, 2000); Lil' Wayne, "Loud Pipes," *Tha Block Is Hot* (Cash Money 153919, 1999).

10. B.G., "Bling Bling."

11. Ibid.

12. Raekwon, "Ice Water," *Only Built For Cuban Linx* (Loud 66663, 1995).

13. Notorious B.I.G., "I Love the Dough."

14. Missy Elliott, "Slide," *Under Construction* (Elektra 62813, 2002).

15. Jay Z, "Money Ain't a Thing," *Vol. 2: Hard Knock Life* (Roc-A-Fella 558902, 1998).

16. Snoop Dogg, "Tha Shiznit," *Doggystyle* (Death Row 50605, 1993).

17. Lil' Rob, "Peek-A-Boo," *Can't Keep a Good Man Down* (Lideres 950226, 2001).

18. Ibid.

19. Lil' Wayne, "Hey DJ," *The Carter* (Cash Money 27JYPI, 2004).

20. 50 Cent, "You Are Not Like Me," *Get Rich or Die Tryin'*, (Interscope 493544, 2003); Clipse "I'm Not You," *Lord Willin'* (Star Trak 4735, 2002).

21. Prodigy, "Y.B.E," *HNIC*, (Relativity 1873, 2000).

22. Critics influenced by Cornel West's account of black "nihilism" (*Race Matters*, Boston: Beacon Press, 1993) have seen rap as an expression of negative, antisocial attitudes plaguing the black inner city.

23. Paul Gilroy, *Against Race* (Cambridge, MA: Harvard University Press, 2002), 199.

24. Sanneh, "Gettin' Paid," 74.

25. Adam Krims, *Rap Music and the Poetics of Identity* (Cambridge: Cambridge University Press, 2001), 83.

26. Tricia Rose, "A Style Nobody Can Deal With," in *Microphone Fiends*, ed. Andrew Ross and Tricia Rose (London: Routledge, 1994), 80.

27. Elijah Anderson, *Code of the Street* (New York: W. W. Norton, 1999), 73.

28. Thorsten Veblen, *The Theory of the Leisure Class* (1899; New York: Penguin, 1994), 8.

29. Charles Taylor, "The Politics of Recognition," in *Multiculturalism*, ed. Amy Gutmann, (Princeton, NJ: Princeton University Press, 1994), 26; Martha Nussbaum, "Invisibility and Recognition: Sophocles' *Philoctetes* and Ellison's *Invisible Man*," *Philosophy and Literature* 23:2 (1999): 257–83; Homi Bhabha, *The Location of Culture*, London: Routledge, 1994.

30. Taylor, "Politics of Recognition," 64.

31. Anderson, *Code of the Street*, 73.

32. 50 Cent, "Life on the Line," *Get Rich or Die Tryin'*.

33. Puff Daddy feat. Mase, "Been Around the World," *No Way Out* (Bad Boy 39QD), 1997.

34. Mike Jones feat. Slim Thug, "Still Tippin,'" *Who Is Mike Jones?* (Warner Brothers 7YMV1K), 2005.

35. Brennan, "Off the Gangsta Tip," 681.

36. Houston Baker, *Black Studies, Rap, and the Academy* (Chicago: University of Chicago Press, 1993), 74–5.

37. Lil' Rob, "Peek-A-Boo."

38. T.I., "Be Easy."

39. I am particularly indebted to Fried's *Absorption and Theatricality: Painter and Beholder in the Age of Diderot* (Chicago: University of Chicago Press, 1988).

40. Notorious B.I.G, "I Love the Dough."

41. Westside Connection, "Gangsta Nation," *Terrorist Threats* (Priority 24030, 2003).

42. Eric B. and Rakim, "I Ain't No Joke" *Paid in Full* (6th and Broadway 444005, 1987); "Lyrics of Fury," *Follow the Leader* (Uni UNID3, 1988).

43. For an influential example of this stance drawn from spoken word poetry, see Saul Williams' performance in the film *Slam Nation* (New Video Group B000BB152O, 1998).

44. Brennan, "Off the Gangsta Tip," 692.

45. Jay-Z, "Come and Get Me," *Vol. 3: The Life and Times of Sean Carter* (Roc-A-Fella 558906, 2000).

46. *The Spoken Word Revolution*, 143.

47. Big Pun, "Whatcha Gonna Do," *Endangered Species* (Relativity 1963, 2001).

48. Clipse, "I'm Not You."

49. Jay-Z, "Heart of the City," *The Blueprint* (Roc-A-Fella 586396, 2001).

50. Jay-Z, "The Takeover," *The Blueprint*.

51. Scarface feat. W.C., "I Ain't the One" *The Fix* (Def Jam 986909, 2002).

52. B.G., "Niggaz In Trouble," *Chopper City* (Cash Money 9690, 1996).

53. Sanneh, "Getting Paid," 73.

54. Ibid.

55. Ibid.

56. Krims, *Rap Music and the Poetics of Identity*, 51.

FURTHER READING

Baker, Houston, *Black Studies, Rap, and the Academy* (Chicago: University of Chicago Press, 1993).

Bradley, Adam, *Book of Rhymes: The Poetics of Hip Hop* (New York: Basic Books, 2009).

Clover, Joshua, *1989: Bob Dylan Didn't Have This to Sing About* (Berkeley: University of California Press, 2009).

Ellison, Ralph, *Invisible Man* (New York: Random House, 1952).

George, Nelson, *Hip Hop America* (New York: Penguin, 1998).

Krims, Adam, *Rap Music and the Poetics of Identity* (Cambridge: Cambridge University Press, 2001).

Rose, Tricia, *The Hip Hop Wars: What We Talk About When We Talk About Hip Hop and Why It Matters* (New York: Basic Books, 2008).

Sanneh, Kelefa, "Gettin' Paid," *The New Yorker* (August 20, 2001).

Tiffany, Daniel, *Infidel Poetics* (Chicago: University of Chicago Press, 2009).

Veblen, Thorsten, *The Theory of the Leisure Class* (1899; New York: Penguin, 1994).

15

JENNIFER ASHTON

Poetry of the Twenty-First Century:
The First Decade

It is more or less a commonplace of our recent literary history that late-twentieth-century poetic discourse was driven by what Hank Lazer refers to as "opposing poetries."[1] I want to begin, however, by suggesting first (uncontroversially) that the most prominent form of that opposition – between an avant-garde (understood as hostile above all to the lyric) and a perceived mainstream (identified precisely with lyric) – has, in the twenty-first century, begun to disappear and second (more controversially), that, in a certain sense, the lyric has won. A 1989 manifesto, written collectively by six poets affiliated with the Language movement, offers a succinct enough version of the concept I mean to invoke. The poetry that Language writing sought to overturn – what the authors of the manifesto call the "autonomous, New Critical lyric" – is, as they put it, a poetry with "the self as the central and final term of creative practice."[2] That "self," moreover, would seem to be indistinguishable from the "speaker" that remains the primary currency of contemporary close reading: "What we mean by self," they write, "encompasses many things, but among these is a narrative persona, the fictive person (even in autobiography, who speaks in his or her poem about experience raised to a suitably aestheticized surface."[3] From the perspective of the lyric genre, this definition of "self" looks familiar because it is virtually identical to the "speaker" inhabiting the definitions of lyric codified in handbooks and textbooks of literary study. Take, for instance, this one from 1957 first edition of M. H. Abrams's *Glossary of Literary Terms*, which remains in the most recent edition, published in 2011: "[A] lyric is any short poem, consisting of the utterance by a single speaker, who expresses a state of mind or a process of perception, thought, and feeling."[4]

What I want to argue for early-twenty-first-century poetry – let's call it, for the sake of convenience, First-Decade poetry – is that it enables us to see the entire post-1945 era of American poetic production as an era distinctively committed to building a literary art around the value of self-expression. That is, not only lyric poetry understood *as such*, but even explicitly

216

anti-lyric poetics such as those of the Language movement or, more recently, of a resurgent conceptualism that claims to be "against expression" are equally committed to the valued representation of subjectivity, if not of "self." Hence, even though the lyric genre that, as Virginia Jackson has observed, is "now identified with an expressive theory" may be a distortion, it is one that, as I have argued elsewhere, provides an extremely useful perspective.[5] Indeed, it is precisely in distorting the recent history of American poetry – that is, by seeing lyric self-expression everywhere – that an entire set of material social relations, relations that have tended to remain obscure even in the most overtly political poetry, can be made visible and in turn make visible what might count as the poetic alternatives.

But before I get to the alternatives, I want to run through a few brief examples that lead us to this "lyric impulse" (to borrow a phrase from C. Day Lewis) in the first place.[6] Its starkest instance resides in the most virulent attack on lyric that I know of, namely that of the Language movement that I have already mentioned. Take for example, the codification of the "open" text, articulated most prominently in Lyn Hejinian's 1983 talk "The Rejection of Closure," variations of which can be found throughout the literature of the movement, from Ron Silliman's idealization of prelinguistic "chant" to Steve McCaffery's insistence on sound as a way to remove poetry as far as possible from the register of meaning.[7] If the Language text's emphasis on the visual and aural materiality of language is intended, as Hejinian put it, to "invite participation" by "foreground[ing] process, either … of the original composition or of subsequent compositions by readers," it is hard not to see this as simply replacing one locus of "perception, thought, and feeling" with another, replacing the subjectivity of the traditional lyric speaker with the subjectivity of the poet on the one hand and the reader on the other.[8] In other words, a represented subjectivity in lyric has simply been replaced with a literal subjectivity in Language writing, but in both instances, lyric and anti-lyric, it is in the subjectivity itself that we find the principle poetic investment.

Furthermore, if we look back for example, at the so-called anthology wars of the early 1960s, often cited as a key instance of the hallmark "avant-garde/mainstream" divide in twentieth-century American poetry, we find that the "avant-garde" poets of Donald Allen's *New American Poets, 1945–1960* – poets like Charles Olson, LeRoi Jones/Amiri Baraka, and Frank O'Hara – are just as committed to self-expressivity as the supposedly conventional poets – like Robert Lowell, Robert Bly, and W. D. Snodgrass – who had been collected three years earlier in Donald Hall, Robert Pack, and Louis Simpson's *New Poets of England and America*. How, in other words, are the vision of visceral bodily projection through the breath of Olson's "Projective

Verse," or the authenticity of voice called for in Jones's "How You Sound??" or even the abstraction of self proposed by O'Hara's "Personism" any less tied to subjectivity than the poetry of Lowell, Bly, and Snodgrass that we have come to call "confessional"?

Keeping the lyric goggles on, let's pan ahead now to the start of the twenty-first century. I would point out first another installment in the anthology wars with two anthologies in particular. First is Juliana Spahr and Claudia Rankine's 2002 *American Women Poets in the Twenty-First Century: Where Lyric Meets Language*, in which a new generation of poets, drawing on the formal techniques of their Language movement predecessors, discover that these techniques are not inhospitable to lyric after all. And when Language techniques "make room" for lyric and vice versa – "where language meets lyric" – the "lyric" that is both accommodated and accommodating refers, as Spahr puts it in the volume's introduction, "to interiority and/or intimate speech that avoids confession, clear speech, or common sense."[9] Even if, as Spahr goes on to say, the poetry resists "too easily separated and too easily declarative identities," its commitments to interiority and intimate speech are nothing if not committed to highly particularized subject positions, in this case with the particularities of gender in the foreground.[10] Second, an anthology that appeared in 2010, presenting itself as evidence that the anthology wars of the previous decades had definitively come to an end, Cole Swensen and David St. John's *American Hybrid* starts with the observation that "American poetry finds itself at a moment when idiosyncrasy rules to such a degree and differences are so numerous that distinct factions are hard, even impossible to pin down."[11] But even in their highly individualized commitments, what the poets of this "post-avant" moment share, Swensen argues, is a tendency to "honor the avant-garde mandate to renew the forms and expand the boundaries of poetry – thereby increasing the expressive potential of language itself – while also remaining committed to the emotional spectra of lived experience."[12]

For some examples of poetic projects that would seem to defy any attributions of "lyric" and which nonetheless keep poetry pegged to subjects and subjectivities, we can turn to Craig Dworkin's 2007 essay, "The Imaginary Solution."[13] In it, Dworkin discusses several digitally mediated projects (produced from the 1970s through the turn of the century), which he also has chosen to include in a recent anthology of conceptual writing that he and Kenneth Goldsmith have edited, titled, provocatively, *Against Expression*.[14] Consider projects like Kenneth Goldsmith's *Day*, consisting of the author's transcription, word for word, of a single day's issue of *The New York Times*; Bill Kennedy and Darren Wershler's Apostrophe Engine program, which searches the Internet for the locution "you are" and spins out a text whose lines anaphorically enact the apostrophic address; Dan Farrell's *The Inkblot Record*, which alphabetically organizes phrases randomly drawn from recorded responses to Rorschach inkblots; or Douglas Huebler's much earlier *Variable Piece #4: Secrets*, which collages photocopied "secrets" that had been written down and deposited by visitors to a gallery exhibition.[15] For Dworkin, the upshot of these kinds of works is the degree to which they foreground algorithms, taxonomies, rules, and tactics for organizing information in such a way that "the mode of poetic production in the books described above is indistinguishable from" and presumably, Dworkin seems to imply, serves to remind us of "the database logic at the core of other, far more ominous, activities," such as "unchecked mass surveillance."[16]

But what Dworkin frequently manages to observe and yet also manages to treat as incidental is the extent to which these projects depend on reminding us, even in their absence, of the subjects that produced the data in the first place. Like most of Goldsmith's work, *Day* is explicitly attached to the poet's own activity and physical presence in the process of producing the work, in this case in transcribing and scanning for hours and weeks and months on end, and becoming excruciatingly bored in the process.[17] Farrell's *Inkblot Records* may be a tour-de-force of fictive cataloging methods, but what they catalog are the records of clinical subjects expressing their most deeply subjective responses to the solicitous forms of the inkblots, and precisely in the context of a project of self-analysis. Dworkin admires the "inscriptive relay" of Douglas Huebler's project, and the degree to which it reveals the formal similarity of the secrets – in their syntax especially, which overwhelmingly predicates the secret on the first-person "I" followed by a present- or past-tense verb, with "I love you" emerging as a kind of refrain – that visitors deposit.[18] But, as even Dworkin acknowledges, the force of the secrets is that their capacity for self-revelation – our "most personal psychological reflexes" – is made all the more vividly personal by their imposed anonymity. Kennedy and Wershler's Apostrophe Engine is probably the most successful in accomplishing what Dworkin describes in *Against Expression* as a "laying bare" of "linguistic self-reflexivness" and an insistence on "impersonal procedure."[19] Moreover, unlike, the source material of Farrell's *Inkblot Record* or Huebler's *Secrets*, the source material for the Apostrophe Engine is as likely to come from a user support page or corporate mission statement as from anything like a personal confession. But even if the sense of "intimate personal address" is merely an index of "the extent to which Web pages in fact attempt to interpellate readers," the form that Kennedy and Wershler choose for the poetic outputs their engine produces is nevertheless that of the "intimate personal address," a staple of the lyric genre.[20]

I could point to other recent projects: Joshua Clover's *The Totality for Kids*, a book-length ode to the Situationists of the 1960s, and particularly to the exhortations of one of its leaders, Ivan Chtcheglov, to defy prescriptive institutions and structures through an individually driven practice of "psychogeograpny"; Noah Eli Gordon's *Inbox*, a seamless collage of all the e-mail in the poet's inbox on September 11, 2004, resulting, much like the outputs of the Apostrophe Engine, in a long anaphoric second-person address, and more than that, a self-portrait, if for no other reason than that the referent for every single "you" in the text is the poet himself; Katie Degentesh's *The Anger Scale*, a contribution to the Google-based "Flarf" movement, in which the poet Google-searched phrases from the Minnesota Multiphasic Personality Inventory (MMPI) – a now-discredited personality test – and then collaged the search results into poems with fairly transparently correct grammar and syntax and often with a first-person speaker; or in another recognition of the subject by its negation, Gnoetry, which uses a computer program to generate poems in established verse forms by sampling hallmark stylistic features of canonical works of literature in the public domain (you could program it to generate a sonnet from *Moby Dick*, or a free-verse poem from *Little Dorritt*) as a way of announcing that "the chemical author is dead."[21]

My point here is that lyric – more precisely, lyric equated with the expression of a subject, whether as an absence marked by a mere index or trace or a voluble presence in the form of a unified speaking voice – is never far from view even when it is supposed to have been rendered irrelevant or immaterial to the project at hand. And if we ask ourselves why the end of the twentieth and the beginning of the twenty-first century have seen this intensification of commitment to the self (an intensification so great that even opposition to it becomes a form of it), we can begin to get an answer by looking at more explicitly social and political claims made on behalf of lyric's value. Two important theoretical projects in particular exemplify that effort in its strongest form. The first is a lifelong project, the systematization of poetic history and principles of poetic practice that Allen Grossman first presented in a comprehensive form in his 1990 *Summa Lyrica*, and that he continued to develop and refine in *The Long School-Room: Lessons in the Bitter Logic of the Poetic Principle* and most recently in *True-Love: Essays on Poetry and Valuing*.[22] One of these essays, "The Passion of Laocoön," offers an especially succinct version of the project's central claims: that *"poetry is the civilizational means of last recourse,"* and that the principle by which it operates, the "human interest" that it serves, is "the construction of persons."[23] The second theoretical project in this vein (and a direct descendant of the first) is Oren Izenberg's 2011 *Being Numerous: Poetry and the Ground of Social Life*, in which "'poetry' names an ontological project: a civilizational wish to reground the concept and value of *the person*."[24] Izenberg's grounding of poetry in a more capacious account of "person-hood" is designed to redress what Grossman calls "the exclusionary difference that effects recognition," and "produces the archetype of economic scarcity."[25] We can imagine one very concrete meaning of economic scarcity for most of the period covered in this volume, but particularly beginning in the late 1960s up to our present moment, simply by noting that this period has coincided with a massive redistribution of wealth in the United States in which, since 1969, all of the increase in wealth has accrued to the top 10 percent. But scarcity goes with recognition in a more abstract sense as well. In other words, the distinctions on which recognition depends inevitably entail categories in which only some are included and all others are excluded, so that however we may wish to think there is no hierarchy in pure difference, recognizing difference depends on criteria that some meet and some do not. For Izenberg, the poetics that yields a sufficiently "minimal" account of personhood, one that will "tolerat[e] no exemptions or exclusion," is one that would successfully neutralize the condition of scarcity that necessarily grounds any project of "recognition."[26]

The poetic projects that I have tracked briefly so far are completely legible within the framework of persons and personhood offered to us by Grossman and Izenberg. Even a project like Gnoetry, for example, designed to displace persons altogether ("the chemical author is dead"), is only intelligible in the context of a wider poetic practice defined by its commitment to persons.[27] But the persistence of this poetic investment makes me wonder if the grounding of poetry in personhood might not be as symptomatic as it is descriptive of these post-1945 lyric and anti-lyric investments. Indeed, in some sense, it can be seen as part and parcel of the same commitment to the subject that I am arguing we see when we see through the lens of lyric, whether it takes the generalized form of personhood or the highly particularized forms of identities or of selves. If there is to be a break in the lyric/anti-lyric circuit, the project that poetry names will have to relinquish the ground of personhood and enter into a serious consideration of the ground of "scarcity" on which the recognition of persons is constructed, which is just what the poetry of the First Decade begins to reveal as a possibility.

In this connection, we turn to two poets who, in very different ways, suggest what such an undertaking might look like. One is Tao Lin, who, at the age of twenty-nine, belongs to the youngest generation writing in the First Decade. The other is Michael Fried, primarily known as an art critic and historian. Lyric is central to both poets' projects, just as I have been arguing it is for the poetry of the preceding half-century, but the difference these poems make is that they deploy the conventions of lyric, above all the expressive trappings of "perception, thought, and feeling" identified with it, to make claims for poetry's social and aesthetic functions that cannot be sustained on anything like the ground of the personal.

Since 2006, Lin has published two books of poetry, a collection of short stories, a novella, two novels, and directed and produced three feature-length films. While I will be focusing here on his poetry, his best-known works are fiction. But Lin is probably less appreciated as either poet or fiction writer than notorious as a publicity hound and overproducer, his notoriety including his promiscuous use of social media (constant updates on Twitter, Tumblr, and Facebook); writing his own self-promoting reviews and articles about himself as the new literary phenomenon, as in the Tao Lin cover of the Seattle magazine, *The Stranger*, parodying the *Time* magazine cover that presented Jonathan Franzen as the next "Great American Novelist"; his claim to having made a living for a time by selling items on eBay, including his crudely drawn cartoon sketches, along with items he had shoplifted (including those from American Apparel); in 2008, selling public shares in the as-yet-unwritten novel *Richard Yates*; giving ridiculously short readings (often no more than ten minutes long), sometimes while on hallucinogenic drugs, and even when not on drugs, speaking consistently in a mumbled, barely comprehensible monotone; for forming a film production company whose first release is a mind-numbing "feature film" of himself and his soon-to-be wife Megan Boyle on ecstasy, engaged in unscripted wandering and chatting around New York; in other words, for engaging in gimmicky antics that seem on the face of it more or less empty.

My point is not exactly to make Lin into a world-historical genius. But I do want to suggest, first, that the distinctive poetic exercise of Lin's work (including the fiction) is oriented toward the same "civilizational wish" that Grossman and Izenberg identify, and then, more crucially, I want to argue that, rather than regrounding personhood, Lin exposes, in multiple genres, through writing that is in every case the functional equivalent of the persona poem – indeed, of the same persona, "Tao Lin" (scare quotes required) – the terrain of scarcity where a regrounding would need to occur if it were to occur. And Lin accomplishes this by foregrounding something like his own market operations – the circulation both of "Tao Lin" and of the literary works he produces.

Like the title of Lin's first collection, *you are a little bit happier than i am*, many of the poems Lin writes are delivered first-person and are littered with "I"s and "you"s – pronouns, importantly, of traditional lyric address. On the surface, which we can see even in the title of a poem like the aptly named, "i am about to express myself," his poetry constantly evinces something like waiting or anticipation.[28] After all, this poem (along with others) repeatedly stages the prospect of greater happiness to come, always by receiving something from the world or by effecting a change in oneself or one's condition: "i wish i loved everything,"; "i know that good news will arrive only by email"; "there will be shockingly good news about my life inside of my email"; "i think something happened to me."[29] About half-way through the poem, there is a "change" that takes place literally in the space between pages, where the speaker goes from saying "i want to end my life" at the bottom of one page to "i don't want to end my life anymore / i changed... / i am expressing myself pretty good right now" at the top of the next page.[30] (The next page is the reverse side of the previous page, so it is a change that involves literally, as we say, "turning a new page.") More often Lin's poems stage the opposite disposition, however, pointing to the *lack* of what is wanted and the despair, sadness, and anger (often violent) that accompanies it, with an abiding sense of the futility of change. But in both kinds of propositions, I want to insist, Lin is not interested in the hoped-for (or unattained) change itself.

Unlike, say, Joshua Clover, Lisa Robertson, or Kevin Davies, poets whom Christopher Nealon describes in "Camp Messianism, or, the Hopes of Poetry in Late-Late Capitalism" as writing from a standpoint of waiting for something that the global expansions of capitalism have rendered impossible to conceive – in effect, the end of capitalism – Lin's hope for change is doing something else.[31] What interests Lin is the extent to which the disposition to change and achieve fully adequate forms of subjective expression and thereby of self-actualization is part of what enables (has enabled) capitalism to persist and continue its "damage to material life" in the form of over-whelming scarcity.

The fallback locution in *you are a little bit happier* is "i want," and some-times "i wish," often followed by some formulation involving personal change or projecting a response from the (often unspecified) "you" whom most of the poems address. The "I want" locution gives way at the start of Lin's second collection, *Cognitive Behavioral Therapy*, to the more insistent "i will," whose accompanying action often projects a further action that "you will" do as a projected result of what "i will" do. In their conversation with the therapeutic aims of the mental health practice known as Cognitive Behavioral Therapy, the poems of Lin's book (both of which I will refer to from now on as *CBT*) revolve around questions about what feelings and behaviors, both the speaker's own and those of the "you," are and are not within an individual's conscious power to change.

This brings me to Lin's signature obsession with facial expressions, which perform these questions of conscious control not only in the poems of *CBT*, but throughout *you are a little bit happier* and all of Lin's fictional work as well. The two volumes of poetry alone include eighty-seven references to faces and facial expressions. This persistent tendency serves to represent an embodied equivalent of the generic situation of lyric address, otherwise denoted by the speaking "I" in its address to a "you." In Lin's fiction, narrators repeatedly register characters' facial expressions (as "neutral," "bored," "sad," "alert," "concerned"). And the characters themselves are often depicted striving to read other characters' emotional states off of their faces, at the same time striving to make their own facial expressions legible or illegible according to what they think the situation requires, or in some cases recognizing the limit of their ability to exercise such control. Take this passage from the long poetic sequence that concludes *CBT*: "all instances of sad crying are actually carefully rendered exhibitions / of 'sad crying'; my face is actually a highly instructional message."[32] These lines happen to occur in the context of a simultaneously imagined literary failure ("he did not solicit my poetry") and success ("I think he is coming to solicit my poetry"), precisely in terms of available market structures (solicitation and submission of one's work for publication). For Lin, the effort to alter or control emotional expression, in the interest of communicating the desired message and soliciting a desired response – selling the expression, as it were – has a correlate in Lin's extraliterary activity, which relentlessly documents the sale of, and efforts to sell, his work – a constant endeavor in which the author's very life has become a kind of *reductio ad absurdum* of the market. It also has a correlate in what Michel Foucault has described as a foundational moment in the turn from liberalism to neoliberalism, namely the moment when "the worker himself appears as an enterprise for himself" (rather than, say, as a worker whose labor may be exploited by enterprise).[33] The value of the person in Lin's work exists, that is, in purely economic terms. For what Lin's work delivers is the conflation of a highly codified genre – lyric as self-expression – with an economic concept of human value, "human capital."[34] What Lin's work offers is thus a vision of what lyric and capital have in common: the fantasy of self-determination through self-transformation. Or rather, what Lin's work offers is the revelation of their collusion: the degree to the one is the ideological means of production of the other.

The generic features of lyric that Lin exploits are a measure of scarcity in economic terms. My second example, the poetry of Michael Fried, like much of the art history and criticism on which he has made his primary career, delivers another report of scarcity, but in this case in strictly aesthetic terms. Fried has published only two slim volumes of poetry: *To the Center of the Earth* (1994) and *The Next Bend in the Road* (2004).[35] Like Lin's poetry, many of Fried's poems present themselves in unambiguously autobiographical terms. And many of these deal with deeply personal responses to intimate situations, often building toward an epiphanic turn, features that could easily fall into line with the expressive stereotype that has attached to the "mainstream" lyric. Take for example, "The Drought":

> We wake in the dark
> to great flashes of light.
> The drought is history.
>
> Each time the thunder
> crashes the barn walls shake.
> Is that our daughter crying?
>
> No: she's sound asleep
> in the arms of the storm.
> Oh firm-fleshed Anna!
>
> *We stand over your crib*
> *scarcely breathing.*
> *Though we're not needed*
> *our lives are complete.*[36]

Anna is the poet's daughter, whose adoption in China is the subject matter of several poems in *The Next Bend in the Road*. And there is no question in this poem, or in any of the others on the subject, as to whether the people in the poem really are Fried, his wife, Ruth Leys, and their adopted daughter Anna. In short, these poems are nothing if not personal. Moreover, insofar as this poem conveys a very powerful emotional response from "we" in the poem to the presence of the daughter and the changes she has brought to their lives, it is nothing if not profoundly expressive (there is even a rapturous apostrophic "oh!" to seal the deal). Indeed, we might even go so far as to say it risks sentimentality, one of the great forbidden sins of modern and contemporary poetry, and a frequent charge against lyric poems in this highly emotional, subjective mode. We might thus ask why this sort of poem is not simply a regression to lyric of the most conventional and least interesting kind; why it is not simply another addition to the vast body of similar first-person autobiographical poetry that those who have struggled "against expression" have felt compelled to attack, whether on the side of lyric's defenders or its detractors.

Admittedly, the short, simple sentences, and often monosyllabic vocabulary that make up the lines of this poem create a smooth veneer of plain-spoken, even spontaneous, ease that is difficult to see past. But the poem's surface begins to change if we register the proliferation of internal rhymes that move our ear and eye against the regular grain of the line and stanza lengths: "Wake" rhymes with "shake," the effect preceding both a familiar cause (we shake people to wake them) and the very particular cause of the waking of the parents that is the occasion for the poem. Then we have "flashes" rhyming with "crashes," further causes of waking (again, both in general experience and in the particular situation of the poem), all of which have successfully wakened the parents and spectacularly failed to waken the child: "No: she is asleep." But something shifts when the speaker then addresses his sleeping daughter directly: "Oh, firm-fleshed Anna!" The phrase "firm-fleshed" is both descriptive of the child's ability to withstand the violence of the thunder and serves to fuse two of the preceding tracks in the internal rhymes of the poem: from "flashes" and "crashes" we have "fleshed," and from "arms" and "storm," we have "firm." Both "fleshed" and "firm" are slant rhymes with respect to their antecedents, therefore less easy to recognize, and insofar as it is only the root word that rhymes in both cases, these rhymes are all the more deeply embedded within the material texture of the poem.

The series of gestures, both deliberate and obscure (we can now abandon any idea that this poem is simply a spontaneous expression of a father's love for his daughter), then leads directly into the poem's coda, a stunning assertion of the child's autonomy from her parents ("we are not needed") even as we infer from the fact that she is in a crib that her actual relation to them must be one of near if not complete dependence. It is no accident that the figure on whom the poet bestows that autonomy is *asleep*, the epitome of a state in which one cannot help but be oblivious to being observed. For Fried, it is also the epitome of a technology in visual art, but particularly in painting, exemplified for him most strikingly in the eighteenth-century French painting that he addresses in his seminal art historical work, *Absorption and Theatricality: Painting and Beholder in the Age of Diderot*.[37] The most vivid instances of what Fried calls "absorption," works by such painters as Jean-Baptiste-Siméon Chardin or Jean-Baptiste Greuze, depict figures who appear to be absorbed in what they are doing, in reading, studying, drawing – or in the case of the great *Sleeping Hermit* by Joseph-Marie Vien, so unselfconscious in his absorption as to be unconscious. But of course such absorption achieves its full force only by virtue of the fact that these paintings, like all paintings, are made to be beheld. The address to a beholder is never *not* implied. If we replace the term "beholder" with "reader" or "listener," we can see that the same condition obtains for poetry. The concise statement of that condition is John Stuart Mill's famous dictum that "eloquence is *heard*; poetry is *over*heard."[38] Unlike poetry, which in this idealized form speaks as if there were no audience, "[e]loquence supposes an audience."[39] For Fried's eighteenth-century French painters, the opposite of absorption is "theatricality." Like Mill's eloquence, painting that is theatrical actively solicits the audience, indeed, depends on that audience's acknowledgment or response, while the absorbed figures in Greuze or Chardin are an idealization of the opposite state of affairs, "the supreme fiction," as Fried puts it, "that the beholder [does] not exist."[40] The sleeping child in Fried's lyric poem thus becomes an allegory of the autonomous work of art, whether we conceive that work as visual or textual. The fact that "we are not needed" pertains, in other words, as much to us, the poem's readers, as to the awe-struck parents of the child.

The insistence on the autonomy of the work of art has been identified, in both poetry and painting, more with the modernism of the first half of the twentieth century than with work produced during the period with which this volume is concerned. Indeed it has been a hallmark of the art and poetry that followed modernism – namely, of postmodernism – that they have repudiated claims to the autonomy of the work of art precisely by insisting on the reader/beholder's *necessity* to the work of art. Minimalism in art and Language writing in poetry staged this conviction most vividly with their insistence that the reader/beholder is as responsible for producing the art as the artist him- or herself. For Fried, the difference between the work of art that is autonomous with respect to the beholder and the art that depends on the response of the beholder is the difference between what truly is art and what is merely, literally, an object in the world. In his 1967 essay, "Art and Objecthood," autonomy would mark the divide between modernism and literalism, but more importantly, between art and *non*-art.[41] Moreover, throughout his account of the history of art, this divide has functioned at all moments dialectically to limit the range of what can count as art, and even more to the point, what can count as art of any value.

Aesthetic scarcity, unlike economic scarcity, obviously involves no question of ethics – the world is no more or less just if the number of works of art that truly count as art are twenty or twenty thousand. We could not say the same for the increase in the gap between the rich and the poor, the steady reduction of workers' real wages and general concentration of wealth in the hands of a small elite, that has characterized the United States during the period covered by this volume, an incline that has reached its steepest since the start of the twenty-first century. But by insisting on these forms of scarcity – economic in the case of Lin and aesthetic in the case of Fried – as the ground of a patently lyric poetic mode, these First Decade poets allow us to see the extent to which that ground has been obscured, for at least the past sixty-five years, by poetry's investment in its emotional and experiential effects. What these poets give us are poems whose individual and experiential effects are irrelevant, immaterial, while the poems' and their world's formal structure is what matters above all. The force of the work is to remind us that neither it nor the world it inhabits can be altered by our responses to it or by its effects on us – by, say, our feeling "complete"; they can only be altered by a change to their form. In this respect, we may well have arrived at a crucial dialectical shift in the social and aesthetic history of poetry: a new modernism, post-postmodernism.

NOTES

1. See Hank Lazer, Chapter 11 in this volume, but also his *Opposing Poetries Volume One: Issues and Institutions* (Evanston, IL: Northwestern University Press, 1996).
2. Ron Silliman, Carla Harryman, Lyn Hejinian, Steve Benson, Bob Perelman, and Barrett Watten, "Aesthetic Tendency and the Politics of Poetry: A Manifesto," *Social Text* 19/20 (Autumn 1988), 274, 263.
3. Ibid., 263.
4. M. H. Abrams and Geoffrey Galt Harpham, *A Glossary of Literary Terms, Ninth Edition* (Boston, Wadsworth Cengage Learning, 2009, 2005, Kindle Edition, loc. 2963).
5. Virginia Jackson, *Dickinson's Misery: A Theory of Lyric* Reading (Princeton, NJ: Princeton University Press, 2005), 10; Jennifer Ashton, "Lyric, Gender, and Subjectivity in Modern and Contemporary Women's Poetry," in *The Cambridge History of American Women's Literature*, ed. Dale Bauer (Cambridge: Cambridge University Press, 2012).
6. C. Day Lewis, *The Lyric Impulse* (Cambridge, MA: Harvard University Press, 1965).
7. Lyn Hejinian, "The Rejection of Closure," in *The Language of Inquiry* (Berkeley and Los Angeles: The University of California Press, 2000); Ron Silliman, "Disappearance of the Word, Appearance of the World," in *The New Sentence* (New York: Roof Books 1987); Steve McCaffery, "Language Writing: From Productive to Libidinal Economy," in *North of Intention: Critical Writings 1973–1986* (New York: Roof Books, 1986).
8. Hejinian, "Rejection," 43.
9. Juliana Spahr, "Introduction," in *American Women Poets in the 21st Century* (Middletown, CT: Wesleyan University Press, 2002), 2.
10. Ibid., 3.
11. Cole Swensen, "Introduction," in *American Hybrid: A Norton Anthology of New Poetry* (New York: W. W. Norton, 2009).
12. Ibid, xxi.
13. Craig Dworkin, "The Imaginary Solution" *Contemporary Literature* 48.1 (March 2007): 29–60.
14. Craig Dworkin and Kenneth Goldsmith, *Against Expression: An Anthology of Conceptual Writing* (Evanston, IL: Northwestern University Press, 2011).
15. Kenneth Goldsmith, *Day* (Great Barrington, MA: The Figures, 2003); Darren Wershler-Henry, Darren S., and Bill Kennedy, *Apostrophe* (Toronto: ECW, 2006, and http://www.apostropheengine.ca/); Dan Farrell, *The Inkblot Record* (Toronto: Coach House Press, 2000); Douglas Huebler, *Variable Piece #4: Secrets* (New York: Printed Matter, 1973).

16. Dworkin, "Imaginary," 56.
17. See Kenneth Goldsmith, "On Being Boring," http://epc.buffalo.edu/authors/goldsmith/goldsmith_boring.html
18. Dworkin, "Imaginary," 44.
19. Craig Dworkin, "The Fate of Echo," in *Against Expression*, xliii.
20. Dworkin, "Imaginary," 48.
21. Joshua Clover, *The Totality for Kids* (Berkeley, Los Angeles, and London: The University of California Press, 2006); Noah Eli Gordon, *Inbox: A Reverse Memoir* (Kenmore, NY: BlazeVOX, 2006); Katie Degentesh, *The Anger Scale* (Cumberland, RI: Combo Books, 2006); "The Gnoetic Manifesto," http://beard-ofbees.com/manifesto.html
22. Allen Grossman, *Summa Lyrica: A Primer of the Commonplaces in Speculative Poetics*, in *The Sighted Singer: Two Works on Poetry for Readers and Writers*, ed. Allen Grossman and Mark Halliday (Baltimore: The Johns Hopkins University Press, 1992); *The Long Schoolroom: Lessons in the Bitter Logic of the Poetic Principle* (Ann Arbor: The University of Michigan Press, 1997); *True-Love: Essays on Poetry and Valuing* (Chicago and London: The University of Chicago Press, 2009).
23. Grossman, *True-Love*, 117.
24. Oren Izenberg, *Poetry and the Ground of Social Life* (Princeton, NJ: Princeton University Press, 2011), 1.
25. Grossman, *True-Love*, 85.
26. Izenberg, 4.
27. "The Gnoetic Manifesto."
28. Tao Lin, *you are a little bit happier than i am* (Notre Dame, IN: Action Books, 2006), n.p.
29. Ibid.
30. Ibid.
31. Christopher Nealon, "Camp Messianism, or, the Hopes of Poetry in Late-Late Capitalism," *American Literature* 76.3 (September 2004): 580–602.
32. Tao Lin, *Cognitive Behavioral Therapy* (Brooklyn, NY: Melville House, 2008), 80.
33. Michel Foucault, *The Birth of Biopolitics: Lectures at the Collège de France, 1978–1979*, ed. Michel Senellart, trans. Graham Burchell (New York: Palgrave Macmillan, 2008), 226.
34. In the neoliberal sense of the term, coined in Gary Becker's *Human Capital: A Theoretical and Empirical Analysis, with Special Reference to Education, 3rd Edition* (1975; Chicago: University of Chicago Press, 1994).
35. Michael Fried, *To the Center of the Earth* (New York: Farrar, Strauss and Giroux, 1994) and *The Next Bend in the Road* (Chicago: The University of Chicago Press, 2004).
36. Fried, *Next Bend*, 20.
37. Michael Fried, *Absorption and Theatricality: Painting and Beholder in the Age of Diderot* (Chicago and London: The University of Chicago Press, 1980).
38. John Stuart Mill, "Thoughts on Poetry and Its Varieties" (1833), http://www.laits.utexas.edu/poltheory/jsmill/diss-disc/poetry/poetry.html, n.p.
39. Ibid.
40. Fried, *Absorption and Theatricality*, 103.

41. Michael Fried, "Art and Objecthood" (1967), in *Art and Objecthood: Essays and Reviews* (Chicago and London: The University of Chicago Press, 1998).

FURTHER READING

Armand, Louis, ed. *Contemporary Poetics*. Evanston, IL: Northwestern University Press, 2007.

Burt, Stephen. *Close Calls with Nonsense: Reading New Poetry*. St. Paul, MN: Graywolf Press, 2009.

Chiasson, Dan. *One Kind of Everything: Poem and Person in Contemporary America*. Chicago and London: The University of Chicago Press, 2007.

Dworkin, Craig, ed. *The Consequences of Innovation: 21st-Century Poetics*. New York: Roof Books, 2008.

Grossman, Allen. *True-Love: Essays on Poetry and Valuing*. Chicago and London: The University of Chicago Press, 2010.

Izenberg, Oren. *Being Numerous: Poetry and the Ground of Social Life*. Princeton, NJ: Princeton University Press, 2011.

Jackson, Virginia. *Dickinson's Misery: A Theory of Lyric Reading*. Princeton, NJ: Princeton University Press, 2005.

Nealon, Christopher. *The Matter of Capital: Poetry and Crisis in the American Century*. Cambridge, MA and London: Harvard University Press, 2011.

Perloff, Marjorie. *Unoriginal Genius: Poetry by Other Means in the New Century*. Chicago: The University of Chicago Press, 2010.

50 Cent, 204, 206

Abrams, M. H., 176, 216
Abramson, Seth, 160
abstract expressionism, 6, 48, 51, 53, 80, 83
academic poetry, 1, 10
Adam, Helen, 70–71, 74, 77
Adorno, Theodor, 29
Allen, Donald, 6
    The New American Poetry, 1945–1960,
      24, 32, 81, 144, 217
Altieri, Charles, 29, 72, 134
Ammons, A. R., 9, 139
    "Corson's Inlet," 138
    Garbage, 139
Anderson, Elijah, 205–206
Andrews, Bruce, 145, 151–152
Andrews, Bruce and Charles Bernstein
    The L=A=N=G=U=A=G=E Book,
      145, 149
Anzaldúa, Gloria, 110, 115
Apollinaire, 148
Armantrout, Rae, 75, 119–120, 165
artlessness as style, 35
Ashbery, John, 6, 11, 51–53, 58, 62–63
    Reported Sightings, 56
audience, 13
autonomy
    poetic, 33
    of the work of art, 227
avant-garde
    versus mainstream, 1
Ayler, Albert, 8

B. G., 203–204, 211
Bachelard, Gaston, 99
Baker, Houston A., 94, 208
Bakhtin, Mikhail, 151

Baraka, Amiri, 3–5, 7–8, 10, 86, 94–95, 99,
    101, 103–104, 106–107, 217
    "An Agony. As Now.," 104
    *Black Fire: An Anthology of Afro-
      American Writing*. *See also* Neal,
      Larry
    "How You Sound??," 8
    "It's Nation Time," 94
    "SOS," 103
Barthes, Roland, 152, 175
Bartlett, Lee, 146
Bataille, Georges, 150, 152
Bate, Jonathan, 132
Beat poetry, 3–4, 67, 74, 90
Benjamin, Walter, 19
Benson, Steve, 74, 151
Bernstein, Charles, 4, 14, 26, 119, 144–145,
    151, 158, 164, 167
Berry, Wendell, 9, 130, 132
    "The Clearing," 132
    "The Morning's News," 131
Berryman, John, 31–32, 34–35, 40–42,
    146, 184
    77 Dream Songs, 41
Bhabha, Homi, 206
Bidart, Frank, 173
Big Pun, 211
Bishop, Elizabeth, 178, 195
Black Arts, 3–4, 6–7, 86–87, 94–97, 99,
    101–106, 108, 110, 114
Black Arts Repertory Theater School, 8
Black Mountain College, xvi, 16, 23–25,
    27, 188
Black Rob, 203
Blaser, Robin, 6, 68
Blasin, Mutlu Konuk, 177
bling, 13, 203–207, 209
blogs, 168

Bly, Robert, 217
Bök, Christian, 156
Boone, Bruce, 74, 76
breath, 22
Brennan, Timothy, 208, 211, 213
Brenton, Myron, 37
Brock-Broido, Lucie, 175
Brodsky, Joseph, 198
Brooks, Gwendolyn, 106, 180
    "In the Mecca," 102
    "We Real Cool," 101
Brother Antoninus. *See* Everson, William
Broughton, James, 70
Brown, Michael R., 211
Bryson, J. Scott, 129
Buddhism, 72, 74, 81, 89, 135
Buell, Lawrence, 129
Bunting, Basil, 20
Bürger, Peter
    Theory of the Avant-Garde, 149
Byrd, Don, 26
Byrd, Rudolph, 114

Cage, John, 152
California Renaissance, 4, 6
California School of Fine Arts, 68
Cameron, Sharon, 181
capitalism, 137, 147–148, 150, 223–224, 227
Carson, Rachel, 9, 128
    Silent Spring, 9
Cassady, Carolyn, 74
Cézanne, Paul, 47
Cha, Theresa Hak Kyung, 122
chant, 85, 97
City Lights Books, 81
Civil Rights Act of 1964, 8
class politics, 18
Clifton, Lucille, 94
Clipse, 204, 211
Clover, Joshua, 223
    The Totality for Kids, 220
Cobbing, Bob, 146
Cold War, the, 37
Cole, Norma, 74, 165
collective subjectivity, 209
Collins, Billy, 202, 212
Collins, Jess. *See* Jess
Collis, Stephen, 196
Coltrane, John, 8
commodities
    poems as distinct from, 159
communism, 3–4, 18
conceptualism, 14

confessional poetry, 1, 5, 35, 110,
    177–178, 218
conspicuous consumption, 207
Coolidge, Clark, 6
Cooney, Seamus, 28
Corman, Cid, 23–24
Corso, Gregory, 4, 83, 85, 89
craft, 165
Crane, Hart, 9
Crawford, Robert, 199
creative writing programs, 1, 10–11, 26, 146,
    159–165
Creeley, Robert, 7, 22–26, 69, 81–82, 88,
    144, 149
Cronon, William, 131
Cruz, Victor Hernández, 74
Cubism, 47
Culler, Jonathan, 177

Dadaism, 148
Dahlberg, Edward, 22
Davies, Alan, 151
Davies, Kevin, 223
de Chirico, Georgio, 56–57
Degentesh, Katie
    The Anger Scale, 220
Deleuze, Gilles and Felix Guattari, 152
Dembo, L.S., 25
description, 61
Dewey, Anne Day, 28
di Prima, Diane, 4, 7, 74, 82, 87–89
Dickinson, Emily, 173, 177, 196
Diebenkorn, Richard, 68
Dolven, Jeffrey, 198
Dorn, Edward, 23
Douglas, William, 44
Dove, Rita, 173
Duff, David, 198
Duncan, Robert, 3–4, 6, 23–25, 68, 74–75,
    77, 82, 147
    Faust Foutu, 77
    "The Homosexual in Society," 73
    The Opening of the Field, 72
    "Towards an Open Universe," 147
DuPlessis, Rachel Blau, 20, 27, 64–65,
    117–119, 121
    Drafts, 119
    *The Pink Guitar: Writing as Feminist
        Practice*, 119
Dworkin, Craig, 162, 219
Dylan, Bob, 90

ecocriticism, 129. *See* ecopoetry

ecology, 9, 72, 75, 81, 139
ecopoetics, 132
ecopoetry, 10, 129
  differientiated from nature poetry, 130
Eigner, Larry, 25, 144
elegy, 182
Elgin, Catherine, 64
Eliot, T. S., 5, 17, 32, 188, 198
  "Tradition and the Individual Talent," 175
  The Waste Land, 21
Ellingham, Lewis, 78
Ellison, Ralph, 208
Emerson, Ralph Waldo
  "Nature," 130–131
Epstein, Andrew, 62
Equal Rights Amendment, 9
Everson, William, 67–68, 72

Faggen, Robert, 130
Farrell, Dan
  The Inkblot Record, 219
feminism, 2, 8, 40, 75, 82, 87–88, 109–111,
  114–116, 123
Fenza, D. W., 171
Ferlinghetti, Lawrence, 4, 69, 81, 84
"field" poetics, 7, 22, 24, 27, 72, 76, 138
Fields, Julia, 104
Finkelstein, Norman, 27
Fischer, Norman, 74
Fisher, Alllen
  Place, 146
Flarf, 14, 176, 220
Fletcher, Angus, 129
form, 18, 22
Forrest-Thomson, Veronica, 146, 184
Foucault, Michel, 224
Foxy Brown, 213
Frank, David J. and Jay Gabler, 199
Fraser, Kathleen, 117–118
Fredman, Stephen, 143
free verse, 94
Freilicher, Jane, 6, 53, 57–58
Fried, Michael, 209, 221, 227
  *Absorption and Theatricality: Painting
    and Beholder in the Age of Diderot*,
    227
  "Art and Objecthood," 227
  "The Drought," 227
Friedan, Betty, 8, 40, 109
Frost, Elisabeth A., 198
Frost, Robert, 9, 127–128, 139
  "The Gift Outright," 128–129
  "The Oven Bird," 130

Fulton, Alice, 173

Garrard, Greg, 132
Gifford, Terry, 128
Gill, Jo, 44
Gilroy, Paul, 205
Ginsberg, Allen, 3–4, 7, 33, 66, 72, 80–82,
  93, 148, 189, 198
  "Howl," 33, 69, 81
  obscenity trial, 69, 81
Giovanni, Nikki, 4, 8, 97, 103–104
  "Of Liberation," 104
  "The True Import of the Present Dialogue,
    Black vs. Negro," 98
Gleason, Madeline, 70, 74
Glotfelty, Cheryll, 129
Glück, Louise, 11–12, 146, 175, 177, 181,
  183–184
  "Against Sincerity," 177
  The Wild Iris, 181
Glück, Robert, 74
Gnoetry, 220–221
Goldsmith, Kenneth, 218
  Day, 218–219
Gomringer, Eugen, 150
Goodman, Nelson
  Languages of Art, 59
Gordon, Noah Eli
  Inbox: A Reverse Memoir, 220
Graham, Jorie, 11, 15, 146, 173, 175, 179
  and Language writing, 179
  "Self-Portrait as Apollo and Daphne,"
    178
Grahn, Judy, 74–75, 113
Grand Piano, The, 76
Grandmaster Flash, 211
Grenier, Robert, 26, 76, 144
  "I HATE SPEECH," 26, 76, 144
Griffin, Joanna, 75
Griffin, Susan, 74
Griswold v. Connecticut, 38, 40
Grossman, Allen, 1, 11, 187, 189–192,
  196–197, 220
  "Flax: A Ballad of Schools and Dreams,"
    193
  "Flora's ABC," 196
  "The Great Work Farm Elegy," 192
  "The Lecture," 191
  "The Passion of Laocoön: Warfare of
    the Religious against the Poetic
    Institution," 220–221
  The Philosopher's Window, 194
  "The Piano Player Explains Himself," 200

Grossman, Allen (*cont.*)
  Summa Lyrica, 191, 193
  Sweet Youth, 194
  "Wash Day," 195
  "Whoever Builds," 200
  "The Woman on the Bridge Over the
    Chicago River," 194
Guest, Barbara, 6, 53–54, 59, 62, 64
  "Brown Studio," 59
  "Nebraska," 62
Guilbaut, Serge, 62
Gunn, Thom, 175, 183, 186
  The Man with Night Sweats, 183

Hacker, Marilyn, 113
  *Love, Death, and the Changing of the
    Seasons*, 113
Hagedorn, Jessica, 74–75
Hall, Donald
  New Poets of England and America, 24
Hardwick, Elizabeth, 32
Harjo, Joy, 9, 116
Harlem Renaissance, 7
Harryman, Carla, 75, 119
Hartley, George, 146
Hass, Robert, 75, 165
Hejinian, Lyn, 4, 6, 12, 26, 75, 119–121,
    165, 173, 175, 217
  "La Faustienne," 120
  My Life, 121
  "The Rejection of Closure," 149, 217
Heller, Michael, 27
Herbert, George, 181
hip hop, 202
Hitchcock, George, 70
Hodes, Ida, 77
Hoffman, Hans, 53
Hogan, Linda, 116
Howe, Susan, 1, 11, 26, 121–122, 151, 165,
    187, 189–191, 196–198
  The Europe of Trusts, 122
  "Fragment of the Wedding Dress of Sarah
    Pierpont Edwards," 197
  My Emily Dickinson, 122
  Secret History of the Dividing Line,
    122
Huebler, Douglas
  Variable Piece #4: Secrets, 219
Hunter, Sam, 62

identity, 2
imagism, 3, 20
impersonality, 33, 35

indeterminacy, 12, 135, 179, 190
Inman, Peter, 149, 151, 155
intention, 12
internet, 164
intersubjectivity, 209
Iowa Writers' Workshop, 10, 159, 171
Izenberg, Oren, 220–221
  *Being Numerous: Poetry and the Ground
    of Social Life*, 221

Jackson, Virginia, 179
Jarman, Mark, 182
Jarnot, Lisa
  "Tell Me Poem," 139
Jay-Z, 204–205, 211–212
jazz, 70, 74–75, 80, 84, 96
Jess, 77
Jim Crow, 8
Joans, Ted, 83–84, 86
Johns, Jasper, 51
Johnson, Barbara, 185
Johnson, Ronald, 27
  ARK, 27
Johnson, W. R., 174, 183
Jones, Hettie, 74
Jones, LeRoi, 7, 82, 85–86, 95. See Baraka,
  Amiri
Jordan, June, 114
Joyce, James, 18

Kandel, Lenore, 82–83
Karagueuzian, Catherine Song, 179
Kaufman, Bob, 4, 69, 83–84, 86
Kaufman, Eileen, 74
Kaufman, Robert, 64
Kelley, Robin, 213
Kennedy, Bill and Darren Wershler-Henry
  Apostrophe, 219
Kenner, Hugh, 17
Kentridge, William, 64
Kerouac, Edie Parker, 74
Kerouac, Jack, 4, 66, 69, 79–85, 88–89, 93
  Dharma Bums, The, 67
Kerridge, Richard, 132
Kgositsile, Keorapetse, 105–106
  "Exile," 106
Khrushchev, Nikita, 36
Killian, Kevin, 78
Kitaj, R. B., 58
Kizer, Carolyn, 113
Knapp, Steven, 179
Koch, Kenneth, 53
Krims, Adam, 205, 212

Kumin, Maxine, 113
Kyger, Joanne, 69, 74, 84–85, 87–89

L=A=N=G=U=A=G=E, 145, 150–151.
    See Language writing
labor, 4, 72, 138, 163, 194, 224
Lamantia, Philip, 66, 68, 81
Lamm, Kimberly, 53, 62
Language writing, 1, 3–4, 6, 10–12,
    14, 26, 29, 74–76, 118–120,
    143–149, 151–153, 165, 173,
    198, 216–218, 227
Lansing, Gerritt, 26
Last Poets, The, 8
Lazer, Hank, 216
Lee, Don. *See* Madhubuti, Haki
Lehman, David, 62
Levertov, Denise, 7, 24, 82, 88, 147
Levinas, Emmanuel, 163, 168
Lewis, C. Day, 174, 217
Lil' Kim, 213
Lin, Tao, 221, 224
    Cognitive Behavioral Therapy, 224
    "i am about to express myself," 222
line, 22
Lombardi, Marilyn May, 185
Longenbach, James, 183
Lorde, Audre, 9, 104, 114–115
    The Black Unicorn, 115
    "Naturally," 105
Lowell, Robert, 31–32, 54, 146, 194,
    198, 217
    Life Studies, 34
    "Skunk Hour," 31
lyric, 11, 14, 43, 118, 136, 173–175,
    193, 202, 217–218, 220–222,
    224–225
    and musicality, 174
    voice, 12, 120, 146, 180
lyric "I" as convention, 177

Mac Low, Jackson, 152
Mackey, Nathaniel, 75
Madhubuti, Haki, 96, 102, 106
    "Gwendolyn Brooks," 96
mainstream, 1, 14, 110, 146, 174–175, 179,
    183, 188, 225
    versus avant-garde, 166
Mallarmé, Stéphane, 185
Mangan, James Clarence, 197
Marinetti, F. T., 148
markets, 2
marxism, 18

Marxism, 145, 148
Mason, David, 182
materiality
    of language, 3–4, 12, 18–19, 25
    of the text, 26, 119, 121, 152
May, Elaine Tyler, 36
Mayer, Bernadette, 151
McCaffery, Steve, 144, 217
    "Writing as a General Economy," 150
McCarthy, Joseph, 37, 67
McCarthyism, 5, 44
McClure, Joanna, 74
McClure, Michael, 66, 68, 77, 81, 89
McDonald, Gail, 198
McGann, Jerome, 29, 146–147
McGurl, Mark, 170, 199
meaning, 59–60
Melnick, David, 149, 151, 155
Melville, Herman, 197
Menand, Louis, 171
Merwin, W. S., 130, 132, 134
    "For a Coming Extinction," 133
    "Losing a Language," 134
metaphor, 60
Mezzrow, Mezz, 84
MFA, 26, 146, 160, 167, 170–171.
    See creative writing programs
Michaels, Walter Benn, 200
Middlebrook, Diane, 44
Mike Jones, 207
Mill, John Stuart, 5, 202, 212, 226
Miller, Paul Allen, 184
Milton, John, 184
Mirikitani, Janice, 74
Missy Elliott, 204
Mitchell, Joan, 6
Mobb Deep, 203
modernism, 5, 18, 48, 67
Monroe, Harriet, 3, 16
Moore, Marianne, 5
Mor, Amus, 98
    "Poem to the Hip Generation," 99, 103
Moraga, Cherríe, 9, 115
    Loving in the War Years, 116
mp3 recordings, 168
Mullen, Harryette, 122
Museum of Modern Art, 53
music, 3, 18, 20
Myers, D. G., 170
mythology, 6, 17

Naropa Institute, 72, 82, 88
National Endowment for the Arts, 167

National Organization of Women, 8
NEA. *See* National Endowment for the Arts
Neal, Larry, 7, 96, 106
   "The Narrative of the Black
     Magicians," 97
Nealon, Christopher, 223
Nelly, 204
neoliberalism, 224
New Criticism, 33
New Formalism, 182
New Masses, 18
New Narrative, 76
New York School, 1, 6, 48, 51, 53–54, 62,
   65, 82
Niedecker, Lorine, 3–4, 16, 18–20, 24, 27,
   136–137
   "Paean to Place," 137
Nielsen, Aldon Lynn, 95
Nixon, Richard, 36
Notorious B.I.G., 210
Nussbaum, Martha, 206

objectivists, 3–4, 19
O'Hara, Frank, 5–7, 33, 47, 53–54, 56–57,
   62–63, 65, 217
   "Clepsydra," 63
   "In Memory of My Feelings," 63
   "Joe's Jacket," 63
   Lunch Poems, 33
   "Personal Poem," 55
   "Personism: A Manifesto," 5–7, 218
   "Poem (When Your Left Arm
     Twitches)," 63
   as portrait subject, 51
   techniques of lineation, 63
   "To the Film Industry in Crisis," 63
Olson, Charles, 3–5, 7–8, 16, 21, 80, 82–83,
   137–138, 146, 188, 217
   "The Kingfishers," 21
   "Projective Verse," 4–5, 7–8, 10, 12,
     21–24, 84, 89, 147
online poetry magazines, 168.
   See also internet
open text, 3, 6–7, 22, 75, 138, 149–150, 217
Oppen, George, 3, 16, 18–20,
   24–25, 27
Oppenheimer, Joel, 23
ordinary language, 2
Ostriker, Alicia, 9, 113, 116
Oulipo, 152, 156

Pack, Robert. *See* Hall, Donald
Palmer, Michael, 6, 27, 74, 151

pastoral, 9, 129
Peirce, Charles Sanders, 196
Penberthy, Jenny, 28
Perec, Georges, 156
Perelman, Bob, 12, 14, 75, 165
performance, 13, 72, 74, 95, 203, 210
Perloff, Marjorie, 81, 143, 146
Philip, M. NourbeSe, 122
Phillips, Carl, 175, 181, 183
Phillips, Dana, 132
Piombino, Nick, 151
Plath, Sylvia, 31–32, 34–35, 39–42, 45–46,
   122, 146, 174, 178, 185
   "Lady Lazarus," 42
poetic value, 2
Pollock, Jackson, 6, 47–48, 56
Porter, Fairfield, 6, 49, 57–58
portrait painting, 51
postmodernism, 24–25, 132, 190
Pound, Ezra, 2–5, 16–19, 21–23, 59, 68, 80,
   85, 188–189, 191, 198
   Cantos, 18
privacy, 5, 31, 36, 40, 43
   and the body, 43
   private versus public, 2
prizes for poetry, 164, 170
Prodigy, 204
professionalization
   of poetry, 159
Prothero, Stephen, 88
Prynne, J. H., 146
psychotherapy, 33
publishing, 163, 168, 170
Puff Daddy, 207

Quartermain, Peter, 20

Raekwon, 204
Rainey, Lawrence, 198
Rakim, 210–211
Rakosi, Carl, 17, 19–20, 24–25
Rankine, Claudia and Juliana Spahr
   American Women Poets in the 21st
     Century: Where Lyric Meets
     Language, 218
Ransom, John Crowe, 73
rap, 13, 202, 205, 207, 212
Rasula, Jed, 29, 158, 166
referentiality
   critique of, 149–150
Retallack, Joan, 117
Rexroth, Kenneth, 6, 66–67, 80
Reznikoff, Charles, 17–20, 25

Rich, Adrienne, 9, 110–112
  "Diving into the Wreck," 112
  "When We Dead Awaken: Writing as
    Re-Vision," 110
Rivers, Larry, 6, 51, 53, 57–58
Robertson, Lisa, 223
Robinson, Kit, 6
Robles, Al, 74
Roe v. Wade, 40, 43, 45
romanticism, 151, 187
Romanticism, 5, 72
Rose, Jacqueline, 185
Rose, Tricia, 205
Rosenthal, M. L., 31, 44
Rueckert, William, 128
Rukeyser, Muriel, 9, 111
  "Theory of Flight," 111
Run DMC, 211–212
Ryden, Kent C., 129

San Francisco Art Institute. See California
  School of Fine Arts
San Francisco Renaissance.
  See also California Renaissance
San Francisco School of Fine Arts, 77
San Francisco State College Poetry Center,
  68, 78, 82
Sanchez, Sonia, 104, 114
Sanders, Pharoah, 8
Sandoval, Chela, 114
Sanneh, Kelefa, 205, 211, 213
Scalapino, Leslie, 74, 119
Scarface, 211
Schlegel, Friedrich, 151
Schulte-Sasse, Jochen, 149
Schuyler, James, 53, 58, 62, 65
self-expression, 13, 33, 42–43, 54,
  110–111, 118, 164, 173,
  175–177, 216–218, 224
Sexton, Anne, 31–32, 34–36, 38–42
  "For John Who Begs Me Not to Inquire
    Further," 36, 39
  "Menstruation at Forty," 34
  "The Operation," 42
  "Self in 1958," 39
  "Unknown Girl in a Maternity Ward," 42
sexuality, 74, 76, 82, 112, 181
Shange, Ntozake, 74
  For colored girls who have considered
    suicide/when the rainbow is enuf, 75
Sharp, Tom, 28
Sherry, James, 158
Showalter, Elaine, 110

Shurin, Aaron, 74
Silko, Leslie Marmon, 116
Silliman, Ron, 4, 26, 75–76, 144–145, 147,
  149, 152, 154, 158, 168, 170, 217
  "Disappearance of the Word, Appearance
    of the World," 145
  In the American Tree, 146
  "The New Sentence," 152
  Preface and Notes to "The Dwelling Place:
    9 Poets," 144
Silvers, Sally, 151
Simpson, Louis. See Hall, Donald
sincerity, 17–19, 23, 35, 48
Sixties counterculture, 4
Slam poetry, 5, 8, 10, 80
slavery in the US, 8
Smith, Patti, 85
Smith, Richard Candida, 77
Smith, Rod, 154
Snodgrass, W. D., 31, 217
  "The Operation," 41–42
Snoop Dogg, 204
Snyder, Gary, 7, 9, 66–67, 72, 74, 79, 81–82,
  134, 136, 141, 158
  "Riprap," 135–136
  "The Straits of Malacca," 136
  Turtle Island, 135
  "A Walk," 73
sound poetry, 70
Spahr, Juliana, 218
speaker, 2, 5
Spellman, A. B., 94, 96–97
  "friends i am like you tied," 97
Spicer, Jack, 4, 6–7, 66, 68–71, 73–77
  dictation, 71
spiritualism, 4
spoken word, 5, 8, 13, 94–95, 202, 207,
  211, 214
St. John, David and Cole Swensen
  American Hybrid, 218
Stein, Gertrude, 2, 18, 25, 152
Stevens, Wallace, 20, 129
Still, Clyfford, 68
Stone, Christopher D., 10
Strand, Mark, 176
subjectivity, 4, 12, 14, 22, 117, 173, 219
Sun Ra, 8, 99
surrealism, 47, 54, 58, 64, 70, 81
Swensen, Cole, 14, 218

T.I., 209
Tarlo, Harriet, 136
Taylor, Charles, 206

Thoreau, Henry David, 158
Too Short, 212

Umbra Workshop, 8
University of California, Berkeley, 68
utopianism, 19

Veblen, Thorstein, 205
Vega, Janine Pommy, 74, 87–88
Vendler, Helen, 12, 179
Vickery, Ann, 123
Vietnam War, 5
    protests, 5
voice, 14
Vollmer, Joan, 74
von Hallberg, Robert, 29

Walcott, Derek, 175
Waldman, Anne, 81–82, 87
Warsh, Lewis, 82
Watkins, William, 62, 64
Watten, Barrett, 26, 75, 144–145, 152–153
Welch, Lew, 69
Wellman, Donald, 26

West, Cornel, 213
Westside Connection, 210
Whalen, Philip, 66, 74, 81
White, Byron, 43
Whitehead, Kim, 116, 122
Whitman, Walt, 4, 134, 177
Wieners, John, 23
Williams, Jonathan, 23
Williams, Saul, 214
Williams, William Carlos, 2, 4, 9, 16, 19,
    21–22, 24, 27–28, 32, 68, 80, 83–84,
    129, 136, 146–147, 173, 184
    Paterson, 44
Witt-Diamant, Ruth, 68, 82
Wordsworth, William, 5
Wright, C.D., 11, 14
Wright, Charles, 12, 174

Yeats, W. B.
    "Among School Children," 192

zaum, 151, 155
Zukofsky, Louis, 2–4, 7, 16–25, 27–28, 187
    "'Objectivists' 1931" *Poetry* issue, 19

Cambridge Companions to...

AUTHORS

Edward Albee edited by Stephen J. Bottoms

Margaret Atwood edited by Coral Ann Howells

W. H. Auden edited by Stan Smith

Jane Austen edited by Edward Copeland and Juliet McMaster (second edition)

Beckett edited by John Pilling

Bede edited by Scott DeGregorio

Aphra Behn edited by Derek Hughes and Janet Todd

Walter Benjamin edited by David S. Ferris

William Blake edited by Morris Eaves

Brecht edited by Peter Thomson and Glendyr Sacks (second edition)

The Brontës edited by Heather Glen

Bunyan edited by Anne Dunan-Page

Edmund Burke edited by David Dwan and Christopher J. Insole

Frances Burney edited by Peter Sabor

Byron edited by Drummond Bone

Albert Camus edited by Edward J. Hughes

Willa Cather edited by Marilee Lindemann

Cervantes edited by Anthony J. Cascardi

Chaucer edited by Piero Boitani and Jill Mann (second edition)

Chekhov edited by Vera Gottlieb and Paul Allain

Kate Chopin edited by Janet Beer

Caryl Churchill edited by Elaine Aston and Elin Diamond

Coleridge edited by Lucy Newlyn

Wilkie Collins edited by Jenny Bourne Taylor

Joseph Conrad edited by J. H. Stape

H. D. edited by Nephie J. Christodoulides and Polina Mackay

Dante edited by Rachel Jacoff (second edition)

Daniel Defoe edited by John Richetti

Don DeLillo edited by John N. Duvall

Charles Dickens edited by John O. Jordan

Emily Dickinson edited by Wendy Martin

John Donne edited by Achsah Guibbory

Dostoevskii edited by W. J. Leatherbarrow

Theodore Dreiser edited by Leonard Cassuto and Clare Virginia Eby

John Dryden edited by Steven N. Zwicker

W. E. B. Du Bois edited by Shamoon Zamir

George Eliot edited by George Levine

T. S. Eliot edited by A. David Moody

Ralph Ellison edited by Ross Posnock

Ralph Waldo Emerson edited by Joel Porte and Saundra Morris

William Faulkner edited by Philip M. Weinstein

Henry Fielding edited by Claude Rawson

F. Scott Fitzgerald edited by Ruth Prigozy

Flaubert edited by Timothy Unwin

E. M. Forster edited by David Bradshaw

Benjamin Franklin edited by Carla Mulford

Brian Friel edited by Anthony Roche

Robert Frost edited by Robert Faggen

Gabriel García Márquez edited by Philip Swanson

Elizabeth Gaskell edited by Jill L. Matus

Goethe edited by Lesley Sharpe

Günter Grass edited by Stuart Taberner

Thomas Hardy edited by Dale Kramer

David Hare edited by Richard Boon

Nathaniel Hawthorne edited by Richard Millington

Seamus Heaney edited by Bernard O'Donoghue

Ernest Hemingway edited by Scott Donaldson

Homer edited by Robert Fowler

Horace edited by Stephen Harrison

Ted Hughes edited by Terry Gifford

Ibsen edited by James McFarlane

Henry James edited by Jonathan Freedman

Samuel Johnson edited by Greg Clingham

Ben Jonson edited by Richard Harp and Stanley Stewart

James Joyce edited by Derek Attridge (second edition)

Kafka edited by Julian Preece

Keats edited by Susan J. Wolfson

Rudyard Kipling edited by Howard J. Booth

Lacan edited by Jean-Michel Rabaté

D. H. Lawrence edited by Anne Fernihough

Primo Levi edited by Robert Gordon

Abraham Lincoln edited by Shirley Samuels

Lucretius edited by Stuart Gillespie and Philip Hardie

Machiavelli edited by John M. Najemy

David Mamet edited by Christopher Bigsby

Thomas Mann edited by Ritchie Robertson

Christopher Marlowe edited by Patrick Cheney

Andrew Marvell edited by Derek Hirst and Steven N. Zwicker

Cormac McCarthy edited by Steven Frye

Herman Melville edited by Robert S. Levine

Arthur Miller edited by Christopher Bigsby (second edition)

Milton edited by Dennis Danielson (second edition)

Molière edited by David Bradby and Andrew Calder

Toni Morrison edited by Justine Tally

Nabokov edited by Julian W. Connolly

Eugene O'Neill edited by Michael Manheim

George Orwell edited by John Rodden

Ovid edited by Philip Hardie

Harold Pinter edited by Peter Raby (second edition)

Sylvia Plath edited by Jo Gill

Edgar Allan Poe edited by Kevin J. Hayes

Alexander Pope edited by Pat Rogers

Ezra Pound edited by Ira B. Nadel

Proust edited by Richard Bales

Pushkin edited by Andrew Kahn

Rabelais edited by John O'Brien

Rilke edited by Karen Leeder and Robert Vilain

Philip Roth edited by Timothy Parrish

Salman Rushdie edited by Abdulrazak Gurnah

Shakespeare edited by Margareta de Grazia and Stanley Wells (second edition)

Shakespeare and Contemporary Dramatists edited by Ton Hoenselaars

Shakespeare on Film edited by Russell Jackson (second edition)

Shakespeare and Popular Culture edited by Robert Shaughnessy

Shakespeare on Stage edited by Stanley Wells and Sarah Stanton

Shakespearean Comedy edited by Alexander Leggatt

Shakespearean Tragedy edited by Claire McEachern

Shakespeare's History Plays edited by Michael Hattaway

Shakespeare's Last Plays edited by Catherine M. S. Alexander

Shakespeare's Poetry edited by Patrick Cheney

George Bernard Shaw edited by Christopher Innes

Shelley edited by Timothy Morton

Mary Shelley edited by Esther Schor

Sam Shepard edited by Matthew C. Roudané

Spenser edited by Andrew Hadfield

Laurence Sterne edited by Thomas Keymer

Wallace Stevens edited by John N. Serio

Tom Stoppard edited by Katherine E. Kelly

Harriet Beecher Stowe edited by Cindy Weinstein

August Strindberg edited by Michael Robinson

Jonathan Swift edited by Christopher Fox

J. M. Synge edited by P. J. Mathews

Tacitus edited by A. J. Woodman

Henry David Thoreau edited by Joel Myerson

Tolstoy edited by Donna Tussing Orwin

Anthony Trollope edited by Carolyn Dever and Lisa Niles

Mark Twain edited by Forrest G. Robinson

John Updike edited by Stacey Olster

Mario Vargas Llosa edited by Efrain Kristal and John King

Virgil edited by Charles Martindale

Voltaire edited by Nicholas Cronk

Edith Wharton edited by Millicent Bell

Walt Whitman edited by Ezra Greenspan

Oscar Wilde edited by Peter Raby

Tennessee Williams edited by Matthew C. Roudané

August Wilson edited by Christopher Bigsby

Mary Wollstonecraft edited by Claudia L. Johnson

Virginia Woolf edited by Susan Sellers (second edition)

Wordsworth edited by Stephen Gill

W. B. Yeats edited by Marjorie Howes and John Kelly

Zola edited by Brian Nelson

TOPICS

The Actress edited by Maggie B. Gale and John Stokes

The African American Novel edited by Maryemma Graham

The African American Slave Narrative edited by Audrey A. Fisch

Allegory edited by Rita Copeland and Peter Struck

American Crime Fiction edited by Catherine Ross Nickerson

American Modernism edited by Walter Kalaidjian

American Novelists edited by Timothy Parrish

American Realism and Naturalism edited by Donald Pizer

American Travel Writing edited by Alfred Bendixen and Judith Hamera

American Women Playwrights edited by Brenda Murphy

Ancient Rhetoric edited by Erik Gunderson

Arthurian Legend edited by Elizabeth Archibald and Ad Putter

Australian Literature edited by Elizabeth Webby

British Literature of the French Revolution edited by Pamela Clemit

British Romantic Poetry edited by James Chandler and Maureen N. McLane

British Romanticism edited by Stuart Curran (second edition)

British Theatre, 1730–1830, edited by Jane Moody and Daniel O'Quinn

Canadian Literature edited by Eva-Marie Kröller

Children's Literature edited by M. O. Grenby and Andrea Immel

The Classic Russian Novel edited by Malcolm V. Jones and Robin Feuer Miller

Contemporary Irish Poetry edited by Matthew Campbell

Creative Writing edited by David Morley and Philip Neilsen

Crime Fiction edited by Martin Priestman

Early Modern Women's Writing edited by Laura Lunger Knoppers

The Eighteenth-Century Novel edited by John Richetti

Eighteenth-Century Poetry edited by John Sitter

English Literature, 1500–1600 edited by Arthur F. Kinney

English Literature, 1650–1740 edited by Steven N. Zwicker

English Literature, 1740–1830 edited by Thomas Keymer and Jon Mee

English Literature, 1830–1914 edited by Joanne Shattock

English Novelists edited by Adrian Poole

English Poetry, Donne to Marvell edited by Thomas N. Corns

English Poets edited by Claude Rawson

English Renaissance Drama edited by A. R. Braunmuller and Michael Hattaway (second edition)

English Renaissance Tragedy edited by Emma Smith and Garrett A. Sullivan Jr.

English Restoration Theatre edited by Deborah C. Payne Fisk

The Epic edited by Catherine Bates

European Modernism edited by Pericles Lewis

European Novelists edited by Michael Bell

Fantasy Literature edited by Edward James and Farah Mendlesohn

Feminist Literary Theory edited by Ellen Rooney

Fiction in the Romantic Period edited by Richard Maxwell and Katie Trumpener

The Fin de Siècle edited by Gail Marshall

The French Novel: From 1800 to the Present edited by Timothy Unwin

Gay and Lesbian Writing edited by Hugh Stevens

German Romanticism edited by Nicholas Saul

Gothic Fiction edited by Jerrold E. Hogle

The Greek and Roman Novel edited by Tim Whitmarsh

Greek Lyric edited by Felix Budelmann

Greek Mythology edited by Roger D. Woodard

Greek and Roman Theatre edited by Marianne McDonald and J. Michael Walton

Greek Tragedy edited by P. E. Easterling

The Harlem Renaissance edited by George Hutchinson

The Irish Novel edited by John Wilson Foster

The Italian Novel edited by Peter Bondanella and Andrea Ciccarelli

Jewish American Literature edited by Hana Wirth-Nesher and Michael P. Kramer

The Latin American Novel edited by Efraín Kristal

The Literature of the American South edited by Sharon Monteith

The Literature of the First World War edited by Vincent Sherry

The Literature of London edited by Lawrence Manley

The Literature of Los Angeles edited by Kevin R. McNamara

The Literature of New York edited by Cyrus Patell and Bryan Waterman

Literature on Screen edited by Deborah Cartmell and Imelda Whelehan

The Literature of World War II edited by Marina MacKay

Medieval English Culture edited by Andrew Galloway

Medieval English Literature edited by Larry Scanlon

Medieval English Mysticism edited by Samuel Fanous and Vincent Gillespie

Medieval English Theatre edited by Richard Beadle and Alan J. Fletcher (second edition)

Medieval French Literature edited by Simon Gaunt and Sarah Kay

Medieval Romance edited by Roberta L. Krueger

Medieval Women's Writing edited by Carolyn Dinshaw and David Wallace

Modern American Culture edited by Christopher Bigsby

Modern British Women Playwrights edited by Elaine Aston and Janelle Reinelt

Modern French Culture edited by Nicholas Hewitt

Modern German Culture edited by Eva Kolinsky and Wilfried van der Will

The Modern German Novel edited by Graham Bartram

Modern Irish Culture edited by Joe Cleary and Claire Connolly

Modern Italian Culture edited by Zygmunt G. Baranski and Rebecca J. West

Modern Latin American Culture edited by John King

Modern Russian Culture edited by Nicholas Rzhevsky

Modern Spanish Culture edited by David T. Gies

Modernism edited by Michael Levenson (second edition)

The Modernist Novel edited by Morag Shiach

Modernist Poetry edited by Alex Davis and Lee M. Jenkins

Modernist Women Writers edited by Maren Tova Linett

Narrative edited by David Herman

Native American Literature edited by Joy Porter and Kenneth M. Roemer

Nineteenth-Century American Women's Writing edited by Dale M. Bauer and Philip Gould

Old English Literature edited by Malcolm Godden and Michael Lapidge

Performance Studies edited by Tracy C. Davis

Popular Fiction edited by David Glover and Scott McCracken

Postcolonial Literary Studies edited by Neil Lazarus

Postmodernism edited by Steven Connor

The Pre-Raphaelites edited by Elizabeth Prettejohn

Renaissance Humanism edited by Jill Kraye

The Roman Historians edited by Andrew Feldherr

Roman Satire edited by Kirk Freudenburg

Science Fiction edited by Edward James and Farah Mendlesohn

Scottish Literature edited by Gerald Carruthers and Liam McIlvanney

The Sonnet edited by A. D. Cousins and Peter Howarth

The Spanish Novel: From 1600 to the Present edited by Harriet Turner and Adelaida López de Martínez

Travel Writing edited by Peter Hulme and Tim Youngs

Twentieth-Century British and Irish Women's Poetry edited by Jane Dowson

The Twentieth-Century English Novel edited by Robert L. Caserio

Twentieth-Century English Poetry edited by Neil Corcoran

Twentieth-Century Irish Drama edited by Shaun Richards

Twentieth-Century Russian Literature edited by Marina Balina and Evgeny Dobrenko

Utopian Literature edited by Gregory Claeys

Victorian and Edwardian Theatre edited by Kerry Powell

The Victorian Novel edited by Deirdre David

Victorian Poetry edited by Joseph Bristow

War Writing edited by Kate McLoughlin

Writing of the English Revolution edited by N. H. Keeble

For EU product safety concerns, contact us at Calle de José Abascal, 56–1°,
28003 Madrid, Spain or eugpsr@cambridge.org.

www.ingramcontent.com/pod-product-compliance
Ingram Content Group UK Ltd.
Pitfield, Milton Keynes, MK11 3LW, UK
UKHW010037140625
459647UK00012BA/1433